Nineteenth-Century Women Learn to Write

Feminist Issues: Practice, Politics, Theory

ALISON BOOTH AND ANN LANE, EDITORS

Nineteenth-Century Women Learn to Write

Edited with an Introduction by
Catherine Hobbs

University Press of Virginia
Charlottesville and London

THE UNIVERSITY PRESS OF VIRGINIA

First published 1995

Library of Congress Cataloging-in-Publication Data
Nineteenth-century women learn to write / edited with an introduction
by Catherine Hobbs.
p. cm. — (Feminist issues)
Includes bibliographical references (p.) and index.
ISBN 0-8139-1605-4
1. Women—Education—United States—History—19th century.
2. Literacy—United States—History—19th century. 3. Feminist
theory—United States. I. Hobbs, Catherine. II. Series: Feminist
issues (Charlottesville, Va.)
LC1757.N56 1995
376'.973—dc20 94-25198
CIP

Printed in the United States of America

In memory of

James A. Berlin, 1942–1994

Contents

CARROLL SMITH-ROSENBERG

Foreword

THIS VOLUME REPRESENTS a significant contribution to the series "Feminist Issues: Practice, Politics, Theory." Responding to the series editors' charge that scholars reconsider history and thought from an interdisciplinary feminist perspective, *Nineteenth-Century Women Learn to Write* interweaves thick feminist social history with theoretical perspectives garnered from such diverse fields as linguistics and folklore, feminist literary theory, and African American and Native American studies.

Issues of literacy raise pressing questions for both feminists and poststructuralists. Contemporary feminist analyses assume the discursive nature of gender and sexual identities, see women caught in the prison house of the master's language, valiantly struggling to emerge as resisting readers and as authors of alternative discourses. Literacy and its engendering are central to the discursive construction of gender and subjectivity. At the same time, literacy is the product of public policies. It is saturated with economic considerations. Literacy, in short, embodies social, economic, and political practices. To fully explore literacy's twinned ties to literature and the material, scholars must embed literary perspectives in thick social analyses, must carefully locate readers and writers on a detailed map of social and discursive relations. This the editors of this volume and their contributors have done. The result of their efforts is an exciting, pathbreaking collection of essays.

Nineteenth-Century Women Learn to Write constitutes a major addition to traditional social science studies of literacy. Anthropologists and folklorists, linguists and social historians have traditionally explored patterns of literacy in terms of modernization theory, social recruitment processes, the emergence of public cultures, and the deployment of power in industrial and third world contexts. Rarely have they built considerations of gender into their analyses. Yet gender constitutes one of the basic components of any social picture of literacy practices, at the same time as degrees of literacy among women are central to analyses of fertility patterns, to studies of women's social mobilization, or to examinations of the emergence of women as public subjects.

The essays in this volume engender the history of American literacy, contextualizing nineteenth-century American literacy practices within a close reading of women's experiences. Nineteenth-century American society constituted women, especially white middle-class women, as private, domestic creatures. It denied them legal and political subjectivity, enjoined them to the practice of such traditional virtues as modesty, humility, passivity, and obedience, worried obsessively about the appearance of women's respectability. Yet women, as Nathaniel Hawthorne bitterly complained, were "damned scribblers," not only in the privacy of their homes and diaries but in the public prints. Prolific and successful writers, women were also indomitable readers, increasingly the mainstay of America's commercial popular press. Indeed, when we talk of the burgeoning of America's print culture in the nineteenth century, we refer to a print culture sustained by female consumers.

How can we address the contradictions that marked male proscriptions and female practice, between the print culture's marginalization of women and its dependence upon them for its commercial success? How can we trace the ways that women misread and fused divergent hegemonical discourses to constitute alternative resisting voices? To answer these questions, scholars must trace the complex ways the discursive, the social, and the material weave in and out of one another in constructing literacy as a political phenomenon and as a personal experience. The combined contributions to this volume go far to accomplish this goal.

True to its sophisticated vision, *Nineteenth-Century Women Learn to Write* refuses monolithic descriptions of women. Its varied essays explore differences between women along generational, regional, "racial," class, and ethnic lines. They compare the diverse perspectives on literacy taken by white middle-class women and such socially constructed "other" women as African American and Native American women. The attractions and perversities of white middle-class women's discourses on literacy as interpreted by other groups become more apparent through the cultural and ideological approaches of the contributors. Cultures and contexts, voices and practices of literacy interweave in an effort to provide a "thick description" of women's literacy, especially in the second half of the century.

A product of its culture, literacy is simultaneously constitutive of culture. Responsive, it is also productive. In the increasingly print-oriented culture of nineteenth-century America, individuals, as reading subjects, were formed by what and how they read. Their reading, be it of fiction, advice books, devotional literature, or news, informed the ways they imagined and represented and experienced their material surroundings, their social relations, their political and legal identities, their sexual pleasures and fears. Women's texts cannot be read simply as mirrors, reflecting actual experience. The more literate the woman, the more complex the influence of discursive forces upon her perceptions, her sense of self, her ability to resist and transform those discourses that shaped her. It is this vision that drives the essays in this volume. Together, they constitute an intricate mosaic exploring the processes of interpellation, internalization, adaptation, resistance, and transformation.

Finally, this volume leads us to appreciate and wonder at the quality of literacy women achieved during the nineteenth century, a quality and level of literacy that the pressures of the twenty-first century threaten. Examining nineteenth-century women's achievements, aware of the dangers posed by the coming century, we are impressed with the need to again confront the ways American society engenders literacy and, hence, power. The force that drives this volume is the gritty knowledge that women who do not have "effective literacy" will be left without the ability to either understand the postmodern world or to act in it. Admittedly, late-twentieth- and early-twenty-first-century literacy is qualitatively different from that of the nineteenth century. These essays sharpen our appreciation of that difference—at the same time as they remind us that women's struggle for equal literacy must never end.

Acknowledgments

The editor is pleased to acknowledge financial support from Illinois State University in the form of a summer research grant in 1990 and subsequently from the University of Oklahoma, which provided a timely grant from the Research Council in 1993 to support editing. Press director Nancy Essig, C. Jan Swearingen, Winifred Bryant Horner, and an anonymous reader for the University Press of Virginia, as well as Janice M. Lauer from Purdue, Jean Ferguson Carr, and Cecil L. Peaden, provided other kinds of support to make this project possible, as did my sisters Susan Carol Cessna and Jeanne Ann Rogers and my mother Betty Ray Hobbs. We are grateful for the careful editorial work of Pamela MacFarland Holway and Alice Falk provided through the university press. Finally, I and several of the contributors studied at the University of Texas at Austin or Purdue University with the late rhetoric and composition historian James A. Berlin, in memory of whom this volume is dedicated.

Nineteenth-Century Women Learn to Write

CATHERINE HOBBS

Introduction: Cultures and Practices of U.S. Women's Literacy

Teach a woman letters? A terrible mistake:
Like feeding extra venom to a horrifying snake.
—Menander (c. 342–291 B.C.)

As to your extraordinary Code of Laws, I cannot but laugh. We have been told that our Struggle has loosened the bands of Government every where.
—John Adams to Abigail, 1776

He [Horace Mann] will not help the cause of woman greatly, but his efforts to educate her will do a greater work than he anticipates. Prepare woman for duty and usefulness, and she will laugh at any boundaries man may set for her.
—Sarah Grimké, 1853

LITERACY, THE KEYWORD of the information age, often connotes rudimentary skill in reading or the basic consumption of texts. This commonsense meaning can, however, obscure more complex practices such as the production of texts, whether spoken or written. Indeed, the little historical knowledge we have about the extent of women's literacy comes from measures of basic reading skills found in census reports or from inferences researchers have made about reading levels when they found women's signatures instead of marks on legal documents. The history of women's struggle for literacy, especially advanced practices of literacy that assume text production, has only begun to be written.

Literacy in its broadest sense denotes not only the technical skills of reading and writing but the tactical—or rhetorical—knowledge of how to employ those skills in the context of one or more communities. What is entailed by this literate know-how always varies according to its situation of use. Thus one helpful concept implied in some definitions of literacy might be called "effective literacy," meaning a level of literacy that enables the user to act to effect change, in her own life and in society.

"The power to act in society," a phrase suggesting both empowerment and transformation, encompasses many of the functions we mean by the term effective literacy. This definition is a pliable rule, allowing us to designate someone like the powerful African American orator Sojourner Truth, often called functionally illiterate, as effectively literate.[1]

However, most investigations, especially and perhaps necessarily those relying on statistical methods, employ a more strict concept of literacy as rudimentary reading skills and sometimes also basic writing skills. From these inquiries we have learned that half as many women as men in early colonial America had the ability to read and write. Yet after the Revolution, northern white women began to close the literacy gap. At the start of the nineteenth century perhaps half or more white women qualified as reading at some level, compared to men's illiteracy rate of only 25 percent. Nonetheless, by 1870 women had nearly equalled men in basic literacy, with women's illiteracy rates only one percentage point above men's 9 percent. Immigrant, Latino, Native American, and southern women remained behind them. African American women, many of them prohibited by law from reading and writing just when white women were making great strides in literacy, ended the century about where white women had begun it.

Throughout the century women's texts from all regions and races reflect the aspiration that achieving literacy would bring economic gain, social status, freedom, or suffrage, and would surely construct a more ethical society. These hopes, part of an ideology of literacy, endure in some form today, yet the history of women's achievement in literacy and its meaning and consequences for us are not yet fully understood.[2]

Questions that are now being asked include whether women gained equality in literacy with men and when, which of them did so, how this literacy was achieved, and what cultural contexts best supported it. Our knowledge would be enriched if we understood the value of literacy to women's lives and how they felt about their reading and writing. If an ideology of literacy has promised economic or social gains, have women who gained equal literacy shared equally in these rewards or have they been taken in by "the myth" of literacy?[3] Have women closed the literacy gap, or has men's advanced literacy been raised or transformed so that a gender gap yet remains? Has the meaning of literacy shifted to include types of literacy bearing more cultural capital—such as numerical, computer, or visual literacy—leaving women again with less effective, lower-valued print literacy?

We will not be able to deal responsibly with contemporary issues of women's literacy either at home or abroad without historical knowledge of our own literacy, its contradictory assumptions and differential processes.[4] Yet understanding the process of nineteenth-century women's entrance into literacy becomes even more complex when we treat literacy itself as a historical phenomenon. This means we must recognize that literacy is not static but is a moving target that has been continually in flux as it interacts with other factors. These factors include economic, political, religious, and local and national forces shaping the development of schooling and the modern university. Further, rising participation by women in public life after the growth of industrialization and the need for women to assist in educating the young changed the economy and education itself. This feedback loop in which women affect the processes and institutions in which they participate complicates the question "How did literacy affect women?" and forces us to ask, "How did women change literacy?" Yet these kinds of questions, which are just now being posed, have not been addressed in our mainstream histories of education and writing instruction.

Major transformations in literacy over the century took place as society moved from an oratorical culture revering classical and neoclassical texts to a literate, mass print culture based on English and American literature.[5] The English department as we know it today, centered on the reading and criticism of vernacular literary texts, came about only in the last decades of the nineteenth century, and separate speech departments are a twentieth-century phenomenon. For much of the nineteenth century, rhetoric—the theory and practice of male public discourse—was at the center of college curricula and represented the pinnacle of the nation's education and literacy. Literature still carried a broader meaning of written texts in general; belletristic texts including history, poetry, and by midcentury popular fiction were important, especially for women.[6] In 1800 the canon of valued texts was headed by Latin or Greek literature, but by century's end that had shifted to English and American texts. Over the same period the university as we know it came into being, evolving from a male collegiate institution designed to prepare the nation's elite for public leadership to a departmentalized research institution designed to educate and certify professionals—both men and women—in industrial society.

Most of these transformations began with industrialization before the Civil War, taking on their modern cast in the last quarter of the century when women's entrance into higher education, both in formal institutions and informal study groups, boomed. Ironically, Vesey notes that during this same business-oriented period, men's interest in attending college stagnated. We have not yet examined the multiple ways women's entrance into literacy interacted with these broad shifts: the various ways in which changing patterns in women's lives helped construct modern life have been little studied, and women's participation in transforming literacy has not yet been thoroughly explored.[7]

Like the census figures whose averages are not differentiated by sex, stories of women's learning to write and the effects of women's literacy have often been collapsed into men's. It is true that at another historical moment, men's and women's literacies might more nearly converge. However, in the nineteenth century men's and women's lives were carried on with little overlap, in such parallel fashion that the metaphor of separate spheres applied much more than it does today.[8] Even when girls came to be educated side by side with boys, their educations might differ, as did the meanings of their literacy and the expectations of what they could or should achieve. Thus it becomes important to inquire into how girls and women learned to read and write because we cannot assume, especially at the level of advanced literacy, that their experience was the same as that of boys and men in the nineteenth century. Yet histories of nineteenth-century education and writing instruction most often generalize from elite male experience, using records of the century's prestigious all-male institutions such as Harvard, Princeton, or Yale. Even when coeducation was allowed, as at Oberlin, men's and women's educational tracks might be quite different. The value of our having histories of girls' and women's experiences of literacy need not be argued, yet the work of writing these histories and listening to women's "voices" from our past has only begun.[9]

Stories of women's struggles to achieve effective, advanced literacy have now begun to be told, most often in the last decade with its treasure trove of histories of women's education. Yet because of their scope and different purposes, these valuable histories cannot focus on women's reading and writing. So much lies outside institutional histories that accounts of nineteenth-century women and writing must be broader—so broad that this volume can only begin to provide a sample of the various cultures and practices that informed women's literacy. These cultures were sometimes as widespread and resilient as an ideal of womanhood or a religious faith, sometimes as local and evanescent as a literary circle, but each grew out of specific historical situations and institutions—the family, church, school, workplace, and social group—in which women both learned to write and wrote.[10]

Introduction

Gender and U.S. Literacy History

Historical Frames and an Emerging Ideology of Literacy

In colonial America, women were routinely taught to read—and a few might have read on a highly sophisticated level—without being taught to write. It is likely that most feminine hands willingly accepted the needle rather than the pen as a necessary form of early American career tracking; yet the resounding protests of a few linger, in print. The most memorable of these may be the frequently cited lines of Anne Bradstreet's poem, "I am obnoxious to each carping tongue / Who says my hand a needle better fits . . ."

As the population increased and concentrated in urban centers and the economy changed, more and more women were taught rudimentary reading and writing. But if they wanted advanced literacy, they had to struggle, either with the help of a mentor (perhaps a father or brother) or alone. Yet, even so, in the economic and social transformations following the Revolution, women came to play a greater role in literacy as participants in and promulgators of an ideology of literacy that swept the new country.

First, as Republican Mothers they became responsible for the basic education of their children. Although they themselves were not fully recognized as citizens, they took upon themselves the task of forming their sons as citizens of the new Republic. Next, women's participation in the religious revivals of the 1790s to the 1850s called the Second Great Awakening helped form the discourse of True Womanhood that underlay Victorian women's commitment to both literacy and service to family. Their own economic needs, the educational needs of a developing nation, and these discourses of Republican Motherhood and True Womanhood led women to teaching first as a vocation, but then as paid work and a profession. The ideology of literacy was a resilient thread that bound the early- and late-nineteenth-century women's cultures, and, in interlocking fashion, men's and women's spheres. By century's end, basic literacy rates of white northern men and women were about equal.[11]

In other ways white, primarily middle-class women were, equally with men, the executors of this ideology of literacy, which, bound up with Protestant morality and evangelism, underlay the shift to an industrial capitalist economy. As such, these women helped construct and police their own elevated—but restricted—identities and activities in society, all the while creating strong communities of women that pushed at the boundaries of women's sphere. Their struggles and, for a small but growing number of women such as Jane Addams, Charlotte Perkins Gilman, and E. D. E. N. Southworth, subsequent advances in literacy throughout the nineteenth century produced at century's end a women's movement with remarkable power: its like was not seen again until the women's rights movement of the 1960s and '70s. The "New Women" of the Progressive Era, many of them representing what would later be termed the first generation of college women, led the way.

The history of women's efforts to learn to write in the nineteenth century is composed of multiple strands. For instance, one narrative strand is that of women's heroic struggles toward the Enlightenment ideal of equality in literacy, found in Mary Wollestonecraft and some discourses of Republican Motherhood. This Enlightenment strand continues in the nineteenth century in an egalitarianism such as Cogan describes in the ideal of Real Womanhood (see chapter 1). But in other narratives, as in ideals of True Womanhood, even women's separate spheres education and work experience—often undertaken from religious motivation—could ironically produce unintended consequences. Moreover, conservatives like Catharine Beecher and Sarah J. Hale, writers who celebrated women's domesticity, exemplify how literacy may have effected a growth in public power and broadened alternatives for women's lives throughout the century.

However, historical revisionism in literary and literacy studies has complicated the notion that we can easily attribute consequences to literacy outside of schooling and other specific contexts and has questioned the naturalness of the relation of progress to literacy. The contexts of literacy, including beliefs about literacy and the purposes and content of what was read and written, are now considered more important than the mechanical skills of literacy alone. Some have pointed out that inequalities in schooling could keep women unequal, in their place, as docile and obedient domestic and factory workers. Women's studies scholars have also challenged an earlier view of women's educational history as seamless progress in empowering women. Nonetheless, changing patterns of literacy, seen in the context of family and community, work, and schooling for women, did seem to offer more women the prospect of wielding greater control over their lives by the century's end. Not the least significant evidence of such control is the correlation of higher literacy with lower fertility rates.[12]

Gender and Colonial Literacy

The separation of reading and writing for reasons of gender, vocation, and class was common in the pre-Revolutionary era. Only a few upper-class women such as Abigail Adams, Anne Bradstreet, and Mercy Otis Warren learned to write and wrote well. Yet a few women who could not write may still have developed solid reading skills. Just how many nonsigning women were fluent readers is impossible to determine.

Scholars now debate just how many women could claim even rudimentary literacy in colonial New England. Monaghan's discussion of colonial literacy instruction and gender argues that Lockridge and others who portray women in seventeenth-century New England as dramatically less literate than men have misinterpreted the evidence. Auwers, for example, found that the proportion of late-seventeenth-century women in Windsor, Connecticut, who could sign their own names to deeds rose from 27 percent (for the birth cohort born between 1650 and 1669) to 90 percent for the 1740–49 birth cohort. Gilmore reports nearly universal literacy for men of all classes by the 1780s and 60 to 90 percent female literacy, depending on the commercial character of their towns. Lockridge's work relies on counts of signatures on wills, yet it is not clear how levels of literacy correlate to marks or signatures on wills, deeds, and other documents. Kaestle reports a general agreement by scholars that signatures represent modest reading ability; nonetheless, this is a generalization more easily applied to men, and what is more, women are often underrepresented in archival evidence, especially legal documents.[13]

Geographical region, age, race, occupation, and other factors also affected literacy rates. For example, we know that from about 1820 to 1835 (and in four states continuing through the Civil War), black literacy was intentionally suppressed by slave owners after slave rebellions led by literates. Despite the odds and hardships, some slaves still learned to read and a few to write well enough to forge passes to freedom.[14]

Along with other variables, gender remains a key factor in U.S. literacy because from its start, colonial literacy education was a gendered process. As Monaghan writes, learning to read in colonial New England generally followed Locke's late-seventeenth-century characterization: "the ordinary road of the horn-book, Primer, Psalter, Testament, and Bible." In a "major pedagogical shift" occurring about the beginning of the eighteenth century, the spelling book, in particular Webster's Blue-Back speller, began its ascendancy in American pedagogy. Spellers were used as an orally based method of reading instruction that could be taught by nonwriting mothers without requiring a child to write.[15]

The teaching of basic reading was considered a female province with mothers and dame schools (child-tending and basic reading schools) providing the instruction. Town schools were often used to perfect students' reading, not to teach it from scratch. Reading was considered easy to teach. In contrast, writing was male terrain, as the word penmanship implies, and men taught it. Writing technologies were more complex, and copybooks were imported and scarce. Writing itself was vocational training, intended for men from clerks to ministers. The corresponding skill for girls was sewing.[16]

Reading, writing, and arithmetic—the three R's—were taught separately. That the colonies placed greater importance on reading was shown by early colonial laws requiring that children (which often meant "sons") be taught to read. In her discussion of Massachusetts' Poor Laws, Monaghan notes that not until 1771 was legislation regulating education for apprentices amended to include writing for both males and females. This is an important date because apprenticeship was as important in this era as schooling as an institution transmitting literacy. Apprenticeship often served to educate children of the poor in order to keep them from being a drain on public charity. Thus these new laws seem to show that, at least in Massachusetts, economic incentives to teach girls to write rose toward the end of the colonial period.[17]

Literacy in the Early Republic

Englishwoman Hannah More's efforts to teach reading at adult working-class Sunday schools in the eighteenth century represents another example of how blending literacy, religion, and social control could have unintended consequences. More, the conservative author of evangelical tracts, poetry, and sacred drama, did not teach writing to the poor attending her schools but stressed habits of industry and thrift to reinforce dominant social values. Yet in England at that time reading was considered an ability with potential for social disruption, and More was branded a rabble-rouser and radical, something she surely never intended. Soon, however, America took up More's brand of literacy. As Solomon notes, it was More's feminine benevolence model rather than Wollestonecraft's egalitarian model that became the standard for female education in both Britain and the United States.[18]

The use of basic literacy as a means of social control, which began with Sunday schools and religious tract societies after the English model, had made inroads by the time of the Revolution and stood ready to ease the upcoming shift to industrial and commercial capital in North America. Graff believes that the relative absence of social turmoil during the transformation of the United States into an industrial society can be linked to the regularizing and disciplining of the population brought about by the promotion of literacy in such a context. Stressing the importance of religious revivalism to reading, Tompkins points out that at midcentury, when the entire population was only 11 million, the number of tracts the American Tract Society alone claimed to have published stood at 37 million. But the ideology of literacy soon required a widespread system of public education. Before that system could be put into place, women were needed to teach rudimentary literacy skills at home and in dame schools. And for common schooling to succeed, women would be needed to provide cheap, dedicated labor in order to produce literacy on a broad scale. Concomitantly, U.S. literacy ideals would broaden to include writing by women.[19]

Gender, Literacy, and Education: Formal and Informal *Schooling in the Early Republic*

In the colonial period, girls who learned to read were taught by their families or sent to dame schools. Nonetheless, for most women, further education was seen as unnecessary, even dangerous. There was, however, a tradition of higher education for women associated with Renaissance humanism. Perhaps it was in this tradition that ministers and other elites provided higher education to their favorite daughters. Thus a few women—Margaret Fuller and Catharine Beecher, for example—learned classical languages and literatures, the true mark of higher education. Classically trained Mary Moody Emerson helped teach her nephew Ralph Waldo to write. And even late in the century Jane Addams shared her father's love of classical language and literature, following the classical as well as the modern line of scientific and literary studies at Rockford (Illinois) Female Seminary.[20]

Even though doting fathers may have indulged their daughters, true grammar schools, which taught Latin and Greek, usually excluded girls. But as early as the end of the seventeenth century, several factors had begun to make additional, if not classical, education for females more desirable. Monaghan notes that after 1680, women were more and more needed to teach beginning reading at the town schools. The increased production of secular reading material, including novels, was a significant factor in the growth of women's literacy.[21]

After the Revolution, as summer sessions covering basic reading became increasingly open to girls, and with curricula more often including writing, literacy for New England white women rose. At that time, a host of public arguments over women's education—from the pens of such notables as Benjamin Rush, Judith Sargent Murray, Emma Willard, and Susanna Rowson—articulated the discourse of republicanism and civic virtue, linking it with the ideology of literacy and with women's roles. A feminine version of republican culture arose, formed on the ideal of the patriotic Republican Mother. But by the early nineteenth century, even as the burgeoning ideology of literacy provided a cozy image of a mother with child and book in lap, common schools were beginning to take over the burden of primary literacy. By midcentury, school reform had begun to equalize the numbers of white, native-born men and women, at least in the North, who could claim basic literacy. Literacy had become a key element in the social transformation to Victorian culture and the Cult of True Womanhood, with its tenets of piety, purity, domesticity, and submissiveness, as described by Welter, including the existing imbrication of literacy and morality.[22]

The Rise of Common Schools and the Spread of Literacy

A frequently used metaphor for literacy is that of the double-edged sword. This metaphor acknowledges that literacy can be used for social control yet suggests that it also has the tendency to become private and idiosyncratic, veering off in unexpected and unsettling directions. Nonetheless, literacy cannot be easily wrenched from the institutions and contexts that teach it, and most of these institutions themselves harbor mixed radical and conservative motives. Women's own power of active resistance to, or covert subversion of, efforts to socialize them remains another factor to consider. Despite efforts to restrict them, literate women acting privately for groups acting collectively used their literacy to construct their own imagined societies and reforms. They then learned to bring these to public political attention through lecture tours and through various print media. Both black and white women often resisted the intended uses of the literacy they were taught in order to achieve social reform instead of social control.[23]

Yet such uses of literacy may entail that those reading and writing have what many call critical literacy, a self-conscious attitude toward language and its uses for social reproduction or transformation. Literacy studies based on operationally countable definitions of literacy and illiteracy often remain blind to the implications of critical literacy. Critical literacy is difficult to test or measure.[24]

Indeed, even countable rudimentary levels of nineteenth-century women's literacy in the United States are difficult to compare with men's. Few measures exist before 1900, and many works on literacy are stark reminders of just how recently gender has become a category of analysis in history and other disciplines. Even the most helpful studies, including Soltow and Stevens's analysis, do not treat gender as a central factor in literacy, although they and some other authors do discuss women's literacy relative to men's and acknowledge race and class differences.[25]

According to Soltow and Stevens, the United States entered the nineteenth century with an overall illiteracy rate in the North of about 25 percent and in the South of 40 to 50 percent. However, there are wide variations in state and county levels, in part because of urbanization and commercialization, but also because not all locations had common schools. By the 1840 census the adjusted illiteracy rate had drooped to about 9 percent of all adults. In 1870 census figures again show about 9 percent were illiterate, although there had been a slight decrease to 7 percent in 1860. A question included on the census for the first time in 1870 distinguished reading and writing, and it was found that about 25 percent fewer people could write than could read.[26]

Soltow and Stevens ascribe gender differences in literacy to occupational experience demanding the use of letters and to the dominant view that women belonged in the home. In 1860 only 2 percent fewer white women than men were literate, while by 1870 the figure had dropped to 1 percent: overall, 10 percent of women were illiterate. The figures show southern women at a marked disadvantage, with illiteracy rates in 1860 at 15 percent for women compared with 11 percent for men. In contrast, in 1860 northern women were only 6 percent illiterate, compared with 4 percent for men.

Most notably, in midcentury women's literacy increased, with a definite overall trend toward equality in men's and women's basic literacy, especially in the urban North. By 1870 foreign-born and native-born men had similar literacy rates (but not foreign-born women). Soltow and Stevens attribute the general rise in women's literacy to "a general improvement from decade to decade, from 1830 to 1860, in the schooling of women. By 1840, common schools did not discriminate in terms of the number of hours of instruction they provided females and males in reading and writing." While acknowledging that women who were not enrolled at all could not be counted, they ultimately conclude that "native born [white] women in [northern] cities did not suffer from sex discrimination in basic education after the Civil War."[27] This gain, admittedly limited, marks a significant development in the history of women's literacy.

Just as we will never have exact figures for women's literacy earlier in the century, we cannot measure literacy among enslaved African Americans. Black literacy can usually only be surmised from traces left in oral testimony and some slave owners' records as well as slaves' own biographies and church records. Male slaves are more often reported than female slaves to have learned to read and write. However, this is not certain, and slave narratives show that many girls did learn to read and write and that more house slaves than field slaves were taught. While Du Bois estimated that by 1860 perhaps 5 percent of slaves were literate, Cornelius argues that about 10 percent may have been. Graff's study of three Canadian towns in the nineteenth century shows a literacy rate for free Canadian blacks of over 50 percent in 1861, about the same as the 50 percent census rate for free blacks in the United States. The material consequence of the ideology of literacy for slaves was more control over their lives, if not actual freedom.[28]

Soltow and Stevens's work shows the significance of access to equal formal schooling for the equalization of literacy rates on the part of men and women. Thus it is not surprising that literacy-hungry African Americans were the initiators of public education at public expense in the South. Until blacks and other groups gained public formal education, private and informal education was required to serve as a supporting matrix for literacy.[29] Just as access to common schooling helped to narrow the literacy gender gap, access to institutions of higher education supported many women's entrance into advanced literacy and text production.

Formal Higher Education and Advanced Literacy

The nineteenth-century development of seminaries and colleges for women and the later rise in coeducation marked a revolution in advanced literacy for a privileged group of women. Yet because women required preparation at the lower levels to succeed at higher levels, the development of higher education for a few broadened educational horizons for many more. As the sites of training in advanced literacy, these higher institutions with their diverse and conflictual histories and motivations provided a variety of purposes and contexts for women's literacy.

After the Revolution and until midcentury, common schooling for girls expanded rapidly. At first few of the boys' academies admitted girls;

meanwhile, female academies, seminaries, and normal and training schools appeared, along with the prestigious women's colleges. While early in the century the boundary between lower and advanced education was clearly delineated by the latter's concentration on classical languages and literatures, by midcentury vernacular studies were gaining in popularity. This produced a shift in writing pedagogy from rhetoric to composition, coinciding with the burst of women authors decried by Hawthorne as "that damned mob of scribbling women." Yet, for many classical learning remained the sign of a true college education until the century's end. Nonetheless, as women's institutions appeared and developed, ideals of literacy in the United States evolved away from those classics and from oratory-centered ideals. The entrance of women into higher education did not cause the transformation to vernacular literature and scientific educational programs, but an ongoing shift from an oratorical to a literary print culture coincided with women's (and the growth of nonelite men's) presence in higher educational institutions by century's end.[30]

Further Development of Women's Education and Advanced Literacy

From late in the eighteenth century to early in the nineteenth, women's academies and preparatory education greatly expanded. Then, from about the 1820s through the Civil War, seminaries proliferated and experiments in women's collegiate education began. But overlapping the growth of true collegiate education, from 1862 through the century's end, coeducation began to flourish. State-supported colleges began to admit women, in the last quarter of the century many of the Seven Sisters colleges were founded, and many seminaries transformed their curricula into true collegiate studies.

With a base laid in common schools and preparatory institutions early in the nation's history, alternatives for higher education of women expanded during the first half of the century. As Solomon describes it, "an informal, unplanned process evolved: girls not only attended district schools but taught in them: then some used the money they earned to attend academies, where they studied and taught. In time some opened schools of their own."[31] Women themselves were primarily responsible for ensuring the continuance and improvements of institutions in which women gained advanced literacy, and teaching itself was often the bootstrap by which they raised themselves into higher literacy. Many early seminary founders, often remarkable women, followed the pattern of educating themselves through their teaching.

The most important of these seminary founders included Emma Hart Willard, who theorized her teaching and set principles for other institutions to follow. Her founding of Troy Female Seminary in 1821 serves as an important milestone because her seminary consolidated gains made by female academies in previous decades and because her formalized Willard Plans for education were published and widely copied.[32] Acclaimed for promoting teaching as a woman's profession, Catharine Beecher, who had attended Litchfield Female Academy in 1810, began a day school in 1823 that was incorporated as Hartford Female Seminary in 1828. Despite her conservative stance on many women's issues, Beecher's efforts moved women's education closer to that of men's. Also in 1828 Zilpah P. Grant and her friend Mary Lyon opened the Ipswich Academy, and Lyon later founded the influential Mount Holyoke, a missions-minded school that opened in 1837.[33]

The educational values of Emma Willard, Catharine Beecher, Zilpah Grant, and Mary Lyon spread throughout the country. Troy, Hartford, and Mount Holyoke became prototypes for women's institutions in the Midwest and far West as well as the South. Most of these highly structured institutions provided a solid Protestant foundation, often sending missionaries both west and east. Mount Holyoke, for example, sent young women graduates east to Persian harems and west to Native American reservations to spread the ideology both of literacy and of Christianity.

The 1833 opening of coeducational Oberlin, with its evangelical foundations, has long been seen as a watershed in women's higher education. At first coed only in the preparatory department, in 1837 Oberlin allowed women into the collegiate course.[34] However, the gender tracking of its students in both curriculum and domestic chores, a common invisible curriculum in coeducation, must have taught many women they were not men's equals. Nevertheless, Oberlin became important especially for African American women who earned degrees there in the nineteenth century when they could do so nowhere else. These included Fanny Jackson Coppin, 1865; Anna J. Cooper, 1884; and Mary Church Terrell, 1884 (see chapter 8). Early public normal schools such as Illinois State Normal University, which opened in 1857, taught men and women on a more equal basis, producing many women leaders who contributed not only to improving education in their states but to wider vocations for women (see chapter 3).

Although slavery was abolished in the North in the late 1700s and early 1800s, African Americans were not equally educated even after the common school movement. Most northern blacks were educated in private institutions, but throughout the first half of the century they were denied access to most colleges and universities. Except for a privileged few, higher education for African Americans would not come until the twentieth century. More than half the African American women listed in *Notable American Women* who lived between 1790 and 1870 taught school at some point in their lives. But educational opportunities for black women were limited, and late in the century black women lost ground to black men. Most institutions founded for blacks in the nineteenth century were coeducational, except for schools founded by whites such as Spelman College (1881). Even though some may have preferred women's schools, black men needed education, too. Lucy Laney had intended the Haines Normal and Industrial School she founded in Georgia in 1866 to be a women's school, but the needs of both sexes won out.[35]

In addition to going south, women went west from eastern seminaries to help school, Christianize, and "civilize" their students, while women who remained at home wrote literature to promote missionary activities. Talented eastern-educated women often traveled as Protestant missionaries to teach in schools for Native Americans. For example, missionaries from Mount Holyoke helped design the curriculum for Cherokee Female Seminary in Indian Territory in midcentury (see chapter 4). Alice Robertson, who had grown up as the daughter of missionaries in what today is Oklahoma, studied at Elmira Female College before returning to head a Presbyterian school for girls in the Creek Nation in 1885. She built such a fine facility near Muskogee, Indian Territory, that her denomination took it from her in 1894 to reestablish it as a coeducational institution for white settlers. Her "home school" is the true predecessor of the University of Tulsa. Robertson went on to become the second woman and so far the only Oklahoma woman to be elected to Congress.[36]

True Collegiate Education and Coeducation

The Morrill Land Grant Act, signed by Lincoln in 1862, supported states in establishing institutions for agricultural and technical education. When the act was renewed in 1890, a provision ensured that funds would go to both races, improving existing black institutions or establishing separate black institutions. Although the act made no provisions for women's education, its commitment of public funds to higher education put pressure on those institutions to accept daughters of taxpayers. The act thus had an enormous impact on women's access to higher education.[37]

Only late in the century, at the same time as universities were opening to women, was true collegiate education also becoming available at a large number of women's colleges. Several early colleges, including Mary Sharp College (1851) in Winchester, Tennessee, and Elmira New York Female College (1855), had preceded Vassar (1865), one of the first to have an adequate endowment. In the final quarter of the century, the female college era ended with true degree-granting colleges such as Wellesley and Smith (1875); Bryn Mawr (1885); and Barnard (1889).[38]

But the Progressive Era, the age of the New Woman, was the era of coeducation. Slow to arrive in the South, coeducation was pioneered in the Midwest with schools such as Antioch College in Ohio (1852), the University of Iowa from its opening (1856), and Michigan (1870). With few changes made in curricula or texts, women students were allowed to sit in on the male curriculum, a phenomenon producing what Florence Howe terms one of the myths of coeducation: the myth that the curricula were gender neutral. At the same time, their presence did affect the curriculum, accelerating the shift in many institutions away from declamation and speech making and toward theme writing (see chapters 2 and 13).[39]

Informal Education: Women's Clubs, Literary Societies, and Effective Literacy

More girls than boys were graduating from high school by the last decade of the century, yet few were able to go to college. But the numbers grew: the 11,000 enrolled in 1870 rose to 56,000 in 1890 and 85,000 in 1900. Meanwhile, inspired by the ideal of higher education for women, many more women worked to achieve greater literacy through the women's study club movement. Throughout the century, women worked in collaborative groups to improve their reading and writing; after the Civil War, study clubs or literary societies became common and their spread interacted with the growth in higher education. Theodora Penny Martin believes that the popularity of the study club movement helps explain the rapid increase in the numbers of women entering college in the first decade of the twentieth century.[40] Martin points out that while only 14 women were graduated from the University of Wisconsin in 1874, thousands of ordinary women were involved in study clubs. These were primarily "middle-aged and middle-class women," most often white, Anglo-Saxon, and Protestant, studying art, music, history, geography, and literature. Their primary activities usually centered on higher literacy, the refinement of women's abilities to speak and write.

Precursors of women's study clubs can be found as early as Anne

Hutchinson's discussion groups in Boston in 1635. In the third decade of the nineteenth century, Lucy Larcom—educator, writer, and an early proponent of women's groups—received her education in improvement circles at the mills of Lowell, Massachusetts. In 1827, Elizabeth Peabody held her "Historical School" in Boston and took part in "Reading Parties" by women. Later, in the 1840s the transcendentalist Margaret Fuller held her weekly conversations on literature and culture for women in Peabody's bookshop. She remained seated, not standing, so as not to be taken for a public lecturer. Women were not always welcome in the Lyceum movement, but a number of women's groups evolved from Chautauqua literary circles.[41]

These clubs spanned the century, including such groups as the Women's Literary Society of Chelsea, Connecticut (1800); the Minerva Society of New Harmony, Indiana (1825); and Sorosis of New York (1868), founded by Jane Croly, the historian of the women's club movement, after she was denied admission to a reading by Charles Dickens at the Press Club. Later activist groups include the Women's Christian Temperance Union (1874) and the National Women's Suffrage Association (1869). Martin notes that by 1906 five thousand local groups had formed the General Federation of Women's Clubs, which represented only 5 to 10 percent of all such clubs in existence.

Women's clubs helped fill middle-class women's increasing leisure time, gave them self-esteem, and enlarged what had heretofore been considered their proper sphere. While primarily educational in spirit throughout much of the nineteenth century, late in the century women's groups turned to political action, working for kindergartens and other educational and civic improvements. Importantly for the spread of literacy, 75 percent of U.S. libraries were begun by women's groups.[42]

African Americans usually could not join white clubs. So they formed their own associations that provided libraries and reading rooms to encourage their members' writing and speaking endeavors. In addition to their educational purpose, many benevolent organizations worked to serve other urgent needs of African Americans. These societies included such early groups as the African Union Society of Newport, Rhode Island (1780); in the first half of the nineteenth century in the Philadelphia area alone, the Dorcas Society, the Sisterly Union, the United Daughters of Wilberforce, and the African Female Union were founded. The black club movement gained momentum in the last decade of the century with the Colored Women's League of Washington, D.C. (1892) and the New Era Club of Boston (1893); a number of clubs federated under the National

Association of Colored Women in 1896. Frances Harper's novel *Iola Leroy* (1892) contains a chapter describing an African American women's literary circle.[43]

Women's collaborative work in voluntary associations may have appeared to be self-culture in the American individualistic model of an Emerson or Thoreau. Yet much of the self-culture and development of personal skills aimed to serve social or religious goals, as in the case of missionary societies or women's abolitionist or temperance activities. Women's literacy ideals often centered on creating community rather than differentiating their selves, an emphasis that contributed to an alternative model of literacy. This collective model proved powerful to reform-minded Progressive Era women, but it went against the grain of the individualism gaining dominance in U.S. culture.

The Impact of Advanced, Effective Literacy

By midcentury, with its burgeoning industrial development, a transformation in literacy itself was taking place as North America turned from a culture of oratory to one of print literacy. Clark and Halloran write of this shift as part of a larger transformation in U.S. culture from a society with a moral base in communal values into an individualist culture based on professional values determined by field-specific experts. The shift from oratory to composition can be seen in writing curricula over the century, a phenomenon linked with women's success in popular fiction writing and journalism. By midcentury women wrote nearly half the best-selling novels, and by 1872 women were authors of nearly three-quarters of all novels published.[44] By century's end speaking and writing together became common in women's literacy training, both institutional and extrainstitutional.

High culture remained closed to most women, but by midcentury popular writing became a career open to them. Many women wrote fiction because they needed the money, because they had sociopolitical motivations, or for both reasons. In her valuable *Revolution and the Word,* Cathy Davidson argues that the popular and democratizing activity of vernacular novel reading expanded women's literacy. Women's sentimental novels were often monitory tales of seduction featuring a woman's perspective on marriage in an era before birth control. Nearly all these novels discuss women's education along with the subject of marriage, both topics of importance to women. Social historians tell us that in 1800 women's life expectancy was only forty-two years, leaving a much higher proportion of a woman's life in the precarious premarital state than is common today. After marriage, a woman in 1800 could expect to have about seven children, excluding miscarriages and stillbirths. Yet women's premarital lives were more and more often being filled with education, and the growth of women's literacy seemed to give women more control over their fertility. The fertility rate declined by 23 percent by 1850, and 50 percent by 1900.[45]

It is not surprising that an era that produced unprecedented opportunities for women's literacy and formal education should nurture a bumper crop of productive women writers—women such as Harriet Beecher Stowe, Susan Warner, Elizabeth Stuart Phelps and her daughter Mary, and Maria Cummins. By century's end a critical mass of African American women had also gained advanced literacy and produced what historians have termed the Black Woman's Era. Authors from this era include Amelia E. Johnson, Frances Ellen Watkins Harper, Octavia Victoria Rogers Albert, and Pauline Hopkins.[46]

Women's fiction writing grew out of a history of women's personal writing of autobiographical materials such as diaries and letters. Although school literacy probably served as the foundation for much fiction writing, fiction writers learned their craft informally, using previous models they had read and internalized. Women also worked collaboratively with family, friends, editors, or in writing groups to improve their writing (see chapters 6 and 8). Successes of earlier women novelists must have empowered many to attempt the genre women claimed as their own.[47]

Compared with women's fiction, we currently know less about the many works of nonfiction on such subjects as history, language, moral philosophy, medicine, and other sciences. Yet we know that women produced texts on most topics of interest to nineteenth-century readers. Women such as Lydia Maria Child wrote across genres, publishing the first U.S. magazine for children as well as writing novels, poetry, speeches for abolitionists, and journalism. Journalism and publishing work opened doors for many women. For example, Margaret Fuller edited the *Dial,* while Lucy Stone, the first woman in Massachusetts to receive the A.B. degree (Oberlin, 1847), edited the *Woman's Journal* in Boston with her husband Henry Blackwell. Sarah J. Hale edited *The Ladies Magazine* then went on to edit *Godey's Lady's Book* for more than fifty years. Fighting for freedom for blacks, Mary Ann Shadd Cary published the *Provincial Freeman* out of Canada (1854–59), and Ida B. Wells edited the *Free Speech* out of Memphis in the last decade of the century. Women also became publishers and writers for the growing number of women's rights newspapers such as Amelia Bloomer's *Lily* (1849–56); the *Agitator,* Chicago (in 1869); the *New Northwest,* Portland, Oregon (1871–87); the *Queen Bee,* Denver (1882–95); and the *Woman's Chronicle,* Little Rock (1888–93). By midcentury, aided by their personal writing experience, school preparation, and on-the-job training, more women could become—and could imagine themselves becoming—writers when economics and the scarcity of men in the North and East forced them to support themselves.[48]

In the broad transformation from an oratorical into a professional culture women can be more easily associated with the privacy of writing, yet orality and literacy were never distinctly separated in their learning to read and write. An important part of women's struggle for equal education entailed the right to speak in public. Elocution texts popular for female use in both school and home taught girls and women the arts of reading aloud pleasantly and effectively. Whereas male public speaking had long been associated with the ministry, law, and politics, female speaking connoted radical religious views or women's rights advocacy. In 1847 Lucy Stone refused to write her Oberlin commencement address because she would not be allowed to read it herself. It would take a decade before Oberlin would allow women to speak publicly. However, a few women like Fanny Wright, Lucy Stone, Elizabeth Bacon Custer, Charlotte Perkins Gilman, and Frances E. W. Harper were able to support themselves by public lecturing. Women's approach to speech writing as personalized craft would differentiate the styles of their oratory from those of formally trained male orators. Oratory and print literature became so interwoven that, like men's, many women's texts—including Gilman's *Women and Economics,* Jane Addams's *Democracy and Social Ethics,* and Anna J. Cooper's *A Voice from the South*—began as nineteenth-century lectures and were later refined into books. Women's achievement of effective literacy, their ability to speak, write, and enjoy the benefits of a broad range of rhetorical powers, was becoming accepted, even common, by century's end. Women would struggle anew in the twentieth century, but the literacy they would strive for would be a different literacy. Nineteenth-century women had transformed the cultures and practices of literacy, transforming themselves in the process.[49]

Women's Literacy Studies: Tales from the Armchairs and Archives

Most essays in this volume represent a hybrid of self-reflexive, theoretical interpretation and speculation crossed with empirical/archival research into women's history. Reflecting the introductory themes, the book divides into two parts. In part 1, "Cultures and Contexts of Literacy," the writers present a panoply of sites and cultural contexts in which women learned to write, including ideological contexts, institutional sites, and informal settings such as literary circles. In part 2, "Practices and 'Voices' of Literacy," essays examine specific genres, texts, and "voices" of literate women and students of writing and speaking. Throughout the book, authors themselves speak with different voices on theoretical issues such as the value of theories of separate spheres and women's difference in the writing of history. Most of the authors, including the editor, write from the standpoint of their institutional situations in university writing programs. Other contributors work in literature programs in English and in women's studies, American studies, and history departments. Several of the essays were initially part of a panel on nineteenth-century women's writing instruction at a College Composition and Communication Conference.

Surveying the competing ideologies contextualizing nineteenth-century women's literacy is Jane E. Rose's "Conduct Books for Women, 1830–1860: A Rationale for Women's Conduct and Domestic Role in America." Rose strategically complicates two models—"True Womanhood" and "Real Womanhood"—with various responses to patriarchal social codes that competed but nevertheless upheld the dominant interests of male culture in the century. These varying patterns are drawn from her genre study of more than twenty conduct books from the antebellum period. She goes on to critique these ideals for women that, in Althusser's term, "interpellated" women in the first half of the century. Her work reminds us that women such as the authors of these conduct-of-life books had a hand in constructing and maintaining the ideologies that worked to contain women's potential for effective advanced literacies.

Using a hybrid of theory and archival research, Vickie Ricks investigates the environment for literacy at three turn-of-the-century women's colleges: Mount Holyoke, Vassar, and Radcliffe. She has found that women seeking a public voice often were caught in a cultural bind: they may have been offered equality in literacy, but they had to struggle with a literacy defined only in male terms. Thus the teaching of rhetoric and composition both aided and hindered women in their pursuit of a public voice in speaking and writing. However, in exploring the everyday world of these academic women, Ricks concludes that the three colleges were different and responded in diverse ways to women's entrance into the public discursive sphere.

Schwager has called for more histories such as Sandra D. Harmon's "'The Voice, Pen, and Influence of Our Women Are Abroad in the Land':

Women and the Illinois State Normal University, 1857–1899." This university, begun in 1857, was one of the country's earliest state-supported normal schools. The oldest state-supported school in Illinois and the first normal school in the Mississippi Valley, ISNU was a coeducational school where women students slightly outnumbered men, and women held teaching positions. Such an environment, with its greater freedom of association between men and women and greater equality, contrasts with that of many eastern schools. That this environment enabled women to succeed is shown by the numbers of women leaders produced by ISNU. Harmon's research reveals how training in literacy was diffused throughout the curriculum and extracurriculum at ISNU, resulting in many successful women writers and speakers.

Another contribution from the discipline of history, Devon A. Mihesuah's "'Let Us Strive Earnestly to Value Education Aright': Cherokee Female Seminarians as Leaders of a Changing Culture" describes the environment and literacy activities of a nondenominational boarding school in Indian Territory in what is now Oklahoma. The Female Seminary and its corresponding Male Seminary, both established by the Cherokee Council in 1851, were the first nonsectarian schools of higher learning west of the Mississippi River and were notable for being run by a tribe, not by the federal government or missionaries. The female curriculum was based on that of Mount Holyoke, and seminary women with their high academic achievements often surpassed Cherokee males as well as white settlers in the territory. Such an institution did little to preserve Cherokee culture, but it did produce women civic and business leaders who contributed to the Cherokee adaptation to the "white man's world."

In her essay "His Religion and Hers in Nineteenth-Century Hymnody" June Hadden Hobbs explores religion as a context of literacy, in particular women's practice of hymn text writing. She contends that women in Protestant denominations formed a muted subculture that could speak only through the language and forms of the dominant male order. In this article, Hobbs uses Ginzburg's metaphor of the filter to describe how women used the dominant forms to inscribe their own voices in the texts of hymns they wrote. These women hymn writers wove their life experiences into texts by using images of nurturance or aesthetics as opposed to male hymn writers' mercantile or military imagery. Hobbs further suggests that this difference, based on life experiences in the home and kitchen versus the marketplace implies that nineteenth-century women and men experienced spirituality differently.

Nicole Tonkovich's "Writing in Circles: Harriet Beecher Stowe, the

Semi-Colon Club, and the Construction of Women's Authorship" also turns to informal education, examining one literary circle: Cincinnati's Semi-Colon Club. The club serves as a site for her inquiry into the role membership in such a social group played in advancing women writers, in particular Catharine Beecher and Harriet Beecher Stowe. She shows how the club provided a social forum in which both women and men could learn to write and have their compositions critiqued, often by powerful men in a position to further—or to be credited with furthering—women's careers. Tonkovich assesses how the club served women writers and also how the interactions of members—the real social basis of text production—helped construct contrary notions of the individual author-genius. She next turns to a little-known autobiography by an African American in Cincinnati, Eliza Potter's *A Hairdresser's Experience in High Life,* to help reveal the grid of assumptions that undergirded the Semi-Colon Club's existence.

The essays in part 2 examine specific genres, texts, and voices of women previously unheard or, like Elizabeth Bacon Custer, misheard in previous analyses. Whether these are the voices of African American orators and authors or women students of rhetoric and composition, contributors have tried to present nineteenth-century women's own responses to their training in advanced literacies and the development of their intellectual selves.

Shirley Wilson Logan's "Literacy as a Tool for Social Action among Nineteenth-Century African American Women" emphasizes how African American women valued as well as placed their hopes and faith in literacy. Logan describes how five prominent black women acquired literacy and employed it as a key to open minds closed to social action and to change. Beginning with the first women to deliver public lectures, Maria Stewart, and proceeding chronologically to Sojourner Truth, Frances Harper, Ida Wells, and Anna J. Cooper, Logan relates how these women learned their literacies, whether alone or through mentors or literacy study clubs. Addressing both black and white audiences, these women faced different rhetorical situations than did white women speakers. Logan notes that these five serve to represent hundreds of other nineteenth-century black women who used their literacy to serve their people and bring about social change.

In the volume's only overtly collaborative effort, Judy Nolte Temple and Suzanne L. Bunkers explore how "literacy was life" for diarists Emily Gillespie and her daughter Sarah. In "Mothers, Daughters, Diaries: Literacy, Relationship, and Cultural Context," Bunkers and Temple narrate strands from the ninety-four years, and six thousand handwritten pages, of the Gillespies' diaries. They show how women, culturally muted in the public sphere, could construct their lives and subjectivities in the private spheres of their diaries. They observe that the diary, which they believe to be the essential form of female autobiography, was also an essential part of literacy instruction by mothers. The dramatic narrative told here also reveals how gendered knowledge and values could be transmitted along with literacy.

The writing of women on the frontier has been little examined, and a frequently overlooked group of frontierswomen is that of military wives who joined their husbands on military campaigns. In "Women and the Western Military Frontier: Elizabeth Bacon Custer," Maryan Wherry looks at how women's descriptions of their experiences differ from the male texts that have given us our standard myths of the frontier. Custer, the wife of General George Armstrong Custer, wrote a trilogy about life on the frontier. Although her work is often read as a defense of her husband, Wherry reads it as Elizabeth Custer's story of her own life and her interpretation of frontier life.

The next three essays highlight women's experiences in rhetorical training in eastern and southeastern girls' schools, at an eastern coordinate college (Radcliffe), and at a midwestern coeducational college (the predecessor of Butler University in Indianapolis). The essays reveal conflicts as women students learned existing conventions and norms of male discourse, but also triumphs as they learned to mediate forms and construct their own purposes and language.

P. Joy Rouse's "Cultural Models of Womanhood and Female Education: Practices of Colonization and Resistance" uses theories of colonization as a framework to explore education in eastern and southeastern girls' schools. Ideals such as "Republican Motherhood" and "True Womanhood" she sees as social and political forces strengthened through educational institutions and thus as colonizing efforts to control women. In the second part of her essay she presents archival evidence of women's struggles to resist these restrictive ideals, which were often defended in terms of biological determinism, and to construct their own identities. Rouse joins Ricks and Simmons in listening to the resisting and conflictual voices of women students struggling to enter the literate communities of their time and construct their own identities as educated girls and women.

Heidemarie Z. Weidner's "Silks, Congress Gaiters, and Rhetoric: A Butler University Graduate of 1860 Tells Her Story" adds to the narrative of women's experience with coeducation in higher education. Although women at coeducational Oberlin at midcentury were tracked separately in the oratorical curriculum, at Butler in Indianapolis women's educational experience was more similar to men's. There was even a chair of English specified for a woman, the Demia Butler chair. After 1869 the Butler board made no distinction between men's and women's education. But when Lydia Short (the second woman to graduate) attended, there was still a Female Collegiate Course. Weidner focuses on Short's rhetorical training as described in her college diary, giving us another woman's voice from the nineteenth century. As Short later founded Butler's first women's literary society, Weidner's article also illuminates extracurricular activities that enhanced instruction in literacy.

Sue Carter Simmons's essay, "Radcliffe Responses to Harvard Rhetoric: 'An Absurdly Stiff Way of Thinking,'" presents a study of one of the first women to study Harvard rhetoric. Annie Ware Winsor, one of the first women at Radcliffe, was thus one of the first women students Harvard professors taught in the 1880s. The study reveals conflicts with her composition professor Barrett Wendell, who served as a writing mentor. But Simmons's article portrays this conflict as part of Winsor's conflictual initiation into mastery of academic discourse. She describes how women early on critiqued academic writing, developed strategies of resistance to it, and also became masters of it. Winsor's ambivalent feelings about discursive forms developed in masculine contexts are similar to many women's attitudes toward academic forms today.

Finally, in an article reprinted from the Rockford Female Seminary magazine of 1875, the pseudonymous Jerusha Jane Jones shows how even when men and women were educated together, women's education could be different because of their distinct cultural contexts. Jones, the name likely symbolizing a composite figure representing the ideal RFS student, details the differences between her life and that of her college brother John Jones, differences that give her less time to spend on studies and self-development. The piece may have been written by Julia Lathrop, who spent 1874 at Rockford, earned her degree from Vassar College in 1880, and returned to the Midwest to live with Jane Addams and Ellen Gates Starr at Hull House, becoming a nationally recognized child welfare expert. The article, "Is John Smarter than I?" follows a toast to Jerusha Jane Jones, recounted in a letter written by Rockford teacher Mary Ashmun in 1874.

In an afterword reflecting on and synthesizing the histories told in the volume, JoAnn Campbell notes the parallels between the book's nineteenth-century women seeking a public voice and the contributors seeking a voice in academia today. So that these accounts may be historically situated, not read as yet another presentation of indisputable truth from above, she calls for a version of autobiographical literacy criticism to counteract the omnicient historical voice sometimes present. She notes that the book's essays themselves, however, recount how the voices their scholarly authors use today were constructed. Campbell views these histories as oriented to such present-day questions and political issues, and therefore useful for teaching us more about the range of literate practices as well as historical, institutional, and social obstacles to women's literacy. Finally, she sums up the chapters as forming "a history of possibility, a celebration of the ways women have used literacy to challenge oppositional structures, subvert dominant discourses, and create spaces in which to work and play."

Many of these essays conclude that training in literacy for women of the nineteenth century was at once a social disciplining and a liberating and enabling phenomenon. In learning to write women were subjected not only to male conventions and norms, but also to dominant ideologies such as the True Woman ideal. Nonetheless, women were also empowered as subjects, subjects who could not only resist restrictive socialization, but who could imagine alternatives and broader spheres of action. Women who achieved effective literacy—whether in institutional training, in study groups, alone, or with mentors—found a voice and learned to use it to create and enhance their own lives and to bring about social change.

Notes

My thanks to those who read drafts of the introduction, especially contributors Nicole Tonkovich, Shirley Logan, Vickie Ricks, Heide Weidner, Sandra Harmon, Jane Rose, June Hobbs, and Joy Rouse; also to C. Jan Swearingen, who advised on this volume from its inception; my colleagues at Oklahoma, Kathleen Welch, Susan Laird, and Peter Smagorinsky; former colleagues at Illinois State, Anne Rosenthal and Janice Neuleib, as well as Carol Mattingly, Anne Ruggles Gere, and Tom Miller, for helpful readings. William Wright supplied a helpful manuscript on women's clubs. Finally, thanks especially to Cecil Peaden for his help with early drafts.

1. Definitions and taxonomies of "literac(ies)" are numerous, but most distinguish basic or "functional" literacy from advanced, critical, or even "hyperliteracy" (a term from C. A. Perfetti). See Keith Walters, "Language, Logic, and Literacy," in *The Right to Literacy,* ed. Andrea A. Lunsford, Helene Moglen, and James Slevin (New York: MLA, 1990), pp. 173–88, esp. p. 174. For Deborah Brandt's concept of "literate know-how," see "Literacy and Knowledge," *Right to Literacy,* pp. 189–96, esp. p. 194. Brandt differs theoretically from Myron Tuman, *A Preface to Literacy:*

An Inquiry into Pedagogy, Practice, and Progress (Tuscaloosa: Univ. of Alabama Press, 1987), but Tuman also frames critical literacy as active: "Praxis, not coding, explains literacy, for literacy is ultimately best described, not as coded speech, but as verbal praxis; that is, literacy comes to life only in the efforts of people to use written language in acts of praxis" (p. 88). Tuman also extensively surveys and critiques definitions of literacy, as do articles in Eugene R. Kintgen, Barry M. Kroll, and Mike Rose, ed., *Perspectives on Literacy* (Carbondale: Southern Illinois Univ. Press, 1988), and Robert Pattison, *On Literacy: The Politics of the Word from Homer to the Age of Rock* (New York: Oxford Univ. Press, 1982). The definition of literacy as "the power to act in society" is from Janice M. Lauer and Andrea A. Lunsford's "The Place of Rhetoric and Composition in Doctoral Studies," in *The Future of Doctoral Studies in English*, ed. Andrea Lunsford, Helene Moglen, and James F. Slevin (New York: MLA, 1989), p. 106.

2. I agree with Deborah Brandt's view that we do not yet understand the amazing complexity of "basic" reading and writing. As long as this is true and Americans suffer the consequences of illiteracy and poor teaching, we must not disparage studies focusing on the "mere ability" to read and write texts. See her *Literacy as Involvement: The Acts of Writers, Readers, and Texts* (Carbondale: Southern Illinois Univ. Press, 1990), p. 10. Brandt's later ethnographic studies of writing in society represents the kind of work Shirley Brice Heath calls for in her "Toward an Ethnohistory of Writing in American Education," in *Writing: The Nature, Development, and Teaching of Written Communication*, ed. Marcia Farr Whiteman (Hillsdale, N.J.: Erlbaum, 1981), pp. 25–45. Figures on nineteenth-century literacy rates as well as the concept of the ideology of literacy are from Lee Soltow and Edward Stevens, *The Rise of Literacy and the Common Schools in the United States: A Socioeconomic Analysis to 1870* (Chicago: Univ. of Chicago Press, 1981); for literacy rates, see pp. 39, 155–58. The men's rate is my inference from their military enlistment record rate, although the authors use this figure for the overall literacy rate at the beginning of the century (p. 153). Stevens and Soltow (pp. 58–88) discuss ideology as linking literacy with "economic progress, public and private virtue, and nationalism" (p. 63). According to Stevens and Soltow, this ideology maintained that literacy strengthens the social order by binding the family to codes of proper behavior, encourages economic values such as wise use of time and hard work, and promotes economic opportunity for individuals. Its moral and worldly uses were seen as compatible.

3. Harvey J. Graff, *The Literacy Myth: Literacy and Social Structure in the Nineteenth-Century City* (New York: Academic Press, 1979).

4. For an introduction to women's literacy in the developing world, see Marcela Ballara, *Women and Literacy* (London: Led Books, 1992).

5. My understanding of the history of English departments is informed in general by Gerald Graff, *Professing Literature: An Institutional History* (Chicago: Univ. of Chicago Press, 1987). In relation to rhetoric and composition, see James A. Berlin, *Writing Instruction in Nineteenth-Century Colleges* (Carbondale: Southern Illinois Univ. Press, 1984); Sharon Crowley, *The Methodical Memory: Invention in Current-Traditional Rhetoric* (Carbondale: Southern Illinois Univ. Press, 1990); Albert R. Kitzhaber, *Rhetoric in American Colleges, 1850–1900* (Dallas: Southern Methodist Univ. Press, 1990); and Robert J. Connors, "Rhetoric in the Modern University: The Creation of an Underclass," in *The Politics of Writing Instruction: Postsecondary*, ed. Richard Bullock and John Trimbur (Portsmouth, N.H.: Heinemann, 1991), pp. 55–84. The editors' introduction to Gregory Clark and S. Michael Hallor-

an's *Oratorical Culture in America: Essays on the Transformation of Nineteenth-Century Rhetoric* (Carbondale: Southern Illinois Univ. Press, 1993) was particularly helpful in analyzing social and economic transformations in the century in relation to rhetorical education. A valuable collection, John C. Brereton, ed., *The Origins of Composition Studies in the American College, 1875–1925: A Documentary History* (Pittsburgh: Univ. of Pittsburgh Press, forthcoming), is scheduled to be published in 1995.

6. Nina Baym, "Between Enlightenment and Victorian: Toward a Narrative of American Women Writers Writing History," *Critical Inquiry* 18 (1991): 22–41, and also her *Novels, Readers, and Reviewers: Response to Fiction in Antebellum America* (Ithaca: Cornell Univ. Press, 1984); Cathy N. Davidson, ed., *Reading in America: Literature and Social History* (Baltimore: Johns Hopkins Univ. Press, 1989), and her *Revolution and the Word: The Rise of the Novel in America* (New York: Oxford Univ. Press, 1986); Mary Kelley, *Private Woman, Public Stage: Literary Domesticity in Nineteenth-Century America* (New York: Oxford Univ. Press, 1984); and Jane Tompkins, *Sensational Designs: The Cultural Work of American Fiction, 1790–1860* (New York: Oxford Univ. Press, 1985).

7. Laurence L. Vesey, *The Emergence of the American University* (Chicago: Univ. of Chicago Press, 1965), pp. 4–7. See also Lawrence A. Cremin, *American Education: The National Experience, 1783–1876* (New York: Harper and Row, 1980).

8. Linda Kerber in "Separate Spheres, Female Worlds, Woman's Place: The Rhetoric of Women's History," *Journal of American History* 75 (1988): 9–39, critiques historians of women for reifying the metaphor of separate spheres, warning that this reification has produced a sloppy, static model that excludes women of color and slights the relationships between men and women, gender and society. Her critique is part of a general reevaluation of the concept of separate spheres in historical scholarship.

9. Gerald Graff, *Professing Literature;* Vesey, *American University;* Berlin, *Writing Instruction;* Connors, "Rhetoric"; and Burton Bledstein, *The Culture of Professionalism: The Middle Class and the Development of Higher Education in America* (New York: Norton, 1976). Miriam Brody's *Manly Writing: Gender, Rhetoric, and the Rise of Composition* (Carbondale: Southern Illinois Univ. Press, 1993) is an important analysis of the historical gendering of textual practice in institutional rhetoric and composition. Janet Carey Eldred and Peter Mortensen's unpublished manuscript "Monitoring Columbia's Daughters: Writing as Gendered Conduct" (from their forthcoming work *Imagining Rhetoric: Composing the Women of Early America*) examines rhetorical textbooks targeted for women in the eighteenth century. See also their "Gender and Writing Instruction in Early America: Lessons from Didactic Fiction," *Rhetoric Review* 12 (1993): 25–53. Following Drucilla Cornell, *Beyond Accommodation: Ethical Feminism, Deconstruction, and the Law* (New York: Routledge, 1991), I place the word "voice" in quotation marks both to emphasize writing and to acknowledge a dilemma: feminism relies on a feminine "voice" and feminine "reality," while such usage threatens to "reset the trap of rigid gender identities" and cover over real differences between women (p. 3).

10. This "treasure trove" includes, besides the classic work by Thomas K. Woody, *A History of Women's Education in the U.S.* 2 vols. (New York: Science Press, 1929), contributions in John Mack Faragher and Florence Howe, eds., *Women and Higher Education in American History: Essays from the Mount Holyoke College Sesquicentennial Symposia* (New York: Norton, 1988); Helen Lefkowitz Horowitz, *Alma Mater: Design and Experience in the Women's Colleges from Their Nineteenth-Century Beginnings to the 1930s* (New York: Knopf, 1984), and her

Campus Life: Undergraduate Cultures from the End of the Eighteenth Century to the Present (New York: Knopf, 1987); Jacqueline Jones, "Women Who Were More Than Men: Sex and Status in Freedman's Teaching," *History of Education Quarterly* 19 (1979): 47–59, and her *Soldiers of Light and Love: Northern Teachers and Georgia Blacks, 1865–1873* (Chapel Hill: Univ. of North Carolina Press, 1980); Linda Kerber, "'Why Should Girls Be Learn'd and Wise?': Two Centuries of Higher Education for Women as Seen through the Unfinished Work of Alice Mary Baldwin," in Faragher and Howe, *Women and Higher Education in American History,* pp. 18–42; Elizabeth Minnich, Jean O'Barr, and Rachel Rosenfeld, eds., *Reconstructing the Academy* (Chicago: Univ. of Chicago Press, 1988); Florence Howe, *The Myths of Coeducation—Selected Essays, 1964–1983* (Bloomington: Indiana Univ. Press, 1984); Maris Vinovsky and Richard Bernard, "Beyond Catharine Beecher: Female Education in the Antebellum Period," *Signs* 3 (1978): 856–69; Barbara Miller Solomon, *In the Company of Educated Women: A History of Women and Higher Education in America* (New Haven: Yale Univ. Press, 1985); and Sally Schwager, "Educating Women in America," *Signs* 12 (1987): 333–72.

11. A rich body of literature exists on ideologies of nineteenth-century womanhood. Sources on "Republican Motherhood" include Linda Kerber's "The Republican Mother: Women and the Enlightenment—An American Perspective," *American Quarterly* 28 (1976): 187–205, *Women of the Republic: Intellect and Ideology in Revolutionary America* (Chapel Hill: Univ. of North Carolina Press, 1980), and "The Paradox of Women's Citizenship in the Early Republic: The Case of Martin vs. Massachusetts, 1805," *American Historical Review* 97 (1992): 349–78; see also Mary Beth Norton, *Liberty's Daughters: The Revolutionary Experience of American Women, 1750–1800* (Boston: Little Brown, 1980). For the "True Womanhood" ideal, see Nancy F. Cott, *The Bonds of Womanhood: "Women's Sphere" in New England, 1780–1835* (New Haven: Yale Univ. Press, 1977); Carroll Smith-Rosenberg, *Disorderly Conduct: Visions of Gender in Victorian America* (New York: Knopf, 1985); Frances Cogan, *All-American Girl: The Ideal of Real Womanhood in Mid-Nineteenth-Century America* (Athens: Univ. of Georgia Press, 1989); and Barbara Welter, "The Cult of True Womanhood, 1820–1860," *American Quarterly* 18 (1966): 151–74. For evaluation of these as historical constructs, see Kerber's "Separate Spheres" as well as Suzanne Lebsock, *The Free Women of Petersburg: Status and Culture in a Southern Town, 1784–1860* (New York: Norton, 1984). On the history of teaching as a woman's profession, see Nancy Hoffman, *Women's "True" Profession: Voices from the History of Teaching* (Old Westbury, N.Y.: Feminist Press, 1981); for a philosophical-historical view, see Susan Laird, "The Ideal of the Educated Teacher—'Reclaiming a Conversation' with Louisa May Alcott," *Curriculum Inquiry* 21 (1991): 271–97. For literacy rates, see Stevens and Soltow, *Rise of Literacy,* pp. 156–58.

12. On the "consequences" of literacy, see Soltow and Stevens, *Rise of Literacy;* Brian Street, *Literacy in Theory and Practice* (Cambridge: Cambridge Univ. Press, 1984); Harvey Graff, *Literacy Myth* as well as his *Legacies of Literacy: Continuities and Contradictions in Western Culture and Society* (Bloomington: Indiana Univ. Press, 1987); and Sylvia Scribner and Michael Coles, *The Psychology of Literacy* (Cambridge, Mass.: Harvard Univ. Press, 1981). For feminist challenges to the myth of progress, see Schwager, "Educating Women"; Kerber's "Separate Spheres"; Lebsock, *Free Women of Petersburg;* and Jill Conway, *The First Generation of American Woman Graduates* (New York: Garland, 1987), and "Women Reformers and American Culture, 1870–1930," *Journal of Social History* 5 (1972): 164–77.

13. For general background, see E. Jennifer Monaghan, "Literacy Instruction and Gender in Colonial New England," *American Quarterly* 40 (1988): 18–41. Kenneth A. Lockridge's *Literacy in Colonial New England: An Enquiry into the Social Context of Literacy in the Early Modern West* (New York: Norton, 1974) reports that early in the colonial period, about 60 percent of the men and 30 percent of the women could sign their names. Lockridge estimates that by the end of the colonial period the proportion of men signing had advanced to 80 percent or higher, while female literacy judged by signatures had stagnated at 40 to 50 percent (p. 38). However, others such as Auwers and Gilmore have argued that Lockridge's figures for women's literacy are too low. Later studies have found a higher level of signatures than Lockridge did by using deeds and other sources in addition to wills. See Linda Auwers, "Reading the Marks of the Past: Exploring Female Literacy in Colonial Windsor, CT," *Historical Methods* 13 (1980): 204–14, figures on p. 209; and William J. Gilmore, "Elementary Literacy on the Eve of the Industrial Revolution: Trends in Rural New England, 1760–1830," *Proceedings of the American Antiquarian Society* 92 (1982): 114–26, as well as his *Reading Becomes a Necessity of Life: Material and Culture in Rural New England, 1780–1835* (Knoxville: Univ. of Tennessee Press, 1989). Kaestle's remarks on interpretation of signatures by scholars is found in Carl F. Kaestle et al., *Literacy in the U.S.: Readers and Reading since 1880* (New Haven: Yale Univ. Press, 1991), p. 5.

14. For information on African American literacy, see especially Janet Duitsman Cornelius, *"When I Can Read My Title Clear": Literacy, Slavery, and Religion in the Antebellum South* (Columbia: Univ. of South Carolina Press, 1991). See also Linda M. Perkins, "The Education of Black Women in the Nineteenth Century," in Faragher and Howe, *Women and Higher Education in American History,* pp. 64–86; Dana Nelson Salvino, "The Word in Black and White: Ideologies of Race and Literacy in Antebellum America," in Davidson, *Reading in America,* pp. 140–56; Dorothy Sterling, ed., *We Are Your Sisters: Black Women in the Nineteenth Century* (New York: Norton, 1984); James D. Anderson, *The Education of Blacks in the South, 1860–1935* (Chapel Hill: Univ. of North Carolina Press, 1988); W. E. B. Du Bois, *Black Reconstruction in America: An Essay toward a History of the Part Which Black Folk Played in the Attempt to Reconstruct Democracy in America, 1860–1880* (1935; rpt. Cleveland: Meridian Books, 1962); and Robert C. Morris, *Reading, 'Riting, and Reconstruction: The Education of Freedmen in the South* (Chicago: Univ. of Chicago Press, 1981). For oratory, see the anthology edited by Robbie Jean Walker, *The Rhetoric of Struggle: Public Address by African American Women* (New York: Garland, 1992).

15. Monaghan, "Literacy Instruction," esp. pp. 19, 21–23.

16. "Easy to teach": Monaghan, "Literacy Instruction," p. 34; on writing technologies, see pp. 24–25.

17. Information on apprenticeship and literacy is in Monaghan, "Literacy Instruction," p. 27, and Stevens and Soltow, *Rise of Literacy,* pp. 30–33, 37.

18. Soltow and Stevens, *Rise of Literacy,* p. 13; Solomon, *Educated Women,* p. 16.

19. Harvey Graff, *Literacy and Social Development,* pp. 259–60; Tompkins, *Sensational Designs,* p. 153.

20. Lucia Bergamasco, "Female Education and Spiritual Life: The Case of Minister's Daughters," in *Current Issues in Women's History,* ed. Arina Angerman et al. (London: Routledge, 1989), pp. 39–60; Kathryn Kish Sklar, *Catharine Beecher: A Study in American Domesticity* (New Haven: Yale Univ. Press, 1973); Allen F. Davis,

American Heroine: The Life and Legend of Jane Addams (New York: Oxford Univ. Press, 1973); Catherine Hobbs Peaden, "Jane Addams and the Social Rhetoric of Democracy," in Clark and Halloran, *Oratorical Culture in America,* pp. 184–207.

21. Monaghan, "Literacy Instruction," pp. 35–36.

22. On summer sessions, see Cott. *Bonds of Womanhood,* p. 103; on the paradoxical images of motherhood and reading, see Soltow and Stevens, *Rise of Literacy,* p. 38; and on early egalitarian theories of literacy, see Baym, "Between Enlightenment and Victorian," p. 24.

23. The image of literacy as a double-edged sword is found in Soltow and Stevens, *Rise of Literacy,* where discussion of literacy as social control is also discussed; see p. 60. Also see H. Warren Button and Eugene F. Provenzo Jr., *History of Education and Culture in America* (Englewood Cliffs, N.J.: Prentice-Hall, 1983).

24. This controversial point about language awareness is made by Pattison in his introduction and throughout his book, *On Literacy.*

25. Joan Scott, "Gender: A Useful Category of Historical Analysis," in *Gender and the Politics of History* (New York: Columbia Univ. Press, 1988), pp. 28–50; Soltow and Stevens, *Rise of Literacy,* pp. 156–58.

26. Soltow and Stevens, *Rise of Literacy,* pp. 153, 155–56.

27. Ibid., p. 157.

28. On sources for slave literacy, see Cornelius, *When I Can Read,* pp. 7–10; also see Harvey Graff, *Literacy Myth,* pp. 58, 68; for testimony of the value of literacy to slave women, see Harriet Jacobs, *Incidents in the Life of a Slave Girl* (1861; rpt. New York: Oxford Univ. Press, 1990), and Susie King Taylor, *Reminiscences of My Life: A Black Woman's Civil War Memoirs,* ed. Patricia W. Romer and Willie Lee Rose (1902; rpt. Princeton: Marcus Weiner, 1992). The interactions of gender and genre in regard to black literacy have been explored by Katherine Bassard in "Gender and Genre: Black Women's Autobiography and the Ideology of Literacy," *African American Review* 26 (1992): 119–29.

29. Anderson, *Education of Blacks,* p. 6, and Du Bois, *Black Reconstruction in America,* pp. 641–49. Of slaves' secret training in literacy, Anderson tells of Elizabeth Sparks, for example, who was part of a group taught by free blacks who held literacy sessions in slave quarters (p. 17).

30. See Tompkins, *Sensational Designs,* p. 217 n. 5, for references to Hawthorne's familiar quotation. On the shift from rhetoric to composition, see Brereton, *Origins of Composition Studies* as well as David Russell, *Writing in the Academic Disciplines, 1870–1990: A Curricular History* (Carbondale: Southern Illinois Univ. Press, 1991), and Susan Miller, "The Feminization of Composition," in Bullock and Trimbur, *Politics of Writing Instruction,* pp. 39–53. Walter J. Ong's *Rhetoric, Romance, and Technology: Studies in the Interaction of Expression and Culture* (Ithaca, N.Y.: Cornell Univ. Press, 1971) discusses the disappearance of Latin and the education of women (pp. 14–15).

31. Solomon, *Educated Women,* p. 17.

32. Anne Firor Scott, "The Ever-Widening Circle: The Diffusion of Feminist Values from the Troy Female Seminary, 1822–1872," *History of Education Quarterly* 19 (1979): 3–25.

33. On Litchfield Female Academy, see Lynn Templeton Brickley's "Sarah Pierce's Litchfield Female Academy, 1792–1833," (Ph.D. diss., Graduate School of Education, Harvard Univ., 1985). On the self-construction of the female pedogogue, see Sarah Robbins, "Domestic Didactics: Nineteenth-Century American Literary Pedagogy by Barbauld, Stowe, and Addams" (Ph.D. diss., Univ. of Michigan, 1993).

34. Woody, *History of Women's Education,* 2:231. Other dates and information in this passage are from Woody; Schwager, "Educating Women"; and sources listed in n. 11. On Mount Holyoke, see Kathryn Kish Sklar, "The Founding of Mount Holyoke College," in *Women of America: A History,* ed. Carol Ruth Berkin and Mary Beth Norton (Boston: Houghton, 1979), pp. 177–201.

35. Schwager, "Educating Women," p. 356, and Perkins, "Education of Black Women," pp. 80–82.

36. Guy William Logsdon, *The University of Tulsa: A History, 1882–1972* (Norman: Univ. of Oklahoma Press, 1977), p. 34. See also chapter 4. The term "home school" was used by Robertson in her correspondence in the late nineteenth century in the same sense that Jane Roland Martin uses it today.

37. Elizabeth Ihle, "Black Women's Education in the South: The Dual Burden of Sex and Race," in *Changing Education: Women as Radicals and Conservators,* ed. Joyce Antler and Sara Biklen (Albany: State Univ. of New York Press, 1990), pp. 69–80, n. 3.

38. Woody, *History of Women's Education,* 2:470, 148–50, 183–84.

39. Ibid., 2:231–45. See also LeeAnna Lawrence, "The Teaching of Rhetoric and Composition in Nineteenth-Century Women's Colleges" (Ph.D. diss., Duke Univ., 1990).

40. The figures on women's enrollment are from Solomon, *Educated Women,* p. 63; Theodora Penny Martin's comment is from *The Sound of Our Own Voices: Women's Study Clubs, 1860–1910* (Boston: Beacon Press, 1987), p. 2.

41. Martin, *Our Own Voices,* pp. 2–3, 7. See Anne Ruggles Gere, *Writing Groups: History, Theory, Implications* (Carbondale: Southern Illinois Press, 1987), and William Winfield Wright, "Extra-Institutional Sites of Composition Instruction in the Nineteenth Century" (Ph.D. diss., Univ. of Arizona, 1994).

42. Martin, *Our Own Voices,* p. 3; Anne Firor Scott, "Women and Libraries," *Journal of Library History* 21 (1986): 400–405.

43. Martin writes almost nothing about the black club movement; see black clubwoman Fannie Barrier Williams, "The Club Movement among Colored Women of America" (1900), excerpted in *Early American Women: A Documentary History, 1600–1900,* ed. Nancy Woloch (Belmont, Calif.: Wadsworth, 1992), pp. 490–92, as well as Perkins, "The Education of Black Women."

44. Susan Coultrap-McQuin, *Doing Literary Business: American Women Writers in the Nineteenth Century* (Chapel Hill: Univ. of North Carolina Press, 1990), p. 2.

45. See Baym, "Between Enlightenment and Victorian," and Tompkins, *Sensational Designs.* Statistics on life expectancy and fertility are from Davidson, *Revolution and the Word,* pp. 113, 116.

46. See Henry Louis Gates, Jr., "In Her Own Write," foreword to *The Journal of Charlotte Forten Grimké,* ed. Brenda Stevenson (New York: Oxford Univ. Press, 1988), pp. vii–xxx; Frances Smith Foster, *Written by Herself: Literary Production by African American Women, 1746–1892* (Bloomington: Indiana Univ. Press, 1993); and Jacqueline Jones Royster, "Dark Spinners of Word Magic: Literacy as an Authorizing Event" (paper presented at the Composition, Rhetoric and Literacy Seminar, Univ. of Oklahoma, Sept. 1992).

47. See Cinthia Gannett, *Gender and the Journal: Diaries and Academic Discourse* (Albany: State Univ. of New York Press, 1992) on the gendered tradition of diary writing; for issues concerning women novelists of the period, see especially Kelley, *Private Woman, Public Stage;* Nina Baym, *Woman's Fiction: A Guide to Novels*

by or about Women in America, 1820–70, 2d ed. (Urbana: Univ. of Illinois Press, 1993); and Coultrap-McQuin, *Doing Literary Business.*

48. Nina Baym's work on women's historical writing is a valuable contribution to our knowledge of women's nonfiction. See her *Feminism and American Literary History,* containing essays on the historical writing of Emma Willard, Sarah Hale, Elizabeth Peabody, and Lydia Sigourney (New Brunswick, N.J.: Rutgers Univ. Press, 1992). On women's periodicals, see Patricia Smith Butcher, *Education for Equality: Women's Rights Periodicals and Women's Higher Education, 1849–1920* (Westport, Conn.: Greenwood Press, 1989), and Penelope L. Bullock, *The African-American Periodical Press, 1838–1909* (Baton Rouge: Louisiana Univ. Press, 1981). See also Nicole Tonkovich, "Rhetorical Power in the Victorian Parlor; *Godey's Lady's Book* and the Gendering of Nineteenth-Century Rhetoric," in Clark and Halloran, *Oratorial Culture,* pp. 158–83.

49. Nan Johnson, *Nineteenth-Century Rhetoric in North America* (Carbondale: Southern Illinois Univ. Press, 1991); see also her article "The Popularization of Nineteenth-Century Rhetoric: Elocution and the Private Learner," in Clark and Halloran, *Oratorical Culture in America,* pp. 139–57; Karlyn Kohrs Campbell, introduction to *Man Cannot Speak for Her,* vol. 1, *A Critical Study of Early Feminist Rhetoric* (Westport, Conn.: Greenwood Press, 1989), p. 13; also see Walker, *Rhetoric of Struggle.* The masculine nature of written institutional rhetoric is described in Brody's *Manly Writing,* which provides an interesting contrast.

I

Cultures and Contexts of Literacy

I

JANE E. ROSE

Conduct Books for Women, 1830–1860

A RATIONALE FOR WOMEN'S CONDUCT AND DOMESTIC ROLE IN AMERICA

Woman's empire is Home; *and, by adding spirituality to its happiness, dignity to its dominion, and power to its influences, it becomes the best security for* individual integrity, *and the surest safeguard for* national virtue.
—Mrs. A. J. Graves, *Woman in America* (1843)

CONDUCT-OF-LIFE books, a distinct genre written by both men and women in the mid-nineteenth century, provide an important textual site on which to explore social ideals for women's roles in antebellum America. They were concerned with women's self-culture, but for reasons different from the transcendentalist Margaret Fuller's. My study of antebellum conduct books demonstrates that Republican Motherhood or ideal womanhood, the term I prefer to use, reinforced a doctrine of separate spheres and, similar to earlier ideologies of women's education, fostered both positive and negative consequences for women's education and literacy.

The epigraph from Mrs. A. J. Graves's *Woman in America* (1843) best illustrates how conduct books glorify Republican Motherhood and domesticity. First, the home is characterized as woman's appropriate sphere. More importantly, the home, described in terms suggesting sanctity, piety, and dignity, becomes instrumental in fostering religion, uprightness, and virtue. Next, the home is viewed as women's empire, thereby suggesting the importance of a domestic vocation. Women—mothers in particular—can best serve the Republic by raising virtuous citizens, especially sons, who will become future leaders and statesmen. "Woman's empire," in this view, is a key element in the American Republic, and republicanism thus understood is a capacious, synthesizing concept that has to do with a collective way of life. If children become virtuous adults, then "national virtue" is more likely to be strengthened, and the republic is less likely to degenerate.[1]

Mrs. Graves's *Woman in America* is only one example of the many antebellum conduct books for women that promoted such tenets aimed at preserving the social order. Its publication suggests that women's gaining education and therefore literacy also enhanced their abilities to set forth ideas, couched in terms of a moral and civic agenda, through writing and publishing about womanhood and women's roles and vocations. However, as Hobbs points out in the introduction to this volume, the acquisition of literacy can be a double-edged sword used to achieve different goals: social control, "private and idiosyncratic" aims, and mixed radical and conservative motives. In conduct books the rationale for woman's role can be considered both radical and conservative: radical, because it promotes both the literacy and education of women. At the same time, however, the rationale qualifies literacy by dictating reading material compatible to the model of ideal womanhood and also restricts the education of literate women to preparation for a domestic vocation. It is social and cultural rather than private and idiosyncratic, for many authors espouse similar ideas.

Both literary reviewers and publishers praised works that provided high moral content. Domestic writing was produced prolifically because it served the needs of the reading public, sustained the ethos of moral aesthetics, and shaped and reinforced prevailing moral codes regarding femininity and women's roles. Ironically, female authors of conduct-of-life books argued for a limited separate sphere for women at the same time as they enlarged their own sphere of influence by becoming well-known authors. For example, Catharine Sedgwick and Lydia Sigourney disseminated their views of women's culture and contributed to the lucrative enterprise of publishing works with a decidedly moral agenda. Clearly empowered by literacy and education, these authors had the opportunity to shape women's culture significantly.[2]

The conduct book for women usually took one of two forms: a collection of essays, sermons, or letters, or a treatise of closely linked chapters covering conventional topics. Such subjects might include domestic, religious, and wifely duties; advice on health and fashion; rules for dating, mental improvement, and education; the art of conversation and avoidance of "evil-speaking" and gossiping; and advice on fostering harmonious marital relations. Conduct books for women constitute one species of the advice book; other species include the guidebook or success manual for men, the etiquette manual, and the domestic treatise.[3]

Placed in the genre of the conduct-of-life books, the conduct book should be distinguished from the etiquette manual or courtesy book. There is a fundamental difference in purpose: the conduct book promotes social goals for the progress of the Republic whereas the etiquette manual emphasizes individual goals for raising one's status in society. The conduct book prescribes a certain way of life for women to follow. Concerned with the moral and intellectual improvement of women for the good of the Republic, it emphasizes gender-role distinctions and recommends methods of self-culture for women and of fulfilling one's purpose in life. That purpose is delineated as cultivating one's full potential, thereby meeting the components of ideal womanhood: serving God and the Republic by raising virtuous children, and ministering to one's husband by rendering the home a welcome refuge from the world of commerce.

In contrast, the etiquette manual or courtesy book offers rules for appropriate manners and social decorum for polite society, with tips for fashion and beauty. Its major purpose is to educate the reader for self-advancement without regard to the formation of the Republic. If individuals become refined and shed any appearance of vulgarity, then they are more likely to improve their position or status in society and, therefore, gain a place among the upper classes.[4]

Fundamental to the argument that domesticity is the best vocation for women, as promoted in conduct books, is the profile of the ideal woman: wife and mother. But what type of woman is necessary for and capable of reigning in the empire of the home and instilling morality and virtue in future citizens of the Republic? Whose interests does such an ideal serve? What arguments regarding women's conduct and vocation do the authors of conduct books employ? What limitations upon women result from the expectations placed upon them? Questions of this order provide the generative impulse of this essay and guide my investigation of the relation of these texts to their idea of social order, a relation that in most general terms could be characterized as reifying or reinforcing the idea or ideal—or, to quote Jane Tompkins, "redefining the social order."[5]

In the case of the conduct books the authors posit an ideal of womanhood and present their ideas as to how middle- and upper-class women should lead their lives. In this way, they redefine the nature of women and their vocations; by restricting women to the domestic sphere, they redefine the social order. At the same time, taken collectively conduct books reinforce or reify their vision of the social order, placing ideal women in the home and responsible, virtuous men in the public sector. They do not prove that nineteenth-century women really were pious, submissive, virtuous, and domestic or that women served only in the vocations of marriage and motherhood. As these books were being published, many women were working in the mills as textile workers and in households as domestic servants. In this regard there is not anything "true," as the label "True Womanhood" would suggest, about the nature of all women living in antebellum America. Thus, "ideal" is a more appropriate qualifier. The ideal serves to place white, middle-class women on a pedestal as superior moral human beings rather than considering them as individuals with unique personalities and human frailties.[6]

The idealization of white womanhood is one of many criticisms that can be made of conduct books. This essay offers a critique, within the contexts of nineteenth-century gender ideology and women's culture, of the portrait of ideal womanhood promoted in conduct books and addresses larger issues ignored by previous scholarship. My purpose is not to draw conclusions about women's lives from the conduct books. Criticizing scholars who rely on advice books to extrapolate conclusions regarding women's roles, Mary Beth Norton notes that advice books are "expressions of social norms formulated largely by men, outlining ideal types of female behavior."[7] However, my study reveals that a number of women also wrote prescriptive literature, thereby demonstrating that women played active roles in shaping women's culture.

As I have found, conduct books offer an ideal of womanhood that acts as a rationale for the social control of middle-class white women, particularly in their conduct and role in the family circle and society. This rationale promotes the idea of women's influence in advancing the progress of humanity and in reforming and compensating for the negative aspects of mainstream male culture. In many ways, it also serves the interests of a patriarchal culture. By patriarchy, I mean the political and social structures that privilege men at the expense of women by promoting male domination and female subordination. Emphasizing women's subservient roles as wives and mothers, conduct books propose an intellectually circumscribed life for women by placing certain limitations and restrictions upon women's autonomy, literacy, and educational and vocational opportunities.

Over the past three decades, scholars have extrapolated the characteristics of womanhood conducive and necessary to the domestic sphere, as understood in prescriptive literature, but they have chosen not to consider the antifeminist implications of such ideals. The best-known and most often cited study is Barbara Welter's. Through an examination of women's magazines, gift books, religious tracts, sermons, and cookbooks published from 1820 to 1860, Welter identified "four cardinal virtues" associated with what she calls "the cult of true womanhood": piety, purity, submissiveness, and domesticity.[8] While not dismissing the contribution of this landmark study, I suggest that much has been omitted in her analysis of woman's advice books. First, she ignores the style and substance of the arguments prescribing woman's role and character. For example, the authors of conduct books often rely on exalted rhetoric, religious arguments, and republican ideological imperatives, as illustrated by Graves's statement, to promulgate their views regarding women's appropriate conduct and vocation. A woman's mission, ordained by God and acknowledged by the author, is to maintain the harmony and sanctity of the home for the sake of husband and children. Mothers must train upright children for the good of the Republic.

Second, Welter places too much emphasis on women's *passive* role within the domestic domain. She points out that "submission was perhaps the most feminine virtue expected of women" and that men were "the movers, the doers, the actors," while women were "the passive, submissive responders." She implicitly links activity to men's work in the public sphere.[9] However, the numerous duties required of women, ranging from the mundane tasks of cooking, cleaning, and sewing to the momentous projects of instructing children and fulfilling churchly obligations, could not possibly be accomplished by the weak or passive. Female submissiveness, as argued in the prescriptive literature, presents a contradiction. The evidence is clear that women are expected to take an active and major role in maintaining the home as empire. Of course, in doing so, they are acting under the orders or guidance of their husbands. Wives are advised, however, to take a submissive stance in their marital relationships. While noting the kinds of advice recommended to women, Welter overlooks the reasons or arguments behind these prescriptions, thus neglecting their social implications. One such implication, for example, is that giving women special authority in the domestic sphere also largely denies them the right to make other vocational choices and enter the public domain.

More recently than Welter, but in a somewhat similar vein, Frances Cogan has discovered another ideal operating in advice literature. She questions the assumption accepted by scholarship—for example, Carroll Smith-Rosenberg's *Disorderly Conduct,* Catherine Clinton's *Other Civil*

War: American Women in the Nineteenth Century, and Lois Banner's *American Beauty*[10]—that "Welter's monolithic paradigm of True Womanhood . . . was the *only* popular ideal." By examining popular didactic literature, advice books, domestic novels, and periodical fiction published from 1840 to 1880, Cogan identifies a competing ideal at work in these popular sources. The ideal of Real Woman or Real Womanhood, as she labels it, promotes "intelligence, physical fitness and health, self-sufficiency, economic self-reliance, and careful marriage." She also privileges this ideal as the one that really counts. For many women, she argues, this ideal became a survival ethic. It was grounded on the "triple bases of absolute necessity, health reform precepts, and observable clinical reality." Furthermore, the ideal of Real Womanhood views American women "as biologically equal (rationally as well as emotionally) and in many cases markedly superior in intellect to what passed for male business sense, scholarship, and theological understanding."[11]

Like Welter's work, Cogan's study is problematic. First, her partisan focus on a "Real" ideal is a political strategy that seeks to substitute a good ideal for a bad one. By linking ideal womanhood to reform movements in health and education, she deems Real Womanhood a positive influence on the lives of middle-class American women. She does not address the purpose such an ideal served in perpetuating gender roles and in restricting women to a domestic vocation. Nor does she consider the local consequences or ramifications of "real" womanhood. In other words, her ideal exists outside time and place as a counter to another "universal" construct developed by scholars—that of True Womanhood. Second, she claims that Real Womanhood was independent of the "thrust of nineteenth-century feminism," yet she explains neither what she means by nineteenth-century feminism nor how Real Womanhood could remain independent of it. Third, like Welter, Cogan merely offers an explanation of the ideal instead of a critique of it.

I do not dismiss Welter's and Cogan's contentions that ideals of womanhood operate within advice books, but it is not enough merely to identify such ideals without attempting to understand the function or purpose they serve. To do so requires examining their historical and cultural significance. For example, one needs to ask what purpose an ideal of womanhood was expected to serve in a middle-class, republican, democratic, and increasingly capitalist culture. Moreover, a close textual analysis enables one to see how domestic rhetoric was employed not only to teach women appropriate modes of conduct but also to persuade them of the importance of literacy and education in training them for marriage, motherhood, and domesticity.

It is not surprising that the authors of conduct books conclude that domesticity is the most crucial vocation for white middle-class American women, particularly for those able to meet the prescriptions of ideal womanhood. Scholars have traced ideologies prior to the antebellum period that elevate the status of the home and the housewife primarily for civic purposes, thereby reinforcing the notion of separate spheres for men and women. For example, Mary Beth Norton locates the origin of domesticity in the period of the American Revolution. She challenges the commonly held view that white female colonists held equal positions with their partners in the home, that they participated in business, and that as a result women felt high self-esteem. After analyzing women's private writings, Norton concludes that eighteenth-century colonists clearly understood which duties were properly "feminine," what conduct was suitable for women, and what functions women were expected to perform. Furthermore, a hierarchical structure existed within the household, with women holding the inferior position. Before the Revolution American men and women neither questioned the restrictions of the feminine sphere nor systematically defended the scope of woman's domestic role: as they viewed it, woman's destiny was decided at birth. However, during the war the boundaries of woman's sphere became less restrictive as women became politically active and, out of necessity, managed their family property independently. As a result of their wartime accomplishments and the development of republican ideology, after the Revolution women were no longer uniformly viewed as inferior, nor was domesticity disparaged.[12]

In fact, it was during the Revolution that arguments advocating mothers' roles as moral exemplars became so prevalent. Based on her analyses of letters and diaries written by both men and women as well as court records, petitions to legislatures, pamphlets, and other political documents, Linda Kerber has determined how republican ideology modified woman's sphere. As she explains, according to eighteenth-century republican ideology, which borrowed ideas from Aristotle, women were assumed to make moral decisions in the context of the domestic setting, "a woman's domain that Aristotle understood to be a nonpublic, lesser institution that served the polis." Republican ideology called on educated, righteous mothers to raise virtuous male citizens on whom the wealth of the Republic depended. Thus a political context, acceptable to women, in which private female virtues coexisted with civic virtue gradually emerged. This notion has been called "Republican Motherhood." Infusing political values into domestic life and ultimately virtue into the Republic, the mother, not the masses, became the custodian of civic morality.[13]

Clearly, women's patriotic roles as moral exemplars and caretakers of civic morality (by instilling it in men) came to be viewed as a means of maintaining social order and national virtue. In his insightful study *On the Man Question: Gender and Civic Virtue in America,* Mark E. Kann follows Kerber's lead and explains how an ideal of womanhood was formulated through the rhetoric of Republican Motherhood and encouraged by a fear of unmanageable, passionate, untrustworthy women perceived as threats to the social order. As he points out, at the time of the American Revolution it was believed that "women were not born with natural rights" and that they could not be "granted rights until their passions were subdued and their informal powers [influences in town meetings and courts] were constrained." To be given liberty women must be sober, civil, patriotic. The affectionate, pious, nurturing, and patriotic mother could be the model of womanhood to counteract female passion, viewed as a catalyst to disorder. Furthermore, Kann asserts, self-sacrificing patriotic women could help hold the Republic together by creating a domestic haven to counterbalance the market economy of the public sphere where men might be drawn to material excess, intemperance, gambling, and prostitution.[14] Of course, to fulfill their roles, these women were not to be educated for the sake of "self-development and public good," as Judith Sargent Murray and Mercy Otis Warren argued they should be, but for the cause of domesticity linked to preparation for teaching children civic duties. Independent, educated women might turn away from the fireside to pursue masculine professions, business, and law. As Norton's, Kerber's, and Kann's studies indicate, eighteenth-century republican ideology planted the seeds for the glorification of motherhood during the antebellum period.

At the time the conduct books were written, especially during the Jacksonian Age of the 1830s, a number of factors threatened the social cohesion and therefore the stability of the Republic. The depression of 1837–39 put thousands of people out of work: numerous religious denominations broke away from established churches; mass immigration hit cities, causing disorder; and industrialization increased. Amid all these changes, the home more and more symbolized a haven of social stability. And with mass production relieving housewives of duties like making bread, candles, soap, and cloth, women could have more time to attend to husband's needs and to instruct children.[15]

The authors of conduct books rely heavily on the concept of Republican Motherhood. In their view, through domesticity patriotic wives and mothers can fulfill their civic mission by raising upright children to maintain the stability of the nation. Because many of the authors are ministers, they emphasize women's religious mission as well. But the successful execution of these missions requires a certain kind of woman, and the proponents of domesticity seek to profile her. Patriotic domesticity is a tenuous social construct in part because of its reliance on an ideal. As the word suggests, an *ideal* as a conception of something in its absolute perfection, that which may exist only in the mind or imagination, is a standard impossible to meet. But if women are unable to fulfill the civic and religious missions prescribed, then the ideological assumptions of domesticity and Republican Motherhood fall apart.[16]

However, despite the impossibility of meeting an ideal, many authors still argue that the female character is capable of reaching perfection (completion of potential). Thus the primary purpose of the conduct book for women, both polemical and didactic, is to persuade and encourage young women to strive for the authors' purported versions of human perfection—spiritually, mentally, emotionally, and physically—and to teach them how to reach that goal. William Alcott states emphatically that no reason exists to think that a woman cannot be all that she can be, that she cannot reach "the beau-ideal": the beautiful ideal or "the perfect type or model," as the nineteenth-century use of the term is defined in the *OED*. "We ought to do all in our power to emancipate and elevate her," he exhorts.[17] In the context in which Alcott uses it, "to emancipate" woman means to allow her opportunities to develop her potential to its fullest, but only insofar as that potential is linked to a domestic vocation. "To emancipate" suggests neither the freedom of women from economic and political restraints nor a freedom to pursue vocations in the public arena.

Mrs. A. J. Graves also believes in the potential of women to accomplish great things and so fulfill that mission, and she explains in her treatise how to rectify the cultural problem of women's lack of preparation. She assigns to mothers the task of training their daughters to be industrious, active, and useful at home so that they will not lapse into languor and idleness nor choose to become fashionable objects to be admired only at fancy balls. Furthermore, like Catharine Beecher in *A Treatise on Domestic Economy,* Graves urges mothers to teach their daughters how to practice domestic economy so "that the great result—a happy and well-ordered home—can be secured." Moreover, in preparing women for their mission, attention should also be given to physical fitness (to be achieved through domestic tasks) and intellectual development. In Graves's view, a woman should acquire knowledge not to voice her own opinions in the public arena but to be "better qualified to train up her sons in the love of their country and of their fellow-men, by instilling into their minds the lofty and generous principles of liberty and of equal rights for just laws and rightful authority."[18] Clearly, Graves is advocating republican ideological imperatives, not woman's rights initiatives.

For a number of authors, a necessary attribute of the beau-ideal is virtue, a key word in American republican ideology. Because of her powerful, positive influence, the virtuous woman can promote the individual and collective good and can deter corruption and degeneracy. Equally important, according to Jonathan Stearns, female virtue buttressed by piety can keep the dangerous actions of men in check: "It is a holy influence, which the virtuous and pious sister diffuses over the fraternal circle. Wayward passion is awed by it, and the demon of vice and dissipation hides his head, and is ashamed in its presence."[19] As his statement implies, women are capable of being more virtuous than men, and the influence of the virtuous female is needed to counteract or perhaps counterbalance what many authors of conduct books fear—the sexual licentiousness and viciousness of men, a clear threat to the fortunes of social order. Men may turn to greedy pursuits, drinking, and gambling and consequently become abusive and irresponsible husbands, fathers, and citizens. Like Stearns, William Eliot believes in the moral superiority of women in directing men to stay on the right path of virtue.

> Woman's perception of virtue is generally understood to be more nice than that of men; and what satisfies her is sure to meet with their approval, and, generally speaking, they will not come quite up to the mark. We [men] seldom rise quite up to the standard of morality and religion which woman holds before us. We never rise above it. In this respect she is the lawgiver and we are the subjects. The only hope for the moral advancement of society is to keep woman in the advanceguard. Let her point the way and lead it, and the right progress is secured.[20]

This passage has several implications for women's roles in the private and public spheres. First, if a woman is placed on a pedestal and viewed with such respect because of her virtue, she cannot possibly refuse the important project of either guiding or reforming the actions of husbands, sons, and brothers. Second, the passage questions, indeed implicitly criticizes, the behavior of mainstream male culture of the time: men's conduct may harm society and women. Writers like Stearns and Eliot are counting on the influence of virtuous women to counter and dispel evil influences that tend to corrupt men. Third, if women possess moral power to advance society, they are clearly a factor in republican millenarianism. Indeed, the destiny of the young Republic is largely in their hands. Why they should not thus be given voting privileges and allowed equal participation with men in the political arena is an obvious question that nonetheless occurred to relatively few until the turn of the century. Would not the addition of virtuous women to the legislature help check the power of vicious males? Yet the proponents of domesticity offered strong reasons for restricting female influence to the domestic realm while at the same time linking that influence to the public good.

Etymologically and historically, the concept of virtue has been associated with men. For example, the Aristotelian concept of virtue deemed men to be fully virtuous human beings whose chief virtue lay in commanding, whereas women and slaves were not viewed to be fully virtuous human beings. Their only value lay in obeying. I am more concerned here, however, with the understanding of virtue in Revolutionary and post-Revolutionary America, especially its gendered aspects. In a wide-ranging article, Ruth Bloch explores the gender-based meanings of virtue in Puritan ethical theory and in Revolutionary thought. Distinguishing between public and private virtue, she notes that Puritan ethical theory subscribed to the notion that women could practice private Christian virtues—"temperance, prudence, faith, charity." Public virtue—"active, self-sacrificial service to the state on behalf of the common good"—was thought to be an inherently masculine characteristic. Only exceptional women might be capable of public virtue. According to Bloch, masculine qualities (energy, manliness, courage) associated with public virtue were emphasized in the mid-1770s. In the 1780s and 1790s female public spirit emerged through the image of women as custodians of domestic morality and civic virtue. In Bloch's analysis, the public virtue that remained after the Revolution was situated outside the state—"the virtue of a diffuse, patriotic public whose allegiance was not to particular rulers or to the common interest of a homogeneous property holding social order but to a large and impersonal republican nation."[21]

The proponents of domesticity adhere to the same gender-based meanings of virtue applied in classical texts and apparent in Puritan ethical theory and Revolutionary thought. In arguing that women as wives and mothers can train men to be virtuous, they complicate the distinctions between private and public virtue. If public virtue is not an inherently feminine trait, then how is it that women are capable of instilling it in men? In the authors' assessment, because the ideal woman is capable of exercising private Christian virtues, she is somehow enabled to instill public virtue in men, but she herself is not expected to exercise public virtue in the political arena. Thus, the conflict between private and public virtue points to an irony that the conduct experts fail to reconcile. Although the authors link moral superiority to civic virtue, they separate the moral from the political. In their view, women can be moral leaders/guardians in the private domain but not political leaders/activists in the public realm.

Greatly concerned with the moral character of women who guide men, the conduct experts impose yet another limitation upon womanhood: Virtuous women should also be dispassionate. They deem piety to be an essential component of ideal womanhood because it will check women's emotions. They prefer women to be passionless because such females will maintain the social order and will tame men's passions. According to Mrs. L. G. Abell, in the development of one's character piety should be the first thing cultivated, because "it subdues the passions, controls the temper, regulates the feelings, and presides over the affections, and gives beauty, dignity, and symmetry to the character, and destroys the taste for unlawful pleasures."[22] According to the *OED*, "piety" is an early form of "pity," meaning a feeling of compassion or sympathy for the suffering, distress, or misfortune of another. In its Christian sense it means "habitual obedience and reference to God" and "devotion to religious duties." In a secular sense piety also denotes "faithfulness to the duties naturally owed to parents, relatives, and superiors." In the eighteenth and early nineteenth centuries piety was used in the context both of religious devotion and obedience and of devotion to family members. In the context in which Abell uses it, piety denotes her expectation that women will be compassionate, obedient to God, and devoted to religious duties, as well as faithful to duties owed to family members. Obviously, if a woman is to meet the restrictive criteria of the beau-ideal, then she cannot or should not exhibit the full range of emotions inherent in human nature, or she should express them only in acceptably feminine ways. Abell's statement implies that a woman as an embodiment of piety should be incapable of expressing any negative emotions—for example, anger.

Perhaps to frighten their readers into compliance, certain religious writers are quick to point out both the positive and negative consequences to women if they do or do not cultivate piety. Both Daniel Wise, a Methodist minister from New England, and John S. C. Abbott, a Congregationalist minister also from New England, maintain that a woman's happiness is dependent upon her piety. Furthermore, according to Abbott, if a young girl does not practice piety, she will be excluded from heaven, banished from God's preserve without anyone to love her, and left to the will of the wicked of the world who surround her. He promises that the reward of consecrating one's affections and conduct to God can be a rich one, since physical beauty will evolve through generosity: "There is no countenance so pleasant to look upon, so desirable to possess, as that which is animated by the expression of a warm and generous heart." Moreover, such a cheerful disposition will bear immediate fruit by attracting the attention and kindness of others. A disagreeable disposition prompted by impiety, in contrast, creates an ugly countenance—upturned nose, frowning mouth, and wrinkled brow. Such a young woman is avoided.[23]

Although the authors of conduct books view female passion and impiety as detrimental to the social order, they argue for the importance of certain female affections in creating a happy marriage, in raising children, and in improving society. The beau-ideal would not be complete without nurturance, love, and benevolence, qualities associated with the "heart" and accentuated by piety. Pointing out that women are inferior to men in intelligence and physical strength, Eliza Leslie declares that women's power lies in their nurturing qualities and strength of character. They meet tragedy with fortitude and withstand pain with patience, work cheerfully and industriously for their families, and lovingly tend the sick. Finally, according to Leslie, their strength lies in their ability "to smooth the ruggedness of man; to soften his asperities of temper; to refine his manners; to make his home a happy one; and to improve the minds and hearts of their children." A. I. Cummings, too, notes women's gift of nurturance and sympathy, "that deep and unfathomable principle of universal love."[24] Clearly, these authors privilege qualities assumed to be exclusively female—nurturance, compassion, gentleness—to emphasize that a major role for women is to alleviate the hardship of others. In addition, they expect the qualities of female character to tame or counterbalance certain traits usually associated with the male—aggression and unrefined ruggedness.

Closely related to woman's capacity to nurture is her capacity to love, another attribute associated with the heart. William Alcott claims that it is woman's nature to love.[25] A. I. Cummings also believes in woman's natural tendency to love and particularly celebrates a mother's love: "It is that love that smiles over our infant joys, and weeps over our infant sorrows; that watches over us in sickness and in health, by night and by day, with the same untiring constancy and arduous zeal."[26] More importantly, like virtue and piety, woman's love empowers her with a benign influence. With his typical rhetorical flourish, Daniel Wise describes the power of woman's kind and loving spirit: "The loveliness of spirit is woman's sceptre and sword, for it is both the emblem and instrument of her conquests. Her influence flows from her sensibilities, her gentleness, her tenderness. It is this which disarms prejudice, and awakens confidence and affection in all who come within her sphere; which makes her more powerful to accomplish what her will resolves than if nature had endowed her with the strength of a giant."[27] Interestingly, in his description Wise relies on words seemingly incongruous to women's kind and loving spirit. "Sword," "conquests," and "disarms" are warlike terms, suggesting the conflict and aggression men experience in battle. Yet these words from a male lexicon connote the power of woman's love to conquer the negative aspects of human nature and to foster the positive. Obviously, authors like Wise are unable to view the world in any framework other than from a perspective of male/female opposition. In this context, woman can be aggressive but only in a manner compatible with her perceived feminine qualities of love, gentleness, and tenderness.

Because virtue, piety, and nurturing qualities can empower a woman with a renovating influence, according to the conduct experts' rationale, the ideal woman should hold a public role as an agent of religious and social reform. Indeed, if women have such remarkable capacity for love and compassion, it follows that they are naturally benevolent and should perform charitable acts as long as they do not neglect domestic duties. According to Stearns, "the cause of benevolence is peculiarly indebted to the agency of woman"; she can cheer the afflicted and elevate the depressed.[28] Because of women's moral character and high station, both Alcott and Graves believe that they, in particular housewives, are especially suited for the noble work of evangelical redemption. For the cause of charity, Mrs. Abell appoints the lady of the house as the chief instrument in spreading the gospel and in mitigating the adversity of the poor and uneducated.[29]

Scholars have argued that the doctrine of woman's sphere and woman's benevolent influence made women special agents of social reform, thereby granting them social power.[30] However, while the model of ideal womanhood may have empowered women to a certain degree, it also disempowered them by dictating restrictions in their roles as agents of social reform. Although women were encouraged to participate in moral, temperance, and benevolent activities, they were instructed not to assume the minister-like role of publicly promoting their views and proselytizing others to them. When women ignored social customs and used public speaking as means to their reformist ends, they were censured. For instance, when Sarah and Angelina Grimké lectured to mixed (male and female) audiences on behalf of abolitionism in New England in the late 1830s, the Council of Congregationalist Ministers of Massachusetts castigated them for both their unchristian and unwomanly conduct. Recognizing how such a cultural prescription impedes the progress of women, nineteenth-century feminists like Sarah Grimké, Margaret Fuller, and Elizabeth Oakes Smith argued that women's roles as moral guardians and agents of social reform are dubious and limited without political rights and a voice and vote in government to initiate reform and enact laws.[31]

Perhaps the severest limitation placed on women's progress is the intellectual model that the ideal of womanhood imposes, which makes education a highly contradictory endeavor. On the one hand, women are encouraged to become well educated and literate. On the other hand, the advocacy of female education is tempered by restrictions determined by the doctrine of separate spheres, the assignment of women to a domestic vocation, and the fear that if they receive education equal to men's, they may become unsuitable for marriage. Or they may enter the public sphere to pursue a male profession and, therefore, become unsexed and masculine. Declaring that "woman is formed for the calm of home," Daniel Wise identifies the dire consequences for the woman who enters man's sphere: "She may venture, like the land-bird, to invade the sphere of man, but she will encounter storms which she is utterly unfitted to meet; happiness will forsake her breast, her own sex will despise her, men will be unable to love her, and when she dies she will fill an unhonored grave."[32] To some degree, this intellectual model is based on a consensus that women's intellectual capacity is inferior to men's. As can be seen from the authors' notion of woman's nature, the conduct books reach this conclusion by following the conventional belief, common in the early nineteenth century, that men provide the head or intellect (mind) and that women complete men by providing the heart, or love, affection, and compassion. Eliza Leslie states that "the female sex is really inferior to the male in vigor of mind as in strength of body" and dismisses as anomalies women like Joan of Arc and Augustina of Saragossa who have proved the opposite. Her groundless view of women's intelligence is reflected in her advice. She advises that when women converse with gentlemen, they should not argue with the men on political and financial topics because "all the information that a woman can possibly acquire or remember on these subjects is so small, in comparison with the knowledge of men that the discussion will not elevate them in the opinion of masculine minds."[33] In "Is John Smarter than I?" reprinted in this volume, Jerusha Jones disputes the notion of women's inherent intellectual inferiority by showing how the treatment of women as intellectual inferiors, prompted by views and attitudes like Leslie's, denies them an education that will develop the intellect.

Other authors share Jones's more positive view of women's intellectual capacity, but even so, they relate women's intellectual improvement to their missions in the home, not to individual interests and aspirations. William Eliot stresses that a young woman "should be treated as a rational being, who has a mind to think with, duties to perform, and a soul to save." He notes that an educated mother can lead her children in their search for truth and knowledge. Also espousing women's ability to learn advanced subject matter, Daniel Clark Eddy argues that women should be taught subjects usually reserved for men only: the sciences, political economy, and the theoretical and practical applications of religion. The strongest plank of Eddy's position is that mothers need to be well versed in these subjects in order to educate their sons.[34]

Although the authors of conduct books do not directly endorse the education of women at female seminaries, the instructional activities they suggest correspond closely to the educational opportunities at such schools. To a larger degree, their program of education centers on mental and moral improvement. To achieve such improvement, many authors advocate literacy by encouraging women to read because they believe the reading of good books is an effective means of cultivating the mind and character. Indeed, literacy is important so that women will be able to understand and be influenced by works like theirs that promulgate domesticity and a religious and moral agenda. Not surprisingly, they limit freedom of choice by prescribing what is and is not appropriate reading material for female self-culture. Charles Butler recommends that every woman, whether married or single, should allot some time regularly to reading works that will "contribute to her virtue, her usefulness, and her innocent satisfaction, to her happiness in this world and in the next." Lydia Sigourney concurs that reading is essential to all intellectual beings and that leisure time should be devoted to some worthwhile book. Alcott suggests that the Bible and books on physiology and chemistry are suitable reading material for women. A respected author of historical romances and moral and didactic tales, Catharine Sedgwick also advocates reading because books can make one think, and she, too, cites the Bible along with histories, travelogues, biographies, and English literature as necessary for study.[35] Given the emphasis on Bible reading and the fact that many authors were clergy, one might expect moral instruction to be incorporated into an educational program for women. Thus in Eliot's view moral and religious culture should take precedence over the cultivation of manners and the accomplishments of music, drawing, and dancing. Similarly, according to Alcott a woman should pursue appropriate studies as a means of forming her character as a missionary and should study both moral and mental philosophy.[36]

The conduct experts are quick to advise women against reading works that might jeopardize the conduct experts' teachings, incite certain unacceptable desires and ambitions, and thus threaten the social order. For example, Sedgwick warns against reading seductive novels, licentious romances, and popular tales published in newspapers and periodicals, which weaken the mind. Similarly, Timothy Shay Arthur encourages reading to develop the mind, but "for a young girl to indulge in novel-reading is a very serious evil." He claims that many novels are not suitable for young women because they present false views of life. He prefers that women read only novels that "give right views of life" and "teach true principles," and he endorses the works of authors like Miss Sedgwick, Miss Edgeworth, Miss Bremer, Mrs. Howitt, and Mrs. Opie. Other experts on women's conduct condemn novel reading altogether. According to Abell, novel reading is an undue stimulus to the brain and a source of evil, and Wise asserts that novels distract one from more serious reading and may harm one's religious interests; therefore, he recommends the Bible for improving the mind and the heart.[37]

Although some authors recommend a curriculum for female education similar to a curriculum for males and urge the development of mental and moral self-culture through reading, the purpose in educating women, whether through a female or male curriculum, is tightly linked to their role in the domestic sphere. They are obligated to use their knowledge to assist young men in preparing for professions and young women in cultivating private virtue. Women are not expected to use knowledge to pursue careers and fulfill roles in the public realm. There is no call to educate or train women for professions such as law, medicine, and politics, which are considered appropriate for men only. That some women may not marry, may choose not to marry, or may lose a husband is not considered in the argument. Catharine Sedgwick is a lonely voice promulgating the view that women be allowed to choose and pursue their own professional goals. God, she opines, has not limited women's powers to one sphere. Hence her advice: "Be sure to be so educated that you can have an independent pursuit, something to occupy your time and interest your affections: then marriage will not be essential to your usefulness, respectability or happiness. Then you will not be the *old maid,* touched by every ill word, and dependent on every chance kindness, but you will secure an independent existence, and the power of dispensing to others." Furthermore, because the educational program outlined in most conduct books is limited to a domestic vocation or one closely related to domesticity such as the teaching profession, these authors support the notion of total economic dependence of women upon men; yet they do not consider what may happen to women when they become widowed or when husbands fail to be good providers. In this matter, too, Sedgwick is an exception. She recognizes the need for women to be educated so that they are able to support themselves, live independently, and avoid being forced into marriage out of economic consideration. Similar to Sedgwick in her views, Lydia Sigourney believes women should become well versed in either art or science so that they may earn a living "should they be reduced to poverty."[38]

Ironically, in a sense the authors of conduct books for women can be regarded as promoters of progress and reform in society. After all, these authors create a model of the ideal woman because they see the need to improve society. They firmly believe that the woman who exemplifies virtue, piety, nurturance, and benevolence can exert her moral and religious influence for the good of society at large. In particular, her influence can counter the negative aspects of mainstream male culture. But this so-called progress places restrictions upon women. It dictates criteria that serve a beau-ideal of sorts, but that in practice may be impossible to meet. The model of womanhood promoted in the conduct books, especially because it is so idealized, reinforces the self-abnegation of women and perpetuates their powerlessness. Women are asked to forswear both freedom of choice and freedom of mind to meet the demands imposed upon them by others. These demands, albeit dressed up as sharing responsibility for the fortunes of the Republic, in fact require submitting to male power in general and supporting a range of "respectable" male interests in particular—for example, training men to be successful in professions and giving them guidance in being responsible husbands and fathers.

Not at all clear from the texts is why so few authors question the burden placed on women as the primary caretakers of republican virtue and Christian piety—at least within the domestic realm—and also as the caretakers of men's actions. To a major extent, wives are held accountable for their husbands' conduct, and yet questions regarding failure of their influence are not addressed. If husbands turn to drinking and gambling or become abusive, then how and why has the redemptive and refining influence of wives failed? The answer, or at least part of the authors' answer, is that the woman has failed to cultivate private virtue. She has failed to reach the beau-ideal. Blaming the victims (women) and excusing the wrongdoers (men) are unmistakable implications of the gender roles in marriage fostered by the model of ideal womanhood. Also, by arguing that women must fulfill civic and religious missions, the proponents of domesticity perpetuate an idealistic view of a domestic vocation yet do not attach a public and economic value to it. Thus, what by logic can be seen as the high status of the domestic sphere and women's roles in it translates, in practice, into a tenuous situation for women by making them economically dependent upon and politically subservient to men. In addition, women are encouraged not to enter professions outside the home. All in all, by advocating their ideal of womanhood, the experts on conduct are implying that the beau-ideal *is* or *should be* the norm in social arrangements. As such, because the ideal aims at socially controlling white, middle-class American women, it circumvents any real gains in radical social reform in behalf of all women, especially in the areas of legal and political rights and educational and vocational opportunities, serving instead the interests of a patriarchal society.

As the following chapters demonstrate, fortunately, by the turn of the century the strictures on women's education and literacy imposed by ideal womanhood and the doctrine of separate spheres were gradually loosening, primarily because of the actions of goal-oriented women not content to be uneducated and illiterate. For example, Shirley Wilson Logan discusses how African American women sought literacy as a means of achieving liberation, citizenship, and the power to voice their people's concerns. As Nicole Tonkovich's and other studies reveal, many women empowered themselves and each other by joining with others in writing and literary groups. Finally, other essays (see chapters 2, 3, and 11) document that, given the opportunity to participate in a curriculum centered on language, literacy, and rhetoric, women could excel as both orators and authors, working up to their intellectual potentials and gaining the power to effect social change.

Notes

1. Mrs. A. J. Graves, *Woman in America; Being an Examination into the Moral and Intellectual Condition of American Female Society* (New York: Harper, 1843), p. [i].

2. See Nina Baym, *Novels, Readers, and Reviewers: Responses to Fiction in Antebellum America* (Ithaca: Cornell Univ. Press, 1984); Lawrence Buell, *New England Literary Culture: From Revolution through Renaissance* (New York: Cambridge

Univ. Press, 1986); and Susan Coultrap-McQuin, *Doing Literary Business: American Women Writers in the Nineteenth Century* (Chapel Hill: Univ. of North Carolina Press, 1990).

3. The publication of advice books flourished during the antebellum years. According to Arthur M. Schlesinger Jr., whose study focuses on etiquette books, approximately twenty-eight such manuals were published in the 1830s, thirty-six in the 1840s, and thirty-eight in the 1850s; see *Learning to Behave: A Historical Study of American Etiquette* (New York: Macmillan, 1946); p. 18. Advice books for men went through numerous editions and sold thousands of copies, suggesting the popularity of this genre. For instance, William Alcott's *Young Man's Guide* went through twenty-one editions between 1833 and 1858, and in its first edition, Daniel Eddy's *Young Man's Friend* proved to be a bestseller at ten thousand copies; see Karen Halttunen, *Confidence Men and Painted Women: A Study of Middle-Class Culture in America, 1830–1870* (New Haven: Yale Univ. Press, 1982), p. 1. Advice books for women were also popular. Lydia Maria Child's *The Frugal Housewife* underwent thirty-three editions between 1829 and 1870; see Nancy Woloch, *Women and the American Experience* (New York: Knopf, 1984), p. 133.

4. Academic scholarship has largely ignored the conduct genre. However, in her recent study of conduct books for women published in the eighteenth century, Sarah Emily Newton notes some of the same conventions that I have observed in mid-nineteenth-century conduct books: a profile of the ideal woman, a focus on a domestic vocation for women, distinctions between male and female character, and guidelines for ideal behavior and conduct. See Newton, "Wise and Foolish Virgins: 'Usable Fiction' and the Early American Conduct Tradition," *Early American Literature* 25 (1990): 139–67. For a discussion of using the conduct book as a tool in understanding the domestic novel, see Jane E. Rose, "Gender Politics in American Literature of Domesticity, 1830–1860" (Ph.D. diss., Purdue Univ., 1992).

Scholarship has mainly focused on the etiquette manual. For a superficial review of etiquette rules for men and women, see Dixon Wecter, *The Saga of American Society: A Record of Social Aspirations, 1607–1837* (New York: Scribners, 1937), pp. 157–95, and for a discussion of behavior manuals for men, see Carol Bode, *The Anatomy of Popular Culture, 1840–1861* (Berkeley: Univ. of California Press, 1959). For a history of manners, see Gerald Carson, *The Polite Americans: A Wide-Angle View of Our More or Less Good Manners over 300 Years* (New York: Morrow, 1966) and Esther B. Aresty, *The Best Behavior: The Course of Good Manners—from Antiquity to the Present—as Seen through Courtesy and Etiquette Books* (New York: Simon and Shuster, 1970). For a bibliography of etiquette manuals, see Mary Reed Bobbitt, "A Bibliography of Etiquette Books Published in America Before 1900," *Bulletin of the New York Public Library* 51 (1947): 687–720.

5. Jane Tompkins, *Sensational Designs: The Cultural Work of American Fiction, 1790–1860* (New York: Oxford Univ. Press, 1985), p. xi.

6. The ethic of ideal womanhood applied to white women of the upper classes. Scholars of black women's literature have criticized the implications of its racial and class biases. Undervaluing black womanhood, it reinforces the stereotyping and status of black women, especially slaves, as inferior moral and intellectual beings. Because slave women were often sexually exploited by their masters, they could never live up to such an ideal. See Hazel V. Carby, *Reconstructing Womanhood: The Emergence of the Afro-America Woman Novelist* (New York: Oxford Univ. Press, 1987); Paula Giddings, *When and Where I Enter: The Impact of Black Women on Race*

and Sex in America (New York: Bantam, 1985); bell hooks, *Ain't I a Woman: Black Women and Feminism* (Boston: South End Press, 1981).

7. Mary Beth Norton, "The Paradox of 'Women's Sphere,'" in *Women of America: A History,* ed. Carol Ruth Berkin and Mary Beth Norton (Boston: Houghton, 1979), p. 141.

8. Barbara Welter, "The Cult of True Womanhood, 1820–1860," *American Quarterly* 18 (1966): 151–74; see p. 152.

9. Welter, "Cult," pp. 158–59.

10. Carroll Smith-Rosenberg, *Disorderly Conduct: Visions of Gender in Victorian America* (New York: Knopf, 1985); Catherine Clinton, *The Other Civil War: American Women in the Nineteenth Century* (New York: Hill and Wang, 1984); and Lois Banner, *American Beauty* (New York: Knopf, 1983).

11. Frances Cogan, *All-American Girl: The Ideal of Real Womanhood in Mid-Nineteenth-Century America* (Athens: Univ. of Georgia Press, 1989), pp. 4, 5–6.

12. Mary Beth Norton, *Liberty's Daughters: The Revolutionary Experience of American Women, 1750–1800* (Boston: Little, Brown, 1980), pp. xiv, 110, 298.

13. Linda Kerber, *Women of the Republic: Intellect and Ideology in Revolutionary America* (Chapel Hill: Univ. of North Carolina Press, 1980), pp. 7, 10–11.

14. Mark E. Kann, *On the Man Question: Gender and Civic Virtue in America* (Philadelphia: Temple Univ. Press, 1991), pp. 248–49; 252–53.

15. For studies on domesticity, see Barbara Epstein, *The Politics of Domesticity: Women, Evangelism, and Temperance in Nineteenth-Century America* (Middletown, Conn.: Wesleyan Univ. Press, 1981); Mary Kelley, *Private Woman, Public Stage: Literary Domesticity in Nineteenth-Century America* (New York: Oxford Univ. Press, 1984); Glenna Matthews, *"Just a Housewife": The Rise and Fall of Domesticity in America* (New York: Oxford Univ. Press, 1987); Mary P. Ryan, *The Empire of the Mother: American Writing about Domesticity, 1830–1860* (New York: Haworth Press, 1982); Kathryn Kish Sklar, *Catharine Beecher: A Study in American Domesticity* (New Haven: Yale Univ. Press, 1973); Gillian Brown, *Domestic Individualism: Imagining Self in Nineteenth-Century America* (Berkeley: Univ. of California Press, 1990), and chapters 7 and 11.

16. Many of the male authors considered in my study were also clergy. Having received religious training at Andover Theological seminary, John S. C. Abbott was ordained as a Congregationalist minister in 1830 and held pastorates in Massachusetts. In 1844 he resigned his ministry to devote time to literature. Daniel Clark Eddy was a Baptist minister. William Eliot graduated from Harvard Divinity School in 1834 and was ordained as a Unitarian pastor. Jonathan Stearns studied theology at Andover Seminary and was ordained a Presbyterian minister. Daniel Wise was a Methodist minister and also an editor of tract publications.

17. William Alcott, *Letters to a Sister; or Woman's Mission* (Buffalo: George H. Derby, 1850), p. 19.

18. Graves, *Woman,* pp. xv, 40, 51, 54, 55, 67–68, 238; Catharine Beecher, *A Treatise on Domestic Economy* (1841; rpt. New York: Schocken Books, 1977).

19. Jonathan Stearns, *Female Influence and the True Christian Mode of Its Exercise* (Newburyport, Mass.: J. G. Tilton, 1837), pp. 6, 8.

20. William Eliot, *Lectures to Young Women* (Boston: Crosby, Nichols, 1856), pp. 32–33.

21. Ruth Bloch, "The Gendered Meanings of Virtue in Revolutionary America," *Signs* 13 (1987): 37–58; see esp. pp. 42, 44, 46, 54.

22. Mrs. L. G. Abell, *Woman in Her Various Relations: Containing Practical Rules for American Females* (New York: J. M. Fairchild, 1851), p. 317.

23. Daniel Wise, *The Young Lady's Counsellor: or, Outlines and Illustrations of the Sphere, the Duties, and the Dangers of Young Women* (1851), in *The American Ideal of the "True Woman" as Reflected in Advice Books to Young Women,* ed. Carolyn De Swarte Gifford (New York: Garland, 1987), p. 37; John S. C. Abbott, *The School-Girl; or, the Principles of Christian Duty Familiarly Enforced* (Boston: Crocker and Brewster, 1840), pp. 9, 12–14.

24. Eliza Leslie, *Miss Leslie's Behavior Book: A Guide and Manual for Ladies* (Philadelphia: T. B. Peterson, 1859), pp. 199–200; A. I. Cummings, *The Young Lady's Present: or Beauties of Female Character* (Boston: J. Buffam, 1854), p. 10.

25. Alcott, *Letters,* p. 214.

26. Cummings, *Young Lady's Present,* p. 13.

27. Wise, *Lady's Counsellor,* p. 103.

28. Stearns, *Female Influence,* p. 10; for a similar view, see also Cummings, *Young Lady's Present,* pp. 46–47.

29. Alcott, *Letters,* pp. 79–80; Graves, *Woman,* pp. 139–41; Abell, *Woman in Her Relations,* pp. 71–72.

30. Nancy Cott, *The Bonds of Womanhood: "Woman's Sphere" in New England, 1780–1835* (New Haven: Yale Univ. Press, 1977), pp. 199–200; Ryan, *Empire,* p. 18; and Sklar, *Beecher,* pp. xii-xiii.

31. Sarah Grimké, *Letters on the Equality of the Sexes and Other Essays,* ed. Elizabeth Ann Bartlett (1838; rpt. New Haven: Yale Univ. Press, 1988); Margaret Fuller, *Woman in the Nineteenth Century* (1855; rpt. New York: Norton, 1971); and Elizabeth Oakes Smith, *Woman and Her Needs,* in *Liberating the Home* (1851; rpt. New York: Arno Press, 1974). For a discussion of the contradictions and commensurabilities between nineteenth-century domesticity and feminism and for analyses of these works, see Rose, "Gender Politics."

32. Wise, *Lady's Counsellor,* p. 92.

33. Leslie, *Miss Leslie's Book,* pp. 197, 199.

34. Eliot, *Lectures,* pp. 101–2, 114; Daniel Clark Eddy, *The Young Woman's Friend; or the Duties, Trials, Love, Hopes of Woman* (Boston: Wentworth and Company, 1857), pp. 132–38.

35. Charles Butler, *The American Lady* (Philadelphia: Hogan, 1836), pp. 111–12; Lydia Sigourney, *Letters to Ladies* (Hartford: W. Watson, 1835), pp. 73–74; William Alcott, *The Young Wife, or Duties of Woman in the Marriage Relations* (1837; rpt. New York: Arno Press, 1972), pp. 302, 314; Catharine Sedgwick, *Means and Ends, or Self-Training* (New York: Harper, 1854), pp. 242–46.

36. Eliot, *Lectures,* pp. 119, 126; Alcott, *Letters,* pp. 69, 74.

37. Sedgwick, *Means,* p. 247; Timothy Shay Arthur, *Advice to Young Ladies on Their Duties and Conduct in Life* (Boston: Phillips and Sampson, 1848), pp. 60, 61; Abell, *Woman in Her Relations,* p. 274; Wise, *Lady's Counsellor,* pp. 189. 190.

38. Sedgwick, *Means,* p. 19; Sigourney, *Letters,* p. 32.

2

VICKIE RICKS

"In an Atmosphere of Peril"

COLLEGE WOMEN AND THEIR WRITING

OVER THE PAST decade, gender studies and feminist thought have transformed the views of communication, rhetoric, and composition held by those of us responsible for college writing instruction. Discussions related to women and discourse have generated books, articles, and university courses—many exploring the impact of gender on composing processes, many looking at interdisciplinary theories that explore how women understand discourse.

Historians of rhetoric and composition have been particularly motivated by these events, by recent developments in liberatory pedagogy, and by changes in political and cultural history—all of which have resulted in a recent upsurge in histories of women as writers and orators. These changes have also helped us examine assumptions about women's learning environnment and the language recording it. Simply put: In the struggle to reshape our thinking about gender and the history of writing instruction, we have run the intellectual gamut in search of a usable past and an appropriate present and future.

For example, early on in my own research and writing, I relied upon analytical tools from a traditional training in classical and modern rhetoric, tools that often failed as immediate resources in understanding nineteenth-century women's beliefs, experiences, and accomplishments. But an interest in gender issues, namely why and how women had been excluded from the rhetorical tradition, kept me searching for a satisfactory critical methodology. My studies at the time focused on reviving lost women in American rhetoric, such as Gertrude Buck at Vassar, and on exploring concepts such as "Republican Motherhood" that supported assumptions about women's limited role in American rhetoric. With women's colleges as a focus, my goal was to critique traditional history and locate what I thought was a history of liberatory pedagogy for these women who had been marginalized in American rhetoric.

At first, my conceptual models included theorists and historians of rhetoric who had written on these and related topics: Mina Shaughnessey, Kenneth Bruffee, Peter Elbow, Paulo Friere, Albert Kitzhaber, Porter Perrin, Edward P. J. Corbett, James Berlin, and Donald Stewart, to name a few. For these writers, composition instruction was mainly defined through standard topics of historical inquiry, and the study merely of how academic women fit into the teaching of rhetoric tended to shut down broader conceptualization by merging women into men's stories, not by opening up women's distinctive voices.[1]

Fortunately, I was not alone in my dissatisfaction with traditional historical approaches, approaches that feminists often have characterized as "add women and stir."[2] Certainly, within the past ten years historians of rhetoric and composition have reacted to these challenges and have turned to interdisciplinary feminist studies in literary, social, psychological, and poststructural theory, to name a few. The result has been a richer texture of history, one opening up unexplained cultural webs that continue to give shape to our theories, practice, and teaching of rhetoric and writing.

For many, inquiry into the history of teaching rhetoric and composition to women at the turn of the twentieth century has profited specifically from new historical and psychological approaches, approaches that have helped many understand how women in different periods acknowledged their developmental processes and assessed the strengths and weaknesses in their educational systems. We find women at times responding to cultural and social forces by voicing discontent or by expressing subversion through violent protest. At other times, women state—or more often imply—their helplessness in affecting those historical forces that control educational processes. In any case, texts and social events of the period do inform one another, and the act of exploring how women and men alike introduced and responded to the formation and reformation of women's educational systems offers us insight into how writers simultaneously assessed, challenged, and encouraged those cultural and social forces engaging them.

Within this framework, however, another gender issue emerges: how women in the American academy came to understand their relationships to males and the politically male-dominated public sphere that culturally sanctioned male speakers and writers but questioned the female's public propriety and therefore her public ethos. Informed by feminist theory, my analysis here does not uncover a simple, objective set of strategies that men or women felt were useful solely to women as public writers or speakers. Rather, three women's institutions—Mount Holyoke, Vassar, and Radcliffe—answered these challenges differently in the formation of their colleges, in the development of their composition and rhetoric programs, and in how they defined women's public and private use of knowledge gained from these programs.

In describing the institutions' conflicts, I draw heavily from college archives, from the private papers of students, professors, and administrators, and from public statements by men and women charged with women's education. And by relying primarily upon these voices—the nineteenth century's imagery and its descriptions of internal relationships—I try to uncover a more practical side of research about women's rhetoric that focuses on everyday lives, experiences, and communication involving academic women. In defining the ways of knowing that educated women valued, however, I cannot overlook a more private substructure associated with institutional conflicts shaping women's higher education. Although in many ways those early arguments clarify what some educated women fought for, namely social equality with men, what finally emerges is a clearer history of how women sought self-definition and self-recognition, not simply how they tried to answer the question of what it meant to gain equal educational opportunity with men.

Men's views, included in the debate, often preoccupied women coming to terms with new images, new roles, and new ways of knowing about themselves. But the struggle to accommodate new expectations to traditional ones proved difficult for many women who tried to rely upon their own notions of reality and not those of the men around them. This discursive transition, filled with women's voices in conflict with themselves and with their world, offers remarkable keys to nineteenth-century women's perceptions of truth, authority, and their own educational development. Their words clearly echo what Carol Gilligan, Mary Belenky, Nancy Chodorow, and others have discovered: "Women's self-concepts and ways of knowing are intertwined."[3]

Like their twentieth-century sisters, nineteenth-century women sought public voices. Often, however, they were caught in a cultural bind that offered women educational equality but only when equality was defined in traditional "mothering" terms. For many of these women raised in nineteenth-century Victorian society, motherhood and its implications of women's separate sphere set the tone for female education and for educational processes that encouraged women's difference and at the same time limited their public voices because of this difference. Traditionalists and feminists wanted women to be well educated—to speak and to write—but both groups wanted women to use education in prescribed ways. Traditionalists who supported women's education and encouraged women as writers and speakers felt education should enhance women's traditional roles. Women we today see as more "feminist," on the other hand, stood on a range of platforms that drew women beyond the limited scope of writing and speaking as mothers or in social extensions of that role. Although many college women's career expectations were raised as a result of early feminist thought, coping with these mixed signals proved difficult for many educated women. Even though they were told to succeed simultaneously as traditional mothers and as leaders in society, they found this an almost impossible task in a society and an educational system founded on male leadership and patriarchal notions of women's physical and mental limitations. Many college women could not overcome cultural pressure and remained immersed in women's traditional role, a role that for years kept women out of many fields of higher education and almost silenced them publicly.

Even when progressive reformers argued successfully that women with an education could function better in their traditional role than women without an education, critics found other reasons to limit women's access to higher edcuation. During the formative years of women's colleges, for example, educators faced criticism from men such as Edward Clarke, the author of *Sex in Education: or, A Fair Chance for the Girls,* who relied upon Charles Darwin, Herbert Spencer, and Alexander Bain to detail women's physical and mental limitations resulting from the evolution of their sex. According to Clarke, a Harvard overseer, women had fallen behind men in intellectual development because of their mothering role in the evolutionary process; thus, they could not mentally or physically tolerate men's educational environment. Consistent with these thoughts, Frances Emily White, professor of physiology at a women's medical college in Philadelphia, argued in 1875 that women should be educated, but educated to enhance their special feminine nature of "tenderness and love . . . and devotional sentiment."[4] Others reacted more specifically to women who desired educational equality. They charged that women were too weak for a traditional male education, that females might become too masculine, or that women would weaken higher education by their feminization of it. Thus in its early stages the popular debate centered on questions about women's cultural role and how educational systems could develop along that separate and distinct line. Few educators sought ways to adapt educational processes to women's ways of knowing, and many in both single-sex and coeducational institutions expressed misgivings about the practicality of teaching women to write and to speak publicly when the public had little need for women's views.

But by the end of the nineteenth century many educators, psychologists, anthropologists, and sociologists had reacted against these and similar accusations that stressed limiting women's position in higher education and in society. At the University of Chicago, John Dewey, who had been ambivalent only a few years earlier, and Marion Talbot, dean of the new institution, responded to President William Rainey Harper's proposal to segregate the coeducational university by establishing a junior college tailored to women's special nature. Protesting Harper's belief that increasing numbers of women threatened the university's educational and financial structure by driving men away, Dewey wrote that such a separation would only emphasize old notions behind "the distinctively feminine" and "distinctively masculine life," not promote equality of the sexes.[5] In arguing for equality, either through coeducation or a system based on "separate but equal" instruction, Dewey and Talbot hoped that women would abandon a separate sphere mentality and strive for education that would integrate women more into a man's world.

Such statements underscore how nineteenth-century college women, in claiming their uniqueness through the separate sphere metaphor, often limited their public potential. Although early educators tried to broaden women's options for public careers, the arguments for a more active public role were unconvincing for many women. When some found their sex the object of this debate, they divided their loyalties along old lines. In 1885 several women, for example, found themselves debating these issues for the first time in a public setting when the newly formed Harvard Annex (later Radcliffe) Debating Club chose to resolve whether or not "it should be as customary for women as for men to enter a regular trade or profession."[6] Although the Annex women were instructed by Harvard professors and the Annex was only a few steps from Harvard Yard, Harvard overseers made it a point to keep the two institutions separate.

Voting prior to the debate and afterwards was consistent: nine of the women were in favor, six opposed. Although the formal debate raised the question of women's general acceptance in public society, the discussion afterward clarified the women's reluctance to trust their own sex in leadership positions. Women, they noted, were doing benevolent and social work without anyone objecting. But leadership on the same level as men became problematic. One of the students, Miss Howe, pointed to the source: "We are and shall be for the next ten years in a transition stage, for men will always argue that we cannot do things until we prove that we can." For Harvard Annex women, if the proof came, it would come from exceptional women. Miss Howe explained, "If a woman has talent, she may afford to devote a larger portion of her time to developing her ability *and* give her time to household cares" (my emphasis). Even when one student suggested that a woman could raise the tone of politics, another replied: "True perhaps in the case of great movements. But ordinarily she would not raise politics but would be degraded herself." If they wanted to be socially involved, women might just as well be satisfied with supporting their politically minded husbands.[7]

It is not surprising that these women in their new role as public debaters would defer judgment to the opposite sex and remain loyal to a system and role models already in place. Gilligan explains: "The difficulty women experience in finding or speaking publicly in their own voices emerges repeatedly in the form of qualification and self-doubt, but also in intimations of a divided judgment, a public assessment and private assessment which are fundamentally at odds."[8] Gilligan's *In a Different Voice* emphasizes how the women she studied constructed moral problems differently from men because their values were centered differently. Drawing from writings of Virginia Woolf, she stresses what has now become commonplace among feminists: women generally function within a morality of responsibility, relationships, and care; men within one of rights, autonomy, and rules. Though unaware of this gender distinction, many leaders in women's education were at odds with American education's basic (male) assumption that knowledge of the rules, laws, and principles of democracy would create literate citizens capable of self-government. Rather than promote an atmosphere that accommodated women, assumptions like these created an ambivalence about women's entry into the public sphere. Those women who focused their education on preparing for motherhood and for careers that integrated characteristics traditionally attributed to women (teacher, nurse, missionary, social worker, and so on) spoke with authority about the usefulness of their education. Those, like Marion Talbot, who wanted to enter the public sphere through other career options took steps to do so, but found that after their hard work in the academy, they had few appropriate places to apply their newly acquired knowledge.

So in spite of the argument that women's special nature made them good community leaders, nineteenth-century America could only accommodate a few women in those traditional female leadership roles. Women's strengths—now known to be human strengths—were regarded by men to be weaknesses, and academic women, more often than not, accepted these prejudices and remained separated from public life. Not only was this ambivalence present in the work place, but it was also felt in a woman's undergraduate school where, as the Harvard Annex and other women's college students admit, they were often ill at ease with men's expectations of them. Even at the turn of the century, when women were instructed in public rhetoric, all lacked the right to vote and therefore were hindered in their access to public forums. Classrooms also provided a mixed bag of experiences as women experimented in that limited setting with a range of freedom and responsibilities that a larger society might never offer. When we begin trying to understand some of the complexities that foregrounded a nineteenth-century woman's entry into the all-woman classroom and that set the tone for her range of reactions, we come closer to identifying those forces that also limited her voice.

Woman's Sphere and Women's Colleges

At first, women were permitted access to American education based on their roles as mothers, wives, and teachers, roles that would maintain the "natural" social order of mothering. Here a restricted education brought women limited access to public speaking. Soon, however, dominant cultural myths that allowed women's speaking only within traditional, essentialist roles were challenged by educators and students. On the one hand, they argued for women's rights to voice their views on the family, social issues, and, finally, all areas of American society, but on the other hand, they found themselves unable to subvert the cultural norms that denigrated or negated women's voices whenever they were heard outside their "natural" sphere. Precisely because women's institutions set women apart from society, however, the schools reaffirmed this ambivalence toward the place of women's rhetoric in American society, a position whose uneasiness is still reflected in our culture's ambiguous response to women in public speaking roles.

Isolated physically and psychologically from men's colleges, women's colleges provide us today with insight into how educated women tried to fashion themselves to fit into the public sphere. But from their beginnings in the 1830s and especially until 1920 when women received voting rights, women's colleges also became the literal grounds where society tried to reaffirm and reproduce its dominant assumptions about women. The struggle was never as simple as between what roles the New Woman would fill and what roles society would allow her to fill. Explicit questions focused on how women learned, on where their intellectual strengths and weaknesses lay, and on whether women could equal men's intellectual work. But more complex issues were present and in contention. Rather than reflect the language and rhetoric of new roles for women and the new rites of passages that would initiate women into those roles, many of the sources at Mount Holyoke, Vassar, and Radcliffe confirm the resulting conflict that often ended in separating women from society, not comfortably initiating them into it. For many nineteenth-century college women, then, higher education became an enlightening experience, but a troubling one. As historian Carroll Smith-Rosenberg explains, by the turn of the century many women students and faculty women no longer saw college as a simple way to prepare themselves for marriage. Women began to view higher education as a path to a new and more complex independent life, one that may have brought opportunities to women but one that also threatened male students, faculty, administrators, and trustees who questioned women's entry onto the public scene.[9]

This tension was felt in 1895 particularly at Radcliffe where noted neurologist Silas Weir Mitchell, who specialized in women's disorders, addressed the president, dean, and students on the topic: "The woman who wants the higher education; the life while winning it; the life after it." Known for his espousal of the rest cure in the 1870s, Mitchell is often remembered today as Charlotte Perkins Gilman's psychiatrist and the object of criticism in her 1892 short story "The Yellow Wallpaper." Consistent with his earlier views that women had enough to manage as busy homemakers, Mitchell warned the Radcliffe women: "If . . . the college life in any way, body or mind, unfits women to be good wives and mothers there had better be none of it." Moreover, Mitchell had no patience with women who judged a career as "finer, nobler, more to their taste than the life of home . . . women's *natural* life." When women's education reached that stage, Mitchell concluded, "better close every college door in the land." Mitchell, despite claiming that he wanted women to be free and independent, could not personally support the idea of women as "preachers, lawyers, or platform orators" any more than men as "seamstresses or nurses of children." Intellectual freedom, then, should come "within the noble limitations of sex."[10]

Turning more to specific issues related to women's "limitations" in a college environment, he left the Radcliffe students with two precautions:

"First, of all, do not conclude that the whole mass of you can assume the man's standard as to what you do in the way of mental labor. It will be your peril. . . . You are women, not men" (p. 13). Not only would mental stress eventually catch up with women, but because they often pushed themselves to study, they ended up neglecting their physical well-being, something men more naturally attended to, Mitchell observed. He was well aware that Wellesley, Bryn Mawr, and Vassar prescribed exercise, but prescription would never overcome the natural tendency of women to avoid strenuous exercise, he claimed. "Trust me, I am right. Do not try to be men when you are women. . . . Be punctual at meals and do not take a book or the thought of work to table, or talk shop there" (pp. 13–14). Drawing from his experiences with women's disorders, he ended by putting women's "wild craving" for a career in perspective. "A woman is *born* to a profession; a man is not. . . . You are here in competition with men. . . . The professor expects of you virile standards of work and results; you are, therefore, as I think, in an atmosphere of peril" (pp. 21–22).

As Gilman's "Yellow Wallpaper" illustrates, women's conflict with society's expectations was evident, especially among self-conscious women who knew the power available to them through rhetoric and writing. New images of women could be created, they mused, and society's definition of the New Woman could change women's actual living conditions—or women would be driven mad in the process. For these and similar reasons, many women, like Gilman, were drawn nationwide to political and social movements at the end of the nineteenth and beginning of the twentieth century.

Within the walls of all-woman colleges, the New Woman honed her rhetorical skills at the same time she developed her aesthetic and social sensitivities, a useful combination throughout the 1890s and into the 1920s; during this period radical and philanthropic women worked together to establish settlement houses, argued for trade unions, lobbied for workers' legislation, and established women's literary societies. As Smith-Rosenberg says, these women were "effective manipulators of public opinion" and soon became "expert" at social change. Their reforms during these years changed the fate of American women more than "any other group of women in American experience." At the same time that educated women were bringing about positive social change and raising the consciousness of American women, however, they found many traditional men, including college presidents and trustees, reacting with hostility and fear.[11]

To make matters worse, a younger generation of women attending college shortly after the turn of the century faced criticism from older women who had established the groundwork for them years earlier. These earlier college women, brought up under the assumptions of the Cult of True Womanhood, saw their education as an extension of the home—a sophisticated preparation for their homemaking and mothering roles—not as preparation to live an independent life or, as some radical reformers urged, to compete with men. Those women raised as "True Women" had altogether different educational values than their more radical sisters and daughters who chose to live as "New Women" outside a well-contained, traditional domestic role. Nowhere are these conflicts more evident than in the turn-of-the-century women's colleges where many of the questions centered on what and how to teach women.

Constructing Women's Curriculum: Controlling Women's Sphere and Speech

Most men who founded and shaped early female education in America tried repeatedly to answer the criticism that education would unsex women and take them away from their natural and special natures. When Matthew Vassar established Vassar College in 1865, he stated that the college would be to women what Yale and Harvard were to men. Vassar women were therefore particularly open to criticism because the college's founding statements committed women to a liberal arts curriculum similar to that of men's colleges and universities and to a curriculum taught by women.

At Vassar, Gertrude Buck's books on the modes of discourse as well as departmental records indicate women wrote and analyzed expository and argumentative essays on commerce, law, politics, and aesthetics in addition to fiction, drama, and poetry. Unlike the seminary model devoted to religious and moral duties (for example, Mary Lyon's approach at Mount Holyoke during the 1830s), Buck's approach implied that women were men's cultural and intellectual equals. Because this position threatened long-held divisions between men's and women's authority, one might think that Vassar College was more open to criticism than Mount Holyoke, an institution that claimed women and men as spiritual equals only. Both institutions, however, received their share of criticism. In anticipation of such challenges, founders of both colleges agreed that women were increasingly coming into public roles, but both were hesitant to have women make the transition too quickly. Women, the founders agreed, needed to be isolated from the hustle of busy city life during preparation for female leadership. In many ways, the language used by both sets of founders expressed the institutions' basic conflict with giving women a public voice.

Mary Lyon assumed that a seminary system modeled after nineteenth-century mental asylums would provide perfect psychic and disciplined intellectual order in a thoughtfully landscaped environment. Influenced by current theories about insanity and experiences of her own family's successful treatments in asylums, Lyon designed a highly regulated daily schedule of private devotion, class attendance, study, communal work, worship, and meals. Accepting the doctrine of separate spheres, the nineteenth-century notion that women had a special "nature and destiny" apart from men's, Lyon emphasized a close teacher-student relationship analogous to that of mother and daughter. At a time when women's influences were limited to the home and direct extensions of it, Lyon and women like her institutionalized women's growing self-consciousness of their unique nature and position in life. As more and more women were made aware of the expansion of their special roles through such magazines as *Godey's Lady's Book,* through sermons, and through higher education, they altered their experiences and expectations. No longer bound by the rhythms of the natural cycles in traditional women's roles, the roles related to mothering and attending to the dying, women flirted with the strict and orderly world of the male sphere. Lyon saw her institution moving women away from their conventional private lives into more unconventional, but more religiously rewarding, public responsibilities.[12]

This scheme of separating women into their own educational society, away from men's direct influence, soon came under criticism from such male educators as E. A. Andrews, Boston gentleman, editor of *The Religious Magazine,* and a spokesperson for his day's religious right. Andrews attacked Lyon's approach on at least two important grounds: its female isolation (which also meant self-governance) and its rigorous discipline, which implied maleness. Rather than seeing Lyon's methods at Mount Holyoke as appropriate for preparing missionaries and teachers, Andrews objected to the entire system on the grounds that it would unsex women. The mind, he argued, would be strengthened, but the graces would remain dormant. Andrews writes: "In place of all which is most attractive in female manners, we see characters expressly formed for acting a *manly* part upon the theater of life. . . . Under such influences the female character is fast becoming masculine." Not only criticizing Lyon's grammar and self-education, he caricatured Mount Holyoke graduates as graceless and "manly" missionaries who traveled west, looking not for teaching positions, but for husbands.[13]

It was this charge of manliness that Vassar presidents also feared. Beginning in the 1860s and intensifying at the turn of the century, the threat of women losing their femininity and assuming men's leadership roles on the Vassar campus became more of a reality as women's rights issues and feminism forced conservative trustees and administrators to react to women's demands.

In building an exemplary women's college, Matthew Vassar had the material means for constructing buildings—organizing the outer structure—but initially he left the curriculum, governing, and teaching decisions to Milo P. Jewett, a Baptist strongly influenced by Mary Lyon's combined seminary/asylum model at Mount Holyoke. Forced to leave the South in 1855 because of his antislavery stance, Jewett settled in Poughkeepsie, opened a girls' school, became friends with Matthew Vassar, and helped build the foundation for Vassar's curriculum. Although Vassar and Jewett wanted to offer women a strictly English curriculum similar to Mount Holyoke's, they also wanted something in the truest sense equal to a college. As Jewett argued, they needed "necessary buildings, libraries, cabinets, apparatus and so on" along with "a full faculty of instructors, men of learning, ability, and reputation"—something that Mary Lyon's all-female institution lacked.[14]

Vassar also listened to Jewett's arguments and placed Vassar women away from the city, "embosomed in Sylvan Bowers, protected by shady Avenues, [on a] site in harmony with the modesty and delicacy which are always associated with the gentler sex." However, Vassar parted company with Jewett over the hiring of an all-male faculty to design and oversee the curriculum. Influenced by Horatio Hale's review in *Godey's Lady's Book,* which called the college's plans for an all-male faculty its "one defect," Vassar accepted the argument that a "woman should be the teacher and guardian of her own sex" and hired several women. But Vassar began with only with one woman, the noted astronomer Maria Mitchell, at the professorial level. Other important positions at this level were filled by men, while women filled the rank of instructor. This pattern of larger numbers of male professors and almost all female instructors slowly was reversed by the turn of the century when the numbers of qualified women graduating from colleges and universities rose. By that time women, such as Gertrude Buck and Lucy Salmon from the University of Michigan and Laura Wylie from Yale, had proven their academic worth primarily at coeducational institutions and brought with them progressive ideas about women's specific place in institutions of higher education and in society in general.[15]

From these shaky foundations, Vassar College experienced gender trouble and continuing conflicts concerning the role of women in higher education. Vassar's founders had reasoned that education for men and women was to be the same because men and women had a shared responsibility for culture and liberal arts. Woman's sphere, however, was traditionally the home and the care and nurture of other women. From two sides, then, the feminist and the maternal, Vassar supported professorships for women, giving women who were trained in the new curriculum a public forum in which to spread and develop their knowledge. The combination, though, brought constant tension to Vassar College, a tension easily plotted in the documents of the period. On the one hand, male administrators continually saw women stepping outside the defined boundaries of social control and thus threatening Vassar's conservative tradition. On the other hand, we find academic women condemning the restrictions, disorder, and power structure, which they saw as distinctively male centered.

President John Raymond spoke for Vassar trustees in the 1860s when he said that "failure" for Vassar would be if its seniors and alumnae became known as "vulgar and extreme woman's rights people." Throughout his tenure Raymond expressed this fear and systematically assured Vassar trustees that a Vassar education—even if it were based on a disciplined mind and the study of liberal arts—would continue to encourage femininity "lest by too close an imitation of the forms and studies and too much cultivation of the Spirit of ordinary colleges, we should impair womanliness of character in our students, and encourage the formation of those mannish tastes and manners which are so disgusting to every right mind and feeling."[16]

This conservative guided Raymond in refusing radical speakers such as abolitionists and feminists who might encourage women to abandon their traditional domestic roles. Likewise, Vassar President James Taylor in 1907 would not allow Jane Addams to speak on the "workingwoman's need of the ballot." Responding to a letter from M. Carey Thomas, president of Bryn Mawr, Taylor would not commit himself and Vassar College to a series of lectures by Addams at six eastern women's colleges. Taylor wrote to Thomas:

> It is not merely in the line of political rights but of all sociological questions that these disputed themes are coming to the front and certainly there should be instruction, and full understanding on the part of the students, regarding them all. Is not the matter somewhat different, however, when it comes, not in the form of education and discussion, but as a part of a propaganda, the attainment of a definite end. I have

> myself been inclined all along to think so and as I look back to the experience of my admirable predecessor, Dr. Raymond, and the careful way in which he was obliged to steer in order to avoid the association of what was then a comparatively new work with movements that were regarded as radical, so saving for the larger work, as it seems to me, and the more fundamental, its own special sphere and its own peculiar influence, I am confirmed in my feeling that it is best not to allow a propaganda of any kind whatever to enter the college.[17]

Two years later, Taylor explained his line of reasoning in the annual address to the Vassar Alumnae, an address that he published and distributed as "The Conservatism of Vassar." Arguing that Vassar undergraduate women needed "teachers" not "agitators," he defined Vassar's chief mission as an undergraduate institution, and calling upon its nineteenth-century roots, he once again distanced women from society:

> The chief mission of the college is to train the young, not for special fields of work or any special theories of reform, but to enlighten and broaden and inspire, to train to the careful weighing of evidence of history, to the testing of theories of what has been already tried, and all as the basis for individual independence in thought and life. It is not the chief mission of an undergraduate to deal with the untried. . . . Vassar College recognizes all good service as worthy. . . . It affirms its belief in the home and in the old-fashioned view of marriage and children and the splendid service of society wrought through these quiet and unradical means. . . . It reiterates what President Raymond said in 1875, after ten years of work and in the midst of questions and agitations reminding us of today: "The Institution was not founded and is not administered in the interest of any doctrine or class of doctrines. Its business is education in the broadest sense, and exclusively that, so to develop and discipline the faculties of the young that they shall be able in due time to form their own opinion."

He added, "The mission of Vassar College was not to reform society but to educate women."[18]

Although they tried, neither Raymond nor Taylor could suppress the radical thoughts of many students and faculty. Maria Mitchell and other feminists on the faculty protested Raymond's tight control over campus speakers. Mitchell regularly invited feminists into her home. Under Taylor's administration, English faculty, including department chair Laura Wylie and Professor Gertrude Buck, openly joined feminist and socialist groups. In 1909 several Vassar faculty gathered with students in organizing a suffragist "debate," where, according to Taylor, who saw the whole affair as propagandistic, "only those favoring suffrage were invited to speak." Taylor quickly called a meeting to reprimand faculty participants, who, he complained, seemed unconcerned over the press coverage and the tone that they had created of an "organized expression of opinion as if official and authoritative." Finally, Taylor's personal notes of the event recorded his awareness that the debate was staged to answer his earlier conservative comments to the alumnae. In the end he refused to acknowledge that suffrage was even an issue, preferring to highlight broad, abstract principles and stress the narrower issue of the faculty's complaints that his guidelines attacked their individual freedom. The following day, Taylor mailed letters to faculty, reiterating his "principle" that propaganda, such as the debate, be avoided at all costs when it applied to "suffrage, socialism, temperance, and other allied questions."[19] The curriculum, Taylor implied, would shape, or rather keep, Vassar women within the conservative myth of education equal to men's.

Shaping the Writing Curriculum

The liberal arts curriculum that Vassar had originally designed was to develop the student's general intellectual judgment and her relationship and responsibility to culture. Therefore, classical languages, history, philosophy, and the abstract sciences were emphasized, unlike Mount Holyoke's or Wellesley's "seminary" approach, which emphasized teacher/missionary preparation. From the middle of the nineteenth century, modern languages and natural sciences had also entered the college curriculum along with debate clubs and literary societies, which at Vassar quickly expanded to include an intercollegiate competitive drama society. By the turn of the century a four-year baccalaureate degree at Vassar had all the marks of the founders' ideas of a real college. The required plan of study included four semesters of English; two semesters of Latin, mathematics, history, physics or chemistry, and Greek, French, or German; and one semester of hygiene, ethics, and psychology. It is within this framework that tension reappears. Typical of the liberal arts tradition was the required junior year course in psychology, a course that according to the catalog description aimed "to further the immediate intellectual discipline of the student and also to lay a basis for the formation of a sound and independent conception of self, the world, and God. Lectures and textbook study are supplemented by essays and free class-room discussion. The student is encouraged in every way possible to think for herself."[20]

Thinking for themselves did become a characteristic trait of Vassar women, as graduates such as Edna St. Vincent Millay or Ruth Fulton Benedict illustrate. But Vassar women rarely describe themselves as forming an "independent conception of self, the world, and God," as the junior course in psychology promised. More often than not, this cultural myth was thwarted by women who, as JoAnn Campbell observes, were "rooted in cooperation," not individualism. As Campbell explains, college life in and out of the classroom was based on a democratic spirit—women working and learning together to lead productive community lives.[21]

Assumptions behind the English curriculum during this period (1890–1920) reflect this philosophy and were particularly aimed at self-realization through an educational principle that began at the departmental level and extended to the individual students. By the end of the nineteenth century when composition and rhetoric had become departmentalized in the liberal arts curriculum as English, the Vassar English Department was conscious of its assumptions in teaching the discipline. College catalogues, departmental reports, and faculty essays and books detail the department's belief that students should have "frequent and regular practice" in composing, and that students' work should be systematically and intelligently critiqued by themselves, by their peers, and by teachers who are "experts in the fields of writing or research or both."[22]

As far back as 1867, Vassar College had stressed student conferences and interviews in freshman composition because both methods gauged a student's work within a larger community. To continue using this approach, the department regularly argued for reduced teaching loads so that faculty could teach English as expression controlled by individual experiences and in relation to an audience. In arguing for both these aspects of English composition, the faculty sought student involvement, not merely dictating mechanical "skills" for future clerks and managers as was the case at Harvard and many men's institutions.[23] Therefore, as at Mount Holyoke, Vassar faculty emphasized a close teacher-student relationship, but Vassar's faculty was drawn to a social model comparable to mentoring and to small group tutoring sessions rather than the mother-daughter model favored at Mount Holyoke. The results, perhaps more like the liberal culture model of the male institutions, did give the Vassar faculty a sense of preparing women for ever-expanding social roles. Although at times the task must have seemed overwhelming, the faculty, according to departmental reports, consistently worked in harmony toward the department's goals. English faculty taught as many as six preparations and more than 150 students while directing student and community activities, serving on college committees, writing articles, and otherwise maintaining a scholarly presence.[24]

After World War I when the president and board of trustees told the department to "retrench" and cut costs, chair Laura Wylie reflected on the department's curriculum and philosophy since her tenure in the 1890s. "English is primarily an art . . . and . . . whether considered from the point of view of literature or of writing, it should be so studied and taught." She added, "If it is to meet the requirements of art-study, it must be taught as individually as possible and must concern itself with the imaginative and perceptive hardly less than with the intellectual training of the student. . . . A series of administrative measures," she continued, was destroying the "coherence" of the departmental structure and would inevitably compromise the "educational ideas" at its foundation.[25] Although Wylie understood budgeting problems, she aptly placed the responsibility for limiting women's horizons on broad cultural values in the form of an administration that failed to see the value in women's imagination and perception, capabilities that Wylie and her colleagues obviously prized. Cooperation among department members had gone a long way in overcoming budget shortcomings in the past, but, as Wylie's exasperation showed, the 1920 cuts threatened the curriculum too much. Cuts would be particularly destructive of what she and Gertrude Buck had spent years developing.

Knowing Women's Ways of Knowing

In 1897, shortly after hiring Gertrude Buck from the University of Michigan, the department boasted of a writing, literature, and language sequence, one similar to many present-day English departments concerned with the connections among reading, writing, and thinking. Buck's textbooks, serving as the basis of Vassar's sequence, challenged the prevailing practices in many college English departments, which separated the creative and interpretative acts. When Wylie resisted post–World War I retrenchment, she was fighting to maintain this interrelationship of reading, speaking, writing, and thinking. At the same time, she was also resisting what had become a national trend in the teaching of college writing, namely, the teaching of isolated "skills." In describing this trend, Edward P. J. Corbett points out that many eastern institutions charged their English programs with preparing a new generation of industrial and business leaders to speak and write. But most English faculty, who lacked interest and training to carry out this charge, soon turned to linguistics and literature as a way of enriching their professional lives in lieu of teaching what they felt were essentially "skills" courses. Consequently, as Corbett explains, "The immensely rich rhetoric course that had been inherited from the Greek and Roman rhetors was replaced with a curriculum primarily concerned with style or even more narrowly with 'correct' grammar, punctuation, spelling, and usage."[26]

In spite of the trend, which Corbett tracks from the 1880s to the 1940s, the Vassar English department consistently opted for a more personal and individualized teaching approach supported by an emphasis on psychology and social theory. Department members taught Vassar students to be aware of individual creative processes, as they came into relationship with other human beings. That meant students would explore language in its complete processes and ranges, from the individual's perceptions to the community's interpretation. More than a strictly individualist liberal arts approach founded on classical literature, the curriculum led each student to search within her own frame of reference, to draw her writing experiences from her own daily experiences, and to sculpt her language in cooperation with someone else's.

Such was the case in first-year writing courses as well as the more advanced creative writing courses, in which students were encouraged to develop reflective, creative, and critical thinking applicable to society's needs. Like John Dewey, who used Buck's grammar textbook in his Chicago Laboratory School, Buck and her colleagues at Vassar viewed learning as a cooperative activity among students, and successful writing as a cooperative activity between writers (or speakers) and readers (or listeners). Buck explained her ideas by describing the "function of language as essentially social," not individual. As such, Buck criticized "anti-social" language, or language used to manipulate an audience (as Buck finds in the work of the Sophists), and termed this "uncooperative discourse." This was language from speakers and writers who disregard the needs of their audiences and simply write to express themselves or to persuade their audiences through deceptive, one-sided arguments. In emphasizing the needs of the audience, Buck stressed that writers and speakers should know the characteristics of their audiences, and, in particular, the shared mental and social processes involved in all communities. Buck specifically noted that writers must know how their audiences think. Consequently, a good communicator must know her audience's reasoning processes (logical, psychological, and cognitive), and a good narrative writer must know the typical structures in a story so as not to confuse the reader's expectations. A good writer of exposition must find a shared experience before she can be assured of successful communication.[27]

More often than not, Vassar's writing courses explored the shared characteristics among writers and audiences rather than those characteristics that divided them or made them distinctively individual. But because Buck's textbooks were written for the Vassar curriculum, they are illustrated with women's experiences and not only quote women authors and critics but also raise issues concerning women's emerging role in a patriarchal society. Getting female students to value their own thinking, speaking, and writing processes in light of their changing roles in society, therefore, enabled them to see themselves as significant participants in society. Buck's books are peppered with a moderate feminism found in the texts' theory, explanations, illustrations, and exercises.

One book's comparison of a society girl and two hunters provides an excellent example. Outlining the areas of shared life experiences of the society girl and the two sportsmen, a diagram illustrates the conclusion that, in spite of having more "life experiences," the two hunters have a "common basis in sense experience" with the society girl. This common basis and a "congenial" disposition make communication successful, and the girl can understand the men's adventures, regardless of the men's belief that a society girl would need a "sixth sense" to do so.[28] Significant to any feminist agenda in the Vassar English department's curriculum, this assumption (namely, that all people "see" alike) helps account for the way women experience and explain their world in relationship to men's.

The resulting guide to successful communication becomes especially helpful to women entering the predominantly male academic, business, and political worlds—arenas into which the textbook exercises thrust the readers. Through this means of socially cooperative language, therefore, the Vassar English faculty thought women's alienation from a male world could be lessened. In place of a world where language becomes another tool of competition and conflict, as with the Sophists, or a wall excluding one group from another, as with the society girl and the hunters, the Vassar curriculum finally suggests a fully democratic linguistic approach to women's place in society. And students had no better example of a successful democratic community than the Vassar English department, a department that overcame financial and political setbacks with its cooperative spirit.

In theory and in practice, the rhetoric institutionalized by Buck and her Vassar colleagues accommodated women's experiences and imaginations, first by asking students to write about their individual mental and intellectual processes, processes they assume are shared by all people (male and female), and then by stressing discourse as a socially constructed process involving the equally important activities of writers and readers. Clarifying her own assumptions of English study, Buck explains in a lecture to freshman students, "We study English in all its forms to open the doors of the thoughts and feelings of others to ourselves and of ourselves to others." She asks, "Why do we write?" and answers, "To make one able better to appreciate good writing." But in order to share those experiences of good writers, one must learn to "extract" experiences from herself, from her own writing. "What to write?" Buck asks. In words that might remind present-day readers of Hélène Cixous, Buck concludes, "Write what you yourself see and think. Write yourself, your individuality and experiences."[29] Buck's inclusion in her 1899 textbooks of women writers and women's experiences also implies the importance of women's roles, behavior, and consequently women's bodies to women's view of socialization. Such an approach is doubly interesting for analyzing changes in rhetoric and in a writing pedagogy that typically relied upon male writers, male speakers, and male experiences. No doubt this inclusion challenged popular classroom rhetoric, which seemingly separated public and private discourse and thereby excluded many women writers and thinkers from the history of rhetoric.

Wylie's and Buck's language does more than suggest remedies and cures under the guise of educational reform. What they have to say about their discipline exposes a disorder in an educational system where important decisions were often placed out of the reach of those charged with creating order. As I have already suggested, in increasing numbers academic women at the turn of the century discovered they did not conform to the conventional world—a world from which they refused to retreat, however—and set about to create a more orderly one for themselves. Whether at Mount Holyoke, Vassar, Radcliffe, or other Seven Sisters colleges, turn-of-the-century women continued to write of their frustration, their voices sometimes only hinting at the world they would like to inhabit.

Radcliffe's Writing Curriculum: Voices in Peril

Although a growing institutional consciousness at the turn of the century focused on the notion that women needed well-trained voices (both speaking and writing) to function effectively in their new public roles, not all went as far as Vassar in realizing the special needs of their female students. At Radcliffe women's educators had asked for treatment equal to that of Harvard men. And women's instruction followed closely along those lines—with Silas Weir Mitchell's warnings well in mind. In locating the historical places from which Radcliffe women have spoken about how their own needs related to those of male students, I have been concerned about how these "survivors" shape their own writing voices and consequently establish their own agency as historical subjects. Thus, defining women's liberating discourse involves not only looking at "public" and "private" papers as artifacts of nineteenth-century women's culture but also valuing the cognitive processes and the developmental problems women identify in their writing. We are reminded again that texts belonging to women students, teachers, and administrators offer insight into a kind of women's knowledge often overlooked by traditional histories with their focus on public speech.

Shifting one's view away from completed text to text-in-process can provide a satisfactory framework for rethinking gender issues in turn-of-the-century writing and writing instruction. Consequently, the rough draft, or the "daily theme"—Radcliffe's (and Harvard's) version of the rough draft—has provided some clues to women's struggle in gaining literacy and in accommodating their personal knowledge to confusing social expectations. Gender issues, for example, surface when Radcliffe women respond to male Harvard professors in their daily themes. Annie Ware Winsor Allen, class of 1888, writes:

> Men who have taught both men and women say that in general women have too much conscience and too little independence. . . . I think, women, besides really lacking independence, add to their apparent servility by their timid silence. Women students often disagree radically and emphatically with their instructors' statements and opinions, often have independent, sensible notions of their own; but they do not dare to express their dissent or knowing themselves ignorant, they do not feel justified in propounding original theories to men who have spent years in study. They are not the mere recepticles [*sic*] which they seem to be.[30]

Annie Allen's scheme of women's intellectual development, or perhaps her lack of intellectual development in her writing class, corresponds to development patterns outlined by Mary Belenky's *Women's Ways of Knowing*. According to Allen, her classmates share "subjective knowing," described by Belenky and her coauthors as one type of women's knowledge: women understand "truth as personal, private, and subjectively known or intuited." They will listen to their own instincts and establish a strong internal authority, often isolating themselves from external authorities. They move into their own worlds and share those only with women in similar circumstances. Such subjectionists are at risk, Belenky notes.[31] No doubt many Radcliffe women overcame such cultural oppression and gender-stereotyping forced upon them by male professors who saw their student's minds, as one Harvard professor wrote in a terminal comment to the Radcliffe student cited above, as "charmingly feminine" and incapable of seeing the "world as it is."[32]

Moreover, on occasions when women at Radcliffe and Vassar speak of being empowered through composition and rhetoric, lines of social and gender division are still felt. For example, Vassar correspondence and pamphlets detail a consortium among four of the women's colleges at the turn of the century and suggest that all worked toward a uniform standard in teaching composition and rhetoric. These types of coalitions created a sense of unity and community. But at the same time, they created conflict. Documents at Radcliffe, for example, hint that uniform standards were quite difficult to maintain in light of individual differences among the colleges' faculties, missions, and administrative structures. Likewise, writing tasks at Radcliffe and Vassar created in many respects a sense of community, especially among students who formed debating clubs for educational and social reasons. But at Radcliffe, the debating club also gave female students an avenue for individual expression, something they felt was often absent in male instructors' classes. Thus rather than end in consensus, the debates and discussions that followed brought out the women's social, political, and cultural differences as students sharply disagreed about public and private roles for women.

In this sense gender becomes a system of cultural representation, and women's rhetoric becomes an important site for exploring new relationships of power. Especially in the case of women's debate societies, as women's teams were ridiculed by both men and women for challenging men's teams, the phenomenon of educated women as public speakers exposes a change in relations of power and systems of belief. Many women, we could argue, were initially unsure of their emerging power, and they became increasingly forceful in demanding it and indeed in claiming it. Others may have taken advantage of social climbing through higher education and used their positions to define "success" for the educated and culturally literate woman. In any case, because women within these sites illustrate difference within difference, their collective interests as "women" become less evident and more a matter of debate for themselves and a matter of investigation for us. Furthermore, their challenges to the earlier definitions and systems of belief help us question the terms that initially kept women out of the public sphere. These debates and other disagreements among educated women obviously became part of a larger dispute involving political and social control. More specifically, during the decade before the turn of the century and until women received the vote in 1920 women's colleges became political backgrounds, not only for defining women's rights but also for redefining and illustrating how one becomes a woman.

Only now are we beginning to realize that as the status of women changed, systems that had once defined women responded to those changes, some advancing women's causes, some trying to ignore them. Departments and areas of study no less than educational institutions serve as sites to illustrate the resulting political and cultural impact as women struggled to have their voices heard. There is little doubt that the teaching of rhetoric and composition at times aided and at other times hindered women in these pursuits. And even now as we write revisionist stories of the American institutionalization of composition and rhetoric, we must admit different perspectives into histories of rhetoric and writing, not construct a single history. Perhaps from these perspectives we may even go beyond a tentative conclusion about women and their views of rhetorical education and reach an understanding about how women experienced widely diverse worlds in their literacy training in turn-of-the-century women's colleges.

Notes

1. See especially James A. Berlin, *Rhetoric and Reality: Writing Instruction in American Colleges* (Carbondale: Southern Illinois Univ. Press, 1987); Edward P. J. Corbett, *Classical Rhetoric for the Modern Student,* 3d ed. (New York: Oxford Univ. Press, 1990); and Albert R. Kitzhaber, *Rhetoric in American Colleges, 1850–1900* (Dallas: Southern Methodist Univ. Press, 1990).

2. See, for example, Catherine Peaden, "Feminist Theories, Historiographies, and Histories of Rhetoric," in Charles W. Kneupper, ed., *Rhetoric and Ideology: Compositions and Criticisms of Power* (Arlington, Tex.: Rhetoric Society of America, 1989), pp. 116–26, esp. p. 218.

3. Carol Gilligan, *In a Different Voice: Psychological Theory and Women's Development* (Cambridge: Harvard Univ. Press, 1982); Mary F. Belenky et al. *Women's Ways of Knowing: The Development of Self, Voice, and Mind* (New York: Basic Books, 1986); and Nancy Chodorow, *The Reproduction of Mothering: Psychoanalysis and the Sociology of Gender* (Berkeley: Univ. of California Press, 1978). The quotation is from Belenky, et al., p. 3.

4. Edward Clarke, *Sex in Education: or, A Fair Chance for the Girls* (Boston:

Osgood, 1873); cited in Rosalind Rosenberg, *Beyond Separate Spheres: Intellectual Roots of Modern Feminism* (New Haven: Yale Univ. Press, 1982), p. 13.

5. Rosenberg, *Beyond Separate Spheres,* p. 46.

6. Ibid., p. 49.

7. Ibid., pp. 53–55.

8. Gilligan, *In a Different Voice,* p. 16.

9. Carroll Smith-Rosenberg, *Disorderly Conduct: Visions of Gender in Victorian America* (New York: Knopf, 1985), pp. 252–53.

10. Silas Weir Mitchell, "Address to the Students of Radcliffe College," Cambridge, Mass., 1986 (delivered 17 Jan. 1885), History of Women Collection, Schlesinger Library, Radcliffe College, pp. 5–6. This work will hereafter be cited parenthetically in the text. Charlotte Perkins Gilman, "The Yellow Wallpaper" (1892), in *The Charlotte Perkins Gilman Reader,* ed. Ann J. Lane (New York: Pantheon, 1980), pp. 3–31.

11. Smith-Rosenberg, *Disorderly Conduct,* pp. 257–58.

12. Helen Lefkowitz Horowitz, *Alma Mater: Design and Experience in the Women's Colleges from Their Nineteenth-Century Beginnings to the 1930s* (New York: Knopf, 1984), pp. 14–17.

13. Ibid., pp. 58, 56–59.

14. Ibid., p. 33.

15. Ibid., pp. 33, 37.

16. Ibid., p. 57.

17. Vassar President James Taylor, letter of 4 Nov. 1907, J. M. Taylor Papers, Box 16, Vassar College Library, Poughkeepsie, N.Y.

18. Vassar President James Taylor, "Re: Faculty Discussion on Freedom, Etc., Apropos of Suffrage—19 Mar. 1909," 3 Nov. 1911, J. M. Taylor Papers, Box 5, Vassar College Library.

19. Ibid.

20. *Vassar Thirty-fourth Annual Catalog* (Poughkeepsie, N.Y.: Vassar College, 1898–99), pp. 24–25.

21. JoAnn Campbell, "Women's Work, Worthy Work: Composition Instruction at Vassar College, 1897–1922," in *Constructing Rhetorical Education,* ed. Marie Secor and Davida Charney (Carbondale: Southern Illinois Univ. Press, 1992), pp. 26–42; see p. 27.

22. Bessie R. Hooker, "The Use of Literary Material in Teaching Composition," *School Review* 10 (1902): 474–85; Gertrude Buck and Elisabeth Woodbridge Morris, *A Course in Narrative Writing* (New York: Henry Holt, 1906); Buck and Woodbridge Morris, *A Course in Expository Writing* (New York: Henry Holt, 1899); Gertrude Buck, *A Course in Argumentative Writing* (New York: Henry Holt, 1899), and "The Study of English," *Vassar Miscellany Weekly* 2 (19 Jan. 1917): 6; and see especially Laura Johnson Wylie, "Report of the Department of English, 1921," Vassar College Library, p. 5.

23. Edward P. J. Corbett, "Literature and Composition: Allies or Rivals in the Classroom?" in *Composition and Literature: Bridging the Gap,* ed. Winifred Bryan Horner (Chicago: Univ. of Chicago Press, 1983) pp. 168–84; see p. 175.

24. Laura Johnson Wylie, "Annual Report of the Department of English for the Second Semester, 1897–98," Vassar College Library.

25. Wylie, "Report, 1921," pp. 2–3.

26. Corbett, "Literature," p. 176.

27. Buck, *Argumentative Writing,* pp. vi, 5–7; Buck and Woodbridge Morris,

Expository Writing, pp. 2, 5–6, and *Narrative Writing,* pp. iv, 100; and Gertrude Buck, "The Present State of Rhetorical Theory," *Modern Language Notes* 15 (1900): 168–74.

28. Buck and Woodbridge Morris, *Expository Writing,* pp. 5–6.

29. Buck, "Study of English," p. 6.

30. Annie Allen, 5 Jan. 1887, Annie Ware Winsor Allen Collection, MC 322, Schlesinger Library, Radcliffe College, Cambridge, Mass. See also Simmons's essay in this volume for an analysis of this student's writing and experience at Radcliffe.

31. Belenky, *Women's Ways,* pp. 54–55.

32. Allen, 9 Dec. 1884, Annie Ware Winsor Allen Papers, MC 322, Schlesinger Library.

3

SANDRA D. HARMON

"The Voice, Pen and Influence of Our Women Are Abroad in the Land"

WOMEN AND THE ILLINOIS STATE NORMAL UNIVERSITY, 1857–1899

A SUBSTANTIAL PORTION of the literature of the history of women's education in the United States centers on higher education, especially on elite, eastern women's colleges, a point highlighted by Sally Schwager in her perceptive review essay on women's educational history. Among the institutions that have received scant attention are nineteenth-century normal schools. Studies of normal schools are underrepresented in the literature despite the fact that normals were important educational agencies for thousands of young women across the country. During the second half of the nineteenth century, more than half of all women enrolled in schools beyond the secondary level were students in normal schools.[1] With their low or free tuition, public normals offered many young women, especially those with limited means, their only opportunity for formal education beyond common schooling.

As institutions primarily dedicated to preparing teachers for the nation's common schools, normals were intimately tied to what was, for all intents and purposes, the only profession open to women during most of the nineteenth century. Because teaching was deemed a respectable occupation for women and one that "could accommodate women from a wide range of backgrounds," it was appealing both to those who needed to become economically self-sufficient and to those who looked forward to eventual marriage. Many female normal students and graduates made teaching their life's work or a springboard to other careers, and, as Schwager points out, "unlike most nineteenth-century women, whose social status was in large part a function of their father's or husband's status, women teachers occupied a position in their communities that was, to some degree at least, a function of their own occupational role."[2] Teaching also was thought to be good preparation for wifehood and motherhood, and, therefore, an appropriate short-term occupation for women until they married.

Normal schools prepared teachers through a curriculum that generally included further study of the "common branches" of learning and classes in the educational theory of the day. Some normal schools offered elements of a classical course of study as well. However, English language instruction was central to the schools' mission of furnishing professional training for teachers. For that reason, it is useful to examine the normal school as one agency of women's rhetorical education in the nineteenth century. Generally, knowing more about the normal schools—their mission, the curriculum offered to students, and the campus environment for women—can help fill in gaps in our knowledge of women's education in the nineteenth century. Knowing more about the students and graduates of the normal schools can lead to a more complete profile of educated women in the nineteenth and early twentieth century. This study of one midwestern normal school of the nineteenth century, the Illinois State Normal University in Normal, Illinois,[3] is an attempt to shed light on women's experiences in a coeducational institution whose primary mission was to train teachers for the state's common and high schools, and to note the kind of careers the graduates chose to pursue. Special attention will be paid to the school's English language curriculum and to the subsequent professional writing of some of the graduates.

On the first morning of classes, Monday, 5 October 1857, thirteen women and six men enrolled for the first term of the Illinois State Normal University. By the second week of classes, their number had grown to forty-three. They came from all over the state to attend a school temporarily ensconced "in a tumble-down hall, tumbled up on the top of a grocery house, at an out of the way corner, in the city of Bloomington," as Charles Hovey, the first principal, described the school's quarters.[4] The permanent location for the school lay a mile or so north of Bloomington on what was then "a lonely prairie, not a tree to be seen, not a house near." Over the next three years, while classes were held in Majors Hall in Bloomington, a three-story building was erected on a rise on the prairie and the new village of North Bloomington, later rechristened Normal, took shape. An alumna of the first graduating class of 1860 wrote, "When the great red brick Normal school building arose in its majesty, it stood a real temple of knowledge."[5]

The school must have seemed that way to other students as well, for in 1857 Illinois was still in the pioneer phase of its history with rudimentary school systems serving a largely rural population. The Illinois State Normal University was itself a pioneering institution. While the country's first state-supported normal schools had been established in Massachusetts in 1839, the Illinois normal was the first of its kind in the Mississippi Valley and the first state-supported school of higher education in Illinois. By 1870, with slightly more than 300 students, the ISNU was the largest state normal in the country and remained one of the largest for the rest of the century. It served as a model for a number of later Illinois and midwestern schools.[6]

The earliest state normals had sought to prepare teachers for elementary schools. Then some normals added the tasks of preparing high school teachers and school administrators. Once the normal school movement arrived in the Midwest, a third purpose arose from the desires of a frontier population for "people's colleges." These, according to Jurgen Herbst, a recent historian of the movement, "would allow their graduates easy transfer into liberal arts colleges and universities" and "would open the door for them to any occupation or profession." While the ISNU served as a "people's college" for many of its students and graduates and was for ten years the state's only public university, it adopted the training of teachers and administrators for all levels of schooling as its primary objective.[7]

Trained teachers were sorely needed to improve the state's public schools, a fact demonstrated time and again by the numbers of normal school applicants who were unprepared for any kind of advanced work. During the first week of classes in October 1857, the editor of the Bloomington *Daily Pantagraph* sat in on the oral examinations of prospective students. He observed, "Some of the scholars were very apt in their answers, and others were more or less backward." Twenty years later the situation was much the same. A third of the applications seeking admission through examination were rejected "on account of imperfect literary qualifications." Other students admitted by certificate from their county superintendents were "afterwards found to be poorly qualified."[8] President Richard Edwards also acknowledged the need to attract already-employed teachers to the normal school for training. In his "Decennial Address" to the school on 27 June 1872 he noted, "every practical man knows that in all communities there are many ill-qualified teachers. . . .

The wise course for the Normal School is to receive these unfinished teachers, and hold them as long as possible. Let help be given them wherever it is needed, whether in the knowledge of the subjects to be taught, or of the science and art of imparting instruction. It is wise to do this, because these are the teachers in fact and will be, whether qualified or not, and every particle of culture imparted to them will be so much clear gain for the schools."[9]

Over the course of the nineteenth century, the academic qualifications of the entering class rose. President John W. Cook reported to the governing body, the Board of Education, in December 1897 that 202 of the 394 students admitted to the school that term were high school or college graduates. Of those graduates, 163 were women, leading Cook to comment: "The great disparity between the number of girls and of boys in the graduating classes of our public high schools shows itself here. But few of our young men have taken such a course. The result is that the women represent a higher degree of culture in our entering classes than the men."[10]

Whatever their academic backgrounds, the students who came to the normal university were a relatively mature lot. Admission standards required males to be at least seventeen and females at least sixteen; however, throughout the nineteenth century the average age of the entering class was considerably higher. For example, the 1862 entering class average was twenty-four years and six months; the 1880 class, twenty-four years and eleven months; and the 1890 class, twenty years and one month. As might be expected with older students, a number were wholly or partially self-supporting. A majority of the students came from farm families.[11]

Early graduates later recalled the humble backgrounds and financial struggles of the students. Elizabeth Mitchell Christian of the first graduating class of 1860 remembered, "Those were pioneer days in this great state of Illinois, and these ambitious boys and girls came from humble homes where courage, stability, and industry were the winning qualities." Those early students were, she said, "earnest, serious minded students, whose one object seemed to be to do their best work." Henry B. Norton of the class of 1861 wrote of himself and his classmates: "We were very poor, but very plucky. . . . [O]ur parents were sad-faced, struggling pioneers of the prairies; but we were cheery, resolute and happy in our life and our work." However, as Charles Harper pointed out in his history of the school, "They were poor in a society where there were not great extremes of wealth. Their poverty was not particularly noticeable because it was so common." He contended that the student body was generally representative of all economic classes in Illinois.[12]

A recurring theme in official school reports, however, is the financial struggles of students to meet room, board, and living expenses even though for most, tuition was free. A glimpse of this struggle is offered in a memoir Flora Adelaide Holcomb Bronson wrote for her children. Bronson first entered the school for the 1869 fall term. Describing herself as shy and lonely, she nearly left until befriended by Professors John Cook and Thomas Metcalf. Soon, "I began to get acquainted and became very happy in my work." Then financial woes beset her. "I wrote Uncle Harvey. When I left Michigan he borrowed my savings to pay his taxes. I wrote that I needed it and he sold a cow and sent me thirty-odd dollars, I think. I began to board. The cash soon began to vanish. I wrote to Uncle Fayette I thought I ought to have the $71 coming to me from the property he held as guardian. Poor little property! He sent it and I finished the fall and winter term." These two terms were all Bronson could afford, but she believed "my Normal training had so improved me I feel I did very good work" as a teacher in the years that followed.[13]

The school was coeducational from the beginning, and women students outnumbered men throughout the nineteenth century. The female enrollment varied from 57 to 69 percent of the total figure in the period 1865–90. However, the fact that around 40 percent of the student body was male set it apart from eastern normals where the percentage of male students was generally lower, especially toward the end of the century. An item published in the school newspaper, the *Vidette,* in 1894 noted that nationally 65.5 percent of public-school teachers were women and added, "It is interesting to note that this is not far from the proportion of girls in the Normal."[14]

Most aspects of the campus environment and school experience were truly coeducational with certain bows to convention. Men and women took the same classes and met in the same classrooms, but Old Main, the only campus building for many years, had separate entrances, cloakrooms, and stairways for the two sexes. Because there were no dormitories constructed in the nineteenth century, students lived with local families or took rooms in boarding houses, with men and women often rooming in the same house. Lida Brown McMurry, class of '74, described how she and her brother, Isaac Eddy Brown, boarded themselves. "I cooked our meals, my brother running the errands. On Friday evenings he helped me do the washing, and on Saturday I ironed. (At that time stiff shirt fronts were in vogue; how I did sweat over them.) Saturday was baking day also—a very full day."[15]

Several years after the Browns attended, student began forming boarding clubs. According to McMurry: "The students who belonged to a club, rented rooms in a large house and engaged a woman to cook for them. One of the boys was appointed steward and did the buying." The boarding clubs proved to be very popular, and "old grads were as loyal to their boarding clubs as if they had been fraternities."[16] In 1898 the school put an end to coeducational rooming houses, although men and women were allowed to continue taking their meals together in boarding clubs. President Cook announced his decision to the board: "I believe the presence of young men and young women at the same table to be advantageous to both. Rooming in the same houses is attended by so many objections, however, that it has been thought best to discontinue it."[17] He did not elaborate on the objections.

In the beginning the school offered a three-year course of study that included seven divisions of classes: didactics, language, mathematics, geography and history, natural science, vocal music, and drawing as well as optional studies in Latin, French, and higher mathematics. Later Greek, German, and advanced study in the natural sciences were available as optional studies. With other periodic modifications, this remained the basic course of study for the rest of the nineteenth century.[18]

While all the common branches of learning were considered important, the study of the English language was especially emphasized. The study of English included a rigorous and, to the students, onerous training in spelling. In his semiannual report to the Board of Education in December 1874, President Edwards noted that, as "many of our pupils are woefully deficient in spelling," the University "does not consider its dignity at all compromised by a thorough daily drill in spelling for such as need the training." Every student had to pass spelling, and most took five terms to do it. According to Charles Harper, "twenty-five words were assigned each day," and "a miss of more than one word in a term meant failure for the term."[19]

Many entering students were not only deficient in spelling, according to President Edwards, but also were "unable to read with any adequate apprehension of nice shades of meaning." Furthermore, he declared, "When we reflect that the English tongue furnishes in itself a 'liberal education,' and that an unskillful and slovenly use of it is disastrous to any accuracy of thought, we can not do otherwise than deeply regret this state of facts. The Normal University considers it a worthy service to do all that is possible to remedy this evil."[20]

In addition to three terms of spelling, the English language curriculum outlined in the 1877 catalog included one term of etymology, one term of syntax that required written and oral exercises, and two terms of reading with practice in elocution. The catalog described the one term of rhetoric as "Diction, including Purity, Propriety, Precision, Clearness, Unity, Strength and Harmony. Rhetorical Figures. Style and its varieties. Original Composition during the term." The final three offerings were one term of literary criticism requiring an original composition, one term of English literature beginning with Chaucer, and one term consisting of a critical study of Shakespeare's *Hamlet* with required orations and essays.[21]

While much of the classroom work was the traditional nineteenth-century form of recitation, in which the students memorized textbook passages and repeated them to the professor, ISNU students were required to write and read original compositions as well. Further experience in reading, writing, and speaking came through the students' involvement in the extracurricular literary societies. Literary societies were a standard feature of nineteenth-century higher education in the United States, a higher education that was primarily the preserve of men. College students often received more practical experience in writing, speaking, and debating in the societies than in the classroom where so much time was devoted to recitation.[22]

In keeping with the male tradition of literary societies, men students organized a debating society four days after classes began in 1857. However, in February 1858 dissension within the group led to the formation of a second society with thirty-three charter members including fourteen women. Thereupon, the original society opened its doors to women. By the fall of 1859 the societies—the Philadelphian and the Wrightonian—were so firmly established and deemed so educationally valuable that the school began assigning all entering students to one or the other.[23] Prevailing sensibilities as to the proper roles of men and women precluded women from taking part in the debates. Instead, women members were put in charge of each society's literary paper, the Philadelphian *Ladies Garland* and the Wrightonian *Oleastellus*. In annual contests men debaters and women writers vied for first-place honors for their societies. The literary papers were replaced by essay contests for women in 1888. Vocal music had been added to the program in 1862 and instrumental music in 1866, with both men and women performing in those competitions. An oration contest was held for the first time in 1869, but no woman contended for honors until 1902. However, a woman had appeared for the first time in the debate contest of 1899.[24]

A similar division of labor prevailed in the first, short-lived series of internormal contests held in 1879 and 1880 between the ISNU and the new state normal school at Carbondale, which had opened in 1873. An

ISNU committee made up of both men and women, Philadelphians and Wrightonians, sent a proposal to Carbondale in December 1878: "Recognizing the importance of the culture to be derived from what is known as Literary Society Work," and because "of our relative status as Normal Schools being debarred from participating in the Inter-Collegiate Contests, in a spirit of friendship and not of rivalry, we hereby send you a challenge for a Literary Contest." The ISNU group proposed contests in debate, oration, essay, and vocal and instrumental music to which the Carbondale committee added declamation. In the two years that contests were held, both men and women participated as musicians and essayists, while only men were debaters and orators, and only women were declaimers.[25]

From the division of labor in the literary societies, it is clear that the world of public speaking and debate was still a male world. The classical, rhetorical idea of men skilled in public speaking was still strong and still gender-specific in the Illinois normals. Women's rhetorical accomplishments were to be found in writing, although in the case of essay contests, women were allowed to read their compositions, and, in the case of declamation contests, women could recite the words of others. Therefore women students did gain experience in appearing before an audience, even if it was not the same experience as men's.

The ISNU societies were a bit more daring in the matter of choosing officers. In 1870 the Philadelphians were the first to elect a woman president, though not without controversy. Alice Emmons, a senior student with previous teaching experience, won a hard-fought election after having been defeated the year before. According to an early history of the society, "the election of a lady caused dissatisfaction, and a committee was appointed to test the election, and it was finally declared illegal." However, that same history lists Emmons as president for two terms.[26] Her classmate, Louisa C. Allen, served as the first woman president of the Wrightonian Society. Emmons died a year after graduating. Her obituary in the alumni register of 1882 called her "a brilliant scholar, thoroughly conscientious and faithful in the discharge of every duty," and noted, "all had anticipated for her a future of rare usefulness." Allen's later career befitted her pioneering student role. She established the first domestic science program at the University of Illinois, where she taught domestic science and physical education and served as preceptress in the late 1870s.[27] Other women also served as society presidents, an office that changed hands frequently to allow greater opportunities for students. An 1882 listing named ninety-six Philadelphian presidents, of whom eleven were women, and ninety-five Wrightonian presidents, of whom fourteen were women.[28]

Over the years, students organized other literary clubs, with men again taking the lead. The all-male Ciceronian Society, dating from the 1870s, did not have a female equivalent until the Sapphonian Society formed in 1887. Once organized, Sapphonians mounted ambitious programs of music, recitations, declamations, orations, and essay readings as well as debates at their weekly meetings. Debate topics covered a wide range of issues: Sunday hours for public parks and libraries; using surplus U.S. treasury funds to build a navy; whether "the maiden lady can do more to benefit humanity than the married lady"; whether "better results can be obtained in separate schools for different sexes"; and whether "woman should compete with man in all possible vocations."[29] On an evening devoted to the poet Whittier, the debate topic was, "Resolved that Whittier should not have been a bachelor." On several occasions, the young women approved motions encouraging every member to take part in society discussions. During an extemporaneous debate on the resolution "that a country life is preferable to a city life," all members were required to speak, "each taking whichever side she wished."[30] In the supportive atmosphere of an all-female society, ISNU women who chose to do so did have the opportunity to debate formally, an activity denied them in the coeducational clubs.

Other nineteenth-century literary extracurricular organizations were coeducational, including the Oratorical Association established in 1887. The *Vidette,* the student newspaper, made its debut in February 1888, with H. Kate Bigham as editor-in-chief. Her tenure was short. She resigned after a month due to a heavy workload and was succeeded by a man. Thereafter, men typically were editors-in-chief and business managers while women were associate editors. However, both men and women wrote for the paper, often on similar topics, with little to distinguish the articles of one sex from the other. The last major nineteenth-century student undertaking was the publication of a yearbook, *The Index,* begun in 1892. It, too, had a coeducational staff.[31]

In English classrooms and extracurricular activities, nineteenth-century ISNU students honed their rhetorical skills. Writing, in the form of journal keeping, also played a part in instruction in pedagogy. In his report to the board in December 1872, President Edwards explained his method of supervising student teachers, which included having each pupil teacher keep a diary "detailing the work of the day, stating the subject of the recitation, pointing out the difficulties that have been encountered, the methods by which they have been surmounted, the various expedients resorted to for securing an interest in the lesson, and the modes of reviewing and thus rendering permanent the acquisitions of the pupils." Edwards found the diaries "useful in many ways. They turn the thoughts of the young teacher to his methods and to the details of his teaching, and prevent him from doing any thing thoughtlessly." In twice-a-week group meetings of pupil teachers, Edwards called upon students to read from their diaries.[32]

Students who took the three-year course of study leading to a diploma faced two final writing projects. One was a senior paper, "discussing either the Geology, Botany, or some department of the Natural History of the district in which he or she resides." This requirement was adopted by the board in June 1865. No reason was put forth for natural history as the subject for the papers. However, the Museum of the Illinois Natural History Society was housed on the third floor of Old Main, and natural history study was an important component of the curriculum. Students helped describe, classify, and catalog specimens for the museum's collections, and this work was an integral part of their science education. From the beginning the board gave enthusiastic support to science education, to the museum, and to its first professional curator, John Wesley Powell, who was appointed to the position in March 1867.[33]

The class of 1868 was the first to fulfill the requirement of completing a senior paper, and the Board of Education took special note of "the carefully-prepared and valuable essay of Miss S. Grace Hurwood . . . upon 'The Mosses of McLean County.'" The following year's board *Proceedings* listed the titles of all senior papers. Women students generally wrote on flora while men students addressed a variety of topics: "Topography of McLean County," "Combustion of Coal," "Ventilation," and "Frogs," among others. Only one woman ventured beyond trees, flowers, and grasses to write a paper entitled "Water." Botany had long been considered an appropriate science for women, and it apparently was appealing to ISNU women. The board was very pleased with the papers, "evincing as they do, much industry and investigation," and declared "several of the papers are of such marked excellence as to be deemed worthy of publication."[34] Several women graduates did eventually publish books and articles on natural science in their later careers as educators. Forty-five years after her paper on mosses so pleased the board, Grace Hurwood, for example, published an article on the French naturalist Henri Fabre in the *American Review of Reviews,* thus combining her interests in French and natural science.[35]

The other writing requirements for seniors was a graduation theme. From 1860 to 1871, each member of the graduating class presented or read his or her theme at the commencement exercises. As the size of the classes grew, the ceremonies became all-day affairs and included a lunch break. In the 1870s, in an effort to shorten the proceedings, students were chosen by lot or according to class rank to make oral presentations, and in the 1880s the board limited the number of speakers to seven. Still, every senior had to prepare a theme. Throughout the nineteenth century, men's themes were denoted orations and women's themes were essays.[36] While both men and women appeared on the platform to make oral presentations, there was, as in the case of literary society work, a clear distinction between masculine and feminine styles. Men orated. Women read.

In the polarized gender system of the nineteenth century, distinctions such as those between orations and essays are not surprising. It is perhaps more noteworthy that campus life at the Illinois State Normal University was very much coeducational. President Edwards was, in fact, an outspoken advocate of coeducation, believing women and men were equally qualified to pursue all knowledge. In an 1868 speech to the Illinois Teachers' Association, he asked, "Is it not the acme of absurdity for you and me, because we happen to grow beards, to step forward, with our little measuring strings, and attempt to fix, beforehand, the scope of women's investigation of truth?"[37]

In classes and extracurricular activities, in rooming houses and boarding clubs, men and women learned together, worked with and lived next to each other, and occasionally competed with each other in society elections and contests. Men students, to be sure, took precedence in debate activities and office holding, although women made inroads in these male preserves. In a period when coeducation was in its infancy, the ISNU offered a good deal of freedom of association to its men and women students. Henry B. Norton of the class of '61 later recalled, "We lived as we pleased, formed our friendships and associations, made our calls, and managed our affairs, entirely at our own choice and pleasure."[38] There were, in fact, rules and regulations regarding conduct, but the maturity of the student body may have contributed to the sense of freedom of association.

Many students attended the Illinois State Normal University. Relatively few graduated. As of 1907, 24,013 students had attended the school since its opening. However, of those, only 1,760 or 7.33 percent had graduated from the three-year course of study. On the occasion of the school's quarter centennial in 1882, President Edwin C. Hewett bemoaned the fact that so few students took their diplomas. He noted: "Our course of study is more extended than that of most Normal schools. We insist rigidly on our rule of requiring each one to reach a fixed standard of attainment in any study before he is allowed to pass that study." However, he continued, "Many of our students . . . are dependent upon their own exertions for means, and, before their course is complete, they are obliged to go out and teach."[39]

The sex ratio of the graduating classes differed from the ratios of the entering classes, with women usually making up a smaller portion of the graduates than of the total student body. The class of '76 had the smallest percentage of female graduates (17 percent) and the class of '98 the highest (76 percent). The average for the decade of the 1860s was 52 percent; the 1870s, 47 percent; the 1880s, 55 percent; and the 1890s, 57 percent.[40]

Most of the women graduates taught upon leaving school. In fact, in return for free tuition, students agreed to teach in Illinois for three years and were to report their teaching positions to the president of the school for the three years following graduation. Those who failed to teach were to repay tuition costs.[41] The school attempted to continue to keep track of its graduates over the rest of their lives and published periodic alumni registers. It is from these registers that information about career choices of the women graduates has been gathered.[42]

Information about 524 out of a total of 541 women graduates from 1860 to 1899 was included in one or more of the registers. The vast majority of them taught for at least the three years required to receive free tuition. Excluding five women who died within three years of graduation, 94 percent of the remaining 519 for whom there is information taught at least three years. In this regard, ISNU women had a high employment rate in comparison with some late-nineteenth-century college graduates. One study of two eastern women's colleges found that 90 percent of the women who graduated from Bryn Mawr and 65 percent who graduated from Wellesley from 1889 to 1908 worked for pay for at least some period of time. A majority of them were employed as teachers, as were most college-educated women in the nineteenth century. A study conducted by the Association of Collegiate Alumnae of 3,500 college graduates from 1869 to 1898 found that 72.4 percent had taught.[43] Not only did ISNU women have a high employment rate, they also worked for relatively long periods of time. Two-thirds worked in education for at least six years. Forty percent had careers that lasted over ten years, including at least eighty-eight women or 17 percent who worked over twenty-five years.

Graduates reported holding teaching and administrative positions in all types of schools—elementaries, high schools, normal schools, and colleges—but most often in elementary schools. Many of the teachers, especially those who taught in normal schools and colleges, had continued their own education beyond that of the three-year ISNU course. A total of 151 women, nearly 30 percent of all the graduates from 1860 to 1899, reported taking course work after leaving the ISNU. The numbers by decade reflect the growing availability and acceptance of higher education for women. Seven women (12 percent) who graduated in the 1860s took further course work; twenty women (20 percent) from the 1870s; thirty women (22 percent) from the 1880s; and ninety-four women (45 percent) from the 1890s. Fewer received additional degrees. Out of the nineteenth-century graduates, five earned M.D.s, forty-one earned bachelor's, and thirteen earned master's degrees.

While education was the primary field of work for ISNU graduates, nearly eighty women listed careers in addition to or instead of teaching. Their choices are representative of the kind of occupations open to middle-class women in the late nineteenth century: physicians and nurses, foreign and domestic missionaries, clerical workers, business owners, journalists, librarians, and matrons of institutions for the aged, blind, and orphaned. Eight single and eleven married women listed themselves as farmers.

Most graduates who left paid employment did so to marry, but not all graduates married. Nationally, about 90 percent of all late-nineteenth-century women married at some point in their lives. College women, however, had a much lower marriage rate. An Association of Collegiate Alumnae survey of 3,600 college-educated women in 1900 found that of those who graduated between 1869 and 1879 only 55.4 percent married; of those graduating between 1879 and 1888, 50.3 percent married.[44] Marriage rates for ISNU alumnae were higher than that but still much lower than the national norm. The average rate for graduates of the 1860s was 56 percent; the 1870s, 60 percent; the 1880s, 66 percent; and the 1890s, 58 percent. A relatively large number, over 35 percent, of the married ISNU graduates worked for pay after marriage. No doubt some of these were widows, but it is clear that many worked while their husbands were living.

Writing professionally was an activity that both married and single women pursued. While very few of the ISNU graduates made a living writing or editing, at least fifty reported having had articles or books published or having worked as editors. Four women were newspaper editors. The two most interesting were Ida Estelle Crouch-Hazlett, class of '88, and Lavinia E. Roberts, class of '90. Both wrote for the *Vidette* as students, and Crouch was the *Vidette's* treasurer and on its board of managers her senior year. In addition, Crouch was a founding member of the Sapphonian Society. She taught for seven years, but her subsequent career was as a lecturer, organizer, newspaper reporter, and editor for the Socialist Party. She was at one time editor of the socialist newspaper the *Montana News*.[45] Roberts was a farmer, a Populist Party speaker, and editor of the *People's Advocate* of Pittsfield, Illinois. In 1894 she was the Populist nominee for State Superintendent of Public Instruction.[46]

The only alumna to list herself as a writer was Augusta Eleanor Root, '83, who taught for eleven years and then apparently supported herself by writing stories for popular adult and children's magazines. She was also a frequent contributor to an educational journal, *The Western Teacher,* published in Milwaukee by owner-editor S. Y. Gillan, a graduate of the ISNU class of 1879. Gillan's sister, Mary Gillan Eastman, class of '81, was a member of his editorial staff from 1902 to 1917 and contributed occasional articles as well. Her editorial career followed twelve years of teaching and her marriage in 1895.[47]

Most of the women who wrote did so for the educational press, and there is evidence of networking among men and women with ISNU connections. *The Western Teacher* is one example. *School and Home Education,* published in Bloomington under a variety of names, often carried the work of ISNU faculty and former students, including at least four of the women graduates. *School News and Practical Educator,* published in Taylorville, Illinois, also carried articles by those connected with ISNU. Alumnae Pauline Schneider, '94, and Mary Steagall, '96, were contributors to the section called "Editorial Paragraphs," solicited from "a number of prominent educators."[48] One of the most prominent educational writers was Lida Brown McMurry, '74. McMurry, "the great primary teacher of the Herbartians," was a nationally recognized leader of the American Herbartian movement along with Charles DeGarmo and her brothers-in-law Charles and Frank McMurry, all fellow alumni of the ISNU. She wrote children's books as well as materials for teachers while she taught first at the ISNU and then at the Northern Illinois Normal in DeKalb.[49]

At least two women wrote science textbooks for children and high school students as a sidelight to their professional careers. One of these was Sarah Hackett Stevenson, perhaps the Normal's most well-known nineteenth-century woman graduate. Stevenson, who graduated in 1863, later became a prominent Chicago physician and club woman and the first woman member of the American Medical Association. Her high school text, *Boys and Girls in Biology,* appeared in 1875 and her book *The Physiology of Woman* in 1890. Alice Jean Patterson, class of '90, whose poetry often appeared in the *Vidette* during her student days, was a prolific writer on natural science topics. In addition to articles in educational periodicals, she authored or coauthored a popular series of science textbooks for grade school and junior high classes. She taught for her alma mater from 1906 until her death in 1929.[50]

In surveying the identified published output of ISNU women graduates, it is clear that most wrote on educational topics. Their educational specialities varied: reading, grammar, Latin, German, nature study, speech and drama, English and American literature, U.S. history, and educational theory and practice. Several wrote stories (both fiction and nonfiction) and poetry for children. One writer, Margaret H. J. Lampe, '86, cast some of her articles on teaching for *School and Home Education* in a fictional mode.[51] Most of the writers were also working teachers. A few—like Eleanor Root, who called herself a writer, and Grace Hurwood, who published in national magazines like *National Monthly* and the *American Review of Reviews*—were former or retired schoolteachers.[52] For all these women, writing was one aspect of their careers in education.

At the jubilee anniversary celebration of the Illinois State Normal University in June 1897, one of the invited speakers was Sarah Raymond Fitzwilliam. A graduate of the class of 1866, Raymond had served as superintendent of Bloomington, Illinois, schools from 1874 to 1892, one of the first women in the state to be named a city superintendent of schools. In her remarks she commented: "The women of this institution feel that they have much of which to be proud, much for which to be grateful, as they gather here today, the wards of the great prairie state, the beneficiaries of the famous and timely act of '57." She continued, "The influence of this institution is not limited to the educational field as narrowly understood. The voice, pen and influence of our women are abroad in the land, in all the various associations and places of honor open to women."[53]

Thousands of young women who attended the ISNU were indeed the beneficiaries of the legislative act that created the school. Students at the normal school received training for the one profession, teaching, that welcomed women in the nineteenth century and that offered women from nonelite families the possibility of upward mobility in terms of occupational status. Among the graduates of the school were a number of women who achieved state and national recognition for their professional work. While many of the graduates eventually left teaching for marriage and some left teaching for other careers, a sizeable portion spent a good many years in education. Their alma mater had afforded them study in the common branches of learning and in the art and practice of teaching with some opportunities for advanced study in languages, mathematics, and natural sciences. Because of the emphasis on English language instruction, young women students could hone their writing and speaking skills, many of them gaining a level of advanced literacy that enabled them to write and speak to forward their careers.

In some respects their experiences as students reinforced common gender stereotyping of the day. While women students were in the majority, the male minority was large enough to ensure men's precedence in a number of extracurricular activities. Training in rhetoric also focused on men as public speakers. Nevertheless, women students had opportunities to read their own work in classrooms and before public audiences in literary society contests and at graduation ceremonies. Within the circle of the Sapphonian Society, women students also practiced speaking and debate. In a number of ways, men and women students were truly colleagues. They took the same classes, were assigned to the same literary societies, lived in the same rooming houses, and took their meals together in boarding clubs. At least one result of the coeducational environment was the possibility of networking with both men and women alumni in seeking teaching positions and in finding publishing outlets.

Sarah Raymond Fitzwilliam was proud of the fact that the "voice, pen and influence of our women are abroad in the land." Many of the women of the ISNU, both the graduates and those who could only attend for a few terms, did make their influence felt in their communities. Multiply their numbers by those attending normal schools throughout the nation, and it becomes evident that normal schools were a significant factor in women's education in the nineteenth century and in the development of American education in general.

Notes

1. Sally Schwager, "Educating Women in America," *Signs* 12 (1987): 333–72, esp. pp. 335–36; Mabel Newcomer, *A Century of Higher Education for American Women* (New York: Harper and Bros., 1959), p. 88.
2. Schwager, "Educating Women," p. 354.
3. Illinois State Normal University became Illinois State University in 1964.
4. Helen E. Marshall, *Grandest of Enterprises: Illinois State Normal University, 1857–1957* (Normal: Illinois State Normal Univ., 1956), p. 39; Charles E. Hovey, "Autobiography of Gen. C. W. Hovey," in *A History of the Illinois State Normal Uni-*

versity, Normal, Illinois, ed. John W. Cook and James V. McHugh (Bloomington, Ill.: Pantagraph Printing, 1882), p. 39.

5. Elizabeth Mitchell Christian, "Impressions of Gen. Hovey," *Alumni Quarterly* 2 (Feb. 1913): 18.

6. David Felmley, "Recent Developments of the Normal University," *Alumni Quarterly* 1 (Feb. 1912): 5; Jurgen Herbst, *And Sadly Teach: Teacher Education and Professionalization in American Culture* (Madison: Univ. of Wisconsin Press, 1989), pp. 116, 118.

7. Herbst, *And Sadly Teach,* pp. 4–5.

8. *Daily Pantagraph* (Bloomington, Ill.), 10 October 1857, 3; *Proceedings of the Board of Education . . . December 16th, 1874* (Peoria, Ill.: N. C. Nason, 1875), p. 4.

9. Richard Edwards, *Decennial Address: Delivered at the Illinois State Normal University, June 27th, 1872* (Peoria, Ill.: N. C. Nason, 1872), p. 26.

10. *Proceedings of the Board of Education . . . December 8, 1897* (Springfield, Ill.: Phillips Bros., 1898), pp. 6–7.

11. Marshall, *Grandest of Enterprises,* p. 33; Charles A. Harper, *Development of the Teachers College in the United States with Special Reference to the Illinois State Normal University* (Bloomington, Ill.: McKnight and McKnight, 1935), pp. 58, 102–3; Herbst, *And Sadly Teach,* p. 112.

12. Christian, "Impressions," pp. 17–18; "Letter from H. B. Norton," in Cook and McHugh, *History,* p. 173; Harper, *Development,* p. 101.

13. Justin Leiber, James Pickering, and Flora Bronson White, eds., "'Mother by the Tens': Flora Adelaide Holcomb Bronson's Account of Her Life as an Illinois Schoolteacher, Poet, and Farm Wife, 1851–1927," *Journal of the Illinois State Historical Society* 76 (1983): 293–94, 296.

14. Harper, *Development,* pp. 103–4; *Vidette,* March 1894, p. 13.

15. Harper, *Development,* pp. 107, 104.

16. Quoted in Harper, *Development,* pp. 104–5; Marshall, *Grandest of Enterprises,* p. 186.

17. *Proceedings of the Board of Education . . . December 7, 1898* (Springfield, Ill.: Phillips Bros., 1899, p. 7.

18. *Catalogue of the State Normal University for the Academic Year ending June 29, 1860* (Peoria, Ill.: N. C. Nason, 1860), pp. 16–21; *Proceedings of the Board of Education . . . December 16th, 1874,* p. 10.

19. *Proceedings of the Board of Education . . . December 16th, 1874,* p. 9; Harper, *Development,* p. 135. There were three terms in each school year.

20. *Proceedings of the Board of Education . . . December 16th, 1874,* p. 9.

21. *Nineteenth Annual Catalogue of the Illinois State Normal University, Normal, Illinois, for the Academic Year Ending June 21st, 1877* (Bloomington, Ill.: Pantagraph Steam Printing, 1877), pp. 26, 28–29.

22. Gerald Graff, *Professing Literature: An Institutional History* (Chicago: Univ. of Chicago Press, 1987), pp. 44–46.

23. *Semi-Centennial History of the Illinois State Normal University, 1857–1907* (Normal, Ill.: Faculty Committee, 1907), pp. 135–36, 138.

24. *Semi-Centennial History,* pp. 140, 145–52.

25. "Contest between Carbondale and Normal, 1878–1881," Letterbook, Special Collections/University Archives, Milner Library, Illinois State University, Normal, Ill., pp. 11–12, 16, 33, 43, 54.

26. Cook and McHugh, *History,* p. 106.

27. Cook and McHugh, *History,* p. 75; Lois Arnold, *Four Lives in Science: Women's Education in the Nineteenth Century* (New York: Schocken Books, 1989), pp. 69, 64.

28. Cook and McHugh, *History,* pp. 106–7, 129–30.

29. Sapphonian Minutes Book, 1887–1896, Special Collections/University Archives, Milner Library, Illinois State University, pp. 10, 17, 19, 23, 24.

30. Sapphonian Minutes Book, pp. 15, 13, 66–67.

31. *Semi-Centennial History,* pp. 161, 173–76; *Index,* 1892, n.p.

32. *Proceedings of the Board of Education . . . December 3d, 1872* (Peoria, Ill.: N. C. Nason, 1873), p. 5.

33. *Proceedings of the Board of Education . . . June 21st and 22d, 1865* (Peoria, Ill.: N. C. Nason, 1865), p. 12; Arnold, p. 71; *Proceedings of the Board of Education . . . Special Meeting . . . March 26th, 1867* (Peoria, Ill.: N. C. Nason, 1867), p. 8.

34. *Proceedings of the Board of Education . . . June 24th and 25th, 1868* (Peoria, Ill.: N. C. Nason, 1868), p. 13; *Proceedings of the Board of Education . . . June 23d, 1869* (Peoria, Ill.: N. C. Nason, 1869), pp. 5–6, 13.

35. Grace Hurwood, "A Letter from an Early Alumnus," *Alumni Quarterly* 4 (Aug. 1915): 36–37; Grace Hurwood, "Fabre, 'The Most Distinguished Naturalist Now Living,'" *American Review of Reviews* 47 (1913): 611–13.

36. Marshall, *Grandest of Enterprises,* p. 163. Titles of all essays and orations were printed in the commencement programs.

37. Quoted in Harper, *Development,* p. 107.

38. "Letter from H. B. Norton," p. 174.

39. Herbst, *And Sadly Teach,* p. 111; "Address of Edwin C. Hewett, LL.D.," in Cook and McHugh, *History,* p. 209.

40. Figures are derived from "Alumni Register, Illinois State Normal University, 1860–1927," *Normal School Quarterly* 22 (July 1927): 5–79.

41. Marshall, *Grandest of Enterprises,* p. 33; Harper, *Development,* pp. 94–95; Cook and McHugh, *History,* p. 89.

42. A register for 1882 is in Cook and McHugh, *History,* pp. 56–102; a register for 1907 is in *Semi-Centennial History,* pp. 249–327; and a register for 1927 is in "Alumni Register, 1860–1927." A more detailed assessment of the marriage and career choices of ISNU women graduates is in Sandra D. Harmon, "'And Gladly Teach'? The Career Choices of Women Graduates of the ISNU, 1860–1899" (paper presented to the Twelfth Annual Illinois History Symposium, Springfield, Ill., 7 Dec. 1991).

43. Roberta A. Wein, "Women's Colleges and Domesticity, 1875–1918," *History of Education Quarterly* 14 (1974): 44; Barbara Miller Solomon, *In the Company of Educated Women: A History of Women and Higher Education in America* (New Haven: Yale Univ. Press, 1985), p. 127.

44. Solomon, *Educated Women,* pp. 119–21.

45. *Vidette,* Feb. 1888, p. 1; "Alumni Register, 1860–1927," p. 40; *Semi-Centennial History,* p. 288.

46. "Alumni Register, 1860–1927," p. 45; *Woman's Journal,* 10 Nov. 1894, p. 354.

47. *Semi-Centennial History,* p. 278; "Alumni Register, 1860–1927," pp. 30, 25, 27. Root wrote under the name Eleanor Root. I am indebted to my research assistant, Monique Leon, for locating the published works of many of the fifty women.

48. *Semi-Centennial History,* pp. 169–73; see, for example, Mary M. Steagall, "The Magnetic Power of the Ideal," *School News and Practical Educator* 23 (1909): 148; Pauline Schneider, "Cultivate an Interest in Public Affairs," *School News and Practical Educator* 24 (1910): 99.

49. Harper, *Development,* pp. 199–216, esp. p. 212.

50. Thomas Neville Bonner, "Sarah Ann Hackett Stevenson," in *Notable American Women, 1607–1950,* 3 vols., ed. Edward James, Janet James, and Paul S. Boyer (Cambridge, Mass.: Harvard Univ. Press, 1971), 3: 375; Harper, *Development,* pp. 375–76; "Alumni Register, 1860–1927," p. 44.

51. See, for example, Margaret H. J. Lampe, "Two Literary Clubs," *School and Home Education* 26 (1907): 342–47.

52. See, for example, Eleanor Root, "Erin, The Undiscovered Country," *National Monthly* 3 (1911): 122–23.

53. *Daily Pantagraph,* 24 June 1897, p. 8.

4

DEVON A. MIHESUAH

"Let Us Strive Earnestly to Value Education Aright"

CHEROKEE FEMALE SEMINARIANS AS LEADERS OF A CHANGING CULTURE

THE CHEROKEE FEMALE Seminary was a nondenominational boarding school established by the Cherokee Nation at Park Hill, Indian Territory (now Oklahoma), in order to provide high-quality education for the young women of its tribe. A male seminary was built at the same time, three miles from the female seminary (it burned in 1910). Because many of the wives of missionaries to the Cherokees had attended Mount Holyoke Seminary in South Hadley, Massachusetts, the curriculum of the Cherokee Female Seminary was based on that of the New England institution. The Cherokee Female Seminary first opened in 1857, but in 1887 it was destroyed by fire. Two years later, a larger, three-story seminary building was erected on the outskirts of the Cherokee Nation's capital, Tahlequah. By 1909, when the building was converted into Northeastern State Normal School by the new State of Oklahoma, approximately 2,300 Cherokee girls had attended the school. The old female seminary building is now a focal point on the campus of Northeastern Oklahoma State University and is known as "Seminary Hall."[1]

The Female Seminary was established by the Cherokee Council in order to educate women according to the ways of the upper-class antebellum South, that is, to produce leaders who would lead the "social salvation" of their tribe by lending stability and solidarity to the "unenlightened"

Cherokees (such as illiterates, non-Christians, and those who did not speak English). These "True Women" would then become knowledgeable, pious, dutiful wives for their prominent Cherokee husbands, whose self-esteem was undoubtedly elevated by placing women in a position that seemed exalted yet was subservient. The Male Seminary, on the other hand, was created to train the future leaders and businessmen of the tribe.[2]

Ironically, while the National Council was controlled by males who wanted to keep women in their domestic sphere (both seminaries were controlled by the same men), many of the Female Seminary alumnae proceeded to equal or surpass the academic achievements of their male counterparts. With the exception of military drills required at the male school, the curricula of both schools were essentially the same. Many of these highly educated alumnae played influential roles within their Cherokee Nation and across the United States. These Cherokee women also received more education than many white females living in Indian Territory, and indeed even in the rest of the country. At least four have been inducted into the Oklahoma Memorial Hall of Fame.

The history of the Cherokee Female Seminary becomes complicated when one delves into the socioeconomic aspects of the school. The seminary did not educate only one faction of the Cherokee tribe; it served students who possessed a wide variety of cultural adherences, social values, and appearances. Students ranged from 1/128 degree Cherokee blood to full-blood; some knew nothing about Cherokee culture, while others enrolled in the seminary to learn about white society. Many girls were blue-eyed blondes, while others looked phenotypically like Cherokees. Appearance played an important part in the seminarians' futures because, ultimately, only the girls who looked Caucasian could realistically aspire to the "True Woman" ideal, especially if they moved outside of the Cherokee Nation.[3]

Obviously, the Cherokees' history is quite different from the histories of other tribes. After the Cherokees' contact with European traders, artisans, and adventurers in the 1690s, many intermarried with whites. The mixed-blood offspring often adopted the white value system of their white fathers, including the lack of interest in traditional Cherokee customs, and because of their inherited wealth, they developed the best farms and plantations and purchased black slaves.[4] By the early nineteenth century, the Cherokees' traditional matriarchal system had faded in favor of the patriarchal family, which recognized males as leaders of the social order. Many mixed-blood children adhered to the whites' view of women as submissive homemakers instead of individuals of political and economic importance.[5]

Among the Europeans to encounter the Cherokees were the missionaries who brought Christianity and the first schools to the tribe. The Cherokees proved to be more receptive to the missionaries' secular educational efforts than to their religious proselytizing, and after the tribe's forced removal west of the Mississippi River over the "Trail of Tears" to Indian Territory in the late 1830s, the Cherokee National Council established public schools in every district of their Nation. In 1851, the elaborate Male and Female Seminaries were opened; both were the largest structures ever built by an Indian Nation within the United States. They were also the first nonsectarian schools of higher learning—Indian or white—west of the Mississippi River, and they were among the few Indian boarding schools to be established, financed, and administered by an American Indian tribe, not by the federal government or missionary agencies.[6]

But not all Cherokees wanted a "white education." Although progressive Cherokees (mostly mixed-bloods, but some full-bloods) were the most vocal supporters of a Cherokee school system, many tribespeople preferred to see tribal funds spent on farming. Many of the "conservatives" wanted to preserve the traditional Cherokee culture and were concerned that high schools, especially, would transform Cherokee culture for the worse. Throughout the seminaries' existence, intratribal debates raged over the practicality of teaching Latin and calculus instead of agricultural methods. In addition, because the seminary did not teach any aspect of Cherokee culture, the school was branded elitist and the students "white Cherokees."

Despite the differing opinions over the necessity of Cherokee high schools, the Cherokee National Council was desirous of establishing the most sophisticated school possible, and in 1851 requested that Mary Chapin, the principal of Mount Holyoke, make out a course of study patterned after her own institution's curriculum. The Cherokee seminary's school year was divided into two sessions of twenty weeks each, with classes meeting five days a week, six hours a day. During the first four years the school was open, students were divided into four "classes" (freshmen through seniors). In 1873 $75,000 was appropriated for a "primary department," grades one through five, and a "preparatory department," grades six through eight. The students in these two departments were collectively known as the "primaries," "indigents," or "beginners." From 1851 to 1856 tuition was free, but after 1872 students were charged a tuition of $5.00 per year (later raised to $7.50). As a compromise with those Cherokees who complained that the seminary was too expensive, fifty children were selected from the "Cherokee speaking class" to attend school in the primary grades free of charge.[7]

Until 1856—when the seminary closed because of financial difficulties and the impending Civil War—students studied geometry, algebra, physiology, geography, Latin, English grammar, and Greek and American history. When the seminary reopened in 1872, the curriculum was broadened and diversified. In addition to the former courses, students devoted their efforts to a more intensive study of French, German, chemistry, zoology, botany, trigonometry, analytical geometry, calculus, and business writing. Aiding the students in their studies were the library's 1,300 volumes of fiction, classics, encyclopedias, reference books, and various newspapers and magazines from around the country.[8]

Juniors and seniors studied the works of Virgil, Livy, Homer, Goethe, Molière, George Eliot, and Shakespeare. Literary clubs, such as the Minervian, Germanae, Sodales, Netrophian, Philomathian, Utopian, and Hypathian societies, gave students an opportunity to develop their "literary, musical, and dramatic talents" and to learn the important qualities "necessary to a pleasing appearance before the public." Students could join the prestigious Glee Club, and all were eligible to audition for the annual Shakespeare play.[9]

The seminary was not associated with any religious denomination, but in accordance with the emphasis placed on piety among the Cherokees and at Mount Holyoke, the students' "Christian Spirituality" was a prime concern of the National Council. In 1852 several tribal members formed the "Cherokee Educational Association," an organization for promulgating a "wholesome Christian influence on the public schools." Its board required students to attend church services of their choice on Sunday, although the choices were limited to Presbyterian, Baptist, Methodist, Moravian, or Congregational churches.[10]

Students also exercised twice each day, calisthenics in the morning and a three-mile walk in the afternoon. All pupils were required to thoroughly clean their rooms and various parts of the seminary on a rotating basis. Occasionally, upperclasswomen were allowed to visit the local dress shops, ice cream "saloon," roller-skating rink, and photography studio in Tahlequah, and several times each year the seminary played hostess to picnics, political rallies, fund-raisers, and concerts.[11]

From 1851 to 1856 seminary teachers were Mount Holyoke alumnae, but after the seminary reopened in 1872 and until it closed in 1909, women who had graduated from the seminary returned to teach at their alma mater. In the 1850s seminary principals were paid an annual salary of $800, the first assistants $600, and the second assistants $500 (salaries increased after 1872). In addition to salaries all faculty members were provided with room and board. Reflecting the importance placed on female education in the Cherokee Nation, Principal Chief John Ross reported in 1855 that the instructors at the Male Seminary had complained about being paid the same as the women at the Female Seminary, but he dryly noted that the latter had "never interposed any objection."[12]

Seminary students were able to publicly express themselves through their school newspaper, the *Cherokee Rose Buds,* which was published by the girls and cost ten cents per copy. Making its first appearance on 2 August 1854, the paper was edited by seminary students and was devoted to "the Good, the Beautiful, and the True." Measuring ten by twelve inches, each page consisted of two columns, one in English and one in Cherokee, so that all the tribe's citizens could read it. The paper contained notices of forthcoming events, editorials, engagement and wedding announcements of prominent persons, short stories, and poetry. In 1855 the name of the newspaper was changed to *A Wreath of Cherokee Rose Buds.*[13]

There is not enough evidence available to reconstruct what the students were taught regarding their gender role and "Indianness," but the editorials and stories in the *Rose Buds* reveal that the race-conscious and ethnocentric students were attempting to define their roles as women and as Cherokees. The females who have been emphasized in works focusing on domesticity and Protestant evangelism are usually white, but the Cherokee students of the Female Seminary were also advocates of the True Woman ideal. They were confident about the influence women could have on humanity, and the stories they incorporated in the *Rose Buds* declared their belief that women's responsibilities were important and distinctive. In the commentary "Female Influence," for example, student Qua-Tay asserts that "the destiny of the world depends on woman . . . [as] the appointed agent of morality[,] . . . the inspirer of those feelings and dispositions which form the moral nature of man."[14] Student Alice further elaborates on the grace of women in her essay entitled "Beauty": "But man, himself, in physical beauty, excels in the works of God. What more admirable than the noble form, erect in God-like majesty, or the more perfect gracefulness of woman? Like flowers, the more they are cultivated the more beautiful they become."[15]

As with women in other parts of the United States, the religious female seminarians were also understandably concerned about the flow of liquor into their communities and the effect of alcohol on their families. They never tired of attending the Sons of Temperance meetings or of discussing ways that they could better their society. According to student comments in the *Rose Buds,* the subject of intemperance "cannot be worn out. . . .

Dissipation or intemperance is one of the greatest evils in our [Cherokee] Nation. . . . Ought we not all try to lend our aid in putting down this great evil? If we are young, we have an influence so let us one and all give our utmost influence for this noble cause."[16] The seminarians may have been repressed by males in some areas of their lives, but by banding together and touting temperance, they were able to rebel at least a little against male dominance. Many of the male seminarians (some of whom were brothers of female seminarians) did in fact break their pledge and were expelled from the school for being intoxicated. By attending the weekly church services, the seminary's daily chapel services, and the temperance meetings, in addition to using the *Rose Buds* to express their opinions, the seminarians felt that they were fulfilling their roles as True Women and doing something worthwhile for society.

The seminaries were established fifty years before W. E. B. Du Bois espoused his philosophy of the "Talented Tenth": "The Talented Tenth of the Negro race must be made leaders of thought and missionaries of culture among their people. No others can do this work and Negro colleges must train men for it. The Negro race, like all other races, is going to be saved by its exceptional men."[17] But the seminarians already subscribed to the philosophy that they had a duty to save their Nation, and the *Rose Buds* reveal that the students were convinced of their superiority over the "unenlightened" members of their tribe. These attitudes reflected the growing class system within the tribe, based not only on differing cultural ideals between the progressives and the traditionals, but also between those who looked "Indian" (i.e., darker skin) and the mixed-blood children who had lighter skin and hair. As time passed, and more Cherokees intermarried with whites, the offspring appeared even more Caucasian. In 1899, for example, the preponderance of mixed-blood Cherokees in Tahlequah was evidenced by *Twin Territories* writer Ora Eddleman, who expressed dismay over the wealthy Cherokees and the "blond Cherokee women."[18]

Rose Bud's editorials reflect the seminarians' deep-seated belief in their duty to "uplift" the Cherokee Nation and their inclination to watch each other's behaviors: "Let us begin now in new energy that we may gain that intellectual knowledge which will reward the hopes of our Nation, fitting us for doing much good among our people"; "Young people—do not forget a remark made at the [recent] temperance meeting. . . . That your character is weighed by those around you." Other poems and compositions focused on the "Power of Kindness," "Tardiness," "Patience," "Angry Words," and "Conscience" (who, "with her small voice, gives no rest for the wicked"). Another, perhaps reflecting the girls' affluent backgrounds, espoused the belief that "however beautiful or wealthy we may be[,] it is but for a moment. . . . Beauty of the soul will, if properly cultivated, flourish long after the Earth with all it contains, has passed away."[19]

During the 1850s there were only two full-blood Cherokee girls enrolled, but no traditionalists, resulting in charges of elitism and prejudice against the full-bloods at the seminary by citizens in the Cherokee Nation. But in 1854 progressive full-blood student Na-Li eloquently defended her seminary by stating in the *Rose Buds* that "it is sometimes said that our Seminaries were made only for the rich and those who were not full Cherokee; but it is a mistake. . . . Our Chief and directors would like very much that they [full Cherokees] should come and enjoy these same privileges as those that are here present." Na-Li, however, had been adopted by a mission at an early age, had a thorough primary education, and could easily pass the entrance examination that was required of potential students in the 1850s (the test was dropped in the 1870s).[20]

In further defense of her heritage and skin color, Na-Li asserted that although her parents were "full Cherokees . . . belonging to the common class," she felt it "no disgrace to be a full Cherokee. My complexion does not prevent me from acquiring knowledge and being useful hereafter. . . . [I will] endeavor to be useful, although I sometimes think that I cannot be."[21] Apparently, the more Cherokee blood a girl had, or the more "Indian" she looked, the more she felt she had to prove herself as a scholar and as a "useful" member of a society that she believed valued only those women who were white in appearance and attitude.

The early seminarians were indeed defensive about their hair and skin coloring, which provided a popular theme of the Cherokee seminary's paper. There were numerous anecdotes and stories in which appearance was a prominent factor, particularly blue eyes. For example, one story tells of the consequences that young "Kate M." faced after plagiarizing a poem for literature class. "Fun and abundance," student Lusette wrote, "peeped from her blue eyes . . . and the crimson blush stole upon her cheeks." In the same issue, author Inez wrote about what her schoolmates might be doing in four years. One was described as a "fair, gay, blue-eyed girl," and another was a "fairy-like creature with auburn hair." Still another story by student Icy, entitled "Two Companions," paired Hope ("the very personification of loveliness") with a "tiny blue-eyed child" named Faith.[22] In an 1855 issue of *A Wreath of Cherokee Rose Buds,* offended seminarians complained in an editorial about the Townsend, Massachusetts, Female

Seminary's paper, the *Lesbian Wreath,* that referred to the Cherokee girls as their "dusky sisters."[23] Evidently, to seminary students blue eyes were the epitome of enlightenment and civilization.

Students took pleasure in comparing the old Cherokee ways with the new and improved lifestyles of the tribe to show that many tribespeople had progressed past savagery and were on their way to equality with whites. In an 1854 issue of *Rose Buds,* student Edith championed the virtues of nineteenth-century white society and boasted of the progress the Cherokees had made. "Instead of the rudely constructed wigwams of our forefathers which stood there [the Park Hill area] not more than half-a-century ago," she wrote, "elegant white buildings are seen. Everything around denotes taste, refinement, and progress of civilization among our people."[24]

The prolific Na-Li collaborated with another student in 1855 to illustrate their uneducated ancestors' backwardness, and more importantly to emphasize the vast improvements the tribe had made. In "Scene One" of the essay, "Two Scenes in Indian Land," Na-Li described a "wild and desolate estate" of a Cherokee family comprising "whooping, swarthy-looking boys" and plaited-haired women, all of whom, she wrote, "bear a striking resemblance to their rude and uncivilized hut." She concluded that the poor imbeciles "pass the days of their wild, passive, uninteresting life without any intellectual pleasure or enjoyment," except, she added, to attend the green corn dance, a "kind of religious festival."[25]

"Scene Two" by author Fanny painted a completely different picture of Cherokee life. In her commentary, even the environment around the family's home has magically blossomed from the influence of the missionaries. "Civilization and nature are here united," she declared. "Flowers, music, and even better, the *Holy Word of God* is here to study, showing that religion has shed its pure light over all." The Indian lad, "in place of his bow and arrow, is now taught to use the pen and wield the powers of eloquence. The girl, instead of keeping time with the rattling of the terrapin shells [around her ankles] now keeps time with the chalk as her fingers fly nimbly over the blackboard." Fanny then professed her hope that "we may advance, never faltering until all the clouds of ignorance and superstition and wickedness flee from before the rays of the Suns of Knowledge and Righteousness."[26] In these tales, then, there was the promise that the "wild Cherokee Indian" could be changed and become a new person. The seminarians were not shy in vocalizing their hope that their unsophisticated tribespeople would make the transition.

The attitude that the Cherokees needed a moral change was also illustrated in the *Sequoyah Memorial,* the newspaper of the Cherokee Male Seminary. One student wrote that "the bow and arrow have been laid aside," and until the Cherokees reached the "summit of civilization and refinement," they could never be happy and contented.[27] Student Estelle's opinion was, "O! that all, especially among the Cherokees could but learn the vast importance of a good education. This and only this will place us on equality with other enlightened and cultivated Nations. . . . If we love our country, if we would have the name of a Cherokee an honor, let us strive earnestly to value education aright."[28]

The seminarians also were convinced of their superiority over members of other tribes. After a group of Osage men visited the seminary in 1855, student Irene wrote a romantic essay—not unlike white authors of the day—on the "lofty, symmetrical forms, and proud, free step of these sons of nature just from their wild hunting ground." She found their war dance amusing: "those tall, dusky forms stomping and stooping around . . . making a wailing sound." In comparing her tribe and theirs, she pointed out that the Osages listened to the seminarians sing "Over There" so attentively because, she concluded, at least the "wild and untutored Savage had an ear for music as well as the cultivated and refined."[29]

Other essays in the *Rose Buds* include anecdotes about "hostile Indians" attacking peaceful Cherokees out on the "wild and unknown regions" on their way to the California goldfields, and about "barbarous Camanches [*sic*]," living in their "wild wilderness." A student named Cherokee described a Seneca Dog Dance in which the drum "made a very disagreeable noise" ("what there was in such music to excite the Seneca belles is more than I can imagine"), and although she judged the dancers to be graceful, she believed they "ought to have been at something better."[30]

No reference to blacks or slavery is mentioned in any of the *Rose Buds* issues or in the memoirs of the early female teachers. The students' ideas on the subject are unknown, although most students' families did own slaves and dozens of male seminarians fought (and died) for the Confederacy. Blacks were not allowed to attend either seminary, but children of the freedmen could enroll in the Cherokee-operated Colored High School.[31]

At the same time that a faction of the seminarians and teachers believed themselves to be elevated above the unenlightened members of their tribe, other tribes as a whole, and blacks, these same girls and teachers felt somewhat inferior to whites, even though many of them had far more "white blood" than Cherokee (especially after 1870). The same *Rose Buds* issue that discussed the "elegance and civilization" of the Cherokee

Nation also compared it unfavorably with the refinement of eastern states: an editorial greeted the new bride of Chief John Ross, Mary Stapler, who admirably left her more civilized surroundings in Philadelphia in order to "dwell with him in his *wild* prairie home" (emphasis theirs).[32] Another editorial, commenting on the completed 1855 spring term, read, "We present you again with a collection of Rosebuds, gathered from our seminary garden. If, on examining them, you chance to find a withered or dwarfish bud, please pass it by[;] . . . we hope for lenient judgment, when our efforts are compared with those of our white sisters." The article "Exchanges" acknowledged the newspapers received from girls' schools in New England. But the Cherokee seminarians did not send copies of the *Rose Buds* in return because, as an editor explained, "We feel ourselves entirely too feeble to make any adequate recompense. . . . We are simply Cherokee school girls." These students appear to have been much like the individuals E. Franklin Frazier has described as the "black bourgeoisie," those blacks who developed feelings of inferiority because they judge themselves by white standards.[33]

But the students can hardly be blamed for focusing upon skin color and the acculturative achievements of their tribe. Many had a white or at least one mixed-blood parent, and if not, they still attempted to emulate whites, who deemed themselves superior to blacks and other races. When one considers the seminary's philosophy ("white is best"), the students' skin coloring (usually dark), and the "backwardness" of many Cherokees, it is little wonder that the seminarians berated themselves for falling short of the white ideal.

Within the larger Cherokee society, the seminarians were in the minority. For instance, in 1852, 1,100 children attended Cherokee schools and approximately 50 of them were enrolled in the seminaries (4.5 percent); in 1880, of the 5,413 children of school age (between six and twenty), 1,308 females and 1,740 males attended the Cherokee schools, but only 184 attended the seminaries (6 percent); in 1899, 4,258 attended public schools, and 215 enrolled at the seminaries (5 percent); and in 1903, 5,505 children enrolled in public schools, while 724 studied at the seminaries (13 percent).[34] It is clear that the ratios of seminary population to public school population were very uneven. However, the male and female seminary alumni had received a rigorous education; they held important jobs in education, industry, social work, and other fields; and they had a high degree of visibility. All of these factors meant that the almost 6,000 alumni of both schools would directly influence not only their families but all who were living in Indian Territory or the State of Oklahoma.

Men appeared to have dominated the Cherokee Nation. Student rolls and government records show that from the 1870s to 1907 the initial enrollment at the Male Seminary each year was often higher than at the Female Seminary, but the average attendance was always lower. In other words, the female school had fewer dropouts each academic year than did the male school. Throughout the Cherokee Nation, there were almost always more females enrolled in school regardless of the male/female population ratio. Despite the similar curricula offered at the seminaries, the higher attendance rate at the female school, and the excellent grades the females earned, men were still able to secure a greater number of professional jobs. At least two hundred alumni received degrees at colleges and universities, and they played important roles within their Nation and the United States. Many became lawyers, physicians, dentists, writers, oilmen, Cherokee chiefs, and attorneys general.[35]

The female seminarians, however, were not passive recipients of whatever opportunities were thrown to them. From 1851 to 1856 the seminary had been a training ground for teachers and housewives, but in the 1870s new teachers with broader ideas about the women's sphere contributed to a shift in values at the school. Many of the later alumnae aspired to have careers, not just become homemakers.

Because of their stringent course of study, seminarians were given sixty-two hours of college credit at Northeastern State Normal School; more than thirty female seminarians took advantage of this offer. At least forty more attended twenty-eight different colleges and universities, such as the University of Oklahoma; Northfield Seminary in Massachusetts; Buena Vista Female Seminary in Virginia; Oswego Female College in Kansas; Drury College, Kirkwood Seminary, Spaulding's Commercial College, and Howard Payne College in Missouri; and the University of Chicago. Interestingly, none attended Mount Holyoke.[36]

Perhaps the most successful seminarians were Rachel Caroline ("Callie") Eaton and Isabel ("Belle") Cobb. Eaton graduated from the Cherokee seminary in 1888, then earned her bachelor of science degree from Drury College and her master and doctor of philosophy degrees from the University of Chicago. She was hired as head of the history department at the State College for Women in Columbia, Missouri, later served as professor of history at Lake Erie College in Painesville, Ohio, and was dean of women and head of the history department at Trinity University in Texas. She produced numerous written works, including *John Ross and the Cherokee Indians, Oklahoma Pioneer Life,* and *History of Pioneer Churches in Oklahoma.*[37]

Belle Cobb graduated from the seminary in 1879, attended Glendale Female Seminary in Ohio for two years, then returned to teach at the Cherokee Seminary until it burned in 1887. The next year she enrolled in the Women's Medical College of Pennsylvania, and in 1892 received her medical degree—the second American Indian woman to do so (the first was an Omaha-Ponca, Susan LaFlesche, in 1889). Even though the Cherokee Nation took great pride in Cobb's status as a physician, she was denied employment as medical superintendent of the Cherokee Female Seminary.[38]

Seminary alumnae found employment in a variety of other professions, such as Works Project Administration supervisors, dental assistants, telephone operators, stenographers, postal clerks, secretaries, and assistants to Cherokee politicians. Teaching was almost the only job available to early alumnae, and most of them remained within the Cherokee Nation to teach at the common schools. Later alumnae had more choices, but many who worked also chose the teaching profession, either in the public schools, the Cherokee Orphan Asylum, the Male Seminary, or their alma mater. At least six alumnae became superintendents of Oklahoma school districts.[39]

Many women of the middle and upper classes who had attended the seminary did not choose professions, usually because their husbands could support them. Instead, they followed the Progressive spirit, as did many white women throughout the country, and joined social clubs. Many Cherokee women were dedicated to social reform, and some became active leaders in the Cherokee Nation and other communities. Alumnae joined organizations such as the Order of the Eastern Star, the White Shrine of Jerusalem, the Society of Oklahoma Indians, various Federations of Women's Clubs, the Hyechka Music Club, the Pocahontas Club, the Fortnightly Club, the Tahlequah Music Study Club, the Red Cross, the War Savings Service, and a number of literary and music societies. Many of these women eventually moved outside of the Cherokee Nation (a few moved to Europe); because of their Caucasian appearance, they were able to blend into white society and encountered no prejudice.[40]

Although women were not allowed to vote until 1920, alumnae were politically active before the turn of the century, probably because of the influence of their teachers and also because many of their fathers were politicians. The majority were Democrats. Nannie Katherine Daniels Fite, for example, served as a delegate to the National Democratic Convention in San Francisco in 1920, was chairman of Oklahoma's Educational Department of the Democratic National Committee, and was vice chairman for Oklahoma's Woodrow Wilson Foundation.[41]

Although many Cherokees were not convinced of the value of the Female Seminary—many of them were farmers and traditionalists with little use for "white education"—the seminary nevertheless educated and influenced hundreds of Cherokees of all backgrounds. The seminary did not contribute to the retention of traditional Cherokee culture, and as a result it was the cause of factional strife among Cherokees—between those who were advocates of education and those who preferred to see the money spent on farming. But strengthening traditional customs was not the seminary's purpose; its alumnae were to promote the facilitation of Cherokee acculturation so that the tribe could compete in the white world on its terms.

The education the women received at the seminary also made them desirable marriage partners, gave them a source of identity and pride, and contributed to their development as individuals healthy both mentally and physically. Although the seminary was the bane of many tribespeople because it imposed the "white ideal" upon pupils, the education it offered provided a strong foundation for those who went on to colleges and universities. The training the school offered was invaluable to the acculturated girls' success in business and in social circles within and outside the Cherokee Nation. Alumnae were hailed by many Cherokees (certainly not all) as the grande dames of Indian Territory, and each year they are celebrated by the Descendants of Cherokee Students Association, Northeastern State University, and the Cherokee Nation.

The Cherokee Female Seminary alumnae led the way for those Cherokees who were desirous of "advancing" Cherokee culture (although many Cherokees saw nothing wrong with the "old" culture). The women did not want to "de-Indianize" their tribe, for despite their belief in the superiority of white culture, they were staunch advocates of keeping their Cherokee Nation distinct from—and superior to—all other Indian and non-Indian nations. Rather, they promoted a new Indianness among educated Cherokees who were good Christians and patriotic citizens of the Cherokee Nation and of the United States, people who could manage their own affairs according to the ways of white, not traditional Cherokee, society.

The Cherokee Nation today is one of the most populous tribes in the country, and thousands of its members are descendants of the seminarians, proud to have been influenced by their ancestors' educational experiences. Many have become physicians, lawyers, educators, tribal administrators, and businessmen and -women. Partly because of the reputation of the seminary, many Americans claim to be Cherokee when they really are not. Indeed, the Cherokee Female Seminary may have contributed little to the preservation of traditional Cherokee culture, but it was an important institution in facilitating Cherokee cultural change and remains a symbol of the Cherokees' commitment to education and adaptation in the white man's world.

Notes

1. For a thorough discussion of the history of the Cherokee Female Seminary, see Devon A. Mihesuah, *Cultivating the Rosebuds: The Education of Women at the Cherokee Female Seminary, 1851–1909* (Urbana: Univ. of Illinois Press, 1993).

2. See Devon A. Mihesuah, "'Out of the Graves of the Polluted Debauches': The Boys of the Cherokee Male Seminary," *American Indian Quarterly* 15 (1991): 503–21. In his book *American Feminists* (Lawrence: Univ. of Kansas Press, 1963), Robert E. Riegel asserts that "education was a method of transmitting traditional social patterns and not of reforming society" (p. 115). Comments of the Cherokee National Council and the seminarians, however, suggest that the purpose of education *was* to reform Cherokee society according to the ways of the acculturated Cherokees.

3. Students' blood quantums were compiled by the author from the 1880 Cherokee Census and Index, schedules 1–6, 7RA-07, rolls 1–4; the 1890 Cherokee Census, (no index), schedules 1–4, 7RA-08, rolls 1–4; the Index to the Five Civilized Tribes, the Final Dawes Roll, M1186, roll 1; and the Enrollment Cards for the Five Civilized Tribes, 1898–1914, M1186, rolls 2–15, cards 1–11, 132 at the Federal Archives. The Final Dawes Roll has many errors in regard to the Cherokees' blood quantums, so cross-references of other family members were used. If the student died prior to the opening of the rolls, the quantum was found via either other siblings, children, or parents. Married names were located on the census records, in newspapers, and in Emmet Starr, *History of the Cherokee Indians: Their Legends and Folklore* (Oklahoma City: Warden, 1979). A few of the early students, graduates, and husbands had died leaving no progeny and thus no clues as to their degree of Cherokee blood, but only two were reported to be full-bloods. Some of the students during the later years (1903–09) were not enrolled, because they were recent arrivals to Indian Territory. It must be remembered that not all mixed-bloods were affluent or advocates of education, nor did they all subscribe to the value system of white Americans. Conversely, full-bloods were not always poor, uneducated, or traditionalists.

4. Histories of the early Cherokee culture include Henry T. Malone, *Cherokees of the Old South* (Athens: Univ. of Georgia Press, 1956); Starr, *History of the Cherokee Indians;* Russell Thornton, *The Cherokees: A Population History* (Lincoln: Univ. of Nebraska Press, 1990); William G. McLoughlin, *The Cherokee Ghost Dance: Essays on the Southeastern Indians, 1789–1861* (Macon, Ga.: Mercer Univ. Press, 1984), and also his *Cherokee Renascence in the New Republic* (Princeton, N.J.: Princeton Univ. Press, 1986); Leonard Bloom, "The Acculturation of the Eastern Cherokee: Historical Aspects," *North Carolina Historical Review* 19 (1942): 323–58, and "The Cherokee Clan: A Study in Acculturation," *American Anthropology* 41 (1939): 266–68.

5. For information on early histories of Cherokee women, see Theda Perdue, "The Traditional Status of Cherokee Women," *Furman Studies* 26 (1980): 19–25; see

also Perdue's "Cherokee Women and the Trail of Tears," *Journal of Women's History* 1 (1989): 14–30; Mary E. Young, "Women, Civilization, and the Indian Question," in *Clio Was a Woman: Studies in the History of American Women*, ed. Mabel E. Deutrich and Virginia C. Purdy (Washington, D.C.: Howard Univ. Press, 1989), pp. 98–110.

6. "An Act making provisions for carrying into effect the Act of the last annual session of the National Council, for the establishment of one Male and one Female seminary or High School," 12 Nov. 1847, secs. 1, 15, and 19, in *Constitutions and Laws of the American Indian Tribes* (*CLAIT*) (Wilmington, Del.: Scholarly Resources, 1973), vol. 5 (part 2 of volume). The best books on Cherokees and missionaries are William G. McLoughlin, *Cherokees and Missionaries: 1789–1839* (New Haven: Yale Univ. Press, 1984) and idem, *Champions of the Cherokees: Evan and John B. Jones* (Princeton, N.J.: Princeton Univ. Press, 1990). For information on the removal process, see Grant Foreman, *Indian Removal: The Emigration of the Five Civilized Tribes of Indians* (Norman: Univ. of Oklahoma Press, 1932), and William L. Anderson, ed., *Cherokee Removal: Before and After* (Athens: Univ. of Georgia Press, 1991).

7. Devon Abbott, "'Commendable Progress': Acculturation at the Cherokee Female Seminary," *American Indian Quarterly* 11 (1987): 187–201; "An Act in Relation to the Male and Female Seminaries and Establishing Primary Departments Therein for the Education of Indigent Children," 28 Nov. 1873, in *Constitutions and Laws of the Cherokee Nation* (St. Louis: R. and T. A. Ennis, 1975), vol. 7 of the *CLAIT*, pp. 267–69. For information on Mount Holyoke, see Arthur C. Cole, *A Hundred Years of Mount Holyoke* (New Haven: Yale Univ. Press, 1940).

8. *An Illustrated Souvenir Catalog of the Cherokee National Female Seminary: 1850–1906* (Chilocco, Okla.: Indian Print Shop, n.d.).

9. See annual catalogues of the Male and Female Seminaries at Archives, John Vaughan Library, Northeastern State Univ., Tahlequah, Okla., for yearly class schedules, faculty and staff listings, social activities, rules and regulations, and student rolls (the latter are listed sporadically).

10. McLoughlin, *Champions of the Cherokees;* Reese to Butler, 12 October 1854, *Annual Report of the Commissioner of Indian Affairs (ARCIA) for 1854*, 33d cong., 2d sess., S. Exec. Doc. 1 (serial 746), p. 327; Carolyn Thomas Foreman, *Park Hill* (Muskogee, Okla.: The Star Printery, 1948), p. 99.

11. *Eufaula Indian Journal,* 28 June 1877; *Cherokee Advocate,* 11 July 1874; ibid., 23 May 1884; *Fort Smith Elevator,* 1 July 1892; *Tahlequah Arrow,* 24 May 1908; C. Foreman, *Park Hill,* pp. 153–55; Evelyn Suagee Maheres interview, #cLL 219.1, and Susie Martin Walker Albert interview, #CLL 219.3, both in Living Legend Collection (LLC) at the Oklahoma Historical Society in Oklahoma City; Ida Wetzel Tinnin, "Educational and Cultural Influences of the Cherokee Seminaries," *Chronicles of Oklahoma* 37 (1959): 59–67. For a compilation of stores in the historical Tahlequah area, see Melody Lynn McCoy, "Location and Enterprise: A Review of Merchants in the Cherokee Nation, 1865–1907" (M.A. thesis, Harvard Univ., 1981). A thorough discussion of health care at the seminary is in Devon Abbott, "Medicine for the Rose Buds: Health Care at the Cherokee Female Seminary, 1876–1909," *American Indian Culture and Research Journal* 12 (1988): 59–71.

12. Ellen Rebecca Whitmore to Mary Chapin, 16 Mar. 1852, in Cherokee Collection, Williston Memorial Library/Archives, Mount Holyoke College, South Hadley, Mass.; William Potter Ross, "Public Education Among the Cherokee Indians," *American Journal of Education* 1 (Aug. 1855): 121. See Mihesuah, *Cultivating the*

Rosebuds, appendices D and E, for lists of seminary alumnae who taught at their alma mater.

13. Copies of the *Cherokee Rose Buds* and *Wreath of Cherokee Rose Buds* are in the Archives, John Vaughan Library, Northeastern State Univ., and at the Anthropological Archives, Smithsonian Institution, Washington, D.C.

14. *Wreath of Cherokee Rose Buds,* 4 Aug. 1855, p. 5.

15. Ibid., 1 Aug. 1855, p. 2.

16. *Cherokee Rose Buds,* 2 Aug. 1854, p. 5. Also see Barbara M. Welter, "The Feminization of American Religion, 1800–1860," in *Clio's Consciousness Raised: New Perspectives,* ed. Mary Hartman and Lois Banner (New York: Harper Colophon, 1974), pp. 137–57.

17. See Herbert Aptheker, ed., *The Correspondence of W. E. B. Du Bois* (Amherst: Univ. of Massachusetts Press, 1973–78).

18. *Twin Territories,* June 1899.

19. *Cherokee Rose Buds,* 2 Aug. 1854, pp. 2, 7.

20. Ibid., p. 2.

21. Ibid.

22. *Wreath of Cherokee Rose Buds,* 14 Feb. 1855, pp. 2, 5; *Cherokee Rose Buds,* 2 Aug. 1854, p. 6.

23. *Wreath of Cherokee Rose Buds,* 14 Feb. 1855, p. 2.

24. *Cherokee Rose Buds,* 2 Aug. 1855, pp. 1–2.

25. *Wreath of Cherokee Rose Buds,* 1 Aug. 1856, pp. 1–2.

26. Ibid.

27. *Sequoyah Memorial,* 31 July 1856, p. 2.

28. *Wreath of Cherokee Rose Buds,* 14 Feb. 1855, p. 3.

29. Ibid., p. 5.

30. Ibid., pp. 4, 6.

31. "An Act Prohibiting the Teaching of Negroes to Read and Write," 22 Oct. 1841, in *CLAIT,* 5: 55–56. For information on slavery in the Cherokee Nation, see Theda Perdue, *Slavery and the Evolution of Cherokee Society: 1540–1866* (Knoxville: Univ. of Tennessee Press, 1983), and R. Halliburton, *Red over Black: Black Slavery among the Cherokee Indians* (Westport, Conn.: Greenwood Press, 1977). For lists of Cherokees who participated in the Civil War, see W. Craig Gaines, *The Confederate Cherokees: John Drew's Regiment of Mounted Rifles* (Baton Rouge: Louisiana State Univ. Press, 1989). Also see Thomas Lee Ballenger, "Colored High School of the Cherokee Nation," *Chronicles of Oklahoma* 30 (1952–53): 454–62.

32. *Cherokee Rose Buds,* 2 Aug. 1854, p. 3.

33. *Wreath of Cherokee Rose Buds,* 1 Aug. 1855, p. 4; E. Franklin Frazier, *Black Bourgeoisie* (Glencoe, Ill.: Free Press, 1957).

34. *ARCIA for 1852,* 32d Cong., 2d sess., House Exec. Doc. 1, (serial 673), p. 407; *ARCIA for 1899,* 56th Cong., 1st sess., (serial 3916), p. 203; *ARCIA for 1903,* (serial 4646), p. 271; Summary of the Census of the Cherokee Nation for 1880, at Western History Collections, Univ. of Oklahoma Library, Norman, Okla., p. 11; T. L. Ballenger, "Lists of Students of Cherokee Male and Female Seminaries, Tahlequah, Oklahoma, from 1876 to 1904," Special Collections, John Vaughan Library, Northeastern State Univ.; "[Principal] Ann Florence Wilson's Grade Book," or "Cherokee Female Seminary Records of Grades, 1876–1909," in Northeastern State University's Office of Admissions and Records, Administration Building, Tahlequah, Okla.

35. *ARCIA* for the following years: *1872* (serial 1650), p. 387; *1873* (serial 1601), pp. 336–37; *1875* (serial 1680), pp. 110–11; *1876* (serial 1749), pp. 212–13;

1877 (serial 1800), pp. 234–35, 294–95; *1884* (serial 2287), pp. 270–71; *1888* (serial 2637), p. 118; *1899* (serial 3915), p. 92; *1899* (serial 3916), p. 203; *1900* (serial 4101), pp. 113, 168; *1902* (serial 4458), p. 124; *1902* (serial 4291), pp. 293, 319; *1902* (serial 4459), p. 263; *1903* (serial 4645), p. 79; *1903* (serial 4646), p. 269; *1904* (serial 4798), p. 94; *1906* (serial 4959), p. 113; *1907* (120.1: 907), p. 97. Harry F. and Edward S. O'Bierne, *The Indian Territory: Its Chiefs, Legislators, and Leading Men* (St. Louis: C. B. Woodward, 1892); Mihesuah, "'Out of the Graves of the Polluted Debauches.'"

36. Compiled from Starr, *History of the Cherokee Indians,* pp. 489–680, and J. G. Sanders, *Who's Who among Oklahoma Indians* (Oklahoma City: Trave Publishing, 1928).

37. Muriel H. Wright, "Rachel Caroline Eaton," *Chronicles of Oklahoma* 10 (1932): 8; Sanders, *Who's Who,* p. 18; Starr, *History of the Cherokee Indians,* p. 666.

38. Starr, *History of the Cherokee Indians,* p. 489; Sanders, *Who's Who,* last page; manuscript of Belle Cobb in Grant Foreman, ed., *Indian and Pioneer Histories* (Oklahoma City: Oklahoma Historical Society, —c. 1930), 65:184–218; *Record-Democrat* (Wagoner, Oklahoma), 14 Aug. 1947; Valerie Sherer Mathes, "Susan LaFlesche Picote: Nebraska's Indian Physician, 1865–1915," *Nebraska History* 63 (1982): 502–30.

39. Sanders, *Who's Who,* p. 45; Thomas J. Harrison, "Carlotta Archer, 1865–1946," *Chronicles of Oklahoma* 25 (1947–48): 158–60; Cherokee Seminaries Homecoming Program for 7 May 1958, Archives, John Vaughan Library, Northeastern State Univ.; Starr, *History of the Cherokee Indians,* pp. 666, 678–79; Wright, "Rachel C. Eaton"; Mihesuah, *Cultivating the Rose Buds,* appendices B–E.

40. Sanders, *Who's Who,* pp. 19, 26, 28, 45, 77, 90, 185; Starr, *History of the Cherokee Indians,* p. 679.

41. Sanders, *Who's Who,* pp. 90, 185.

5

JUNE HADDEN HOBBS

His Religion and Hers in Nineteenth-Century Hymnody

THE WAY TO tell newcomers from lifelong Baptists in a worship service is to watch how each acts during hymn singing. Newcomers actually look at their hymnals most of the time while old-timers use them only occasionally for a new song or little-sung verse. Congregational singing may seem to be only pleasant tradition or simple entertainment to the outsider; however, memorizing perhaps a hundred or more hymns is significant in a church that lacks formal creeds or liturgy because hymns are an important medium for recording and teaching both history and doctrine. According to seminary professor Robert H. Mitchell, "The scripture does not tell us anything about what the church has done the last two thousand years. . . . The only place we can find this is in the hymn book."[1]

Speaking as someone who can sing from memory all six verses of "Just as I Am," a popular invitation hymn used to elicit personal responses at the end of a worship service, I am constantly amazed by the fact that "old-time religion" is not really very old, judging by the composition dates of the texts that transmit its traditions. Despite a few truly old favorites, such as St. Francis of Assisi's "All Creatures of Our God and King," an occasional eighteenth-century composition by Isaac Watts, John Newton, or Charles Wesley, and a handful of twentieth-century hymns, most of what we Baptists sing every Sunday was composed between approximately 1870 and 1920. (Here I am using *hymn* to refer only to the lyrics, which, though usually associated with one particular hymn tune, can be and are sung, for variety's sake, to a number of songs.) If Mitchell is right, then the religion of Baptists and of the many other evangelical churches who share the same hymn literature is very much a nineteenth-century creation. This fact is particularly interesting in light of the work of scholars, such as Ann Douglas, who view nineteenth-century Protestantism as a Christianity feminized in its departure from the intellectual rigor of Calvinism and its emphasis on personal experience. If Douglas is right, in fact, what I would expect to find in those hymns I know so well is evidence of the female culture that gave Protestantism images of domesticity, the concept of a nurturing God, and a doctrine of salvation more concerned with the emotions than with intellectual activity. Indeed, at first glance, this is exactly what I do find. Consider, for example, the titles of several well-known gospel hymns from the period: "Lord, I'm Coming Home," "I Am Thine, O Lord," "I Need Thee Every Hour," "What a Friend We Have in Jesus," "Leaning on the Everlasting Arms," "Sunshine in My Soul." Most of these titles suggest the importance of a personal relationship with God, who is like a good parent, and the emotional reaction of the Christian to that relationship.

Closer examination of nineteenth-century texts in twentieth-century Baptists hymnals, however, reveals that male and female authors often treat the same theme, image, or metaphor in somewhat different ways even though they both use the language of what Sandra Sizer terms "evangelical domesticity."[2] Men and women create in hymns different models of salvation, contrasting views of God, and different rationales for missionary activity. These differences suggest either that nineteenth-century culture was never fully feminized or that, as I believe, once change began, it was assimilated rapidly into the dominant culture and became the property of powerful men in evangelical churches. But I do not suggest that women lacked power altogether. Although they were denied formal public authority in their churches, they could write; the flourishing market for sacred music after the Civil War created many opportunities for women to join men in publishing gospel hymns that supported evangelical Christianity.[3] And women's use of gospel hymn language challenged the androcentric value system of evangelical churches.

Accounting for the differences in the ways men and women make meaning while using the same language has engaged many literary critics and social historians. Brian Stock, for example, observes that "oral literature in formerly colonial lands has had to adopt the outsider's literary formats in order to be heard. So have women."[4] Similarly, Elaine Showalter, who uses a model originally developed by Edwin Ardener, suggests that women are a "muted" group who must use the language of the dominant group to be taken seriously. She explains that "women's beliefs find expression through ritual and art, expressions which can be deciphered by the ethnographer, either female or male, who is willing to make the effort to perceive beyond the screens of the dominant structure."[5] Both of these explanations are unsatisfying when applied to American gospel hymns in the years 1870–1920 if their application implies that female hymnists have no language of their own—that, at best, they can encode their meaning in rhetorical constructions available but only crudely appropriate for their use.

I argue instead that women had a well-articulated language of spirituality by this time. Nineteenth-century domestic novels had, by 1870, established the home as a center of spiritual development, created a model of the Christian life as a nonlinear walk rather than a journey to a specific destination, given spiritual authority to women—especially to mothers—in the private sphere, and developed a resonant language of the feelings to define spirituality.[6] This rhetoric of domestic religiosity was specifically associated with a culturally constructed notion of gender that empowered evangelical women, and female hymnists used it to their advantage. That male hymnists also used women's language in hymns is obvious; at times, they overlaid the cultural tropes created by the domestic novels with patriarchal values or drew upon an earlier tradition of hymnody that emphasized an androcentric world view. But female hymnists constantly reappropriated their own language. Historian Carlo Ginzburg, though writing of a premodern condition, proposes a useful model for this nineteenth-century phenomenon. He suggests that socially subordinate groups read and express themselves through a filter that effectively blocks what lacks meaning for them or does not accord with their experience.[7] Adapting this notion to the complex use of language in gospel hymns, then, I argue that women filter out patriarchal values that become attached to the cultural tropes made available to all hymn writers through domestic or sentimental novels.

To illustrate and support my thesis, I have chosen four sets of representative hymns written between approximately 1870 and 1920 that demonstrate how male and female hymnists use the same figures of speech and other rhetorical techniques in ways that demonstrate epistemological differences. I do not propose to prove that all female hymnists write hymns centered in female experience or that all men appropriate female language and use it to further an agenda of male domination. Rather, I argue that male and female uses of the language of "evangelical domesticity" represent a struggle between two kinds of authority within the evangelical community. Women in the evangelical community frequently employ the language of influential nineteenth-century literature produced for reading in the private sphere to shape behavior and beliefs, while men often use the rhetorical techniques of sermons and the values of the public sphere to challenge female spiritual authority.[8] From this gendered contest emerge distinctly male and female models of spirituality.

Coming Home to Jesus

As Mary G. De Jong observes, the favorite parable of Victorian hymnists was the Prodigal Son.[9] Gospel hymnists compress this narrative into the figure of coming home to Jesus and use it to describe both conversion and going to heaven. Male and female approaches to this metaphor differ primarily in the position of the narrator or speaker in the hymn. Men tend to identify with the prodigal and to speak as one who is out on the road and being called home. Women, understandably, are more likely to situate themselves within the home and speak on God's behalf, thus identifying themselves with the forgiving father.

Examples of a male approach to coming home to Jesus are William J. Kirkpatrick's "Lord, I'm Coming Home" and Will L. Thompson's "Softly and Tenderly Jesus Is Calling." Kirkpatrick takes the perspective of a man returning home, tired and battered after battles in a sinful world. He says that he's "wandered far away from God" and that, like an adulterous husband, he's "tired of sin and straying." Home is to him an oasis of comfort, and he prays, "My strength renew, my hope restore." This imagery culminates in the chorus, which creates a scene that sounds like an errant husband's plea to his long-suffering wife:

Coming home, coming home,
Nevermore to roam,
Open wide Thine arms of love,
Lord, I'm coming home.[10]

Similarly, Thompson's narrator associates himself with the sinner who is away from home and must heed God's call, which comes "softly and tenderly" like the voice of a beloved woman. Throughout the hymn, he often speaks in first-person plural, emphasizing his identification with other sinners. In the first verse, he encourages the fellow sinner to whom he speaks to visualize Jesus waiting at home:

Softly and tenderly Jesus is calling,
Calling for you and for me;
See, on the portals He's waiting and watching,
Watching for you and for me.

Thompson clearly associates going home with conversion when he urges the sinner to go home quickly because "shadows are gathering, deathbeds are coming." And he envisions God in terms of unconditional welcome, love, and pardon:

Oh! for the wonderful love He has promised,
Promised for you and for me;
Tho' we have sinn'd, He has mercy and pardon,
Pardon for you and for me.

This hymn characterizes God as a good nineteenth-century woman. She is stationary in the home; the sinner must come to her. Her identity is created by family relationships—in Kirkpatrick's hymn, that of husband to wife; in Thompson's, that of child to mother. She shows no anger in the face of transgression, yet her suffering is apparent because she is "pleading" for the sinner to allow her restorative work.[11]

Twentieth-century critic Barbara Welter describes this same woman as a "hostage in the home" who redeems men's contamination in "a materialistic society." In other words, women's sphere is for the nineteenth-century male a retreat wherein to restore emotional, moral, and spiritual wholeness. As Harvey Green argues, the "division between commerce and morality" in nineteenth-century America created a separation between secular and sacred because "by the mid-nineteenth century the economy operated as a theoretical antagonist to the principles of Christian behavior." Green concludes that restoring order in society depended on centering morality and goodness in the home, away from the economic demands of capitalism. In terms of a popular biblical metaphor used to describe the American mission, the idea that American communities would provide a moral "beacon on a hill" was reduced to the notion of the "light in the home" provided by women, who created a retreat from the corrupting world of commerce.[12]

The spiritual values that emerge most clearly from Kirkpatrick's and Thompson's hymns are those created by the division Green suggests between "morality and feeling" and "material well-being." For these hymnists, spiritual reality exists in dichotomies: sin and pardon, traveling and arriving at home, dissipation and restoration of feelings, sinful man and all-accepting God.[13] Conversion is a matter of submission to a female standard that requires privileging one's feelings, the compulsion to give in to that soft and tender voice. However, assigning gender-specific traits to God means that God, like women, can be confined, and thus controlled, in the home. One can apparently continue one's necessary economic activities in the public space so long as one goes home from time to time to set things right.

Female hymnists do not see it that way. In "Jesus Is Tenderly Calling Thee Home," Fanny J. Crosby positions herself in the home calling on behalf of the Savior. The first two stanzas describe the sinner's position as "away" and entreat the sinner to "bring" the burden of sin home, not "take" it to another place:

Jesus is tenderly calling thee home,
Calling today, calling today;
Why from the sunshine of love wilt thou roam
Farther and farther away?

Jesus is calling the weary to rest,
Calling today, calling today;
Bring Him thy burden and thou shalt be blest;
He will not turn thee away.[14]

Like Penelope waiting for Odysseus to return, Crosby's speaker stays at home expecting the sinner to come to her. Kirkpatrick speaks of the past when he regrets the fact that he "wandered far away from God" and "wasted many precious years," and Thompson speaks of future "deathbeds . . . coming." But Crosby's speaker ignores linear time; she exists, like God, in a timeless present. She emphasizes the importance of the present in the phrase "quickly arise and away"; like Penelope raveling her weaving every night, she keeps the future from intruding.[15]

Even more important than a different sense of place and time in the hymn is the implication that a woman's position in the home identifies her with God. Thus, she transcends her confinement by becoming like God, who can move at will through influence. In Crosby's hymn, the speaker, like God, can move the hearer/performer to return home, an action that empowers her. She even envisions the sinner bowing at the feet of the one who calls. Many hymns of the period also present women as ubiquitous in spirit though their bodies stay in the home. In Lizzie DeArmond's "Mother's Prayers Have Followed Me," for example, the speaker goes home "to live my wasted life anew, for mother's pray'rs have followed me . . . the whole world thro'."[16] These elements of female spirituality—emphasis on eternal or cyclical time, operating out of the home, and power in the form of influence—were standard features of domestic novels in the nineteenth century. The most resonant scene of Harriet Beecher Stowe's *Uncle Tom's Cabin* brings together all three. Eliza and Harry, slaves who have escaped and been aided by the underground railroad, are reunited in the Quaker Hallidays' kitchen, where women reign supreme:

> Everything went on so sociably, so quietly, so harmoniously, in the great kitchen,—it seemed so pleasant to every one to do just what they were doing, there was such an atmosphere of mutual confidence and good fellowship everywhere,—even the knives and forks had a social clatter as they went on to the table; and the chicken and ham had a cheerful and joyous fizzle in the pan, as if they rather enjoyed being cooked than otherwise. . . .
>
> It was the first time that ever George had sat down on equal terms at any white man's table; and he sat down, at first, with some constraint and awkwardness; but they all exhaled and went off like fog, in the genial morning rays of this simple, overflowing kindness.
>
> This indeed, was a home,—*home,*—a word that George had never yet known a meaning for, and a belief in God and trust in his providence, began to encircle his heart.[17]

The name Halliday suggests the "holy day of the Lord," or the marriage feast of the Lamb predicted in Revelation 19:7–9. In Stowe's novel, the expected hierarchies that place men over women and free people over slaves dissolve in this scene just as they will at the end of time when all Christians sit down together at the same table. Yet the scene can be enacted over and over because the activities of the kitchen are cyclical. Its actions have deep spiritual significance that can literally change the world because they challenge the social order.

Thus, for Stowe and Crosby heaven does not have to wait for the end of time. It can be a feature of present life within the home. This conflation of home and heaven in domestic novels is also illustrated in Elizabeth Stuart Phelps's *Beyond the Gates,* published in 1883, the same year as "Jesus Is Tenderly Calling Thee Home." Phelps describes heaven in amazingly concrete terms that include details of dress, eating, recreation, and courtship after death. In the novel, Mary, a forty-year-old woman, dies and goes to heaven, where she is taken to "a small and quiet house built of curiously inlaid woods"; surrounded by trees, it has all the accouterments of a pleasant home, including "a fine dog sunning himself upon the steps." She discovers that this home has been prepared for her and asks, "Was Heaven an aggregate of homes like this? Did everlasting life move on in the same dear ordered channel—the dearest that human experiment had ever found—the channel of family love? Had one, after death, the old blessedness without the old burden? . . . Was there always in the eternal world 'somebody to come home to'? And was there always the knowledge that it could not be the wrong person?" Mary quickly learns that the answer to all her questions is "yes." Her father, the first family member to arrive in heaven and himself glad to have "somebody to come home to," explains that Mary's "new life had but now, in the practical sense of the word, begun; since a human home was the centre of all growth and blessedness."[18]

The influence of Phelps's novels on evangelical society in general and evangelical hymnody in particular was enormous. One telling piece of evidence is the constant allusions in gospel hymns to *The Gates Ajar* (1868), the title of the first book in her "Gates" trilogy; Lydia Baxter's hymn, "The Gate Ajar for Me," is a good example. The characterization of the human home as "the centre of all growth and blessedness" implies that relationships provide the context for spiritual growth. This growth within a relationship is another central feature of female spirituality. Mary finds that heaven simply refines what has been a feature of the earthly home. After death, she discovers a "social economy of the new life" in which relationship itself exists in a state of "eternal permanency" because old mistakes are rectified. For example, Mary rediscovers a man she loved and lost twenty years earlier. The woman he committed himself to is fortunately absent, and Jesus himself blesses the resumption of their love. As Mariana B. Slade's hymn "Gathering Home" puts it, heaven is the place where the "dear ones" gather. It is this gathering, the creation of what Carol Gilligan calls a "web of relationships," that distinguishes female spirituality.[19] In a heavenly social economy women acquire the authority denied to them in a capitalistic society and in the churches that support its values.

Submission to Sexual Authority

Despite her empowerment by feminized religion, woman's spiritual influence within the evangelical community came at the price of total submission to divine authority. In fact, the figure of conversion as surrender to sexual authority is common to both male and female hymnists; it implies a common standard for all believers. However, male and female versions of the metaphor differ in meaningful ways. In the male figure, the speaker in one hymn gives advice to the believer and thus implies that the speaker is teaching correct doctrine. In the female version, the speaker addresses God, and the focus is on their relationship. Further, male hymnists view submission to sexual authority as part of an economic exchange, but women emphasize that it leads to transcendence and a mystical union. Hymns by Cyrus S. Nusbaum and Adelaide A. Pollard illustrate these differences.

Nusbaum's hymn, "His Way with Thee," is an address to the sinner by an authority figure giving advice. Each stanza begins with three rhetorical questions that promise a worthy outcome if the hearer takes the speaker's counsel to "let Him have His way with thee." The first stanza, for example, says,

> Would you live for Jesus, and be always pure and good?
> Would you walk with Him within the narrow road?
> Would you have Him bear your burden, carry all your load?
> Let Him have His way with thee.

Other rewards for submission to Jesus include freedom, peace, and rest. Nusbaum also suggests that the convert will work better and be saved from failure, asking, "Would you in His service labor always at your best?" and "Would you have Him save you so that you can never fall?" The chorus reiterates the benefits of Jesus' "power," which can, among other things, "make you what you ought to be." It ends with the claim that "you will see / 'Twas best for Him to have His way with thee."[20]

Although the phrase "let Him have His way with thee" is a euphemistic description of a woman's submission to intercourse, Nusbaum's hymn ignores physical union, focusing instead on conversion as an economic exchange. Those who spend enough ("give all") in the enterprise will profit enormously. Hearing this hymn, one can imagine a loving father admonishing his daughter to submit to the man chosen to be her husband in order to reap the rewards of the relationship. The authoritative male speaker employs rhetorical questions, endorses values of the public sphere, and envisions sex as something to be enacted upon a passive partner. Thus, even though the believer in the hymn is clearly female, the male hymnist can retain social authority by separating his social functions from his spiritual role. And, as De Jong observes, such hymns can resolve the conflict created for men by a religion that requires female-style submission for all believers in an era that "insisted on female inferiority in all realms but domesticity and piety." Hymns that cast Christ as the powerful bridegroom in a marriage contract allowed "male singers" to "perceive their own social dominance as Christ-like."[21]

In contrast, Adelaide A. Pollard's "Have Thine Own Way, Lord" emphasizes the transcendent nature of sexual union. This hymn also concerns itself with power, but Pollard envisions her female believer empowered in a consummation that makes her one with God. "Have Thine Own Way, Lord," still sung every Sunday in evangelical churches as an invitation hymn, is an intimate prayer in which the speaker asks God to use her to His purpose. In the first verse, Pollard writes:

Have Thine own way, Lord!
Have Thine own way!
Thou art the Potter;
I am the clay.
Mould me and make me
After Thy will,
While I am waiting,
Yielded and still.[22]

The god of Pollard's hymn is not a businessman but an artist and, perhaps, a woman. At any rate, the hymnist uses artistic and domestic figures to describe what "have Thine own way" means. She asks God, for example, to "mould" her like a potter, to "wash" her like a housewife, to "touch and heal" her like a mother caring for a sick child. While the language of submission to sexual authority emphasizes the masculinity of Christ and the separation of bride and bridegroom in "His Way with Thee," here it feminizes the deity and endorses a female spirituality in which conversion requires what Ochs describes as "coming into relationship." As if to underscore the priority of relationship, "Have Thine Own Way, Lord" is usually sung to a hymn tune with a waltz rhythm, suggesting fusion in a sort of dance between God and the believer.[23]

Pollard's focus on domestic tasks also provides an important contrast to Nusbaum's mercantile metaphor by making home—not church, a public place where men exercise authority—the locus of spiritual activity. In so doing, Pollard gives sacramental value to the ordinary activities of caring for others. As Josephine Donovan argues, "The housewife is immersed in the daily world of concrete realities in a way that most men are not, and the qualitative nature of her products—that they have been personalized by her touch—gives women an avenue to the sacred that most men, immersed as they are in the profane, alienated world of exchange or commodity production, do not have.[24] Thus Pollard, like Stowe in her description of the Halliday home, endorses the values of the kitchen, where the cyclical process of preparing raw materials, using what is prepared, and beginning again is the norm.

In addition, Pollard's model for conversion stresses the importance of usefulness or benevolent activity, religious behavior assigned to women in the nineteenth century and denigrated as a function of feelings and behavior rather than of reason and the intellect.[25] The metaphor describing God as a potter and the believer as clay alludes to Jeremiah 18:6, Isaiah 64:8, and Romans 9:21, passages in which the relationship between God and the chosen vessel depends entirely on the adaptability of the clay. In other words, the spiritual relationship requires that the believer, like a piece of pottery, be useful to God, not that the believer be a valuable commodity. The form of the vessel—by implication the physical body—is recast by God's spirit and put to use. Thus, sexual differences do not hinder or restrict full spirituality. In the terms of the sexual metaphor, conversion is a penetration of the believer's very essence by the spirit of God. Total submission means God can enter the believer and live through her, an idea articulated in the last line of Pollard's hymn, which prays that God's spirit will fill her so others can see "Christ . . . living in me."

Another version of this figure of speech, Clara H. Scott's "Open My Eyes That I May See," describes a progressive opening of the eyes, ears, mouth, and heart to God. The first verse speaks of receiving God as liberating and compares this reception to being infused with light:

> Open my eyes, that I may see
> Glimpses of truth Thou hast for me;
> Place in my hands the wonderful key
> That shall unclasp, and set me free.
> Silently now I wait for Thee,
> Ready, my God, Thy will to see;
> Open my eyes, illumine me, Spirit divine![26]

Best of all, in the last verse the Spirit of God gives a voice to one restricted from public speaking: "Open my mouth, and let me bear / Gladly the warm truth ev'rywhere." These lines suggest an interesting parallel between physical intercourse, which can lead to childbearing, and spiritual intercourse, which reaches fulfillment when the believer "[bears] . . . the truth." No longer restricted to the functions of her body, Scott's believer can express her creativity with language.

In the Garden

Despite frequent references to sexuality in gospel hymns, evangelical hymnody of the nineteenth and early twentieth centuries lacks the sensuality of earlier Protestant hymns.[27] While gospel hymns retain the erotic theme of conversion as sexual union, they usually reduce the physical aspects of consummation to descriptions of entering closed spaces. In addition, a male version of the relationship between sensuality and spirituality devalues spirituality by associating it with nature rather than culture. The female version, however, separates physical intimacy from sexual expression and makes a romantic friendship between two women the model for idealized spirituality. Both versions describe a relationship with Christ in terms of entering a garden.

C. Austin Miles's version of this metaphor, in his hymn "In the Garden," eroticizes the relationship. Miles describes a meeting with Christ in a garden the believer enters alone "while the dew is still on the roses."[28] Paula Bennett explains the importance of such a setting in her discussion of the erotic suggestiveness of flower imagery for a Victorian audience: "The Language of Flowers has been Western culture's language of women. Most specifically, it has been the language through which woman's body and . . . women's genitals have been represented and inscribed." In addition, Bennett describes "flower language" as "so widely deployed for sexual purposes that Freud, writing in the first decades of the twentieth century, could casually refer to its erotics as "'popular symbolism' and assume his audience would not demur."[29]

Thus, the speaker's withdrawal into an enclosed place filled with flowers suggests sexual intercourse. The intimacy of the relationship and the speaker's sense of privacy and exclusivity reinforce this idea. In the chorus, for example, Miles narrates a scenario of romantic love appropriate for a secular love song:

> And He walks with me, and He talks with me,
> And He tells me I am His own;
> And the joy we share as we tarry there,
> None other has ever known.

The idea of God walking and talking in a garden with a human being recalls the innocence of the Garden of Eden (Gen. 3:8). But attention to sensory details in the hymn suggests both spirituality and sexuality. The voice of Christ, for example, "is so sweet the birds hush their singing."

The third verse of "In the Garden" portrays the believer sorrowfully leaving to return to the real world:

> I'd stay in the garden with Him
> Though the night around me be falling,
> But He bids me go;
> Thro' the voice of woe
> His voice to me is calling.

The pastoral aspects of the garden—its remove from real time and public space and its function as a retreat—make it much like the heavenly home described in *Beyond the Gates*. Leaving the "Son of God" behind in the garden, where He calls the believer to return in a "voice of woe," assigns to Christ the role of a woman and underscores the general irrelevancy of spirituality to real life. Presumably, the believer is sent out into the world because "the night . . . be falling" and the world must be brought to redemption. Time in the garden renews the believer and gives him pleasure so compelling he can scarcely bear to leave, but the real test comes in his separation from the female world.[30]

The hymn allies women with nature and men with culture, which Sherry B. Ortner says "generat[es] and sustain[s] systems of meaningful forms (symbols, artifacts, etc.) by means of which humanity transcends the givens of natural existence, bends them to its purposes, controls them in its interest." Ortner argues that women become mediators between culture and nature—represented in the hymn by references to birds and flowers, the suggestion of sexual intimacy, and the desire to renew the nurturing, exclusive bond between mother and child. Miles's hymn implies that the female world is necessary to salvation, a process described in Puritan sermons as changing a natural man into a regenerated one. As Ortner explains, women engage in "*mediation* (i.e., performing conversion functions)." Though Ortner describes "conversion" in terms of socializing infants and turning raw food into cooked, the word is also used to describe spiritual salvation.[31] As mediators, however, women can be safely confined to "the garden," and their activities can be controlled by making "gardening" their prime activity. Thus, their spiritual authority is unquestioned, but their real power is limited.

In contrast to the sensual implications of "In the Garden," Eleanor Allen Schroll's "The Beautiful Garden of Prayer" seems curiously abstract and flat. Schroll describes the waiting Savior without the intimate, specific characteristics of Miles's hymn. The garden itself has no concrete details; it is simply "wondrously fair," and "it glows with the light of His presence." Jesus is not a lover, but a friend who "waits," "opens the gates," and speaks "words of comfort" rather than expressions of romantic love to the believer who meets him.[32] Like Clara H. Scott in "Open My Eyes That I May See," Schroll is concerned with light—a symbol for spiritual and intellectual insight—and with opening what has been closed. But the garden is spiritualized, shorn of its physical characteristics. As in hymns describing conversion as submission to sexual authority, female hymnists split sexual response into intimate but pure expressions of love and the sexuality that characterizes Miles's garden. Omitting the latter to focus on the former is perhaps a way of asserting spiritual autonomy and of gaining power. Michelle Zimbalist Rosaldo argues, "If assertions of sexuality can give power to women, so too can its denial. Victorian women won status by denying their own sexuality and treating male sex drives as a sin."[33]

Louisa May Alcott aptly illustrates the concept of sexuality spiritualized by references to gardening in *Work*. Near the end of this story set in the early 1860s, Christie Devon marries a gardener named David Sterling shortly before he is to report for duty in the Union army. After the ceremony, the minister tells the young couple, "One hour more is all you have, so make the most of it, dearly beloved. You young folks take a wedding-trip to the green-house, while we see how well we can get on without you."[34] Sarah Elbert explains that the novel draws heavily on the philosophies of transcendentalism, including the idea that "the spirit could transcend the prison of the flesh through an original relationship with Nature." Thus, the consummation of Christie and David's marriage takes place in the context of flowers, symbols of female sexuality that for Alcott replace physical relations with spiritual intercourse. Entering the closed world of the greenhouse is immersion in nature to achieve transcendence rather than a retreat from culture to the periphery where nature and culture meet, and it does not require subordination of either Christie or David.[35] Afterwards both of them go off to war because Christie has decided to "enlist" as a nurse (p. 362). When David conveniently dies of wounds received in battle, Christie is left to the satisfying communion of other women, relationships unvexed by sexuality or, more accurately, by the associations of heterosexual relations with corruption and subordination. Her household consists of her daughter, David's mother, and David's sister. The final scene in the novel describes Christie with her women friends, sitting around a table holding hands as they discuss her part in a reform movement to improve the lot of working women. Her name is, of course, no accident, for she becomes a Christ-like friend to other women.

Symbolic of her connections with female friends are tender physical gestures that occur frequently in the novel. Christie's most eloquent caresses are given to her romantic friend, Rachel, whom she later learns is David's sister. Christie "wooed this shy, cold girl as patiently and as gently as a lover might" when they are seamstresses together. When Rachel finally consents to be her friend, "Christie kissed her warmly, whisked away the tear, and began to paint the delights in store for them" (pp. 131–32). Later, Christie learns that Rachel is a reformed "fallen woman," corrupted by a former sexual liaison with a man that, when discovered by their employer, causes her to lose her position as a seamstress (pp. 134–38). In contrast, the relationship between the two women does both of them good because it is pure love in which physical caresses do not carry the weight of sexual sin or the obligation of subordination.

Despite gaining through their relationship, Christie loses her job when she stands by Rachel. Eventually, reduced to poverty and illness, she decides to drown herself. But Christie is saved at the last moment when Rachel finds her and pulls her back from danger. The scene that follows is a scenario of romantic friendship often associated with Christ in gospel hymns: Rachel "tenderly laid the poor, white face upon her breast, and wrapped her shawl about the trembling figure clinging to her with such passionate delight" (p. 160). Symbolically, Christie has lost her life (as a seamstress) to save it in relationship with her friend.[36] She trades physical security for spiritual security and manages to retain sensory comfort as well.

An example of this version of evangelical spirituality in gospel hymnody is Fanny Crosby's "Safe in the Arms of Jesus," probably her best-loved hymn until well into the twentieth century:

> Safe in the arms of Jesus,
> Safe on His gentle breast,
> There by His love o'er-shaded,
> Sweetly my soul shall rest.

These words describe the believer and Jesus in an embrace appropriate for a woman and her "bosom companion." The second verse of the hymn stresses the purity of the relationship with Christ and contrasts it with figures of decay and corruption: "in the arms of Jesus" the believer is "safe from corroding care" and "free from the blight of sorrow." Like Christie clinging to Rachel, Crosby's speaker is "firm on the Rock of Ages," where "sin cannot harm" her.[37]

Physical expression of love for Christ is thus passionate but pure, representing for the original audience love between women rather than love between a man and a woman.[38] As Crosby reiterates in the first two verses and the chorus, it is "safe." In addition, De Jong argues that both Christ's willingness to suffer and his nurturance are feminine characteristics for the original audience of these hymns:

> Even those who resisted identification with this selfless ideal [i.e., of the Suffering Servant] were reassured that comfort was available to them in Christ. . . . Again and again, hymns appealed to the singers' longing for the warmth and tranquility associated with the constant

> Friend, the Victorian "feminine" and familial version of Charles Wesley's comforting Lover [in "Jesus, Lover of My Soul"]. . . . This nurturant Christ served a function for Protestants similar to that filled for Catholics by the Holy Mother: in their compassion, supportiveness, and self-effacement, both are "feminine"; both afford emotional, even sensual, gratification yet are sexless by virtue of their purity.[39]

In a sense, then, the Christ of "Safe in the Arms of Jesus" is not a male Jesus but his sister.

The Evangelical Imperative

The modern missionary movement, which began around 1800 in the United States, characterizes evangelicals as people devoted not only to hearing but to telling the "good news." Many hymns interpreted and promoted the scripture known as the Great Commission: "Go ye therefore, and teach all nations, baptizing them in the name of the Father, and of the Son, and of the Holy Ghost: Teaching them to observe all things whatsoever I have commanded you" (Matt. 28:19–20, King James Version). Male versions of the missionary imperative cast missions in imperialistic terms of conquest and surrender; female versions of going on mission stress establishing community with others.

A good example of the androcentric version of missions is William P. Merrill's "Rise Up, O Men of God." That this is a hymn about male experience is obvious from the title, which is echoed in the first line, and from Merrill's account of how the hymn came to be written: "Nolan R. Best, then editor of *The Continent,* happened to say to me that there was urgent need of a brotherhood hymn. . . . The suggestion lingered in my mind, and just about that time (1911) I came upon an article by Gerald Stanley Lee, entitled 'The Church of the Strong Men.' I was on one of the Lake Michigan steamers going back to Chicago for a Sunday at my own church when suddenly this hymn came up, almost without conscious thought or effort." In "Rise Up, O Men of God," Merrill creates a picture of strong men going to do battle in service of "the King of kings." He instructs the warriors to "lift high the cross of Christ!" like the banner carried before an army, to gather the resources—"heart and mind and soul and strength"—and to "end the night of wrong."[40] Sandra Sizer claims that the central metaphor in such a hymn is "the spread of empire" because "mission is equated with ideological conquest." As Will Thompson suggests in "The Whole, Wide World for Jesus," evangelical goals of the period sound a great deal like the motivation for the Crusades:

The whole wide world for Jesus!
Be this our battlecry;
The Crucified shall conquer,
And victory is nigh.[41]

As these examples show, mission hymns of conquest focus on the male activity of going to war. In addition, "Rise Up, O Men of God" draws some of its figurative language from a sexuality intent upon domination and display of power. The hymn presents "men of God" as having a machismo that glories in an erection of strength and the impregnation (making great with child) of a feeble woman, which is the way Merrill describes the church in stanza three:

Rise up, O men of God!
The church for you doth wait,
Her strength unequal to her task;
Rise up and make her great!

A mission is, then, both a war to be fought and a way to prove one's manhood since "the day of brotherhood" is what can bring about "His kingdom." De Jong argues that military hymns focus more on the characteristics of the soldier in battle than on those of Jesus, the Captain, as a way of promoting an "energetic, 'martial,' bodily idea of manhood." Her conclusion is that hymns stressing "manly Christianity" indicate a reaction to the feminization of American Protestantism: "The late-Victorian obsession with 'muscular Christianity' coincided with the emergence of the New Woman and the disintegration of the notion of the 'manly' man as a courageous, self-reliant achiever, a dominant but benevolent provider of the material needs of women and children."[42] But muscular Christianity makes missions a restorative activity, not a lifestyle. Like coming-home-to-Jesus and garden hymns, male mission hymns are scenarios of activity that take a man away temporarily from the "real" world of business: Merrill exhorts the "men of God" to "have done with lesser things" in going to battle, but the soldier does return, eventually, to ordinary life. And, like hymns that compare conversion to submission to sexual authority, they stress a solid return for one's investment: a renewed and vigorous masculinity.

A perfect counter to "Rise Up, O Men of God" is Fanny Crosby's "Rescue the Perishing," which describes what Sizer calls a "rescue mission" rather than an "imperial mission."[43] While Merrill's account of writing "Rise Up, O Men of God" emphasizes its call to brotherhood, Crosby's composition narrative shows that it comes from her conscious use of a woman's experience:

> As I was addressing a large company of working men one hot summer evening, the thought kept forcing itself on my mind that some mother's boy must be rescued that night or perhaps not at all. So I requested that, if there was any boy present, who had wandered away from mother's teaching, he would come to the platform at the conclusion of the service. A young man of eighteen came forward and said,
>
> "Did you mean me? I have promised my mother to meet her in heaven; but as I am now living that would be impossible." We prayed for him; he finally arose with a new light in his eyes; and exclaimed triumphantly,
>
> "Now I can meet my mother in heaven; for I have found her God."[44]

In keeping with the story, "Rescue the Perishing" begs the audience to deal with sinners as a loving mother would deal with a wayward child, to "plead with them earnestly" and "gently," to "wake[n]" them with "kindness," to "patiently win them." Crosby's rescue deals with individual human beings, very possibly the sort of "lesser things" that Merrill admonishes men of God to "have done with" in order to fight an abstract battle against "wrong." The concrete reality of sitting down to attend to another's needs is, in Donovan's words, "an avenue to the sacred." And Crosby seems to agree with Alcott's Christie Devon that domestic missions are an important focus for female Christianity. When asked her "opinion of missionaries," Christie replies, "If I had any money to leave them, I should bequeath it to those who help the heathen here at home, and should let the innocent Feejee Islanders worship their idols a little longer in benighted peace" (p. 421).

After she was sixty years old, Crosby devoted her life to home missions, and "Rescue the Perishing" became the theme song of the home missions movement.[45] Thus, she fits Carroll Smith-Rosenberg's definition of the "public mother" who moved the functions of the home into the public sphere.[46] Appropriately, then, "Rescue the Perishing" focuses on life instead of death. Her object is not to "end the night of wrong" and establish the kingdom of God by annihilating the enemy but to save sinners from death:

> Rescue the perishing,
> Care for the dying,
> Snatch them in pity from sin and the grave.

In a deeper sense, her goal is to give new life to the sinner by what Sizer terms the "inward restoration of the emotions."[47] Verse three, for example, reads:

Down in the human heart,
Crush'd by the tempter,
Feelings lie buried that grace can restore;
Touch'd by a loving heart,
Waken'd by kindness,
Chords that are broken will vibrate once more.

Thus, for Crosby religious experience is individual rather than collective, but individual experience leads to connection with others. Harriet Beecher Stowe also emphasizes the restorative value of harmonious feelings for both the individual and the community in the conclusion to *Uncle Tom's Cabin.* The solution to slavery, as she sees it, is proper feelings: "There is one thing that every individual can do—they can see to it that *they feel right.* . . . See, then, to your sympathies in this matter! Are they in harmony with the sympathies of Christ? or are they swayed and perverted by the sophistries of worldly policy?" Excluded from the public world of politics, Stowe endorses a solution to slavery that would not have required the bloodiest war in American history. Her reference to a "*day of vengeance*" in her "Concluding Remarks" is not a call to arms but a prediction of eschatological punishment for those who fail to attend to feelings that affirm life.[48]

His Religion and Hers

Harriet Beecher Stowe's grandniece, Charlotte Perkins Gilman, argues in *His Religion and Hers: A Study of the Faith of Our Fathers and the Work of Our Mothers* that Christianity is a death-based religion because death "was the principal crisis in the life of primitive men." Since hunting and fighting were the main events for a primitive man, death became "the event, the purpose of his efforts, the success, the glory. If he was the dead one, we cannot follow further; but if he triumphed and saw his 'kill' before him, here was cause for thought. The death-crisis, coming as the crashing climax to the most intense activity, naturally focused his attention on the strange result. Here was something which had been alive and was dead; what had happened to it?" To this intense interest in death Gilman attributes Christianity's focus on eternal life after death and the reward for individual merit. However, she claims that this development was actually imposed upon the "teaching of Jesus, heart-warming, truth-filled doctrine of 'God in man,' of 'Thy kingdom come on earth,' of worship in love and service."[49] Hymns by male hymnists illustrate this male version of Christianity. Their coming-home hymns could well be scenes of men returning home after battle to a reward or escape. These texts require a linear concept of time and place their primary emphasis on the future. In addition, male hymnists who envision conversion as submission to sexual authority cast Christ as the lord of the manor who rewards sexual surrender. Further, garden hymns eroticize the relationship with Christ but make pleasure—a vital part of life—something to be left behind upon returning to the real world of military or mercantile battles. Finally, hymns such as "Rise Up, O Men of God" describe going on a mission as riding into battle, ready to die a glorious death for the cause.

In contrast, Gilman argues that if Christianity had developed "through the minds of women," it would have been a "birth-based religion," concerned with the beginning of life rather than its end. Accordingly, "with birth as the major crisis of life, awakening thought leads inevitably to that love and service, to defense and care and teaching, to all the labors that maintain and improve life" (pp. 45–46). Although Gilman proposes woman-based Christianity as a goal, hymns by female hymnists suggest that it was, in a sense, already a fact. Hymns that connect women at home to conversion sacralize a place where service, rather than exchange, is the order of the day. Coming-home hymns by women portray home as heaven on earth; they emphasize the present over the future, cyclical or eternal time over linearity. In addition, female hymns that use submission to sexual authority as a metaphor to describe union with God echo Gilman's vision of a birth-based religion: "Seeing God as within us, to be expressed, instead of above us, to be worshipped, is enough to change heaven and earth in our minds, and gradually to bring heaven on earth by our actions" (p. 292). Female hymnists even retain the concrete pleasure of physical contact with others by making Christ a romantic friend instead of the lord of the manor. Finally, Gilman says, "her" religion can change society by giving it new life through "charity, that social osmosis by which withheld nutrition has forced its way through diseased tissues of the body politic" (p. 281). In a sense, Crosby really can "rescue the perishing" because birth-based religion, in Gilman's words, sees "human life as one unbroken line, visibly immortal, readily improvable" (p. 292). In other words, in "her" religion, eternal life is ours as long as the race of humanity can be nurtured and kept alive.

Thus male and female versions of the same cultural tropes and themes in evangelical hymns written between 1870 and 1920 suggest a struggle for authority between male and female versions of Christianity. As Rosemary Radford Ruether and Rosemary Skinner Keller argue, the nineteenth century represents a unique period for American women, a time in which "progressive feminism" and "progressive Christianity" were closely linked. During this period, the language and epistemology of the private sphere, which were well developed in domestic novels by 1870, gave women a powerful public voice that spoke through evangelical hymnody. Meanwhile, evangelical men faced a choice either of identifying with a feminized Christianity that perhaps failed to accord with their sense of masculinity or of appropriating women's language and repositioning it to restore their lost power. Ruether and Keller observe that by 1920, when American women won the right to vote and began to enter the public sphere on men's terms, Christianity was no longer a power base for women; by the 1960s, "the assumption that the Christian churches are inherently antiwoman" was widespread.[50] But for half a century female hymnists created texts that undermined patriarchal religion by centering power in the home rather than in the church, by locating God within themselves, by separating physical intimacy from sexual submission, and by emphasizing service rather than conquest.

Notes

1. Mitchell is quoted in "Speaker Says Hymns Vital to Worship," *The Tie,* Feb. 1985, p. 8. See also Susan S. Tamke, *Make a Joyful Noise unto the Lord: Hymns as a Reflection of Victorian Social Attitudes* (Athens: Ohio Univ. Press, 1978), p. 24, and Edward S. Ninde, *The Story of the American Hymn* (New York: Abingdon, 1921), p. 60, on the doctrinal and historical functions of hymns.

2. Sandra S. Sizer, *Gospel Hymns and Social Religion* (Philadelphia: Temple Univ. Press, 1978), p. 87.

3. Esther Rothenbusch, "The Joyful Sound: Women in the Nineteenth-Century United States Hymnody Tradition," in *Women and Music in Cross-Cultural Perspective,* ed. Ellen Koskoff (New York: Greenwood Press, 1987), p. 182.

4. Brian Stock, *Listening for the Text: On the Uses of the Past* (Baltimore: Johns Hopkins Univ. Press, 1990), p. 10.

5. Elaine Showalter, "Feminist Criticism in the Wilderness," *Critical Inquiry* 8 (1981): 200.

6. For an illuminating discussion of the walk as a feature of female spirituality, see Carol Ochs, *Women and Spirituality* (Totowa, N.J.: Rowman and Allanheld, 1983), esp. pp. 2, 23, 117. Ochs distinguishes the walk from the male-centered journey, which makes spiritual growth "an extension of the male maturational process that emphasizes individuation—coming into selfhood" (p. 2). A walk, in contrast,

has a way that is not clearly marked, a cyclical time scheme, no specific length, and a less specific destination. The point of the walk is the walk itself (p. 117).

7. Carlo Ginzburg, *The Cheese and the Worms: The Cosmos of a Sixteenth-Century Miller,* trans. John and Anne Tedeschi (Baltimore: Johns Hopkins Univ. Press, 1980), p. 33. To discuss middle-class evangelical women as a group courts a charge of essentializing. But to ignore the similarities in the ways these women constructed a distinctly female epistemology is to fall into the opposite "trap": what Jane Roland Martin calls "false difference." See Martin, "Methodological Essentialism, False Difference, and Other Dangerous Traps," *Signs* 19 (1994): 631. Women as a group were denied speech within evangelical churches, but female hymnists used their collective exclusion as a basis for empowerment. Iris Marion Young points out in "Gender as Seriality: Thinking about Women as a Social Collective" *Signs* 19 (1994): 718, that since women are often treated as a group, discussing them collectively is a practical way to avoid "obscur[ing] oppression."

8. Sizer explains that lyrics for gospel hymns often came from "other songbooks or . . . devotional poems published in religious periodicals" (*Gospel Hymns,* p. 22). Harry Eskew and Hugh T. McElrath also cite the influence of popular songs on hymnody. They claim in *Sing with Understanding: An Introduction to Christian Hymnology* (Nashville: Broadman Press, 1980) that Fanny Crosby "incorporated in her hymns such words of sentiment found in the popular songs of her day as *gentle, precious,* and *tenderly*" (p. 177). I argue that all these sources drew upon the language of the domestic/sentimental novel, which created the most fully articulated narratives or scripts using the notions of female spirituality. Significantly, many popular domestic novelists such as Harriet Beecher Stowe and Elizabeth Prentiss also wrote well-received hymns.

9. Mary G. De Jong, "'I Want to Be Like Jesus': The Self-Defining Power of Evangelical Hymnody," *Journal of the American Academy of Religion* 54 (1986): 467.

10. Kilpatrick, "Coming Home," first published in 1892. For a twentieth-century reprinting, see *Baptist Hymnal,* ed. Walter Hines Sims (Nashville: Convention Press, 1956), p. 237. All of the hymns I analyze have been reprinted many times. I will cite their appearance in three Baptist hymnals published in 1926, 1940, and 1956 because these publications signal denominational approval. Denominational hymnals are very conservative; they usually publish hymns that first appeared in ephemeral Sunday school or camp meeting collections several decades after the original publication. These same hymns also appear in Methodist, Church of Christ, and other evangelical hymnals.

11. Thompson, "Softly and Tenderly," first published 1880; rpt. with slight variations in punctuation in *New Baptist Hymnal* (Nashville: Broadman Press, 1926), p. 339; *The Broadman Hymnal,* ed. B. B. McKinney (Nashville: Broadman Press, 1940), p. 100; *Baptist Hymnal* (1956), p. 236.

For the classic description of the True Woman, who is pious, pure, submissive, and domestic, see Barbara Welter, "The Cult of True Womanhood, 1820–1860," *American Quarterly* 18 (1966): 151–174. God in Thompson's hymn fits the guidelines in Nancy M. Theriot, *The Biosocial Construction of Femininity: Mothers and Daughters in Nineteenth-Century America* (New York: Greenwood Press, 1988), pp. 26–29, 30–31, for the "imperial mother." She centers her identity in her child, stays rooted in her home, does not assert herself by showing anger, in fact suffers on behalf of her child instead of for herself, and achieves adult status through maternity.

Her trade off for "child-centeredness" is an "empire" based on her power to form souls.

12. Welter, "Cult," p. 151; Harvey Green, *The Light of the Home: An Intimate View of the Lives of Women in Victorian America* (New York: Pantheon Books, 1983), p. 181.

13. Green, *The Light,* p. 181. For a discussion of dualism in gospel hymns, see Sizer, *Gospel Hymns,* pp. 24–25. Hélène Cixous argues that dichotomous thinking is characteristic of androcentric rhetoric in "Sorties: Out and Out: Attacks/Ways Out/ Forays," in *The Newly Born Woman,* trans. Betsy Wing (Minneapolis: Univ. of Minnesota Press, 1986), pp. 63–78.

14. Crosby, "Jesus Is Tenderly Calling," first published 1883, rpt. with slight variations in punctuation in *New Baptist Hymnal,* p. 334; *Broadman Hymnal,* p. 57; *Baptist Hymnal* (1956), p. 229.

15. I am indebted to Nicholas Howe for pointing out the narrative parallel with Penelope. See Julia Kristeva, "Women's Time," trans. Alice Jardine and Harry Blake, in *The Kristeva Reader,* ed. Toril Moi (New York: Columbia Univ. Press, 1986), pp. 188–213, for a discussion of time as a feminist issue. Kristeva asserts that "female subjectivity would seem to provide a specific measure that essentially retains *repetition* and *eternity* from among the multiple modalities of time known through the history of civilizations" (p. 191).

16. George Sanville, *Forty Gospel Hymn Stories* (Winona Lake, Ind.: Rodeheaver-Hall Mack, 1943), p. 65.

17. Harriet Beecher Stowe, *Uncle Tom's Cabin; or, Life among the Lowly,* rpt. in *Uncle Tom's Cabin, or Life among the Lowly; The Minister's Wooing, Oldtown Folks,* ed. Kathryn Kish Sklar (1852; rpt. New York: Literary Classics of the United States, 1982), pp. 169–70. See Jane Tompkins, *Sensational Designs: The Cultural Work of American Fiction, 1790–1860* (New York: Oxford Univ. Press, 1985), p. 142, for a discussion linking women with God in the Halliday home. Tompkins calls the meal in the Halliday home "the redeemed form of the last supper," but she does not describe it specifically as an allusion to the marriage feast of the Lamb.

18. Elizabeth Stuart Phelps, *Beyond the Gates* (Boston: Houghton, Mifflin, 1883), pp. 124–28. In *The Feminization of American Culture* (1977; rpt. New York: Anchor Press, 1988), Ann Douglas, who mentions some of these same details, compares the concept of home in a different Crosby hymn to that developed in Phelps's series of novels about heaven. Her point is that nineteenth-century hymns about heaven are examples of consolation literature in which "the subject . . . is not simply heaven, but its accessibility" (p. 220).

19. Phelps, *Beyond the Gates,* pp. 120, 190–94; "Gathering Home," *Broadman Hymnal,* p. 128; Carol Gilligan, *In a Different Voice: Psychological Theory and Women's Development* (Cambridge, Mass.: Harvard Univ. Press, 1982), p. 59.

20. Nusbaum, "Let Him Have His Way with Thee," first published c. 1899; rpt. in the *Broadman Hymnal,* p. 122, and the *Baptist Hymnal* (1956), p. 239.

21. De Jong, "'I Want to Be Like Jesus,'" pp. 468–69.

22. William J. Reynolds theorizes in *Companion to Baptist Hymnal* (Nashville: Broadman Press, 1976) that Pollard wrote this hymn in the 1890s although it was not published until 1907 (p. 83). It is reprinted with slight variations in punctuation in *New Baptist Hymnal,* p. 384; *Broadman Hymnal,* p. 254; and *Baptist Hymnal* (1956), p. 355.

23. Ochs, *Women and Spirituality,* p. 2. For a feminist model of spirituality as a dance with the divine, see Maria Harris, *Dance of the Spirit: The Seven Steps of*

Women's Spirituality (New York: Bantam Books, 1989). Harris contends "that women's spirituality is a rhythmic series of movements, which, unlike the steps of a *ladder* or a *staircase,* do not go up and down. Instead the steps of *our* lives are much better imagined as steps in a dance . . ." (xii).

24. Josephine Donovan, "Toward a Women's Poetics," *Tulsa Studies in Women's Literature* 3 (1984): 103.

25. For an excellent discussion of the concept of "usefulness" as applied to late-nineteenth-century women, see Rosemary Radford Ruether and Rosemary Skinner Keller, eds., *The Nineteenth Century,* vol. 1 of *Women and Religion in America* (San Francisco: Harper and Row, 1981), especially Carolyn De Swarte Gifford's essay, "Women in Social Reform Movements" (pp. 294–303), and Rosemary Skinner Keller's "Lay Women in the Protestant Tradition" (pp. 242–53). Gifford argues that charitable work became the religion of many pious women, "a position of faith as much as a cause espoused" (p. 296). Keller points out that some male church leaders saw benevolence as a way to keep women out of the "real" business of the church, that is, the preaching ministry (p. 252).

26. Scott, "Open My Eyes," first published 1895; rpt. in *Broadman Hymnal,* p. 351, and *Baptist Hymnal* (1956), p. 312.

27. De Jong, "I Want to Be Like Jesus," p. 465; Madeleine Forell Marshall and Janet Todd, *English Congregational Hymns in the Eighteenth Century* (Lexington: Univ. Press of Kentucky, 1982), pp. 21–23.

28. Miles, "In the Garden," first published 1912; rpt. in *Broadman Hymnal,* p. 356.

29. Paula Bennett, "Critical Clitoridectomy: Female Sexual Imagery and Feminist Psychoanalytic Theory," *Signs* 18 (1993): 241–42. Popular songs of the period in which women and courtship are associated with flowers and gardens confirm Freud's conclusion. William Jerome's "I'll Make a Ring Around Rosie" (1910) and Harry H. Williams's "In the Shade of the Old Apple Tree" (1905) are good examples. In addition, Douglas points out that "the garden was the chosen and consecrated terrain of the feminine sensibility in mid-nineteenth-century American culture" (*Feminization,* pp. 370–71 n. 104). See also her discussion of the importance of flower names for women writers (p. 186).

30. See Nancy Chodorow, "Family Structure and Feminine Personality," in *Woman, Culture, and Society,* ed. Michelle Zimbalist Rosaldo and Louise Lamphere (Stanford: Stanford Univ. Press, 1974), pp. 43–66. Chodorow argues that "the attainment of masculine gender identity" requires "denial of attachment or relationship" and "the repression and devaluation of femininity on both psychological and cultural levels" (p. 51).

31. Sherry B. Ortner, "Is Female to Male as Nature Is to Culture?" in Rosaldo and Lamphere, *Woman, Culture, and Society,* pp. 72, 80, 84–85.

32. Schroll, "Beautiful Garden of Prayer," first published 1920; rpt. in *Broadman Hymnal,* p. 342.

33. Michelle Zimbalist Rosaldo, "Woman, Culture, and Society: A Theoretical Overview," in Rosaldo and Lamphere, *Woman, Culture, and Society,* p. 38.

34. Louisa May Alcott, *Work: A Story of Experience.* (1872–73; rpt. New York: Schocken Books, 1977), p. 379. All further references to *Work* will be parenthetical to this edition.

35. Sarah Elbert, introduction to *Work,* by Alcott, xxxiv–xxxv. See Ortner's description of women on the periphery in "Is Female to Male," p. 85.

36. See Matthew 16:25, Mark 8:35, Luke 9:24.

37. Crosby, "Safe in the Arms," first published 1869; rpt. with slight variations in punctuation in *New Baptist Hymnal*, p. 357, and *Broadman Hymnal*, p. 353.

38. For a description of nineteenth-century romantic friendships, see Lillian Faderman, *Surpassing the Love of Men: Romantic Friendship and Love between Women from the Renaissance to the Present* (New York: William Morrow, 1981). Faderman explains that, until the last decade of the nineteenth century, love between women could be perceived as "passionate and spiritually uplifting" without being sexual.

39. De Jong, "'I Want to Be Like Jesus,'" p. 471.

40. Merrill, "Rise Up, O Men of God," first published 1911; rpt. in *Broadman Hymnal*, p. 186, and *Baptist Hymnal* (1956), p. 445. Merrill's account is quoted in Reynolds, *Companion*, p. 186.

41. Sizer, *Gospel Hymns*, pp. 43–44; Thompson, "Whole, Wide World," first published 1908; rpt. in *New Baptist Hymnal*, p. 270.

42. De Jong, "'I Want to Be Like Jesus,'" pp. 475–76.

43. Reynolds notes that Crosby's "Rescue the Perishing" was written in 1869 and first published in 1870 (*Companion*, p. 185). It is reprinted in *New Baptist Hymnal*, p. 329; *Broadman Hymnal*, p. 80; and *Baptist Hymnal* (1956), p. 207. Sizer, *Gospel Hymns*, p. 43.

44. Fanny J. Crosby, *Memories of Eighty Years* (Boston: James H. Earle, 1906), pp. 144–45.

45. Bernard Ruffin, *Fanny Crosby* (Philadelphia: United Church Press, 1976), pp. 104–36. Crosby's enormous popularity is well documented (see, for example, Reynolds, *Companion*, p. 291). In *Memories*, p. 169, she claims to have written at least 8,000 hymns.

46. Carroll Smith-Rosenberg, "The New Woman as Androgyne: Social Disorder and Gender Crisis, 1870–1936," in *Disorderly Conduct: Visions of Gender in Victorian America* (New York: Knopf, 1985), p. 263.

47. Sizer, *Gospel Hymns*, p. 34.

48. Stowe, *Uncle Tom's Cabin*, pp. 515, 519.

49. Charlotte Perkins Gilman, *His Religion and Hers: A Study of the Faith of Our Fathers and the Work of Our Mothers* (1923; rpt. Westport, Conn.: Hyperion Press, 1976), pp. 37–38, 42–47. Further references to *His Religion and Hers* will be parenthetical to this edition.

50. Rosemary Radford Ruether and Rosemary Skinner Keller, introduction to *1900–1968*, vol. 3 of *Women and Religion in America* (San Francisco: Harper and Row, 1986), p. xiii.

I am happy to acknowledge my debt to Joyce Zonana, who taught me feminist theory and guided the writing of the first brief study that led to this essay.

6

NICOLE TONKOVICH

Writing in Circles

HARRIET BEECHER STOWE, THE SEMI-COLON CLUB, AND THE CONSTRUCTION OF WOMEN'S AUTHORSHIP

WHILE LIVING WITH their father in Cincinnati in the mid-1830s, Catharine and Harriet Beecher associated with the Semi-Colon Club, a group whose members constituted a cross-section of those who had access to and control of policy-making forums in the city's schools, churches, hospitals, and newspapers.[1] Unlike many other such nineteenth-century salons, the Semi-Colon Club included both men and women. Here the Beecher sisters, Sarah Worthington King Peter, Caroline Lee Hentz, and Elizabeth, Emily, Anna, and Marian Blackwell socialized with publishers Benjamin Drake, Timothy Flint, James Hall, and James H. Perkins.[2] Lawyers, doctors, clergymen, educators, and their spouses joined these literati as well.

The Semi-Colon's raison d'être, according to several published memoirs, was to provide a forum wherein compositions written by members were solicited, read, and critiqued—often by men who were in a position to further the writers' careers. These memoirists hint or overtly claim that affiliation with such a literary circle was an important formative influence in the lives of well-known writers, particularly Harriet Beecher Stowe.[3] The classic early statement of this developmental thesis is the Reverend E. P. Parker's 1868 assertion that in the Semi-Colon Club, Stowe—whom Parker also characterizes as "the woman of genius"—first became "really conscious of her powers; in it she received . . . recognition, sympathy, and an impulse, and by it found a way for herself out beyond the circle of private fellowships into the wider circles of the great world."[4] Nevertheless, attention to Stowe's writing development and publishing career shows that by the time she joined the Semi-Colon Club, she was no longer a fledgling writer. In addition to having taught composition at Hartford Female Seminary a decade earlier, she had published a popular textbook as well as publishing one of her more famous essays, "Modern Uses of Language," in a student literary magazine at Hartford.

Parker's assertion of Stowe's development through club sponsorship may have derived from an earlier reminiscence "Written by Edw. P. Cranch," who recalls that

> the social enjoyment was in a spirit of perfect simplicity and friendship, a plain repast, dancing, amateur music & conversation filled up the time not given to the reading aloud of literary contributions. In order to discuss these compositions with candor the name of the writer was strictly withheld from all but the hostess, and however keenly curiosity might be excited, it was tacitly understood & agreed that the writer should not be run down or made to confess. This rule gave additional freedom to maturer writers, while it emboldened beginners to a spontaneity of thought and style, which certainly added piquancy to the literary budget of the night. Harriet Beecher Stowe was then a bright & happy girl, running over with genius and sympathy. And it was there she first fledged her wings as a writer.[5]

A photocopy of Cranch's memoir provides the introductory frame to a collection of some 126 essays written by members for club meetings and now held in the archives of the Cincinnati Historical Society. These Semi-Colon Club papers promise to be of inestimable value to the researcher who wishes to investigate nineteenth-century women's involvement in and encouragement by writing groups. For example, Parker's and Cranch's claims that the club was a proving ground for Stowe, combined with the pattern of authorial development delineated by several Stowe scholars,[6] suggest that the Semi-Colon Collection might contain early manuscripts that were the germs of her later published work. And although this is not an entirely incorrect assumption,[7] the researcher who goes to the Cincinnati Historical Society expecting to easily identify manuscripts written by Stowe or by any other specific club member encounters with some consternation a box of unsigned, undated manuscripts. The only outstanding specimens among them seem to be several whose surface features—such as penmanship or illustrations—and not their content make them noteworthy.[8] Nor would an analysis of handwriting help the researcher bent on identifying a writer's earliest work. Anonymity being one of the club's founding principles, members "plott[ed] how [to deliver their essays] without having it known where [they] came from," sometimes asking friends to copy their "pieces" for them.[9] For example, an early version of Harriet Beecher's sketch "The Canal-boat" is included in the Semi-Colon Club collection, but it is unsigned and apparently inscribed by another hand.[10] In fact, Beecher's playful efforts to disguise her writing at times became quite complicated: she "smoked" one of her essays "to make it look yellow, tore it to make it look old, directed it and scratched out the direction, postmarked it with red ink, sealed it and broke the seal, . . . [t]hen . . . inclosed [*sic*] it in an envelope . . . written in a scrawny, scrawly, gentleman's hand."[11]

The undated anonymous manuscripts of the Semi-Colon collection represent only a fraction of the number of essays written under the club's auspices. Thus, these primary sources do not lend themselves to documenting how any given member influenced or was influenced by others. It is impossible to know the context in which any given essay was first heard, the substance of the critique that followed, or the process by which its author was identified so that the essay could be solicited for publication. Our understanding of the club's procedures jumps several chronological and epistemological gaps between an event, its recollection in memoirs written decades later, and that event's transmutation into a determining component of an authorial career. These gaps suggest that the developmental thesis might be modified by a parallel narrative whose purpose it is to trace how women such as Stowe came to be identified as geniuses. It is not a uniformly pleasing story for those who believe in natural talent and inspired authors. It does, however, employ archival materials to illuminate a heretofore occluded network of retrospectively constructed versions of authorship, making clear their bases in privileges of race, class, and gender.[12]

The memoirs and several of the biographies that have derived from the Semi-Colon manuscripts display important similarities. Although they note the cordiality of the meetings, they also uniformly subsume the social nature of the club to its (retrospectively) apparent intellectual mission. Further, Cranch, Mansfield, Parker, Foote, and Venable all assume a category of genius that is the source of Stowe's subsequent "fame," while they assign to Cincinnati publishers the role of patrons in "discovering" her talent. Finally, these memoirists assume that the writer's self-evident gender determined the stages of her development from womanly confinement to worldly approbation. By contrast, manuscripts in the Cincinnati Historical Society suggest that the developmental thesis established by memoirists and adopted by biographers might be usefully revised. They emphasize the social functions of the club over its intellectual benefits, suggesting that the emphasis on camaraderie may have been a way of quelling potential rifts in friendship among club members of differing regional, religious, and political affiliations. The Semi-Colon manuscripts demonstrate that the club, not the author-genius, determined which topics would be deemed successful and that publication was less a matter of "discovery" than of fulfilling the expectations of both writers and publishers. The archival sources throw into doubt the memoirists' assumptions about gendered behavior, suggesting instead that within the Semi-Colon Club, gender was a fluid, performed, and assumed category whose mutability was enhanced by the anonymity that club members treasured. Finally, these materials, read in tandem with other newly discovered sources also housed in the Historical Society, divulge the specific privileges of race and class that enabled the club to meet, gave its members time to write, and provided the foundational stability of shared assumptions against which they were able to experiment, privileges taken as self-evident by the writers of the manuscripts, the memoirists, and the biographers alike.

E. D. Mansfield: "The Influence of Social Sympathy"

The chronological gap between the club's meetings and its members' memoirs has resulted in several retrospective reorderings of detail in order to elevate the club's significance for its members' intellectual development. For example, E. D. Mansfield, writing thirty years after the group dissolved, recalls: "It is enough that I have mentioned out of a small circle gathered in a parlor names which have been renowned both in Europe and America, and whose public reputation has contributed to the fame of our country. I have dwelt more particularly on these meetings to illustrate what I think I've seen in other cases, and to which people in general seldom give due weight. I mean the influence of *social sympathy* in forming and developing individual minds."[13] These writers constructed their recollections at a chronological remove from the events they narrate, a gap that witnessed, for example, the public acceptance of Elizabeth Blackwell as the first accredited woman physician in the United States, the elevation of Salmon P. Chase to the U.S. Supreme Court, and the phenomenal success of *Uncle Tom's Cabin.*

These later recollections of social harmony and intellectual stimulation are, in fact, challenged by texts written nearer to the events they record. Published papers and private letters written by the club's members suggest that its members held irreconcilable political and social views.[14] Specifically, Lyman Beecher had frequently challenged Boston Unitarians in the decade before he came to Cincinnati, hoping to win converts to Calvinism from among their congregations. Nor did he alter his attitude when he arrived in the West. Yet in the Semi-Colon Club he and other Presbyterian clergymen affiliated with the Lane Theological Seminary socialized with a number of Unitarian ministers, some of whom dabbled in transcendentalism. Potential sectarian dispute in Cincinnati was fueled by strong sectional loyalties that divided Semi-Colon members who boosted the West from others, such as Lyman and Catharine Beecher, who as stubbornly urged the predominance of New England values.[15] Lyman Beecher and James Hall disagreed in print over the putative dangers of Catholicism to the West and over the Beechers' characterization of the West as a cultural backwater in need of salvation by New England values. According to Kathryn Kish Sklar, by 1835 Catharine Beecher had openly challenged the cultural leadership of Cincinnati's powerful civic troika—Daniel Drake, James Hall, and Edward King—seeking to destroy their friendship and "to oust Hall from the editorship" of the *Western Monthly Magazine*. Nevertheless, during the period leading up this break all the principals in this struggle had attended the Semi-Colon Club, and Hall had actively sought and frequently published New England sketches attributed to the Beecher sisters.[16]

The explanation for this paradox lies in the importance of the club as a social organism where differences were subordinated to the conventions of mannerly behavior among persons whose bonds of class and family affiliation often quelled the potential divisiveness of their geographical and political diversity. In this regard, we cannot overestimate the importance of women's cooperation in planning, arranging, and facilitating the club's operations to ensure that harmony prevailed. The club met "alternately at the houses of Mrs. William Greene, Mrs. Samuel Foote and Mrs. Charles Stetson."[17] Cranch's identification of each meeting place with the names of women is no accident: within the Semi-Colon Club hostesses fulfilled the role of gatekeepers of class and social propriety. A paper collected in the Cincinnati archives entitled "Receipt for Making a Semicolon" stands in marked contrast to Mansfield's and Cranch's emphasis on intellectual stimulus:

> First, procure a lady of suitable qualifications, and . . . set her down by the fire to write—let her remain there for half an hour or until she has written down the names of some twenty staid, sober, respect-

> able persons; adding thereto ten young and tender lawyers or other young men about town and the same number or more according to taste of pretty young girls to give delicacy and flavor to the whole—she must be careful that all her materials are of the best quality, possessing about equal proportions of wit, humor, good manners, good sense[,] good nonsense, and beauty—
>
> On the evening when the semicolon is wanted let her mix all these ingredients well together until they begin to simper . . . after allowing a short time for them to settle pour over them a decoction composed of droughts, fancies, soarings[,] imaginings[,] rhymes, and reasons—when well saturated with this mixture, introduce the wine, coffee, bread and butter, music and dancing and the Semicolon is Complete.

As the rhetoric of the recipe emphasizes, the hostess's role is to choose guests—not according to their intellect, but with an eye to their suitability in social combination—inviting those whose interests would bridge a potential gap between the older generation of "staid, sober, respectable persons" and the up-and-coming generation of professionals and daughters of the socially prominent. The hostess's role is made clear from the opening irony—the document she writes is not a position paper, nor even a character sketch, but a list composing the perfect mixture of congenial guests.[18]

The respectability sought by this fictional hostess was ensured in fact by the family ties and professional and class loyalties shared among Semi-Colon members. The Beecher family was brought into the club by Lyman Beecher's brother-in-law Samuel Foote, a founder of the group. Foote's sister was the wife of James H. Perkins. Many members had associated in New England before emigrating: C. P. Cranch and William Henry Channing were both Unitarian ministers from Boston. Others had been in the Beecher's New England circle: Edward King, a graduate of Litchfield Law School, had courted Catharine Beecher; he was also the cousin of Lyman Beecher's second (and current) wife. William Greene, at whose Cincinnati home the Semi-Colon Club often met and who served as the group's official reader, had also attended Litchfield Law School; his wife, Abby Lyman Greene, like Catharine and Harriet Beecher, had been a student at Miss Sarah Pierce's Female Academy. Other members included Calvin Stowe, then a professor at Lane Theological Seminary; Daniel Drake, the Beecher's family doctor; and his brother Benjamin, "who was at that time editing a literary paper . . . [for] which he sometimes collected ammunition" from the club.[19]

Cranch's, Mansfield's and Foote's assertions of the "brilliance" of the company and the "superior" intellectual nourishment afforded by the club have, in turn, led a later scholar, Louis Tucker, to observe that "the Club was designed to fill social and intellectual cravings. . . . [Cincinnati's] cultural and intellectual institutions lacked the urbane sophistication of those of Philadelphia and Boston. Practically all of the Semi-Colon members were either emigrants from the East, or had been exposed to literary clubs . . . in . . . this area. . . . To these people, life without intellectual stimulation was unthinkable. The Semi-Colon Club provided them with nourishing intellectual fare." Yet the "Receipt," with its emphasis on "wit, humor . . . manners, . . . and beauty," seems to indicate that if the members were nourished, it was not by way of much sustained intellectual discussion.[20] It suggests that the context for the gathering was not only or primarily the writing and reading of compositions, nor the discussion of intellectual issues, but the sociality and matchmaking that accompanied these activities. Another writer, assuming the persona of an ingenue, identifies the role of intellect within the club: "In the voyage of literary pleasure as in that of life, we are obliged to work our passage. So if you go, you must either look pretty, play cotillions, or write something."[21] This recollection, gender coded as feminine, as is the "Receipt," aligns intellectual display with other social accomplishments, such as the ability to construct a pleasing appearance, to perform musically, or to dance. The writing and critique that memoirists privilege thus must be seen as a part of the evening's entertainment, often taking on the qualities of a game.

The anonymity associated with writing enlivened the sociality of the group, echoing in its form the conundrum and the riddle, genres favored by several members. An evening's contributors either did not sign their pieces or adopted pseudonyms—Samuel Essence, Methuselah Mann, or Cherubina, for example.[22] Members mailed or delivered their compositions to the evening's hostess (who was sworn to secrecy); William Greene read them aloud to the assembled company. If the purpose of this practice, as Cranch implies, was to protect beginning writers and to give additional freedom to "maturer" members, it also served to temper divisive tensions. Anonymity made it difficult or impossible to associate an essay's content with a particular club member, and thus defused ad hominem attacks by essayists and respondents alike. And it is not unreasonable to posit that Greene as the reader and selector of essays—aided by the hostess, who knew the writers' identities—collaborated to censor potentially inflammatory essays.

The emphasis on sociality and entertainment enhanced the nonagonistic quality of the writing, as well. Most essays were short enough that several could be read and commented upon in an evening, still leaving time for music, dancing, and socializing. The surviving Semi-Colon essays average four to eight handwritten pages, hardly enough space to develop a well-supported argumentative position. They took the form of character sketches, essays, travel narratives, poems, riddles, letters, and sermonic and devotional meditations. Their topics, as Anna Blackwell recalled, "ranged from immortality to cranberry sauce, from Adam and Eve to 'old' Dr. Beecher"; their tone is generally light, often satirical or parodic. The absence of argumentative approaches to more substantive topics suggests as well that members may have taken responsibility for preserving the social bonds of a group that included a decidedly volatile combination of members.[23]

Cranch: "A Spontaneity of Thought and Style"

Club memoirists who retrospectively emphasize the presence of a striking number of famous and soon-to-be famous figures assume that the Semi-Colon Club was a kind of forcing ground for new modes of thought and expression. Thus Cranch asserts that anonymity "gave . . . freedom to maturer writers, while it emboldened beginners to a spontaneity of thought and style."[24] Yet the manuscript collection contains few items that seem new or original. Instead, writers seem to have chosen genres, subjects, and approaches that were appropriate to the club's larger social purposes. Indeed, given the homogeneity of class and familial affiliation of club members and its apparent commitment to banishing public antagonisms from the parlor, it is not surprising that members' contributions bear striking similarities to each other. As Cranch quipped ironically in a paper, "I believe that commonplace observations are the best after all—I *hate originality*."[25]

Harriet Beecher Stowe, "the woman of genius," demonstrably took the "inspiration" for several of the sketches she published in her first book, *The Mayflower, or Sketches of Scenes and Characters among the Descendants of the Pilgrims* (1844), from papers she heard read in club meetings.[26] That volume contains a number of character sketches ("Uncle Tim," "Aunt Mary," "Cousin William," "Little Edward," and "Old Father Morris"). Other Semi-Colon Club members frequently worked in this genre, as titles collected in the Cincinnati Historical Society testify: see, for example, "Aunt Katy" and "My Uncle Tim." *The Mayflower*'s "Love versus Law" finds its counterpart in a manuscript essay titled "Sentiment and Charity"; "Feeling" in the *Mayflower* is paralleled by "Brilliancy" in the Semi-Colon Club manuscripts. Nor was Stowe the only Semi-Colon Club member to collect such work: Caroline Lee Hentz, Benjamin Drake, and James Hall also published collections of "sketches" on American themes.[27] Club members' publications in lengthier genres resemble each other, as well. There was undoubtedly lines of influence between Catharine and Harriet Beecher's several books on domestic architecture and those of Charles Elliott.[28] Salmon P. Chase, Ephraim Peabody, James Freeman Clarke, the Blackwell sisters, and James Hall all published papers, wrote legal opinions, or were otherwise involved in abolitionist activities, while the range of literary treatments of the topic is best represented by Stowe's *Uncle Tom's Cabin* (1852) and Caroline Lee Hentz's pro-slavery reply, a plantation romance entitled *The Planter's Northern Bride* (1854).

This homogeneity of topic, approach, and genre is at least partly due to the club's procedures. The tradition of anonymous submission—implemented by Daniel Drake, "the acknowledged chairman"—depended on William Greene, who always served as the reader. Greene exercised the power of choice over what would be read and how it would be interpreted. Harriet Beecher wrote her friend Georgiana May that Greene's verdict on her carefully disguised manuscript was "that it must have come from Mrs. Hall," a "theory" he "elucidated . . . by spelling out the names and dates that I had erased, *which, of course, he accommodated to his own tastes.*" Another member's paper, written in the persona of a "bright & happy girl running over with . . . sympathy" if not with genius, details Greene's control over the procedures: "There were so many pieces that night! I thought Mr[.] Greene should never get to mine! Two or three times he took it up—looked doubtingly at it,—saw the hand was new—ran his eye down the page—shook his head—& then selected something else. . . . At last,—at last! he did take mine up to read——."[29] Given the executive power of Greene, Drake, and the evening's hostess, it is reasonable to infer that members learned to adapt topics, titles, and surface features to accommodate the club's unspoken but powerful adherence to "acceptable" form.

Parker: "Into the Wider Circles of the . . . World"

Within the club, the Reverend Parker asserts, Harriet Beecher's genius was recognized, and through Semi-Colon publishers her work was circulated to a readership outside the parlors of Cincinnati. Parker's narration follows this sequence: James Hall discovered her talent as he heard the "New England Sketch" read to the Semi-Colon Club; he then asked her to enter the essay in a contest sponsored by the *Western Monthly Magazine*. Winning the $50 prize showed Harriet, who had been shy and retiring, that she could make money by writing, and thus launched her career, as she fulfilled the promise of genius that her mentors had recognized and enlarged her circle of influence form the domestic to the global. As I have already established, this line of reasoning is repeated by several of her biographers. Yet both archival sources and simple chronology cast doubt on this sequence.

In the first place, Harriet Beecher was not a particularly retiring writer. Archival materials make clear that she enjoyed writing, had written prolifically, and had published essays prior to joining the Semi-Colon Club. In fact, she had taught composition at Hartford Female Seminary and took her turn editing its student newspaper, *The School Gazette.* "Modern Uses of Language," read to the Semi-Colon Club and published in the *Western Monthly Magazine* in March 1833, had first appeared ten years earlier in *The Levee Gazette,* a Hartford Female Seminary "sorority" newspaper punningly called *chi rho delta.*[30] Nor is there evidence that responses from club members resulted in her revising her work prior to more general publication. The manuscript of "Modern Uses of Language" is virtually identical to its published form.

Like the "New England Sketch," the "Modern Uses of Language" was solicited for publication as a result of Semi-Colon exposure. To Georgiana May, Harriet Beecher wrote: "Some of the gentlemen . . . took a fancy to it and requested leave to put it in the 'Western Magazine,' and so it is in print. It is ascribed to *Catherine,* or I don't know that I should have let it go. I have no notion of appearing in *propria personae.*"[31] It is not clear why Beecher says it was *ascribed* to Catharine, since the version printed in *Western Monthly Magazine* is signed simply "B." Her use of the passive voice suggests the "ascription" was verbal speculation about its authorship among Semi-Colons.

Adherence to the Parker-Cranch developmental thesis leads Stowe's biographer Forrest Wilson to see all this material as evidence of fledgling efforts undercut by womanly reticence: "The Club's tolerance of, indeed its preference for, anonymity was precisely to her young liking. She was still too shy, too sensitive to criticism, to send her own identity uncloaked out upon such a stage. In fact, she was never quite to lose this juvenile shirking from public responsibility. . . . The afternoon of her career found her writing under a pseudonym."[32] Wilson constructs Stowe as a popular but thoroughly unprofessional woman writer who never quite outgrew her amateur status, else she would have authorized her texts by signing her name. Yet a glance at the *Western Monthly Magazine* and other

Cincinnati-area periodicals reveals that anonymous and pseudonymous publication was the norm rather than the exception for this period.

In the second place, inconsistencies and gaps muddle the chronology of the story of the "New England Sketch." Wilson, assuming that Beecher would not have entered the contest on her own accord, "when her own timidity would have told her that she had no chance to win," suggests that she "had the assurance of winning the prize before she ever consented to enter the competition." He bases this assertion on the fact that Hall had extended the contest deadline because of "the disappointing quality of the entries" so that "all who are competent may have the opportunity of entering into the competition." Thus the extension "allow[ed] Harriet to expand into a rounded fiction-tale what was still only an indeterminate sketch."[33] Given this information, and given that the memoirs are curiously silent about how Stowe's identity as the writer of the "Sketch" was discovered, one can only suspect that the entire discovery narrative was formulated years later after Stowe's literary reputation was secure.

It might be more accurate to posit that club members, Harriet Beecher included, were not unwittingly surprised into genius by Hall and his brother publishers. Several of the Semi-Colon women had already seen print elsewhere. In fact, a history of publication seems to have been a requirement for all members except those who were invited to join because of their family ties to publishing authors. Caroline Lee Hentz had published extensively with Hall and in other venues before she and her husband moved to Cincinnati. The Beecher sisters, according to Wilson, were invited "to join with the cultural élite" of the Semi-Colon Club because of the success of their 1833 *Primary Geography for Children.*[34]

These already-published women met socially with the executives of at least six Cincinnati-area periodicals, all of them hungry for material.[35] C. P. Cranch of the *Western Messenger* wrote his sister Margaret, "The poor deserted 'Messenger' seems to beg so hard for an editor. I have contributed several articles, but still there is a large vacancy,—this is the November number. I would stuff it with more poetry, but I am ashamed that so many pieces should go forth with 'C. P. C.' dangling at the end. The numbers should be made up by the fifteenth, and as much as one half, I think, is yet unfinished. . . . I . . . am rummaging my 'Omnibus Book' for scraps and ends to publish anonymously."[36] The numbers of the *Western Monthly* that appeared during the Semi-Colon years reveal Hall's reliance on the club for publishable essays and poems.[37] Thus it seems reasonable to argue that given the regular association of printers hungry for material with writers who knew at least the rudiments of getting their writing into print, "discovery" of "genius" was quite likely driven by demands of the periodical press. It might, in fact, be as reasonable to claim that Harriet Beecher persuaded Hall to extend his deadline to allow her to revise her Semi-Colon essay as to accept Parker's and Wilson's assertion that Hall discovered Stowe.

Nor is it accurate to assert that association within the Semi-Colon Club produced the careers of women writers. Certainly none of the Semi-Colon women, with the possible exception of Caroline Lee Hentz, planned to be a "famous" woman writer, although many had dabbled in publishing their "sketches"—almost a rite of passage for women of their race and class. The opposite assertion seems equally correct: reasoning backward from Harriet Beecher Stowe's fame as the author of *Uncle Tom's Cabin,* the memoirists have claimed an importance for the social groups associated with these writing women, emphasizing the quality of Harriet Beecher's contributions while overlooking essays written by lesser figures. This becomes most obvious in the case of Elizabeth Blackwell, who participated in the Semi-Colon Club during the early 1840s. Anecdotal evidence differs as to the degree of her participation: according to one biographer, while Anna and Marian Blackwell favored the club with essays and music, Elizabeth "sat in shy seclusion, basking in the brilliant company and conversation but seldom daring to open her mouth." Another biography, histrionically entitled *Child of Destiny,* asserts that "the Blackwell sisters felt truly anointed when Harriet Stowe invited them to join the Semi-Colon Club that met once a week at Sam Foote's fabulous mansion overlooking the river. . . . Harriet Beecher Stowe dominated the group, reading her stories and sketches, sometimes in a whimsical way but more often absent-mindedly." Both accounts imply that Elizabeth Blackwell was never destined to write or converse wittily but was focused on other aims. There is reason to question this assessment, however, since in the 1840s Blackwell "wrote stories for the literary magazines so popular in her circles."[38] In 1849, after she had received her medical degree, she returned to Cincinnati and was invited to address the Semi-Colons. It is thus as fair to assume that Blackwell both conversed and wrote in her turn for the club's meetings as that she sat in silence. It also should be emphasized as well that Blackwell wrote prolifically throughout her life, publishing a book of advice, an autobiography, a pamphlet on *Christian Socialism* and a two-volume set of *Essays in Medical Sociology.* But we know Elizabeth Blackwell as a woman physician, and subsequent histories of the club and biographies of Blackwell have erased her as a potential author, ascribing that identity to Harriet Beecher and Caroline Lee Hentz.[39]

Cranch: "A Bright & Happy Girl, Running over with Genius and Sympathy"

The most important assumption underpinning the developmental thesis is that gender determines literary production. Later writers such as Wilson identified as male the club members Cranch characterized as "maturer." They assumed the "beginners," whose "spontaneity" added "piquancy" to club meetings, were "girls." (By my calculations, Cranch was approximately the same age as Harriet Beecher.) Reversing the gendered figure in which Cranch presents Harriet Beecher would not succeed: the figure of "a happy boy" running over with genius and fledging his wings as a writer has no precedent in literary history. And, in fact, the woman Cranch remembers as a "bright & happy girl" had already been a teacher, was currently a school administrator, and had published a successful textbook. The fiction holds, however, that because she was a woman she was necessarily reticent both in demeanor and in writing. Mansfield recalls, "Miss Harriet Beecher . . . was just beginning to be known for her literary abilities. Two or three years after this time, I published in the *Cincinnati Chronicle* what, I believe, was her first printed story. I had heard her read at Miss Pierce's school, in Litchfield, Connecticut, her first public composition. It surprised everyone so much that it was attributed to her father, but was in fact only the first exhibition of her remarkable talents. . . . Her first *little* story, published in the *Chronicle,* immediately attracted attention, and her writings have always been popular."[40] This gender-marked perception demonstrates both Mansfield's condescension toward Beecher's work because it was written by a woman and his retrospective claim to have been the first to acknowledge her genius.

Stowe apparently recognized these gender-based assumptions, parodying them in several of her club essays that also expanded her stylistic repertoire. She wrote Georgiana May: "I have been writing a piece to be read next Monday evening at Uncle Sam's *soirée.* . . . It is a letter purporting to be from Dr. Johnson. I have been stilting about in his style so long that it is a relief to me to come down to the job of common English. . . . My first piece was a letter from Bishop Butler, written in his outrageous style of parentheses and foggification." Although she was annoyed with Butler's "foggification," such imitation was a common way for men and women alike to learn to write. In earlier years, in fact, when Harriet Beecher was a beginning teacher at Catharine's Hartford Female Seminary, her sister had "pounced down upon" her composition of a poetic drama, "and said I must not waste my time writing poetry, but discipline my mind by the study of Butler's 'Analogy.' So after this I wrote out abstracts from the 'Analogy.' . . . I was . . . very much interested in Butler's 'Analogy,' for Mr. Brace used to lecture on such themes when I was at Miss Pierce's school at Litchfield." Harriet Beecher also used her skill at imitation to try to counter the club's (to her, trivial) social agenda. Her letter to May continues.

> The next piece was a satire on certain members who were getting very much into the way of joking on the worn-out subjects of matrimony and old maid and old bachelorism. I therefore wrote a set of legislative enactments purporting to be from the ladies of the society, forbidding all such allusions in the future. It made some sport at the time. I try not to be personal, and to be courteous, even in satire.
>
> But I have written a piece this week that is making me some disquiet. I did not like it that there was so little that was serious and rational about the reading. So I conceived the design of writing a *set of letters* and throwing them in, as being the letters of a friend.[41]

It is unclear whether Beecher succeeded in her attempts to turn the emphasis from noncontroversial matters whose pursuit maintained social decorum to more substantive issues. Her decision to write "legislative enactments" (a genre familiar to the lawyers of the group) suggests, however, that the club's preoccupations with gender-appropriate behavior and gender-determined writing styles led to some fascinating experiments on the part of the club's writers, who played off each other's assumptions about gender and the club's promotion of heterosexual flirtation. Their essays simultaneously assert gender as a stable category and exploit the anonymity of writing to throw these assertions into an eccentric orbit.

Club Essay: "Giv[ing] a Proper Definition of Woman"

Over three decades, several of the club's members published material on women's roles, taking and defending opinions that ranged from Catharine Beecher's conservative defense of women's domestic "roles" and rejection of suffrage to Elizabeth and Emily Blackwell's textual and practical challenges to those notions.[42] Their unpublished manuscripts display a similar range of attitude. Of the 126 papers collected in Cincinnati, some two dozen overtly address gendered and heterosexualized behaviors such as courting, marriage, and family roles; almost every paper takes its foundational assumptions, as well as its characteristic metaphors, from the common notion that men and women thought and behaved differently and in ways tied to their biological sex. Some of these two dozen papers reiterate traditional gender roles; others display an intellectual and sometimes playful resistance to them.

Attention to proper gendered behavior stemmed from the club's emphasis on social interaction; thus active courting was as important a rationale for assembling as were intellectual activities. Under this agenda, intellectual performance became a sort of ritual courtship display. Even the way in which essays were chosen and read in club meetings partakes of sexual flirtation, with a group of likely essays exposed only to the eyes of the man empowered to bring them to voice, the identities of their writers veiled but always able to be inferred and discussed. Heterosexual coupling was actively in the minds of both men and women of the club. The fictive hostess of the "Receipt" took care to invite eligible "lawyers or other young men about town" and "the same number or more . . . of pretty young girls." Cranch proposed that the club meet year round, since "our Semicolons meetings have been truly delightful. . . . Cannot we have Summer Semicolons, on the hills, beneath the shadow of our beautiful trees, by our lovely Ohio?—Cannot we laugh and sentimentalize—and get in love with each other—in the country?" Another essay, apparently written in response to an earlier piece entitled "The Miseries of an Engaged Man," begins, "Yes, thought I to myself the other night at Mrs. G.'s Semi-Colon, I suppose they are miseries; real ones; but they are not the only ones, nor the worst in this life. They are no more to be compared to the miseries of a *man that is expected to be engaged* (and don't desire to be, at least, not yet) than a quiet, peaceful death by chloroform or charcoal, is to be torn by wild horses or broken on the wheel."[43]

Textual preoccupations with courtship and marriage were paralleled by similar activities among members. Harriet Beecher married Calvin Stowe after his wife, her best friend, died. Not all the flirtations between club members had such a happy resolution, although they did serve as grist for literary mills. Caroline Lee Hentz, described in members' reminiscences as "a woman of distinguished grace" "whom none saw without admiring," at some point received an "improper note" from Edward King, one of the group's founders. According to her son, "her agitation [over the note] made her husband suspicious, and so he laid a trap for her. After taking his gun and pretending to go fishing across the river, he shortly returned and, stealthily entering the room, found Mrs. Hentz bending over her desk, preparing to answer and return the unfortunate note. He seized upon the note in a passion, and in the scene that followed sent for Colonel King, slapped him in the face, and 'behaved like a maniac.' [Another Semi-

Colon member] Dr. Drake, for whom Mrs. Hentz sent in this emergency, acted as peacemaker and 'prevented the rupture that seemed . . . imminent.' Mr. Hentz closed his school immediately, and the family left Cincinnati, never to return." Some twenty years later, Hentz wrote a novel based on this incident; *Ernest Linwood, or The Inner Life of the Author* (1856) was published posthumously.[44]

Other essays not overtly engaged in flirtation nevertheless document members' awareness of the social expectations governing gendered behavior. An "Essay on Woman," for example, depends for its humor on the listeners' perception that it is rehearsing some well-worn axioms about women: "Four weeks ago tonight it was found a difficult task to define man, & although the world is four weeks older & wiser, I fear it will be much more difficult to give a proper definition of woman. . . . You will recollect that it was finally settled, four weeks ago, that man was 'all sorts of an animal.' Woman is not all sorts of an animal, for certainly she is not a dumb animal. Man sometimes is dumb as a post, but women never are. Whether they have anything to say or not, they must talk."[45] Consistent with the club's agenda, this essay does not enter the contemporary debates about women's or men's relative rights, roles, and abilities. Rather, it constructs a(n illogical) chain of maxims: man=all sorts of animal; woman≠ dumb animal. The conclusion is foregone: man≠woman.

Other essays, however, challenge those maxims in an attempt to account for the obvious ways in which many of the club's women members had flouted presumptions of behavior understood to define the well-bred lady. Clubwomen were literate, articulate, active in public causes: some earned wages to supplement their husbands'; others supported themselves independently as career professionals. These paradoxes evidence themselves in a number of compositions. One such essay begins, "It is a singular and amusing prejudice which pervades society with respect to that 'rara avis' a learned lady." The writer links the common prejudice against women's possession of "marked superiority of mental ability, or intellectual attainment" with small-town prejudice. Unlike the previous essayist, who argues that [all] women "must talk," this writer asserts that the learned lady "knew how to refrain from loud and ostentatious talking, and really seemed to be aware that it was most consistent with feminine modesty and propriety to make no effort to engross to herself the eyes and ears of the company." The essay, promising to be continued, concludes:

> How many a sage philosopher, and gay writer have inculcated it as a truth, or left it as an irresistible inference, that the pursuit of useful

> knowledge, or any developement [*sic*] of the faculties of the mind, beyond what the most ordinary occasions of life require, are unsuited to the peculiarities of the female character, which can only be preserved in all its amiable weakness, by keeping the higher faculties of the mind as dormant as possible. Such being the liberal and national creed of the intuitively wise and knowing ones of the town in question, as well as of a vast number of equally enlightened and liberal minded people all over the world, it is not surprising that a great proportion of the company assembled on the occasion to which I have alluded, should come to the conclusion that the lady who had excited so much curiosity was by no means entitled to the epithet "learned."[46]

I have quoted from this essay at length because it represents the assumptions about gendered behavior that its writer perceived as characterizing both residents of small towns and many "enlightened and liberal minded people all over the world"—perhaps the "staid, sober, respectable" Semi-Colons among them. It articulates a gendered double bind for the intellectual woman, who, if she talked, was only behaving as an ostentatious *rara avis,* and who, if she were silent, could not possibly be "learned." It also suggests ways in which the women writers of the Semi-Colon overcame this double bind, since any number of them could be classified as *rarae aves*. Associating with the club allowed women to write anonymously, so that "ostentatious" attainment might not be directly attributed to them, and the ventriloquistic voice that read their papers shielded them from the oft-repeated but erroneous maxim that women talked too much.

Club papers define proper social behaviors of men, as well. "About Love and Marriage," written as if by a man, articulates the behaviors of the public man who is able to balance the demands of business and home. The writer deplores some men's "continual absence . . . from their houses & from their firesides . . . [which] they in turn excuse . . . with the convenient plea of 'business.' . . . Think of this, all ye who have the happiness of others depending upon you; and treat your wives, as if they came into your house for some other purpose, than to sit at the head of your table, and pour your tea & coffee! . . . No man of sensibility . . . could ever suffer himself to wound the feelings of the woman he loved, by one unkind word or action, nay! by one unkind thought!" Other manuscripts, often poetic, seem to belie the assumption that sentimental discourse is the property of women writers only. "New England's Snow," a four-stanza verse, celebrates "merry tinkling sleighbell chimes" whose sound a "tale of joyous boyhood tells." Probably the most interesting composition in this regard is "The Babe on my knee—A Song of the Domestic—Inscribed to my wife." Overflowing with the sentiment conventionally ascribed to "lady poets," this verse, initialed "P," declares:

Ah! who, but a Father the rapture may know
With which the deep wells of the heart overflow,
When the first tender scion shoots forth from the tree,—
When the father first holds his dear babe on his knee!

Sweet pledge of a mutual affection most true!
Dear, pleasing relation,—delightfully new!
What rapture so holy on earth, as to be
The Sire of a Cherub like this on my knee![47]

These gender-blurred indistinctions extended into the published work of several of the club's male members, who assembled gift books and published fiction and poetry—such as *Little Henry, the Stolen Child,* and *Home-Made Verses*—that seem to the contemporary eye to epitomize nineteenth-century "domestic sentimentalism."[48] In fact, a brief and suggestive joke in one of the club papers goes so far as to imply that Semi-Colon men did write under female pseudonyms: "Can any of you tell what has become of [the Semicolon Society]? Has Samuel Essence evaporated? Has Methuselah Mann passed into nonentity? Is Rebecca married? Has the dreamer ceased to dream dreams? and the seer to see visions? Is Cherubina—but stop—I will ask no questions of her—*'I like not when a 'oman has a great peard; I spy a great peard under her muffler.'*"[49] The gender fluidity is apparently bilateral: Harriet Beecher assumes the persona of a lawyer to argue for more substantive club discussions; the bearded "Cherubina" pens sentiments deemed appropriate to women. The effect of these reversals is not equal, however. Men had no political advantage to gain by affecting feminine pseudonyms. Their writing under the sign of woman simply reinforces stereotypical understandings of womanly behavior (as, for example, if the writer of the "Receipt" were a man), and the qualities claimed by the writer are already assumed to be part of gentlemanly breeding (sensitivity, appreciation of beauty, or a chivalric acknowledgment of women's rights). But women's appropriation of masculine privilege seems to have different effects. If "The Babe on my Knee" or "About Love and Marriage" were not written by men, their masculine personae nevertheless can address the men of the club as equals, cast them in roles not commonly assumed to be theirs, and instruct them in conduct deemed proper to the "man of sensibility."

As a final case in point, consider how assumptions about the gender of the author of the following essay on the benefits of belonging to such a group affect its interpretation: "Semi-colonism acts upon the *public* welfare, by increasing the amount of the *private* and domestic virtues, by extending the influences of kindly feelings, and the intercourse of friendship, and of the knowledge that public prosperity is better promoted by the exercise of private virtues than by acts grounded on maxims of political expediency."[50] If read as a piece written by a woman, one who would be considered confined to the "*private* and domestic virtues," the essay becomes a plea, much along the lines of any number of other meditations on the efficacy of private (feminine) "influence." If assumed to have been written by a man, it becomes a principled defense of integrity in political life. But our inability (and the inability of those who first heard it) to identify the gender of the writer removes both inflections from the piece, freeing it from both "feminine" pleading and "masculine" agendas of political expediency. Remember, too, that the essay would have been read in Greene's "stentorian voice,"[51] an act that sealed separation of content from writer, and anticipated the estrangement of writer and text that would be the eventual effect of print. Such anonymity, which separated ideas and opinions on the written page from the body of their writer, also suspended gendered conceptions about behavior and sustained the possibility of civil sociality among ideologically divided club members, as I have already argued.

This play with the verbal and social signifiers of gender was possible, I think, precisely because Semi-Colon Club members were so sure of the stability of their social identity and of the categories of gender and behavior. The club's recognition and rehearsal of fictions of heterosexual desire, coupled with larger social activities of singing, dancing, and flirting, ensured that the requisite heterosocial bonding would obtain. Men's display of nostalgia, tenderness, and sentiment would be read not as effeminacy, but as good breeding. Women writing in men's personae or as women were tolerated, even applauded, because it was a safe assumption that these women would promulgate in their public writings the signifying fictions that stabilized gender roles.

Catharine Beecher: "The Combined Exercise of . . . Literary and Domestic Genius"

Indeed, the published writings of clubwomen abetted both the notion of stable gender roles and the idea of "literary genius." Like the writer who defended *rarae aves* to the Semi-Colon, other women writers felt compelled to demonstrate to a larger reading audience that they could be both intellectually and domestically competent. That demonstration depended, in turn, on invoking the presence of humbler avian species: servant women, figured as incompetent obstacles to domestic harmony and the life of the mind. "Trials of a Housekeeper," one of Harriet Beecher Stowe's *Mayflower* essays, perhaps originally read at a club meeting, suggests how the categories of literary and domestic genius depend on equally fictional inventions of bumbling servant women and western provincialism. She begins by invoking an artful simplicity: "I have a detail of very homely grievances to present, but such as they are, many a heart will feel them to be heavy—*the trials of a housekeeper.* 'Poh!' says one of the lords of creation, taking his cigar out of his mouth, and twirling it between his two first fingers, 'what a fuss these women do make of this simple matter of *managing a family*! I can't see, for my life, as there is anything so extraordinary to be done in this matter of housekeeping: only three meals a day to be got and cleared off, and it really seems to take up the *whole of their mind* from morning till night.'" The burden of the "housekeeper's" grievance centers on the impossibility of securing dependable domestic help in the "enlightened West."[52] That ironic phrase exposes the narrator's founding assumption that Cincinnati is really uncivilized and, as it becomes immediately apparent, much too ethnically diverse.

The essay details several encounters with a parade of unfit servants, beginning with "a great staring Dutch girl in a green bonnet with red ribands—mouth wide open, and hands and feet that would have made a Greek sculptor open *his* mouth too" (brought to the home, not incidentally, by the husband of the house). In this succession of ethnic types, only a "tidy, efficient-trained English girl; pretty, and genteel, and neat, and knowing how to do everything" is satisfactory. She immediately departs to be married. The essay concludes, "What shall we do? Shall we go for slavery, or shall we give up houses . . . and sit in our tent door in real patriarchal independence? What shall we do?"[53] Written in the first person, published in company with other "personal" essays introduced by the "Author," this sketch invites its reader/hearer to assume it is autobiographical and, if she is a woman, to identify with the common lot of a (white) woman of refinement trying to survive the deprivations of the West. If the reader/hearer is one of "the lords of creation" sitting in "patriarchal independence" in the parlor, he can only agree that a woman writer's lot is not an easy one and that in order to free "the whole of [her] mind" for writing, she must have reliable domestic help.

An undated memoir written by Catharine Beecher corroborates this essay's agenda, illustrating "the combined exercise of [Harriet's] *literary and domestic genius* in a style that . . . was quite amusing." Much in the same way that Harriet's essay establishes the impossibly inept domestic help as a foil to the narrator's domestic skills, Catharine's account weaves three strands of competing demands on the woman writer's attention: the supervision of Mina, "a dark-skinned nymph waiting for orders"; attending to small children; and completing a "piece for the *Souvenir*" that is due at the publisher. As Mina works, Catharine superintends both Mina and Harriet and acts as scribe. The incident concludes as Harriet dictates the closing lines of her story:

> She continued to dictate,—
>
> "You must take them away. It may be—perhaps it must be—that I shall soon follow, but the breaking heart of a wife still pleads, 'a little longer, a little longer.' "
>
> "How much longer must the ginger-bread stay in?" asked Mina.
>
> "Five minutes," said Harriet.
>
> " 'A little longer, a little longer,' " I repeated in a dolorous tone, and we burst out into a laugh.
>
> Thus we went on, cooking, writing, nursing, and laughing, till I finally accomplished my object. The piece was finished and copied, and the next day sent to the editor.
>
> No wonder Mrs. Stowe describes her writing as "rowing against wind and tide!"[54]

This memoir depends on a complex narratorial agenda, wherein Catharine becomes the administrative heroine ("*I* accomplished *my* object," aiding in the completion of Harriet's writing), and Harriet becomes the literary and domestic genius, an able housekeeper (in contrast to her domestic "help," who are more a hindrance) who is also able to complete her writing of a "piece" that, through her literary genius, transmutes the mundane details of household trivialities into "Art." Finally, Stowe's son and grandson complete the transformation in *Harriet Beecher Stowe: The Story of Her Life* by affirming Catharine's recollection that their mother wrote against overwhelming odds.

Potter: "Why Then Should Not the Hair-dresser Write?"

The Beecher sisters' version of the difficulties of domestic management in the provincial western settlements stands in suggestive contrast to other published memoirs that obscure the nexus of gender, class, and race within which the club met. These accounts assert the plainness of the gathering, insisting that members subscribed in principle to a sumptuary code designed to erase any invidious distinctions of money, possessions, or social advantage. Foote's memoirs make this clear:

> These reunions began and terminated at early hours, and expensive luxuries in food and drink being rigidly prohibited, the health of the members was not endangered, (nor the reputation of their neighbors);—intellectual food of a quality superior to any thing afforded by the highest style of cookery, and more wholesome than personal gossip, not only for the mind, but for the body also, being served up. . . . It was . . . understood to be one of the principles of the club to discountenance extravagance in dress, and luxury in entertainments, both by example, and by avoiding discussions in which they might form a prominent subject.[55]

The gendered implications of this passage are striking when its disdain for "expensive luxuries in food and drink" is read against the "Receipts'" emphasis, both in content and genre, on the hostess's responsibility for her guests' satisfaction and against the Beechers' elaboration of the constituents of domestic genius. Other Cincinnati Historical Society manuscripts—not in the Semi-Colon collection, but written at approximately the same time—further clarify what the memoirs obscure and what the Beechers assume as "natural": the category of Anglo-Protestant "whiteness" that obtained in the Semi-Colon Club. An autobiographical narrative by Eliza Potter, *A Hairdresser's Experience in High Life,* recently reissued by the Schomburg Library of Nineteenth-Century Black Women Writers, exposes the hidden grid of race-, class-, and gender-based assumptions that structure the club, the essays its members wrote, and the woman of genius it purportedly nurtured. The Cincinnati Historical Society copy of the book, from which the Schomburg edition was reprinted, details how an underclass of literate working women, many of them ethnically and racially marked, supported the social life of mid-nineteenth-century Cincinnati.

That the cover of *A Hairdresser's Experience* does not announce an author's name suggests the designation is a privilege linked to race. Only on the title page is the author mentioned, and only as bibliographical data at the bottom of the page: "CINCINNATI: PUBLISHED FOR THE AUTHOR. 1859." The anonymity of this publication differs significantly from that of the Semi-Colon writers. They exercised agency in choosing or revoking their anonymity and were assured that the eventual exposure of their identity would redound to their financial benefit. By contrast, the attribution of Potter's authorship comes only as a result of archival intervention—a librarian has penciled in "by Eliza Potter (colored)" on the title page. There is no related collection of secondary scholarship to invent Potter's genius or chronicle her authorial development.

Semi-Colon Club memoirists, by contrast, do not mark their subjects as white; nor has contemporary scholarship entertained the possibility that any Semi-Colon member was "colored." But Potter's text forces us to recognize the existence of literate African Americans among the intelligentsia of Cincinnati and to account for the existence of salons that paralleled the Semi-Colon among free people of color. Dorothy Sterling, for example, has devoted a section of her book *We Are Your Sisters* to the "small middle class organized literary associations" that "hop[ed] not only to educate themselves but also to combat white racism." These groups met in Boston, Rhode Island, New York, and Philadelphia at precisely the same time the Semi-Colons assembled in Cincinnati.[56]

Potter's introduction to *A Hairdresser's Experience in High Life* likewise asks us to consider how the memoirists' need to celebrate plainness and simplicity obscures the possession of financial, cultural, and intellectual capital by Semi-Colon members. Their emphasis is an affectation available only to the privileged, since class coding assures that simplicity will not be interpreted as bumptiousness, naïveté, or penury. Potter, by contrast, must justify her simplicity:

> The unlettered of all ages have numbered in their ranks many with sufficient observation and intelligence to have written more entertaining books than many which have emanated form cultivated pens, had they only possessed the courage to tell what they knew in *simple, plain language*. . . .
>
> The physician writes his diary, and doubtless his means of discovering the hidden mysteries of life are great. The clergyman, whose calling inspires the deepest confidence . . . sends forth his diary to an eager world, and other innumerable chroniclers of fireside life have existed; but the hair-dresser will yield rivalship to none in this regard. . . .
>
> Nowhere do hearts betray themselves more unguardedly than in the private boudoir, where the hair-dresser's mission makes her a daily attendant. Why, then, should not the hair-dresser write, as well as the physician and clergyman? She will tell her story in simpler language; but it will be none the less truthful, none the less strange.

Potter does not here mention race, but subsumes it into what for her are larger issues of class and gender. She exposes how these determinants combine to justify the writings of some men—doctors and clergy—while trivializing the work of other writers—women who pen simple, "private" stories. Her specific mention of physician and clergyman (and she could have included lawyer) seems to point directly although certainly not intentionally at the affiliative connections structuring the Semi-Colon Club, whose membership was drawn primarily from the ranks of the clergy, the bar, and the medical profession.[57]

Potter's autobiography forces us to read both the Semi-Colon essays and their derivative memoirs with an eye to the assumptions about class and race that we might otherwise overlook. The first paragraph of "Receipt," for example, is permeated with markers of class: its parodic tone does not obviate the writer's references to "the best quality" of society. The writer must be a *lady* and *of suitable qualifications* including, we assume, a capacious home and resources to furnish wine and refreshments—however simple—for upward of forty guests. The essay presumes as well that writing the list of guests was the extent of the hostess's duties, and that recipe writing, as opposed to cooking, was the extent of domestic behavior expected of a "lady of suitable qualifications." Presumably servants would attend to the preparation of the food, the housecleaning, and the cosmetic preparations necessary for the gathering.[58] The essay also assumes that this is not a transactional "Receipt" but a parody; as such, it is a literary and intellectual undertaking, not simply directions for bodily labor. Potter's text, by contrast, demonstrates how such simplicity takes for granted the labor of working women:

> I often laugh at [the eastern ladies] when they come to Cincinnati, as after dashing around a little they find the people are not so green. . . . I have often seen ladies from New York, who moved in a preety [*sic*] good circle at home, struck with perfect astonishment on entering some of our parlors here. . . . One lady, in particular, I combed . . . and advised her to have an elegant head-dress, as I told her she would see some elegant ladies where she was going. She laughed at me, and said if she was in New York she would, but did not think it worth while to take so much trouble for a party in Cincinnati.
>
> The next day on my going to comb her she was very much mortified, and told me if she had known the Cincinnati ladies dressed so well, she would have bought the head-dress. . . . I told her she did not see our prettiest ladies, for some of them are in mourning, and the others are out of town.[59]

Believing Foote's protest of simplicity, and echoing Stowe in asserting Cincinnati's "[lack of] urbane sophistication," Louis Tucker makes the club into a refuge that provides "nourishing intellectual fare" to deprived intellectuals.[60] Potter's invaluable text demonstrates, by contrast, that others felt that Cincinnati shared the intellectual and social sophistication of Philadelphia and Boston. It reminds us, as well, that working women of color were indispensable to the intellectual banquet enjoyed by the Semi-Colons.

"It Will Be Much More Difficult to Give a Proper Definition of [an Author]"

It thus seems impossible to construct a uniformly heroic picture of women's authorship, as seems to have been the agenda of previous memoirists and biographers. Archival collections have shown what is lost when we rely on memoirs and hagiography without attempting to understand their unstated agendas. They suggest that anyone's road to literacy and access to public forums is contestatory and challenge scholars to seek to uncover the conditions against and by which "genius" becomes constructed. When we accept that challenge, we have a fuller picture of just how such claims to power are grounded. Such a perspective forces us to see how women's presence in an early coeducational group sustained that group's agenda. It makes visible the different populations who wrote, the social contexts for writing, and the social relationships involved in the acts of writing and publishing. It challenges us to undertake more textured studies to account for what 150 years of racial and class prejudice has obscured. Then perhaps we will read with new eyes the "beginning," "simple," "little" stories written by women as experiments within and in resistance to the structures of understanding dictated by their social nexus, as well as the subsequent determining fictions of literary history.

Notes

My thanks to Frances Foster, Beth Holmgren, Stephanie Jed, and Pasquale Verdicchio, members of my writing group, whose comments enabled me to revise my insights substantially. Carolyn Haynes's and Shawn Smith's close readings also helped me clarify some muddy positions. Amy Hoffman, Cheryl Reed, and Shawn Smith helped with beginning research. Archival sources for the chapter are found in the Cincinnati Historical Society, the Library of Congress, and the Stowe-Day Library.

1. The Semi-Colon Club met on alternate weeks in the winter from approximately 1829 to 1845. No precise dates exist for the club's founding or dissolution. Several sources suggest that it ended when Samuel Foote lost his mansion in the

Panic of 1837: see Charles H. Foster, *The Rungless Ladder: Harriet Beecher Stowe and New England Puritanism* (New York: Cooper Square, 1970), p. 22, and Dorothy Clarke Wilson, *Lone Woman: The Story of Elizabeth Blackwell, the First Woman Doctor* (Boston: Little, Brown, 1970), p. 197. This date seems to be implied in John P. Foote, *Memoirs of Samuel E. Foote* (Cincinnati: Robert Clarke, 1860), p. 183; however, dated manuscripts, Elizabeth Blackwell's reminiscences, and a short-lived journal entitled *The Semi-Colon* and dated 1845 all indicate that the group met as late as 1846 or 1849.

According to Louis L. Tucker, "Dominated by transplanted New Englanders, the club's membership contained the greatest concentration of intellect in the trans-Allegheny country. . . . Few American cities, east or west, could have boasted of a 'brain trust' of higher intellectual quality. . . . The roster reads like a *Who's Who* of the West of that day." See "The Semi-Colon Club of Cincinnati," *Ohio History* 73.1 (1964): 16.

2. Two recent books trace a general history of writing groups in the United States and of women's study clubs in particular. Gere overlooks the importance of coeducational groups, arguing that "self-improvement societies remained, until the middle of the nineteenth century, largely male provinces. . . . Accordingly, women's self-improvement groups have their own history." Martin's history of women's study clubs begins only in 1860. See Anne Ruggles Gere, *Writing Groups: History, Theory, and Implications* (Carbondale: Southern Illinois Univ. Press, 1987), p. 37, and Theodora Penny Martin, *The Sound of Our Own Voices: Women's Study Clubs, 1860–1910* (Boston: Beacon Press, 1967).

3. In this essay I will follow the general tendency to use Stowe as primary example but will speculate about other women members as well. Another study could be devoted to the issue of men's affiliation with coeducational groups.

4. E. P. Parker, "Harriet Beecher Stowe," in *Eminent Women of the Age,* ed. James Parton et al. (Hartford: S. M. Betts, 1868), p. 307.

5. Cranch's manuscript is held by the Library of Congress, Ac. 9065. A photocopy of the manuscript is the first document in the Semi-Colon collection box at the Cincinnati Historical Society.

According to the Library of Congress, W. H. Venable penned the attribution "Written by Edw. P. Cranch." The writer of this annotation believes, based on information recorded "elsewhere," that the memoir is Christopher Pearce Cranch's. My own research, based on a comparison of handwriting, leads me to believe it was written by Edward P. Cranch, Christopher's brother. Louis Tucker, on the other hand, attributes this memoir and other essays with C. P. Cranch's distinctive caricatures, to *Edwin* P. Cranch ("Semi-Colon," pp. 14, 57 nn. 2, 16). Tucker has wrongly named Edw. as Edwin, as well as mistakenly attributed these essays.

6. See, for example, Joan D. Hedrick: "Harriet Beecher's career formally commenced in the Semi-Colon Club. . . . The step from writing letters for domestic consumption to writing for a literary club was small but significant" ("Parlor Literature: Harriet Beecher Stowe and the Question of 'Great Women Artists,'" *Signs* 17 [1992]: 293). To make such an assertion, Hedrick has to overlook Beecher's writing essays as a student at Sarah Pierce's Academy and her writing and teaching of composition at Hartford Female Seminary. Biographers of Harriet Beecher Stowe rely heavily on memoirs by Cranch, Mansfield, Foote, and Beecher herself to construct a narrative of developmental authorship. See John R. Adams, introduction to *Regional Sketches: New England and Florida by Harriet Beecher Stowe* (New Haven: College and University Press, 1972); Foster, *Ladder;* Gilbertson, *Stowe;* and Forrest Wilson,

Crusader in Crinoline: The Life of Harriet Beecher Stowe (New York: Lippincott, 1941), for examples.

7. Hedrick, "Parlor Literature," pp. 300–301, lists examples. Her assumption is borne out by Stowe's *Mayflower* (1844), a collection of essays that Stowe identified as having been written for the Semi-Colon Club. Only one *Mayflower* essay, "The Canal-boat," is in the Cincinnati collection, however, and is not identified as being Stowe's.

8. See, for example, CHS MS 39, "About Love and Marriage," and CHS MS 84, "New England's Snow," both of which are inscribed in an elegant copperplate hand. CHS MSS 23 and 26 are embellished with caricatures. Louis Tucker identifies these as "Edwin" Cranch's. The handwriting of CHS MSS 23 and 26, however, does not resemble that of the memoir. Instead, the hand, as well as the style of caricature, bears a strong resemblance to that of C. P. Cranch, brother of Edward P. Cranch. Both Cranch brothers lived in Louisville and Cincinnati for a time during the 1830s.

9. CHS MS 10. I am grateful to the Cincinnati Historical Society for permission to quote from unpublished manuscripts from their collections. The Semi-Colon Club collection was donated to the Society by Davis L. James Jr. in 1934.

10. This essay is included in the first folder of the Semi-Colon collection. My photocopy, provided by the Cincinnati Historical Society, is unnumbered and untitled. To my knowledge, no scholar has yet identified this manuscript as Harriet Beecher's.

11. Charles Edward Stowe, *Life of Harriet Beecher Stowe, Compiled from her Letters and Journals* (Boston: Houghton, Mifflin, 1890), p. 70.

12. Sources that refer to particular compositions or that reprint essays identified as having been written for the Semi-Colon Club include Kathryn Kish Sklar, *Catharine Beecher: A Study in American Domesticity* (New Haven: Yale Univ. Press, 1973); Forrest Wilson, *Crusader;* Jeanne Boydston et al., *The Limits of Sisterhood: The Beecher Sisters on Women's Right and Woman's Sphere* (Chapel Hill: Univ. of North Carolina Press, 1988); Anna Blackwell's correspondence; Foote, *Memoirs;* and Harriet Beecher Stowe, *The Mayflower; or, Sketches of Scenes and Characters among the Descendants of the Pilgrims* (New York: Harper, 1844), and *The May Flower and Miscellaneous Writings* (Boston: Phillips, Sampson, 1855).

13. Edward Deering Mansfield, *Personal Memories, Social, Political and Literary, with Sketches of Many Noted People, 1857–1957* (1879; rpt. New York: Arno Press, 1970), pp. 266–67; emphasis added.

14. For example, see Stowe's biographical sketch of Salmon P. Chase: "There was in the general tone of life [in Cincinnati] a breadth of ideas, a liberality and freedom, which came from the consorting together of persons of different habits of living." Quoted in W. H. Venable, *Beginnings of Literary Culture in the Ohio Valley* (Cincinnati: R. Clarke, 1891), p. 420. See also Randolph C. Randall, *James Hall: Spokesman of the New West* (Columbus: Ohio State Univ. Press, 1964), and Sklar, *Catharine Beecher,* as well as manuscript letters upon which these studies are based.

15. Lyman Beecher, Calvin Stowe, and Nathaniel Wright were all associated with Lane Theological Seminary. Unitarians included C. P. Cranch, William Henry Channing, James Hall, Timothy Flint, Ephraim Peabody, and James Freeman Clarke. Clarke, Cranch, and Channing were also transcendentalists. Western enthusiasts included Hall, Flint, Channing, James H. Perkins, James W. Ward, artist Worthington Whittredge, and Daniel Drake. For an example of regional acrimony, see the print feud between Lyman Beecher, who published "Plea for the West," and James Hall,

who responded in his *Western Monthly Magazine* with a review of Beecher's "Plea," later separately published as *The Catholic Question* (1838). See also Catharine Beecher's *An Essay on the Education of Female Teachers* (New York: Van Nostrand and Dwight, 1833), which linked Catholicism, German immigrants, and western ignorance. Alexander Saxton's *The Rise and Fall of the White Republic: Class Politics and Mass Culture in Nineteenth-Century America* (London: Verso, 1990) elucidates the political stakes of this sectional debate.

16. Sklar, *Catharine Beecher,* p. 120. Beecher publications in *Western Monthly Magazine* included "Modern Uses of Language" (March 1833), signed "B."; "Isabelle and Her Sister Kate, and Their Cousin" (February 1834), signed MAY and attributed to Harriet; "A New England Sketch" (April 1834), signed "Miss Harriet Beecher"; and "Aunt Mary" (July 1834), signed "H. E. B."

How the split between Catharine Beecher and the Drakes, Halls, and Kings affected attendance at or behavior in the Semi-Colon Club meetings is difficult to establish because club reminiscences avoid mentioning the feud and because the club manuscripts themselves are undated and unsigned. It is impossible to establish who attended the meetings at any given time.

17. LC, Cranch MS. Unlike Cranch, Venable lists the meetings by hosts' names. I emphasize Cranch's version because the MSS support this gendered interpretation. Venable, by contrast, pays little attention to the club's "nonliterary" women.

Greene, an attorney, lived next to Foote on Third Street, "in the fashionable residential area adjoining the business center" of Cincinnati. See Tucker, "Semi-Colon," pp. 15–16. Foote, brother of Lyman Beecher's first wife, was a sea captain turned entrepreneur remembered for his elegant mansion and the quality of his wine cellar. Meetings may also have been held at the Drake home. Mansfield credits Drake with instituting a salon in 1833 "for the benefit of his daughters, then just growing into womanhood" (*Personal Memories,* p. 262). Mansfield does not say this was the Semi-Colon Club (and the date of founding, if accurate, suggests it was not). However, the details of membership and club procedures duplicate others' descriptions of Semi-Colon meetings. In her biography of Catharine Beecher, Sklar treats Drake's salon and the Semi-Colon Club as separate groups. Venable makes the same separation. For the sake of convenience, I assume they were the same.

18. CHS, MS 36.

19. LC, Cranch MS.

20. LC, Cranch MS; Foote, *Memoirs,* p. 180; Tucker, "Semi-Colon," p. 19. Members may indeed have stimulated each other intellectually. But there is scant evidence that it happened at club meetings. For a dissenting opinion on the brilliance and intellectual stimulation provided by the meetings, see Venable, who includes the reminiscence of an unidentified (adolescent male) member: "We went to different houses of the folks, and certain manuscript articles were read, which were supposed to be interesting and instructive. I suppose they were, as there is no evidence to the contrary. Personally, however, I remember thinking that most of them were stupid. Most of us were glad when the readings were over, for then we did something else, the principal of which was dancing" (*Literary Culture,* p. 420).

21. CHS MS 10.

22. A few club members wrote under their own names. See Hedrick, "Parlor Literature," p. 295 n. 57. My research indicates they were in the minority.

23. Anna Blackwell to William Greene, 18 Aug. 1844, MS letter, Cincinnati Historical Society.

24. LC, Cranch MS.

25. CHS MS 23. Tucker identifies the paper as written by "Edwin" Cranch; see "Semi-Colon," pp. 18, 58 n. 30. I assume it was by his brother Christopher.

26. My point here is in contrast to Hedrick, who credits Stowe with legitimizing a genre she terms "parlor literature" ("Parlor Literature," pp. 199–301). To make this claim, she overlooks the large number of similar essays published by men and women alike before the Beechers' arrival in Cincinnati.

The 1855 edition of *The Mayflower* contains this dedication: "There are those now scattered through the world who will remember the social literary parties of Cincinnati, for whose genial meetings many of these articles were prepared. With most affectionate remembrances, the author dedicates the book to the yet surviving members of The Semicolon."

27. See Hentz, *Aunt Patty's Scrap Bag* (1846); Drake, *Tales and Sketches from the Queen City* (1838); and Hall, *Winter Evenings: A Series of American Tales* (1829) and *Legends of the West* (1832). According to Charles Foster, Hall's *Legends* "could have furnished a model for such scenes in *Uncle Tom's Cabin* as that at the inn in Kentucky where George found the frontiersmen, hats tipped at the angles temperament suggested" (*Ladder,* p. 16).

28. Elliott, also an historian, published *Cottages and Cottage Life* in Cincinnati in 1848. Catharine Beecher's *Treatise on Domestic Economy* was first published in 1841. It was reprinted frequently between 1841 and 1856. In 1869, the *Treatise* was revised and reissued as *The American Woman's Home*, cowritten by Harriet Beecher Stowe. This, in turn, was reprinted under the title *The New Housekeeper's Manual* in 1873. See Sklar, *Catharine Beecher,* pp. 305–6 n. 1, for more details about domestic textbooks published by the Beecher sisters. Elliot published *The Book of American Interiors* in 1876.

29. Mansfield, *Personal Memories,* p. 262; C. E. Stowe, *Life of Stowe,* p. 71, emphasis added; CHS MS 10.

30. These manuscript newspapers are part of the Katharine S. Day Collection at the Stowe-Day Library.

31. C. E. Stowe, *Life of Stowe,* p. 69.

32. Forrest Wilson, *Crusader,* p. 125.

33. Ibid., pp. 125–27.

34. Ibid., p. 122.

35. Benjamin Drake published a local newspaper, the *Chronicle;* Timothy Flint, the *Western Monthly Review;* James Hall, the *Western Monthly Magazine;* and James H. Perkins, James Freeman Clarke, and C. P. Cranch all were associated with the *Western Messenger.* Samuel Foote's *Memoirs* indicate that E. P. Cranch and U. T. Howe also published a newspaper (see p. 178).

36. Leonora Cranch Scott, *The Life and Letters of Christopher Pearse Cranch* (Boston: Houghton, Mifflin, 1917), p. 37.

37. See, for example, Hentz's "Thanksgiving Day" (Dec. 1834) and "The Village Parson's Wife" (Mar. 1835). "Journal of a Pedestrious Tour" (Oct. 1836), signed P. P. and "Shakespeare's Birth Night" (Nov. 1836) are also apparently Semi-Colon productions.

38. Dorothy Wilson, *Lone Woman*, p. 106; Ishbel Ross, *Child of Destiny: The Life Story of the First Woman Doctor* (London: Victor Gollancz, 1950), p. 81; Ruth Fox Hume, *Great Women of Medicine* (New York: Random House, 1964), p. 11. Ross's account is inaccurate and without documentation. There is no evidence that Harriet Beecher read to the group. Compare Mansfield, who recalls, "In the reunion I speak of, she [Beecher] was not distinguished for conversation, but when she did

speak, showed something of the peculiar strength and humor of her mind" (*Personal Memories,* p. 265).

Blackwell's most responsible biographer describes her writings as "short stories steeped in romanticism and Gothic mystery." The surviving manuscripts are entitled "Bradshaw the Traitor," "Dialogue between Gorgo and Praxinoe," "Margaret St. Omer," "Sir Lionel," and "The Relation of Events." All are collected in the Blackwell Family Papers in the Library of Congress. In 1846 she published a "romantic story," "Lyndhurst," in the *Columbian Lady's and Gentleman's Magazine* (5 [1846]: 274–78), "Anna having sent it to the periodical without Elizabeth's knowledge. Elizabeth was indignant that they printed her name as that of the author instead of the more socially acceptable by-line, 'A lady.'" See Nancy Ann Sahli, *Elizabeth Blackwell, M.D. (1821–1910): A Biography* (New York: Arno Press, 1982), pp. 40, 58.

39. Dorothy Wilson, *Lone Woman,* p. 192. The same backward historicism is true of the scholarship on Catharine Beecher, who wrote and published prolifically, but seldom published in "imaginative" genres. Her biographers do not identify the Semi-Colon Club as a formative influence in her career as an author, as do Stowe's, although her history of writing for the club and being published by other club members seems to parallel her sister's. Foote, for instance, says of Catharine Beecher that her "fame and literary works have been widely disseminated before and since, some of whose contributions to the Semi-Colons have been published in annuals and magazines" (*Memoirs,* p. 178).

40. Mansfield, *Personal Memories,* p. 265; emphasis added.

41. C. E. Stowe, *Letters of Stowe,* pp. 69, 32, 83.

42. For example, E. D. Mansfield, *Legal Rights . . . of Women* (1845); J. F. Clarke, *Woman Suffrage for Boston* (n.d.); W. H. Channing, review of *History of Woman Suffrage* (1881); James Ward, "Woman: A Poem" (1852); and Elizabeth Blackwell, "The Position of Women" (1847). Another member, Sarah Worthington King Peter, established "the first school in America to teach girls and women design" (see Gilbertson, *Stowe,* p. 64).

43. CHS MS 23; Foote, *Memoirs,* p. 279.

44. Parker, "Stowe," p. 306; Mansfield, *Personal Memories,* p. 266; Rhoda Coleman Ellison, "Mrs. Hentz and the Green-Eyed Monster," *American Literature* 22 (1950): 346–47.

45. CHS MS 86.

46. CHS MS 65.

47. CHS MSS 39, 84, and 75, respectively.

48. In 1830 Timothy Flint published both *Little Henry* and *The Shoshone Valley: A Romance.* James W. Ward published *Home-Made Verses* in 1857, and James Hall brought out *The Western Souvenir, a Christmas and New Year's Gift* in 1828.

Although I applaud Hedrick's argument concerning Harriet Beecher Stowe's central place in elaborating a "national culture" ("Parlor Literature," p. 290), I do not support her generalization that realistic and conversational "sketches" such as Stowe's constitute "parlor literature," a distinctively feminine genre. Like Judith Butler, I find it more useful to consider gender as a role performed in response to conventional expectation and dissociated from notions of biological sex; see *Gender Trouble: Feminism and the Subversion of Identity* (New York: Routledge, 1990). "Parlor literature," although possibly an identifiable genre, and possibly a discourse gendered feminine, cannot be considered the exclusive province of writers able to be classified as biological women.

49. CHS MS 97; emphasis in original.

50. Foote, *Memoirs,* p. 181.

51. Tucker, "Semi-Colon," p. 17.

52. Stowe, "Trials of a Housekeeper," in *The Mayflower* (1844), pp. 91, 93; third emphasis added.

53. Ibid., pp. 98, 100.

54. Charles Edward Stowe and Lyman Beecher Stowe, *Harriet Beecher Stowe: The Story of Her Life* (Boston: Houghton, Mifflin, 1911), pp. 87, 89, 93; first emphasis added.

55. Foote, *Memoirs,* pp. 180–81. Other accounts, however, emphasize the quality of Samuel Foote's wine cellar. See for example, Forrest Wilson, who writes, "When Capt. Samuel Foote gave the *soirée,* the guest could rely on a glass of that connoisseur's fine old sherry or Madeira with the sandwiches and coffee" (*Crusader,* p. 124). Wealth was an important part of the foundational structure of the club, so much so that several sources assume that the club ceased meeting when Samuel Foote lost his fortune in the panic of 1838 (Foote, *Memoirs;* Forrest Wilson, *Crusader;* Tucker, "Semi-Colon"). But the club continued to meet into the mid-1840s (see n. 1).

56. Dorothy Sterling, ed., *We Are Your Sisters: Black Women in the Nineteenth Century* (New York: Norton, 1984), p. 110. These antebellum African American salons were segregated by gender. A half-century later, Frances Harper's novel *Iola Leroy* represents a coeducational salon. Chapter 30, "Friends in Council," depicts "Mr. Stillman's pleasant, spacious parlors . . . filled to overflowing with a select company of earnest men and women deeply interested in the welfare of the race" (1892; rpt. College Park, Md.: McGrath, 1969), p. 246. At least one other study documents salon activity among ethnic groups: Deborah Hertz's *Jewish High Society in Old Regime Berlin* (New Haven: Yale Univ. Press, 1988) is a study of salon culture in late-eighteenth- and early-nineteenth-century Berlin.

I am indebted to Frances Foster for bringing these sources to my attention and for challenging me to account for race in my work.

57. Eliza Potter, *A Hairdresser's Experience in High Life* (1859; rpt. New York: Oxford Univ. Press, 1991), p. iv. Salmon P. Chase, William Greene, James Hall, E. D. Mansfield, and Timothy Walker were lawyers. Daniel Drake was a physician; Elizabeth and Emily Blackwell received encouragement from fellow Semi-Colons to undertake medical careers. See Sahli, *Blackwell,* p. 50, and Elizabeth Blackwell, *Pioneer Work in Opening the Medical Profession to Women* (London: Longmans Green, 1895), p. 31.

58. I do not mean to assert that the Semi-Colon Club was an occasion for elegant material display, as it is difficult to align Potter's text precisely with the fifteen-year period during which the Semi-Colon Club met. But her account provides a useful stimulus to resistant thinking. And it is important to note that, for all the memoirists' profession of simplicity, biographers emphasize the "elegance" of the Foote mansion, "the seat of a liberal hospitality" (see Foote, *Memoirs,* p. 176).

59. Potter, *Hairdresser,* pp. 276–77.

60. Tucker, "Semi-Colon," p. 19.

II

Practices and "Voices" of Literacy

7

SHIRLEY WILSON LOGAN

Literacy as a Tool for Social Action among Nineteenth-Century African American Women

Many persons may object to the term, Race Literature, questioning seriously the need, doubting if there be any, or indeed whether there can be a Race Literature in a country like ours apart from the general American Literature. Others may question the correctness of the term American Literature, since our civilization in its essential features is a reproduction of all that is most desirable in the civilizations of the Old World. English being the language of America, they argue in favor of the general term, English Literature.

While I have great respect for the projectors of this theory, yet it is a limited definition; it does not express the idea in terms sufficiently clear.

The conditions which govern the people of African descent in the United States have been and still are, such as create a very marked difference in the limitations, characteristics, aspirations and ambitions of this class of people, in decidedly strong contrast with the more or less powerful races which dominate it.

When the literature of our race is developed, it will of necessity be different in all essential points of greatness, true heroism and real Christianity from what we may at the present time, for convenience, call American Literature.
—Victoria Earle Matthews, "The Value of Race Literature" (1895)

ONE MAJOR CHALLENGE facing nineteenth-century African Americans was the acquisition of adequate reading and writing skills. Before the institution of slavery was abolished, the difficulty of this task was compounded by the laws passed in most southern states making it illegal to teach slaves to read during the first half of the century. Such legislation was in part a reaction to rebellions led by literate slaves like Nat Turner and Gabriel Prosser. It became necessary to acquire reading and writing skills surreptitiously, as in the well-known case of Frederick Douglass, who contrived ways to learn from his white associates at a Baltimore shipyard. Even free blacks in northern states faced systematic resistance to their attempts to become literate. Because few were admitted to public schools they developed their own private institutions, most often associated with churches. Throughout the nineteenth century blacks in both the North and South, free and enslaved, were seeking knowledge in a culture in which writing had been valorized over other means of communication. They recognized that literacy was at the center of liberation and that its denial was a primary means of subordination and oppression.[1]

I will examine the ways in which several prominent black women of the nineteenth century acquired literacy and employed it as a weapon against slavery, discrimination, and mob violence in the struggle of African Americans to obtain full citizenship. Literacy allowed these women to mount the platform and voice the concerns of their people. As Salvino reminds us, "The belief in the efficacy of literacy holds powerful currency"; and while these women's facility with language made it possible for them to reach large numbers of people with pen and voice, it was not the case that literacy alone had much of an impact on the success rate of most African Americans who acquired it during the nineteenth century. Studies cited by Salvino suggest a connection between literacy and access to freedom but not to freedom's economic benefits.[2] With this corrective in mind, I will focus on how these women made use of their individual and distinctive literacies for social purposes.

Proceeding chronologically, the essay begins with Maria Stewart, the first woman born in the United States to speak publicly to a mixed group on political issues.[3] The lecture was delivered at Franklin Hall in Boston in 1832. Sojourner Truth is considered next as an example of an outspoken black woman who, according to some definitions, would be considered illiterate. Yet she was probably the best known of these nineteenth-century activists. The sources and uses of literacy for Frances Harper, Ida Wells, and Anna Cooper are also discussed. In acquiring literacy and developing their rhetorical skills, these last three women in particular were faced with the dilemma of representing the causes of those who themselves were without literacy. They had to address predominantly white audiences regarding the concerns of those who did not possess the literacy they so skillfully applied. In some instances, their very facility with language militated against the arguments they would make about the plight of their people. They were faced with the paradox of being both a part of and apart from those they claimed to represent. This was a necessary contradiction, for those in greatest need of representation lacked the essential literacy that would have allowed them to speak for themselves or to speak in a language understandable to those in power.

According to Census Bureau figures, in 1900, out of a black population of 6,415,581, only 55 percent were literate, with the highest concentration of illiteracy in the South. The Bureau considered "literate" only those persons over the age of ten with the ability to write in some language, while persons who could read but not write were classified as illiterate. Such an operational definition excluded many blacks who, in fact, engaged in activities requiring the ability to read. It was more difficult to develop writing skills because special tools and models for imitation were needed. Most contemporary scholars now apply a broader definition of literacy, one that includes the ability to read and write well enough for practical use in particular social settings.[4]

Interestingly enough, records show that between 1880 and 1915 young African American women attended school in greater numbers than young men. These statistics differ sharply from those cited in Hobbs's introductory essay regarding literacy rates among white women during the 1860s and 1870s. According to those figures, in 1860 illiteracy rates among white women were 2 to 3 percent higher than for men. In contrast, only seven black males attended school for every ten females, and by 1910 the literacy rates for black women surpassed those for men. This gender discrepancy can be accounted for in part as the "farmer's daughter effect," or the inclination of black parents to invest in the education of their daughters over their sons because they felt that women had a better chance of achieving their professional goals.[5] It should be understood then that literacy for the nineteenth-century black woman was not an unnecessary frill to enhance the image of ideal womanhood or to make her more marriageable, as was the case for many of her white counterparts. Literacy was an essential source of power needed to address the overwhelming concerns of a people newly released from slavery and struggling to acquire what had been illegal for them to possess only a few years earlier. Given the range of literacy among nineteenth-century blacks generally, how did the women under consideration view literacy, to what extent did they acquire literacy, and how did they employ their literacy to effect change? An examination of their lives and works reveals disparate experiences and motivations, but a common goal.

Maria Stewart

Maria Stewart (1803–79), the first U.S.-born woman to deliver public lectures to mixed race and mixed sex audiences on political issues, presents an interesting case. The sparse biographical details available suggest that she received little formal education. Born in Hartford, Connecticut, in 1803, Stewart was orphaned at five; she went to live with a clergyman's family until the age of fifteen, receiving moral and religious training. Her years "bound out" in this home gave her access to books, possibly including material on the art of public address, and fostered her desire for knowledge. In 1826 she married James Stewart and settled in Boston, where 3 percent of the population was black. She was active in the Massachusetts General Colored Association and a friend of David Walker, one of the association's most vocal members, who in 1829 wrote the incendiary *Appeal, in Four Articles; Together with a Preamble, to the Colored Citizens of the World, but in Particular, and Very Expressly, to Those of the United States of America.* Little else is known about her political activity except what can be gleaned from her essays and speeches. In 1831, two months after Nat Turner's insurrection in Southhampton, Virginia, her first essay, *Religion and the Pure Principles of Morality, The Sure Foundation on Which We Must Build,* was published in pamphlet form by the abolitionist William Lloyd Garrison and his colleague Isaac Knapp. The texts of three of her Boston speeches were printed in various editions of Garrison's newspaper *The Liberator* in 1832 and 1833. In 1832 Garrison and Knapp published a twenty-eight page pamphlet, *Meditations from the Pen of Mrs. Maria W. Stewart.* Moreover, in 1835 *Productions of Mrs. Maria W. Stewart* was published in Boston by the Friends of Freedom and Virtue. These writings embody the ideals of a woman inspired by God, exhorting her people to improve and defend themselves.

A disagreement about the extent of Stewart's literacy stems from comments made by Alexander Crummell, a black Episcopalian priest, in a letter included in a later volume also titled *Meditations from the Pen of Mrs. Maria W. Stewart* (1879). In the letter, he describes Stewart as having "less of the advantages of education" than her associates but as being "full of greed for literature and letters." He expressed surprise "that a person who had received but six weeks' schooling, who could not even pen her own thoughts, who had to get a little girl of ten years to write every word of this book [the 1832 edition of *Meditations*]—that such a person could compose essays of this kind and give expression to such thoughts and be the author of such a work!" Stewart biographer Marilyn Richardson suggests that Crummell's remembrance of what took place forty years earlier was probably flawed, since there is ample evidence that Stewart was able to write before she left Boston in 1832.[6]

What has never been questioned is the high value Stewart placed on literacy and her recognition of its importance, especially for northern free blacks. In *Religion and the Pure Principles of Morality*, she urges her readers to see that their children receive an education, even if they must hire private teachers. In that same essay she challenges black women in particular to acquire an education and to teach, asking: "How long shall the fair daughters of Africa be compelled to bury their minds and talents beneath a load of iron pots and kettles?" In her first public address, "Lecture Delivered at Franklin Hall" (1832), she laments the opportunity denied to the "sons and daughters of Ethiopia" to improve their "moral and mental faculties." In the "Address Delivered at the African Masonic Hall," she urges her auditors to "turn their attention to knowledge and improvement for knowledge is power."[7]

While explicit reactions to Stewart's speeches are not available, early nineteenth-century opposition to women's speaking in public was strong. Women who dared to speak out were often accused of not being "feminine" by those who assumed a natural connection between masculinity and public-speaking ability. In her first published essay Stewart expresses the resulting sense of isolation, proclaiming: "I stand alone in your midst, exposed to the fiery darts of the devil, and to the assaults of wicked men."[8] She may have indeed been alone in her pioneering act as the first American-born woman to speak on political issues before a mixed group. Yellin speculates that white women who read Garrison's *Liberator* must have known of her. Yet those women who later spoke out recognized Angelina Grimké, not Stewart, as their oratorical ancestor: "Either racism or class bias—or both—prevented them from identifying with Stewart."[9] In her 21 September 1833 "Farewell Address to Her Friends in the City of Boston," Stewart expresses her disappointment with the poor reception she received. Her final address clearly implicates the people of Boston in a negative campaign against Stewart's year of public speaking. She justifies her behavior by citing biblical and historical foremothers—judges, queens, messengers of God, preachers, philosophers, and orators. Inspired by God, she persisted in the face of opposition from the black community of Boston. But finally she abandons her efforts, proclaiming, "I am about to leave you, perhaps, never more to return. For I find it is no use for me as an individual to try to make myself useful among my color in this city. It was contempt for my moral and religious opinions in private that drove me thus before a public."[10] Thus her public speaking career lasted exactly one year—from 21 September 1832 to 21 September 1833. Soon after delivering her farewell address, she moved to New York and continued her course of self-education. She became active in black literary societies for women and taught school in New York, Baltimore, and finally in Washington, D.C.

Sojourner Truth

In some ways, Sojourner Truth's background flies in the face of the central thesis of this essay—that these women acquired literacy and used it to advance the cause of the racial uplift. Truth (c. 1797–1883) never learned to read or write. From her narrative we learn that her mother taught her to recite the "Lord's Prayer" in Dutch, along with basic religious principles. Yet it is probably true that she is the most famous of all nineteenth-century African American women and in her own time was known from the eastern seaboard to the western frontier. What then can be said regarding Sojourner Truth's "literacy"?

As its title indicates, Carleton Mabee's article "Sojourner Truth, Bold Prophet: Why Did She Never Learn to Read?" wrestles with Truth's failure to acquire literacy. Mabee concludes that Truth had opportunities to learn that she did not take. He points out that in Truth's home state of New York, slaveholders were actually required to teach their slaves to read the Bible, in preparation for emancipation in 1827. Mabee goes on to document other missed opportunities, finally suggesting that she had a learning disability of some kind, which at the time might not have been understood.[11] My purpose here is not to debate this question; rather, I include Mabee's claims as evidence of the difficulty associated with any attempts to understand the educational experience of women "whose words are described but not preserved." Truth clearly valued the power of the written word, for she traveled from the East to the frontier selling copies of her own story as told to Olive Gilbert, an abolitionist friend who transcribed it. She was selling her narrative at the 1851 Convention. She sustained herself partially through the sales of this written version of her life.

It seems more useful to ask how, in spite of "illiteracy," Truth was able to project such compelling arguments, leaving a lasting impression on those who heard her. Part of her ethos as speaker may have been to heighten her persona as an illiterate black woman speaking from the soul. She may have known that such a persona made her frequently harsh admonitions easier for her white audiences to accept. Frederick Douglass, clearly no fan of Truth, suggests this conscious creation of persona when he describes his initial impression of Truth: "I met here for the first time that strange compound of wit and wisdom, of wild enthusiasm and flint-like common sense, who seemed to feel it her duty to trip me up in my speeches and to ridicule my efforts to speak and act like a person of cultivation and refinement. I allude to Sojourner Truth. She was the genuine specimen of the uncultured negro. She cared very little for elegance of speech or refinement of manners. She seemed to please herself and others best when she put her ideas in the oddest forms."[12] Referring to the famous "Ar'n't I a Woman" transcription of Truth's speech at the 1851 Akron Woman's Rights Convention, black feminist theorist Patricia Hill Collins observes that "by deconstructing the concept *woman,* Truth proved herself to be a formidable intellectual," although she never attained full literacy. Collins here defines an "organic intellectual" as one who appeals to common sense and represents the interests of a specific group. She argues for a redefinition of "intellectual" that validates nontraditional, practical, everyday experiences as a source of knowledge. Fear may have caused mainstream intellectuals like Douglass to reject such thinkers as a threat to the social order.[13]

In another piece, written shortly before his death, Douglass comments again on public perception and reception of speakers like Truth. His language here disparages Truth's manner of speaking and questions what he perceives as an eagerness to reproduce those forms of black speech that allow society to sustain its stereotypical images: "When a black man's language is quoted, in order to belittle and degrade him, his ideas are often put in the most grotesque and unreadable English, while the utterances of Negro scholars and authors are ignored. Today Sojourner Truth is more readily quoted than Alexander Crummell or Dr. James McCune Smith. A hundred white men will attend a concert of counterfeit Negro minstrels, with faces blackened with burnt cork, to no one who will attend a lecture by an intelligent Negro."[14]

One might argue that these white preferences account for Truth's popularity in the nineteenth century and today as representing the convergence of the abolitionist and suffrage movements. Truth fit the stereotype better than her contemporaries. One Truth scholar suggests that "Truth's naive persona did not force her white audiences to reevaluate their stereotypes about black women, as did educated black spokeswomen like Mary

Ann Shadd Cary, Grace and Sarah Douglass, and Frances Ellen Watkins Harper. In a society in which most white Americans assumed that black women were subjects to be instructed and patronized, these better educated and less picturesque figures were hard for many of their white colleagues to stomach."[15]

It has also been suggested that some of those who transcribed Truth's statements may have resorted to a representational "white abolitionist's imagined idiolect of The Slave, the supposedly archetypical black plantation slave of the South," rather than attempt to approximate her actual speech.[16] Such a possibility could account for the linguistic range of Truth's existing speech artifacts. One can compare, for example, the language of Frances Gage's rendering of the 1851 "Ar'n't I a Woman" speech to newspaper accounts of some of her later statements and to Harriet Beecher Stowe's representation in her April 1863 *Atlantic Monthly* article on Truth, "The Libyan Sybil." Truth scholar Painter points out that the Gage version, which most know today, appeared in print some nineteen years after the event and that no contemporary newspaper accounts of the speech mention the "ar'n't I a woman" refrain.[17]

But such arguments, while underscoring representational difficulties, do not and should not deny Truth the compelling force of her arguments. Her appeal rests on more than the questionable renderings of her speech or the fact that most of what we know of her today comes primarily from the remembrances of white abolitionists. Her persona demands a definition of literacy—and of intellect—that transcends knowledge of the written word and takes into account the ability to exploit the word's rhetorical potential.

Frances Harper

Describing conditions at the end of the century, Frances Harper (1825–1911) in the epilogue to her 1892 novel *Iola Leroy* wrote: "The race has not had very long to straighten its hand from the hoe, to grasp the pen and wield it as a power for good." It was Harper who noted in a speech to the Women's Congress that southern black women were stronger supporters of education than men, calling mothers "the levers which move in education."[18] Understanding well the necessity for literacy among black men and women, she grasped her own pen and wielded it as a power for good for more than fifty years.

Born in Baltimore in 1825, Harper lost her parents when she was three. She was raised by her uncle William Watkins, minister and head of the Watkins Academy for Negro Youth, which she attended. By 1835, blacks of Baltimore had established a number of schools like the one Harper's uncle ran behind the African Methodist Church on Sharp Street. She studied the Bible, the classics, grammar, reading, writing, natural philosophy, music, mathematics, and elocution. She attended abolitionist meetings with her cousins, who were well known for their oratorical skills. Her uncle frequently contributed articles to such papers as Garrison's *Liberator* and organized a literary society. Harper completed her formal education at thirteen and took a job as seamstress and nursemaid for a family who owned a bookshop. In her spare time, she read extensively. Although one source indicates that Harper's early education was limited, when she left Baltimore at twenty-six, she was well educated by nineteenth-century standards.[19]

Harper employed her literacy to promote change through poetry, short stories, essays, and a novel, as well as through her speeches. After a brief teaching career, she became a lecturer for the abolitionist cause, one of the few women of the nineteenth century to earn her living with her oratorical skills. Her first lecture, delivered in New Bedford, Massachusetts, in 1854, was on the education and elevation of her people. This was the central theme all of her subsequent lectures. She was active in the Philadelphia station of the Underground Railroad and regularly sent contributions to William Still, one of its officials. After the Civil War she traveled extensively through the South. Frequently, these travels took her into hostile environments. She spoke to white and black audiences, stressing to both their common interests. She spoke on trains and once stood in the door of a church so that she could be heard by those inside and outside. She spent a great deal of time in South Carolina, finding the people there especially cordial.

Harper addressed feminist as well as racial issues. Her first short story, and perhaps the first published by an African American, "The Two Offers" (1859), relates the story of two women. One chose a solitary life dedicated to helping others, while the other married a man who turned out to be a philanderer and caused her to die of heartache. The story ends in praise of the first woman, who chose her career over marriage. Harper herself was widowed after fewer than four years of marriage, and she never remarried. In a speech at the Eleventh Woman's Rights Convention, she related how she was stripped of all her possessions after Fenton Harper's death in Ohio in 1845. This encounter with the male legal structure enabled her to identify with the white women in the audience. But only a year later, she announced her support of the Fifteenth Amendment, although it proposed to give the vote to the black male only. Some women, including Sojourner Truth, argued that such an amendment would encourage black men to exert further authority over the already-oppressed black woman. In Truth's words, "If colored men get their rights, and not colored women get theirs, there will be a bad time about it."[20] Harper, however, felt that racism was the more pressing problem; if she had to choose between race and sex, she would choose race.

But she was not insensitive to the special plight of the southern black woman. When she spoke to audiences of all black women, she accepted no payment. She spoke in the South against the poor treatment many women received from their husbands. Writing to Still, she observed, "The condition of the women is not very enviable in some cases. They have had a terribly hard time in slavery and their subjection has not ceased in freedom."[21] She rehearsed the plight of the female slave in her one novel, *Iola Leroy,* whose hopeful ending spoke to the desires of black women. The title character, a mulatto woman, faced sexual abuse at the hand of a slaveholder. Once the Civil War was over, Iola searched relentlessly for her family. After they were reunited, she married and settled in the South devoting her life to racial advancement.

Harper captivated her audience wherever she went, with oratorical skills nurtured in her uncle's academy and honed by years of experience. Most often she spoke without a prepared text, as this newspaper excerpt confirms: "Without a moment's hesitation, she started off in the flow of her discourse, which rolled smoothly and uninterruptedly on for nearly two hours. It was very apparent that it was not a cut and dried speech, for she was as fluent and felicitous in her allusions to circumstances immediately around as she was when she rose to a more exalted pitch of laudation of the 'Union,' or of execration of the old slavery system."[22] Regardless of genre—poem, short story, essay, novel—or mode of presentation, she took advantage of every opportunity to serve the cause of improving the plight of African Americans. Harper died in 1911, after more than fifty years of such service. Perhaps her life, more than that of any of the other women under consideration, embodied the ideal of literacy, in all its manifestations, for racial uplift.

Ida Wells

While Frances Harper championed the rights of African American men and women in almost all literary arenas, Ida B. Wells (1862–1931) applied her literacy primarily to the writing of fiery editorials and the delivering of forceful oratory at home and abroad. With a strong faith in the persuasive power of evidence, she relied in her speeches and essays on concrete examples and statistics, validating her arguments against the injustice of lynching and the treatment of black women.

She was born a slave in Holly Springs, Mississippi, on 16 July 1862, the oldest of eight children. After emancipation, she enrolled in Shaw University (later renamed Rust College), which included all grade levels. In 1878, when Wells was sixteen, a yellow fever epidemic took the lives of her parents and her youngest brother. Insisting on keeping the rest of the family together, she obtained a teaching job to support them. She eventually moved to Memphis, where she continued to develop her intellect, attending and participating in plays, concerts, lyceums, and lectures, and taking summer courses at Fisk University and Lemoyne Institute, which also served as a cultural center for the black community.

Her first years in Tennessee provided Wells many opportunities to apply her literacy to resistance. In May 1884, when the conductor tried to remove her forcibly to the smoking car of a train, she resisted. She brought a lawsuit against the railroad and won her case, although the railroad appealed and the decision was reversed in 1887. Her journalistic career had its roots in this experience, as well. After an article about it appeared in the *Living Way*, a religious weekly, the publisher invited her to write a weekly column for the paper under the pen name "Iola." Prior to that she had filled a vacancy as editor of the *Evening Star*, another small local paper. Recognizing the importance of making information accessible to those who needed it most, Wells carefully accommodated her writing to this kind of reader: "I had an instinctive feeling that the people who had little or no school training should have something coming into their homes weekly which dealt with their problems in a simple, helpful way. So . . . I wrote in a plain, common-sense way on the things which concerned our people. Knowing that their education was limited, I never used a word of two syllables where one would serve the purpose." The column in the *Living Way* became so popular that newspaper editors in other cities were soon asking her to write for them. By 1886 Wells's articles were appearing in a number of prestigious black newspapers, including the *New York Age*, the Detroit *Plaindealer*, and the Indianapolis *Freeman*.[23]

Perhaps the application of literacy to resistance that had the greatest impact on Wells and ultimately on society was a series of fiery editorials she wrote in 1892. The editorials appeared in the *Free Speech*, a newspaper of which she was part owner and chief editor. Her friends, three black

Memphis entrepreneurs, had opened a grocery store in competition with a white-owned store. The men were arrested for defending their store against white citizens who wanted to put them out of business. Before they had a chance to appear in court themselves, they were removed from their jail cells and murdered. When Wells spoke out against this act in an editorial in her paper, the offices of *Free Speech* were destroyed. Wells, who was in Philadelphia visiting Frances Harper at the time the editorial was published, was advised not to return to Memphis. She was soon hired by editor of the *New York Age,* T. Thomas Fortune, to write a column for his paper. Just as she had been asked to write about her lawsuit against the railroad, she was asked to speak and write about what happened in Memphis. Her first public speech on the matter was delivered in New York City in October 1892 at a testimonial in her honor. Speaking of that occasion in her autobiography, Wells also rehearses some of her uses of literacy up to that point: "I had been a writer, both as correspondent and editor. . . . I had some reputation as an essayist from schoolgirl days, and had recited many times in public recitations which I had committed to memory. In canvassing for my paper I had made talks asking for subscriptions. But this was the first time I had ever been called on to deliver an honest-to-goodness address."[24]

Subsequently she launched a verbal war against lynching that she waged for the rest of her life. As a result of her outspoken offensive against mob violence, the black women's club movement was solidified. In 1895 a group of African American women gathered in Boston to respond to an attack against her character stemming from her political activism. In 1896 these women met in Washington, D.C., to form the National Association of Colored Women, with Mary Church Terrell as its first president.[25]

Anna Cooper

Anna Julia Cooper (1858–1964), by the time of her death at the age of 106, had acquired a level of literacy and formal education surpassing that of most of her female contemporaries, black or white. An educator, Cooper devoted her life to spreading literacy among African Americans. After the war and freedom, she attended St. Augustine Normal School in Raleigh, North Carolina. An early feminist, Cooper demanded and gained admission into an all-male Greek class organized for seminary students only. She subsequently married the professor, George Cooper, who died two years later, in 1879.

In 1881 Cooper left St. Augustine for further study at Oberlin College, where a number of prominent nineteenth-century black women were educated.[26] She obtained the B.A. in 1884 and the M.A. in 1887, teaching at Wilberforce College from 1884 to 1885. Returning to Raleigh and St. Augustine in 1885, she taught mathematics, Latin, and Greek. She applied her literacy and training outside the classroom by establishing a Raleigh community outreach program. She signed a resolution submitted to the state by the North Carolina Teacher's Association claiming the need for "reasonable and just provisions for the training of the colored youth." Two years later Cooper moved to Washington, D.C., to accept a position as math and science teacher at Washington Colored High School. From 1902 to 1906 she served as its principal after it became the M Street School. Due to a controversy, which some claimed stemmed from the Du Bois-Booker T. Washington debate over educational preparation for blacks, the D.C. Board of Education declined to reappoint her principal in 1906. Cooper subsequently left Washington to teach at Lincoln Institute in Jefferson City, Missouri. In the fall of 1910 she was reinstated at the M Street School as a Latin teacher by a new superintendent of schools. In 1916, housed in a new building, the M Street School became Paul Laurence Dunbar High School. Cooper remained active in the school, suggesting its new name and writing the lyrics to the Dunbar school song. In 1925 she completed work toward a doctoral degree from the University of Paris, becoming, at the age of sixty-seven, the fourth African American woman to receive the Ph.D. Upon retiring from public school teaching in 1930, Cooper became the second president of Frelinghuysen University, an evening school for working adults. For a while the school operated out of her own home. Cooper served this institution until her death in 1964.[27]

Cooper biographer Paul Cooke describes her as "continually the scholar. She was in the library when Mary Church Terrell [another turn-of-the-century activist] was picketing the drugstores and cafeterias in downtown Washington, D.C. She chose the lesser limelight, while Terrell chose the Civil Rights route and carried the media."[28] Perhaps the capstone of her scholarly pursuits was *A Voice from the South by a Black Woman of the South* (1892), a collection of essays expressing the urgent need for literacy among black women. The first essay in this collection, "Womanhood: A Vital Element in the Regeneration and Progress of a Race," was an edited version of a speech she had delivered to black Protestant Episcopal priests six years before the book was published. Tracing the changing perceptions and treatment of women over time, the essay culminates in a discussion of the pressing need to educate the southern black woman, claiming that on her advancement hinged the advancement of the entire race. It is of little value, she argued, to brag about the accomplishments of the black male while the black woman suffered from lack of training and preparation. "Only the black woman," Cooper asserts, "can say 'when and where I enter, in the quiet, undisputed dignity of my womanhood, without violence and without suing or special patronage, then and there the whole Negro race enters with me.'"[29] For Cooper, literacy was essential for black women, who bore the primary responsibility for youth training, and she questioned the wisdom of the black Episcopal clergy who appeared to be ignoring them.

"The Higher Education of Women," the second essay, opens with a reference to a book with the curious title *Shall Woman Learn the Alphabet?* According to Cooper the 1801 book, published in France by Sylvain Marechal, proposes a law prohibiting the alphabet to women, and quotes authorities weighty and various to prove that the woman who knows the alphabet has already lost part of her womanliness. In refutation of Marechal and others, Cooper's essay chronicles the progress of women in higher education. Cooper claims for women "a special humanizing influence, the feminine flavor," applying here what Kraditor calls the argument from expediency, or for a separate sphere for women.[30] While the natural rights argument claims that women should be treated equally because they have the same natural rights as men, appealing to sameness, arguments from expediency emphasize difference. Thus Cooper tells her male readers that they need women because of women's unique feminine attributes.

For Cooper, there is clearly "a feminine as well as a masculine side to truth." Education, she feels, nurtures full development of the feminine side, and she laments the fact that this education is limited to only a few women. The argument made by many against educating a woman was that education would "destroy or diminish her capacity for loving." Cooper counters that the emerging educated black woman, rising from the indolent and wretched life of the past, brings this feminine "capacity" with her. In "The Higher Education of Women" she also narrates her experience of gaining admittance into the Greek class at St. Augustine College. Cooper ends this essay with a succinct appeal for gender equality—"not the boys less, but the girls more."[31]

Cooper begins both essays with a universal appeal for improvement in the treatment of all women, but she is keenly and personally aware of the special needs of black women and shortly turns in both essays to a discussion of their plight. The feminist and race-conscious ideas put forth in these essays prefigure the arguments many of her intellectual descendants would espouse. Describing the thinking of these descendants, who follow in the spirit of Cooper, historian Evelyn Higginbotham writes: "At the threshold of the twenty-first century, black women scholars continue to emphasize the inseparable unity of race and gender in their thought. They dismiss efforts to bifurcate the identity of black women (and indeed all women) into discrete categories—as if culture, consciousness, and lived experience could at times constitute 'woman' isolated from the contexts of race, class, and sexuality that give form and content to the particular women that we are."[32]

Conclusion

Cooper used the breadth and depth of her knowledge to express her strong belief in equal access to education for black women. Her own accomplishments demonstrated the possibilities that such an education could allow these women to realize. Her writings directly advocated this belief, while her teaching enacted it. Conversely, Ida Wells in her biography admits to a dislike for teaching and ultimately chooses instead a life of activism, first in the antilynching campaign and later with other social causes. Wells lived the kind of life that Cooper believed was possible for any educated woman. Frances Harper fell somewhere between these two women in her approach to the practice of literacy. She spent a great deal of time at her desk, composing poems, essays, speeches, and finally a novel. But she was also active in the Underground Railroad and traveled throughout South Carolina, Georgia, and other southern states delivering her message of racial progress. Harper and Wells both chose to employ their own literacy directly to effect change while Cooper focused on providing this literacy to others. Sojourner Truth was constantly on the move after her spiritual conversion in 1848. She traveled around the country, speaking directly to the people. She, too, was involved in the Underground Railroad and visited with President Lincoln. Truth's "organic intellectuality" empowered numerous audiences and moved them to action. The effect of her rhetorical appeal on white audiences is summarized in these remarks from Frances Gage, following Truth's famous 1851 speech in Akron: "She had taken us up in her strong arms and carried us safely over the slough of difficulty, turning the whole tide in our favor."[33] Maria Stewart, the first American woman to speak publicly on political issues, stands alone with her act of literacy. Although her speaking career lasted only one year, she managed to attract the attention of many. Her farewell address is, in part, a rebuttal to those detractors who objected to her behavior as inappropriate.

All these women placed a high value on literacy. In the words of Frances Smith Foster, they used language as "both a tool and a weapon to correct, to create, and to confirm their visions of life as it was and as it could become."[34] Yet it should be understood that these women were not anomalies. Throughout the century, hundreds of ordinary, unknown black women, as well as acknowledged educators like Charlotte Forten Grimké, Lucy Laney, Hallie Quinn Brown, Mary Ann Shadd Cary, Mary Peake, and Blanche Harris, subscribed to Frances Coppin's goal: "to get an education and to teach my people"—in the classroom, from the pulpit, through the written word. Literacy for the nineteenth-century African American woman was indeed the essential tool of change.

Notes

1. Janet Duitsman Cornelius, *"When I Can Read My Title Clear": Literacy, Slavery, and Religion in the Antebellum South* (Columbia: Univ. of South Carolina Press, 1991), pp. 1–10.

2. Dana Nelson Salvino, "The Word in Black and White: Ideologies of Race and Literacy in Antebellum America," in *Reading in America,* ed. Cathy N. Davidson (Baltimore: Johns Hopkins Univ. Press, 1989), pp. 141–53.

3. See Lillian O'Connor, *Pioneer Women Orators: Rhetoric in the Ante-Bellum Reform Movement* (New York: Columbia Univ. Press, 1954), p. 53; Dorothy Sterling, ed., *We Are Your Sisters: Black Women in the Nineteenth Century* (New York: Norton, 1984), p. 154.

4. U.S. Department of Commerce, Bureau of the Census, *Negro Population in the United States 1790–1915* (1918; rpt., New York: Arno Press, 1968), pp. 409, 403; for definitions of literacy, see Cornelius, *"When I Can Read,"* p. 8.

5. Figures on comparative school attendance are in Jacqueline Jones, *Labor of Love, Labor of Sorrow: Black Women, Work, and the Family, from Slavery to the Present* (New York: Vintage Press, 1985), p. 91. See E. Wilbur Bock, "Farmer's Daughter Effect: The Case of the Negro Female Professional," *Phylon* 30 (1969): 19.

6. Crummell quoted in Marilyn Richardson, ed., *Maria W. Stewart, America's First Black Woman Political Writer: Essays and Speeches* (Bloomington: Indiana Univ. Press, 1987), p. 94; see also p. 130 n.

7. Richardson, *Stewart,* p. 57.

8. Maria W. Stewart, *Religion and the Pure Principles of Morality, The Sure Foundation on Which We Must Build,* in *Productions of Mrs. Maria Stewart. Presented to the First African Baptist Church and Society, in the City of Boston* (1835), rpt. in *Spiritual Narratives* (New York: Oxford Univ. Press, 1988), p. 21.

9. Jean Fagan Yellin, *Women and Sisters: The Antislavery Feminists in American Culture* (New Haven: Yale Univ. Press, 1989), p. 48.

10. Stewart, *Productions,* p. 78.

11. Carleton Mabee, "Sojourner Truth, Bold Prophet: Why Did She Never Learn to Read?" *New York History* 69 (1988): 60–68.

12. This quote comes from a Douglass memoir, "What I Found at the North-

ampton Association," originally included in Charles A. Sheffeld's *History of Florence* [Mass.] (1984), rpt. in Esther Terry, "Sojourner Truth: The Person Behind the Libyan Sibyl," *Massachusetts Review* 26 (1985): 442.

13. Patricia Hill Collins, *Black Feminist Thought: Knowledge, Consciousness, and the Politics of Empowerment* (New York: Routledge, 1991), pp. 14–18. Collins here relies on Antonio Gramsci's distinction between traditional, academic intellectuals and intellectuals organic to their communities.

14. From a pamphlet by Douglass, *The Lesson of the Hour* (1895), quoted in Wilson J. Moses, *Alexander Crummell: A Study of Civilization and Discontent* (New York: Oxford Univ. Press, 1989), p. 245. James McCune Smith, a graduate of the University of Glasgow, was a New York physician and scholar; Alexander Crummell was the black Episcopalian priest mentioned above.

15. Nell Irvin Painter, "Sojourner Truth in Life and Memory: Writing the Biography of an American Exotic," *Gender and History* 2 (1990): 10.

16. Donna Haraway, "Ecce Homo, Ain't (Ar'n't) I a Woman, and Inappropriate/d Others: The Human in a Post-Humanist Landscape," in *Feminists Theorize the Political,* ed. Judith Butler and Joan W. Scott (New York: Routledge, 1992), p. 97.

17. Both Gage's and Stowe's representations of Truth's speech can be found in Sojourner Truth, *Narratives of Sojourner Truth* ed. Frances W. Titus, (1878; rpt. Salem, N.H.: Ayer, 1988). For a newspaper account, see the *National Anti-Slavery Standard,* 1 June 1867, p. 3; Painter, "Sojourner Truth," p. 15 no. 9.

18. From the 1878 speech "Coloured Women of America," in *A Brighter Coming Day: A Frances Ellen Watkins Harper Reader,* ed. Frances Smith Foster (New York: Feminist Press, 1990), pp. 271–75.

19. Carter G. Woodson, *The Education of the Negro Prior to 1861* (1919; rpt. New York: Arno Press, 1968), p. 141; on Harper's early education, see Monroe A. Majors, *Noted Negro Women: Their Triumphs and Activities* (1893; rpt. Freeport, N.Y.: Books for Libraries Press, 1971), pp. 23, 26.

20. Sojourner Truth, 1 June 1867. Speeches delivered on 9 and 10 May at the First Annual Meeting of the American Equal Rights Association, in *National Anti-Slavery Standard,* 1 June 1867, p. 3.

21. William Still, *The Underground Rail Road* (Philadelphia: Porter and Coates, 1872), p. 777.

22. Ibid., p. 775, quoted from the Mobile (Alabama) *Register* (c. July 1871).

23. Ida B. Wells, *Crusade for Justice: The Autobiography of Ida B. Wells,* ed. Alfreda Duster (Chicago: Univ. of Chicago Press, 1970), pp. 23–24; Sterling, *Sisters,* p. 73.

24. Wells, *Crusade,* p. 79.

25. Paula Giddings, *When and Where I Enter: The Impact of Black Women on Race and Sex in America* (New York: Bantam, 1985), p. 93.

26. Other black women who matriculated at Oberlin during this period included Mary Jane Patterson, Edmonia Lewis, Ida Gibbs, Fanny Jackson Coppin, and Mary Church Terrell (see Sterling, *Sisters,* pp. 192–213).

27. Louise Daniel Hutchinson, *Anna J. Cooper: A Voice from the South* (Washington, D.C.: Smithsonian Institution Press, 1981), pp. 43, 67, 146–47.

28. Paul Cooke, quoted in Mary Helen Washington, introduction to *A Voice from the South,* by Anna Julia Cooper (1892; rpt. New York: Oxford Univ. Press, 1988), p. xxvii.

29. Cooper, "Womanhood," in *Voice,* p. 31.

30. Cooper, "Higher Education of Women," in *Voice,* p. 48; Aileen Kraditor,

The Ideas of the Woman Suffrage Movement, 1899–1929 (Garden City, N.Y.: Doubleday, 1971), pp. 43–74.

31. Cooper, "Higher Education," pp. 60, 70, 79.

32. Evelyn B. Higginbotham, "African-American Women's History and the Metalanguage of Race," *Signs* 17 (1992): 273.

33. Truth, *Narrative,* p. 135.

34. Frances Smith Foster, *Written by Herself: Literary Production by African American Women, 1746–1892* (Bloomington: Indiana Univ. Press, 1993), p. 2; see Sterling, *Sisters,* for a discussion of the contributions of these women to the advancement of literacy.

8

JUDY NOLTE TEMPLE AND

SUZANNE L. BUNKERS

Mothers, Daughters, Diaries

LITERACY, RELATIONSHIP, AND CULTURAL CONTEXT

This book by Any yet unread
I leave for you when I am dead,
That being gone, here you may find
What was yr liveing mothers mind.
—Anne Bradstreet, "To My Dear Children" (c. 1660)

THE AMERICA LEGACY— the dominant story of its Manifest Destiny as well as its physical property—has traditionally been bequeathed from father to son. Henry Adams, as a case in point, inherited both the onerous burden of patriarchal greatness and a special insight provided by his privileged position. Adams suspected that the history he had inherited and continued to write was seriously flawed:

> The study of history is useful to the historian by teaching him his ignorance of women; and the mass of this ignorance crushes one who is familiar enough with what are called historical sources to realize how few women have ever been known. The woman who is known only through a man is known wrong, and excepting one or two like Mme de Sévigné, no woman has pictured herself. The American woman of the nineteenth century will live only as the man saw her; probably she will be less known than the woman of the eighteenth; none of the female descendants of Abigail Adams can ever be nearly so familiar as

> her letters have made her; and all this is pure loss to history, for the American woman of the nineteenth century was much better company that the American man; she was probably much better company than her grandmothers.[1]

Fortunately for those individuals interested in female literacy and life, a few women *were* privately picturing themselves in their diaries, which some dared to leave as legacies for their daughters. In fact, for some women literacy *was* life, for in their diaries they could shape and control their experiences by means of mastering language. As the hard-won legitimacy of diary studies has encouraged historians and literary scholars to bring more texts to light, the growing corpus of women's private writing reveals what may become a female genre. As certain images recur in texts by women geographically isolated but textually connected, it is clear that the world they inhabited—its gender ideology, its images drawn from religious and sentimental literary texts—was itself the text upon which they drew to record and recreate their lives. Images that appear in diary after diary—marriage as a lottery, Home as all, children as the major reason for living, God as ultimate rescue and succor—link women of the nineteenth century in a sorority of like perceptions. Women "culturally muted" in the public sphere were deeply connected in the private sphere of the diary, which, like Nin, Juhasz, Culley, Hogan, and others, we have argued may be the essential form of female autobiography.[2]

Studies of extensive diaries by women show that they are far more than authentic narratives of real life or artifacts of growing Victorian literacy. The diaries contain subtle, cumulative creative characteristics—metaphor, theme, characterization—that require a critical between-the-lines reading attuned to the literary devices of these seemingly disingenuous writers. Just as importantly, such texts reveal the careful attention paid by their writers to a sense of audience.[3] As twentieth-century readers of nineteenth-century diaries, we have found that an intertextual analysis of diaries written by mothers and daughters provides a particularly useful strategy for understanding such texts. Studying paired texts kept while the women were in the same household illuminates similar images as well as contradictions that form a dialogue between lived reality (however elusive that concept may be) and the shaped reality within the mother/daughter dyad.

In the specific texts that we are studying, the daughter's distance from her mother—first imposed by geography, then compelled by the mother's death—reveals how much the text for/of the daughter lived on in her life choices. Few sets of mother/daughter diaries are currently known, yet these texts hint at a genealogy of private autobiography. Writing a book (and most diaries are eventually perceived by their authors to be such) could be legitimated for a woman if she was leaving some sort of legacy for her children. The poem by Anne Bradstreet that opens this essay demonstrates how even an accepted woman author could find it necessary to "explain" her outrageous autobiographical act as a gift for her children. In their great thirst for a confidante, some diarists kept their books as a form of ongoing communication with a daughter still too young to be a companion. Henrietta Bacon Embree wrote in her diary: "how much I would love to have good friend live near me. I have never formed a particular attachment for anyone living here. I suppose I will have no confidant friend until Beulah grows large enough to answer in the place of one. thank God for my children they are so much company to me."[4] Note that it is the *daughter* whom Embree envisions as her future soul mate. Other women, like Madge Preston, confided their innermost thoughts in their journals while simultaneously writing letters containing more conventional confidences to their daughters. In Preston's case, as Virginia Walcott Beauchamp has revealed in a painstaking comparative analysis, the letters hinted at the mother's unease, yet at the same time they obscured a tale of adultery that Preston relentlessly recorded in the diary, which was later bequeathed to her daughter. This diary, then, forms a confidante bridge that initially protects the daughter and later whispers to her from the grave to form a fellowship of wronged women.[5]

The diaries that are the focus of this study are a rare gift: together they cover ninety-four years in over 6,000 pages of handwritten text.[6] The mother-diarist was Emily Hawley Gillespie, who began keeping a diary in 1858, when she was an unmarried woman of twenty living with her parents in southcentral Michigan. The dominant trope in the diary is Home. Emily's first home was "at Father's," where she considered herself the unappreciated eldest daughter. Nevertheless, Emily's diary was occasionally shared with her sister Edna, who was permitted to write comments in its pages. Emily Hawley wrote of trysts in language derivative of the sentimental fiction that she adored. In 1860 her diary mentions that a "bad story" about Emily was circulating in town, but that she would not permit the details of *that wrong story* to enter her diary. So, in essence, the "bad story" does not "happen" in her text. When Emily Hawley, still unmarried, moved in mid-1861 to the "Far West" of eastern Iowa to assist a widowed uncle, she confided more openly in her book/companion, characterizing herself as alone and homeless in the wide, wide world.

> Ah, home, that I could see thee
> Meet once more the warm embrace
> Of those I loved so long. Aye, those
> Who last gave the parting kiss. (1862)

The description of her courtship with James Gillespie, a neighboring farmer's son, is rather foreshortened and cryptic compared to earlier accounts of suitors. This brevity is another indication of the power of the diarist to withhold information and thus shape her narrative. A growing distinction develops in the diary between Emily's book and the book of Emily-and-James:

> this morning after the party had broken up (about 5) and all had gone to their homes I went in the parlor thinking to lie down on the sopha & rest, but James Gilespy came in, commenced talking, so we sat and talked till nearly eight (may we never forget the conversation that passed between us, how much would I give to know he really means all he said) then I went in the kitchen to get breakfast. (26 December 1861)

After her marriage to James Gillespie in September 1862, Emily confided even less within her diary; the entries now became short ones—suggesting the hard life, first of a new wife establishing a home, then a year later of a young distracted mother. Or perhaps the entries indicate that the Gillespies had formed the ideal close emotional bond of marriage and that the diary no longer served as a confidante. Emily calls James her "best friend" in the diary, a term that echoes much Victorian courtship correspondence.[7] If all of Emily's emotions were spent upon James, little would be left unresolved to write down in the diary wherein she had earlier expressed rather unconventional feelings. On several occasions Emily mentions asking James what she should record in the journal for that day, suggesting that at this stage in their marriage the diary was perceived as theirs. In fact, during the last days of her confinements, James's activities take up a good portion of the entries.

The sparse affect that characterizes Emily Gillespie's previously emotional journal can be interpreted through contemporary linguistic theory. During the early years of her marriage, her diary-writing style matches what sociolinguist Basil Bernstein calls a "restricted code." This code has unelaborated prose, few modifiers, concrete language, an emphasis on "how" instead of "why," and implicit rather than explicit emotion. The contrasting code Bernstein calls "elaborated"; it is extended, emotional, explicit. He finds that the restricted code tends to be used by people who share a commonality, while the elaborate code tends to be employed where social connections are weak. In these latter cases, language is used in an attempt to bridge the gap between communicators while still differentiating the speaker.[8]

Marilyn Ferris Motz finds this restrictive code in the diary language of nineteenth-century Michigan women and concludes, "There was little need to differentiate the self or to make explicit values which were generally accepted by the community."[9] In Emily Gillespie's case, her restricted language could reflect a period in her life when she truly felt in harmony with others, when there was little need to explain or differentiate her views. The rare emotional passages in the newlywed's diary refer to sentiments she would probably have tried to keep from her husband because they would differ from his: dislike of his parents, doubts over James's health, fears before childbirth.

The curt wifely diary, then, could indicate that Gillespie was so at peace in "the little family circle," so content to be "at home," that a few words sufficed. Or do the silences indicate that she repressed most of her negative emotions even in her dear diary (which may have been a book open to reading by James) as she strived to be a good-natured helpmate and a perfect mother? Some of the longer diary passages are in the confessional mode, in which she recounts a failure, then asks forgiveness and forbearance in her efforts to be an ideal True Woman.[10] Take, for instance, this entry from the summer of 1863:

> do my mopping, baking, &c; ah I am sad. O why? 'tis this that James came home last evening late. . . . O, Lord wilt thou & him forgive; for James is too kind to be spoken harshly to & God forbid that ever an unkind word or thought from me again. Ah, I feel forgiven now. (11 July 1863)

Only rarely does the diary contain intriguing one-line tags—"why am I blue?"—that are interspersed with the factual narrative, hints that there were incidents or feelings that Emily Gillespie did not feel it appropriate to explore.

Joan N. Radner and Susan S. Lanser's recent research on coding in women's folk culture provides a valuable framework for analyzing what might be happening in Emily Gillespie's early diary entries. Radner and Lanser define *code* not only as "the system of language rules through which communication is possible" but also as a "set of signals—words, forms, behaviors, signifiers of some kind—that protect the creator from the consequences of openly expressing particular messages." In describing and illustrating such coding strategies as irony, indirection, substitution, and trivialization, Radner and Lanser emphasize that, "because ambiguity is a necessary feature of every coded act, any instance of coding risks reinforcing the very ideology it is designed to critique." The challenge facing readers of coded texts, then, is that of inferring intention from the available contextual knowledge, a process dependent on understanding "the conventions for aesthetic production in a given cultural circumstance."[11] As applied to the diaries under consideration here, Radner and Lanser's theory underscores the need for readers to recognize and appreciate the role that literacy played in the diarists' incorporation of ambiguities and contradictions in their texts—and to exercise caution in interpreting a range of possible meanings in those texts.

By the mid-1870s Emily Gillespie's diary was dominated by her children as actors, audience, and ideal models. On 31 October 1875, she addressed her diary itself as her audience:

> Dear journal, 'tis your first sabbath day;
> Good deeds may your pages ever unfold,
> May our Children con thy lines over, and say
> "We love MaMas Diary, though it is old."

It was not enough for MaMa to write a diary, however; the children would also be raised in a tradition of journal literacy. While son Henry soon fell away from the discipline of diary writing, Sarah was a star pupil. Sarah's earliest diary was a tiny (3″ × 5″) copybook handsewn by her mother and given to Sarah when she was about five years old. It contains handwriting exercises and short sentences such as "I am a good girl" and "Learn your lessons well." A second early volume is filled with writing exercises such as "Be gentle, Ever be kind" and "Sarah is a nice girl in school."

Entries in her diary indicate that Sarah was being trained to become a writer and a good Victorian girl. Keeping a diary could be work, but it also had its rewards, especially for a budding diarist like Sarah, who entered into a relationship with her diary as a trusted confidante.[12] On 1 January 1877, at age eleven, Sarah inscribed a new volume of her diary: "Keep well this book and bear in mind / A constant friend is hard to find." The double message that girls like Sarah receive when they are encouraged to write diaries is described by Thomas Mallon: "The little girl is being trained to appreciate dailiness and ordinariness: her lot in life is the quotidian; her brother will do whatever transcending there is to be done. But the bright little girl soon enough recognizes that the cultivated inner life can be a much more powerful and dangerous weapon. . . . It may be in her diary that she discovers how to keep part of herself back, and to take revenge on those who have wounded what part of her has been exposed."[13]

The power of being a literate person was a value that Emily Gillespie infused in her children. It is clear from Emily's diary that James did not agree with many of her ideas regarding the children's upbringing. Emily valued extensive private education, light farm-chore responsibilities to allow time for reading, and fine clothing worthy of town society rather than life on the farm. It could be argued that she "feminized" her son Henry by turning him into a gentleman who infuriated James, in essence rendering Henry a second daughter-confidante.

Early indications of family strife within Emily's diary are characterized not only by what is included but also by what is omitted from individual diary entries, such as the one that Emily made on 11 April 1874:

> I am thirty-six years old to-day; the children wish they might make me a present. I kindly thank them—bless their little hearts. James made a stone-bolt-drag, and drawstone. I sew, mop, etc.:
>
> —This life is but a pleasant dream,
> Things are not *always* what they seem.
>
> *Chilly* wind.

This entry is significant for what it does *not* say as well as for what it *does* say. Although Emily expressed love for her children, Henry and Sarah, she did not do so for husband, James. Instead, she recorded what he did that day and what she did, their separate tasks perhaps a reflection of their increasing coldness toward one another. The "*chilly* wind" may well have been metaphorical as well as literal. By Christmas 1875, when Sarah received another blank journal book, the language in Emily Gillespie's diary clearly defined the lines of division within the family: "Jas wished us all Merry Christmas, we wished him the same."

Soon, however, metaphor was inadequate for naming the stress facing the Gillespie diarists. Both Emily and daughter Sarah became more explicit about James's abuses. At first Sarah merely repeated her mother's account, significantly omitting other sides of the story. As early as 5 March 1881 fifteen-year-old Sarah wrote: "Ma & Pa went to town. they had a '*spat*' I guess. ma told me about it." A year later, on 20 May 1882, Sarah gave a firsthand account of how her father had berated and belittled her mother and how she and her brother Henry had come to Emily's defense. She concluded by remarking about her father, "I'm actually ashamed of him & always will be." The next day, she wrote angrily about how badly James had beaten the family's horses, and she sarcastically noted how well he managed to hide his abusive behavior from those outside the immediate family: "He is too slick tongued to strangers and they *know* him—*not*."

While James was distanced from the rest of the family, the Gillespie women were bonded by the books they were writing. The women's diaries were collaborative and interactive. None of the diaries had a lock and key. To twentieth-century readers, this may seem unusual, but the concept of the diary as a secretive, well-hidden text is a twentieth-century phenomenon. Neither Emily nor Sarah kept her diary a secret from the other. Sometimes, after reading a passage in Sarah's diary, Emily would write a response there. For example, on 16 February 1886 Sarah, now a young country schoolteacher, wrote in her diary about feeling lonesome and discouraged. On 1 March Emily responded by writing this entry in her daughter's diary:

> Sarah, you said last night, "Ma write in my Journal. *I* can't." I just thought I would write a line as I saw it in the Drawer. I tried to not read a word, but Sarah my eyes do take in so much that the above could not quite escape. I get lonesome every day—only that I think of Henry & you. how you are getting along so well. his letters and your sunday visits I should almost give up. I am so thankful that you are both all my heart could wish and can I really appreciate the blessing. You must never get discouraged with the annoyance which some pupils are ever ready to give. do only the best you can and their cutting words and misdemeanor will give them the most inconvenience. *they* will *not* forget. There is no use for us to worry or be made unhappy at the folly of others. just let them pass.

In the case of violent abuses by James Gillespie, however, mother and daughter seem to have agreed to no longer let them pass and to break the code of silence, for now Emily's diary also began to explicitly recount the wounds of a long battle with James. More accurately, it was her version of the battle that she painstakingly chronicled and bequeathed to her children. (After Emily Gillespie's death, as the adult children reread her diaries, they sympathetically wrote in the margins near particularly gruesome entries comments such as "O, how she suffered," thus verifying her account.) Emily's diary of the 1880s records numerous affronts by James, from threatening glances to unkind words. No longer did Emily withhold unpleasant information from her book, which she now called her "only confidant." Her use of the male form of confidante could be interpreted as her transference of the role of male best friend from the disappointing James to the diary that she nourished each day. Several diary passages indicate that James's erratic behavior had been evident to Emily after only two weeks of marriage. The abuses existed in reality, then, long before Emily allowed them to exist within her diary. She wrote on 25 September 1886:

> I tried so hard to live through it without it being known by the outside world, suffered untold sorrow by hearing his abusive language, yet I did not dare to displease him. I have written *many* things in my journal, but the worst is a secret to be burried when I shall cease to be.

Why would the previously reticent wife now become the ruthless journalist who perhaps encouraged her daughter to join in recording an unhappy home? Was Emily's habit of detailing James's abusive behavior in her diary a way of striking back at him, of turning the children against him? Scholars have argued over this point, but it is possible that Emily's description of her husband's behavior was not done strictly out of wifely vindictiveness or out of an overwhelming desire to control her children's lives.[14] Rather, it had two more important and immediate functions. Putting her complaints into writing enabled Emily to verify her belief that her husband's abusive behavior was increasing in frequency and severity, and it validated her refusal to accept such behavior as a "normal" part of married life. Recording instances of her husband's verbal abuse might well have been part of a concerted effort to compile documentation essential if she ever filed for divorce on the grounds of inhuman treatment and endangerment of life. In addition, a sad tradition of "wronged woman" accounts dating back to at least the eighteenth century portrayed women who prayed to God for mercy and at the same time recorded physical abuse and incest for an earthly judge, should it come to that.[15]

Emily Gillespie's diary contains this complicated pattern of resistance and repression. On 4 March 1886 Emily wrote an entry in Sarah's diary in an attempt to explain her problems with James and allay her daughter's well-grounded fears. Near the end of this entry, Emily wrote: "Now do not be offended when you read this—for it is amusing after all to see how *silly upset* and *lose* their *sense some* do. No Sorrow so great but there is somewhere a pleasure mingled in." Emily's diary entry simultaneously emphasizes and minimizes the discord between herself and her husband. In keeping with the pattern evident in many dysfunctional families, Emily apparently felt the need to preserve appearances to some extent, to filter out perceptions that would lead her to see the true danger of the situation. She passed on to her daughter a double message: resist with outrage, endure for the sake of Home.[16]

The story that Emily Gillespie recorded in her diary hinges on the creation of characters, including herself, whom she follows through life. Her own persona, that of underappreciated and misunderstood striver, remains relatively unchanged throughout the thirty-year-long narrative. The characterization of her husband James, on the other hand, undergoes vast changes in Emily's diary. He is originally portrayed as considerate, taking time to pick wildflowers and have pillow fights with his young wife. Later, when the chores of farm life forces a less romantic routine on the Gillespies, James is described as an exhausted man who needs his Sunday sleep and is justifiably short-tempered due to his responsibilities.

Finally, however, when the dam of emotion breaks and Emily permits uncoded criticism of James to enter her book, he is transformed into a rube. The few words by James quoted in the diary are written in uneducated dialect and are often just utterances such as "Ugh." His glances are full of meaning; his mistreatment of farm animals symbolizes his bad nature. His verbal abuse of the children, particularly his exasperation over Henry, is seen as unnatural for a father. In essence, while Emily Gillespie ascribed to middle-class progressive aspirations for the children, James was cast in the older model of semi-illiterate family patriarch. To the outside world, James Gillespie was eventually known as hot-tempered. At one point he chased his family into town with a pitchfork and had to be removed from his property by the sheriff, who feared he would harm himself. James was put under court order to stay away from the farm and his family for one year. What factors compelled James to think and act as he did? As the two of us have mused on more than one occasion, if James Gillespie had written a diary, his side of the conflicts might be known. Unfortunately, no evidence exists that James kept a diary.

Daughter Sarah's diaries are the only other extensive record of interaction within the Gillespie family. In general, her version of events corroborates her mother's and in some cases even shows that Emily downplayed arguments and actions. However, close textual comparison of the few rifts between the two women's accounts suggests that subtle differences give enormous power of creative license to the diarist. Here is Emily Gillespie's version of the events of 8 October 1881 that precipitated a major quarrel during the completion of their new home:

> James help carpenters all day. Henry help too. Sarah help me. Mr Alcock here yesterday and to day—diggin potatoes. we retire to sleep, our hearts filled with sorrow, yet with a prayer and trust that all will end well. James has one of his fits of—well I do hardly know what—whenever he has to pay out any money he seems to think I ought to get every thing for myself & the children without calling on him for it

> Henry & Sarah went out & got him to come in, they were afraid he would hang himself.

Seventeen-year-old Sarah's version of the same event reads:

> At home, the Carpenters done all they could so Henry could finish. After they had all gone, Ma says "James what made you tell Mr Alcock (a man digging potatoes for pa & who owed Ma $2 for pickles) that you would pay him anyway & let it run any length of time," At which Pa said, "*Now* Emily, do for heavens sake dont bring up every little nasty thing, & commenced to tell Ma to pack up & leave."

In the daughter's account, it is Emily who picks the quarrel and James who reacts in self-defense. While a diarist cannot be expected to record every word of a heated argument, Emily's version is consistent with her dramatis persona: she is the martyr, James the lion. Sarah's version of this encounter and of several others, however, suggests more complex interactions in the Gillespie home.

Larger differences in the diaries of Emily and Sarah appear in the characterization of the Gillespie children. The mother presented them as ideal models of young manhood and womanhood, the very reasons for her existence. Sarah, in particular, was seen by her mother as "*myself living over again*" (13 Feb. 1886). Emily's idealization of her offspring may explain why many of the children's quarrels and misdeeds are recorded only in Sarah's diary. One incident shows Emily's omission of a very hurtful wrong done to her by Henry. Her diary entry of 11 July 1884 simply states that she is sleeping that night on the floor in Sarah's room (Emily no longer shared James's bed, sleeping instead in the hallway) and offers no further explanation. In Sarah's diary the painful cause is explained:

> Henry came home earlier to night and went up to Sellens' where Mr. Parkhurst is working and brought him down to stay all night. Ma & I came up to make the bed. Henry camp up & said Ma would have to get up early or Mr. P—— would see her as he has to pass her bed. Ma says—"You ashamed of Ma"? And he said—Yes in the morning—she did not look very handsome in the morning. And she cried & felt so bad about it. He did not mean any-thing wrong. But he and Mr. P—— think a good deal of each other and he wanted every-thing all right I suppose. So Ma put down some quilts at the foot of my bed in my room on the floor & has just retired—Will not sleep in her bed in the hall. I feel real sorry. Ma takes every-thing to heart so. Now I can't half sleep.

If James had insulted Emily so, his words surely would have been recorded. But to protect her son's gentleman persona in the diary, Emily Gillespie omits Henry's thoughtlessness: it simply does not "occur" in her version.

Emily Gillespie created and bequeathed to Sarah an image in her diary of the daughter as virtuous and pure. It was a lesson well-internalized, for in Sarah's dairy, especially after an encounter with a suitor, there was an obsession with purity: Sarah described falling on her knees to pray for continued virtue. In keeping with this characterization, Emily barely alluded to an incident that cast doubt on Sarah's purity and threw the women into a crisis of waiting. On the evening of 7 March 1885, Sarah missed a train connection on her way home from teaching and was compelled to seek lodging in nearby Delaware City. According to the elaborate account in Sarah's diary, a married man offered her the use of his side of his wife's bed while he napped on a chair. But during the night, the woman had a fit and the man lay sideways across the foot of the bed to be near her, making Sarah most uneasy. In Emily's diary version, this bizarre ménage was omitted: "The woman she slept with had two fits in the night. *no sleep*" (8 March 1885).

A week later, when Sarah's menstrual period had not yet started, Emily alluded to her worries, but did not impugn her daughter in the pages of her diary-confidant:

> Tis true she was in danger to stay where she did of being ruined, but I hope nothing wrong will ever befall her. it seems that fellow was a worthless man. O dear! it seems to me if any thing was to befall her or Henry to destroy their purity that life to me could have no more joy. (13 March 1885)

Sarah's diary, on the other hand, records her exasperation at having to defend herself from her mother's suspicions that the man might have assaulted her while Sarah slept. On 15 March 1885 Sarah simply noted in her diary that her period "came around" and continued, "Ma cried for joy when I told her. . . . I will never endanger myself again." This intertextual interplay shows the selective portrayal of the daughter as innocent in the mother's diary, while in real life Sarah was being questioned about her purity. In Sarah's book, the Delaware City incident was recorded in detail because she knew she was blameless, while in the mother's book the suggestive night did not occur, perhaps because she feared that her daughter was no longer innocent and thus was badly out of "character." The task of reliving the mother's life bequeathed to her was a grave one for Sarah, and Emily perceived that her own error during courtship linked her to other devalued women. She wrote: "I only hope Sarah may not see the trouble I have." In the margin of her diary, she added: "Ah, *marriage is a lottery.* how full of Deceit do they come with their false tongues and '*there is no one as dear as thee*' until one is married then '*you are mine now we have something else to do besides silly kissing*'" (25 April 1887).

Sarah and Henry Gillespie indeed became living monuments to their mother's ideals and sacrifices. As they went out into the world of work and college, she lamented their absence in the emotional language she had used twenty years earlier for her young husband. Emily Gillespie's final persona, that of martyred invalid, sadly brought her adult children back into the family circle. In their diaries mother and daughter concurred that the cause of Emily's edema was years of overwork and misuse on the farm. Both women's diaries quote James Gillespie as complaining that his wife had simply quit working and now wanted others to serve her. In this family, as in many others, the daughter bore the major burden of caring for her mother and completing the daily work involved in keeping the household functioning. As a result, Sarah had to grow up quickly.[17]

During the last months of Emily's life, she and Sarah exchanged roles as strokes incapacitated the mother, now physically dependent on the daughter. Sarah had access to her mother's diary, taking dictation from Emily and making many of the last entries. The two women's diaries for 1886 illustrate this point. On 26 May, after Emily had been disabled by increasing paralysis, she dictated a diary entry to Sarah, who wrote it down for her mother and then turned to her own book: "Ma cant write in her journal & wants me to. She is feeling some better is able to sit up awhile. She came very near dyeing. It seems almost impossible to keep her alive every night." Sarah also cried over her mother's will, which included a summary of James's wrongs; after reading passages of the diary with Henry, Sarah wrote that she cried.

Diarist Emily Gillespie, like all writers, created selective portraits of individuals in her diary. She made herself and her children the heroes of their own lives, relentlessly recording their martyrdom and achievements. Misunderstood by her husband, natal family, and most townspeople, Emily Gillespie enumerated her victories and others' irrationality in her book, leaving out "uncharacteristic" incidents. Her diary was a necessary element in Emily Gillespie's "psychic economy," to use Robert Fothergill's term for this type of journal: "the function of the diary is to provide a compensatory outlet for that valuation of [herself] which circumstances conspire to thwart."[18] Unfortunately, while the ideal Sarah within the universe of her mother's diary was a perfect nurse, upon Emily's death Sarah found the outside world to be imperfect. Sarah was twenty-two, unmarried, and in financial straits from not working while she nursed Emily; Sarah's diary indicates that she felt she could not endure her father's home for long. For a time her mother and the diary literacy learned from her were conflated, muted. On 24 March 1888, the day Emily Hawley Gillespie died at the age of forty-nine, Sarah wrote in her diary: "O, my poor dear suffering Mother. I loved her when she was here, but I believe I love her more now." Grief-stricken, Sarah wrote only sporadically in her diary for some time. Emily Gillespie's legacy to her daughter Sarah was a complicated one. It was the legacy of a caring, loving mother; at the same time, it was the legacy of a demanding, troubled mother.[19] The best of her mother's values were reflected in Sarah's eventual work as a teacher and citizen, and in her sense of duty to create a home for other family members. As we shall see, the legacy of literacy was also reflected in Sarah's renewed dedication to her diary, her "constant friend," her own "book of the self."

By some measures, Sarah's life as an adult woman began only after her mother's death. In her own diary Sarah recorded the cordial relations she had with a pawnshop owner, William ("Billie") Huftalen, whom she married in 1892. Billie Huftalen was more than forty years older than Sarah; and her career as a schoolteacher, superintendent of schools, and community leader overshadowed his as a pawnbroker. The diary that Sarah wrote while teaching is a remarkable document in that it records the darker side of the idealized one-room school, that rural icon to literacy: uncleaned outhouses, rude children, petty parents, and salary disputes. Sarah Gillespie Huftalen took literacy a step further, publishing in numerous magazines her observations and pleasing memories of school years. (Emily Gillespie, who had tried her hand at literary contests and was bitter over the success of inferior writers, would likely have been proud of Sarah's list of publications.) While leading an accomplished life, Sarah also kept house and had a companionable relationship with Billie.

Her diary depicts two Sarahs: the public figure and the homemaker. Sarah's diary weaves a rich, vital, colorful tapestry of a life. It illustrates how the diary as a form of autobiography can follow the daily rhythms of housekeeping to inscribe what Ann Romines refers to as *domestic ritual.* Romines defines what she calls the "home plot" as a "complex of narrative strategies" that "respond to, replicate, continue, interrogate, and extend the repetitive rhythms of domestic life, which emphasize continuance over triumphant climax and often subordinate the vaunted individual to an ongoing, life-preserving, and, for some women, life-threatening process."[20]

In 1914, after twenty-two years of marriage, Sarah Huftalen was widowed at the age of forty-nine. Diary entries indicate that Sarah felt sorry for her brother Henry, who remained unmarried on the homestead after their father's death in 1909. In Sarah's view, Henry had never had a home of his own, and she determined to provide one for him, complete with amenities that she had learned to appreciate, such as carpeting and indoor plumbing. Within months of Sarah's return to the family farm, however, the brother and sister reprised the abusive cycle of quarrels that had characterized their parent's relationship. Sarah's diary echoed her mother's. In November 1915 Sarah wrote: "I cannot feel my own free self at all. I feel tied to a granite post that dictates all actions here. . . . I feel too much in suspense. I wish he were married and I were too and in homes of our own." On 14 April 1916 she added: "I am so sorry I came. and that I allowed my things to be brought here. I hope never to misjudge and ill treat anyone. He seems revengeful and to harbor prejudice and bitterness of real or imagined wrongs. Is resentful and crushing. . . . I only wish that I had them [my things] in a little home of my own somewhere *to night*."

Having options that Emily Gillespie did not, Sarah started her deliverance in 1917 by first briefly finding a room of her own at a Chicago sanitarium, then by enrolling as a student at the Iowa State Teachers College in Cedar Falls. By 1924 she had earned a bachelor's degree from that college as well as a master's degree from the State University of Iowa in Iowa City. Sarah Huftalen taught in the Normal Training Department of Muscatine (Iowa) High School from 1924 until 1935, when she reached the mandatory retirement age of seventy.[21] She again returned to the homestead in Manchester, Iowa, where she and Henry lived for almost twenty more years. In her diary, Sarah recorded her daily farm chores, her visits with friends, and her activities in the WCTU and church organizations. She also recorded the wrongs done to her by Henry, with whom she would endure until both Gillespies were almost ninety. Like her mother before her, on occasion Sarah enlarged her personal complaint into a general criticism of men:

> Sometimes it looks as though farmer men think of a woman only as a cattle, estimate her worth by what amount of physical labor she can perform & wait upon them. I had faith to believe that I could make a home for Henry, my only brother whom I was taught to revere & to be a serf for from early childhood & ever have been. . . . [He] treats me as an enemy, dishonest, a foe or a villain; asked me what I came here for.

> Censors everything I do, ought to wear floor length dresses of gray or brown; my voice, "when did I learn to eat with a fork?" "why hold my left hand in my lap while eating," "doesn't look nice to see me walking on the road" & so on & on ad infinitum. Not a day passes that some desultory remark is made about one thing or another until I have gotten so it makes me feel limp & as though my knees would fall out from under me; I pray God give me courage and strength to endure. . . . Maybe I should go away; I've been tempted to a thousand times and not try any longer to make a home for him. He rather be alone. There is no home spirit or atmosphere. (Christmas Day, 1940)

By rebelling against the reverence and serfdom for Henry that she learned from her mother, Sarah broke the code of silence and undermined Emily Gillespie's depiction of the perfect son in her own diary. Sarah relived and thus revised the past. Like many a daughter, Sarah finally broke from her mother, allowing her own diary to split from Emily's, to use her literacy in its fullest power: to create the self. These two women and their books have much to teach us. Emily's diary embodied her internalization of the cultural ideal of becoming the perfect wife and mother, despite seemingly insurmountable odds. Sarah's reflected her internalization of the desire to become the kind of "good girl" she had written about in her childhood copy book, and to become the kind of True Woman her mother Emily had trained her to be.

Yet Sarah's horizons were much broader than her mother's. Sarah was well educated, became a teacher, traveled widely, and became a respected educator. Despite her success as a public figure, however, Sarah continued to place a high premium on making a home—first for her abusive father, James; then for her gentle husband, Billie; and finally for her inflexible brother, Henry. In this respect Sarah was like many women coming of age in the late-nineteenth- and early-twentieth-century United States, and, to some extent, even today. She experienced the complex pressures of being the homemaker as well as the breadwinner.

Sarah Gillespie Huftalen had no daughter who would cherish her and her mother's dairies. But Sarah had an expansive view of history and envisioned future generations as her heirs. In her final years she transcribed parts of her mother's early diaries and "published" typed excerpts by placing them in several state archives. She then carefully gathered together genealogies, family scrapbooks, and the precious volumes of journals and sent them to the State Historical Society of Iowa in Iowa City. Like Virginia Woolf's artist Lily Briscoe, Sarah could inwardly proclaim, "It is finished."

Emily Gillespie also had created two forms of lasting art—her diary and her devoted daughter. Sarah shared not only her mother's sense of history, but also her mother's version of the family saga as the desire to avenge those wronged, to set the record straight. For the most part, mother and daughter were of the same mind, and Sarah achieved Emily's ideal for her "to be all that I could not be." Yet, as we daughters know today, that is cruelly impossible. It is inevitable that in some ways the two women's stories would part ways, for however closely related, Emily and Sarah were also diarists with that itch to record what they perceived as truth. These nuances within the world of mothers, daughters, and diaries illuminate the full measure of their creative power.

Notes

1. Henry Adams, *The Education of Henry Adams* (1918; rpt. Boston: Houghton Mifflin, 1961), p. 353.

2. Both Margo Culley and Rebecca Hogan expand on Anais Nin's and Suzanne Juhasz's recognition of the importance of the diary form to women writing. In her introduction to *A Day at a Time,* Margo Culley analyzes the correlation between the nineteenth-century split into "public" and "private" spheres and the increase in the number of women who kept a diary, traditionally considered a "private" genre (*A Day at a Time: The Diary Literature of American Woman from 1764 to the Present,* ed. Culley [New York: Feminist Press, 1985], pp. 3–26; see esp. pp. 3–6). Yet, as Culley explains, diary keeping "always begins with a sense of self-worth, a conviction that one's individual experience is somehow *remark*able," as well as a sense of audience, whether that be the diarist herself and/or others who might read her text (pp. 8–9). Thus, a diary might have served as an especially appropriate form of life writing for many nineteenth-century American women because it provided a vehicle for constructing a self—and a sense of self-worth. Rebecca Hogan asserts that the diary's "valorization of the detail, its perspective of immersion, its mixing of genres, its principle of inclusiveness, and its expression of intimacy and mutuality all seem to qualify it as a form very congenial to women life/writers" (Rebecca S. Hogan, "Engendered Autobiography: The Diary as a Feminine Form," *Prose Studies* 14 [1991]: 105). See also Suzanne Juhasz, "'Some Deep Old Desk or Capacious Hold-All': Form and Women's Autobiography," *College English* 6 (1978): 663–68, and "Toward a Theory of Form in Feminist Autobiography," in *Women's Autobiography,* ed. Estelle Jelinek (Bloomington: Indiana Univ. Press, 1980), pp. 221–37, as well as Anais Nin, *The Novel of the Future* (New York: Collier Books, 1968).

3. As Culley explains, "The importance of the audience, real or imagined, conscious or unconscious, of what is usually thought of as a private genre cannot be overstated. The presence of a sense of audience, in this form of writing as in all others, has a crucial influence over what is said and how it is said . . . It shapes the selection and arrangement of detail within the journal and determines more than any-

thing else the kind of self-construction the diarist presents" (*A Day at a Time*, pp. 11–12).

4. Henrietta Bacon Embree, quoted in Harriet Andreadi's "True Womanhood Revisited: Women's Private Writing in Nineteenth-Century Texas," *Journal of the Southwest* 31 (1989): 179–204.

5. According to Beauchamp, "Within the private writings of Madge Preston two voices emerge. One is the voice of her diaries, the other the voice of her letters. The tone of the letters is sociable—a kind of written conversation. . . . If the self-portrait displayed in the diary is frequently less serene, it is also unstudied. When Madge writes in this genre, her pen does not pause on the writer viewed from outside herself. It records instead—often movingly, sometimes angrily—her own consciousness as felt from within. It expresses the torment of her private reality" (Virginia Walcott Beauchamp, *A Private War: Letter and Diaries of Madge Preston, 1862–1867* [New Brunswick, N.J.: Rutgers Univ. Press, 1987], pp. xiv-xv).

6. Both Emily's and Sarah's diaries are located in the Sarah Gillespie Huftalen Collection, State Historical Society of Iowa, Iowa City. Bunkers is editor of Sarah's diary, *"All Will Yet Be Well": The Diary of Sarah Gillespie Huftalen, 1873–1952* (Iowa City: Univ. of Iowa Press, 1993). Citations to Emily's diary are from Judy Nolte Lensink, *"A Secret to be Burried": The Diary and Life of Emily Hawley Gillespie, 1858–1888* (Iowa City: Univ. of Iowa Press, 1989). Subsequent citations to the Gillespie diaries will be by date and placed in the text.

7. See Ellen Rothman, *Hands and Hearts: A History of Courtship in America* (Cambridge, Mass.: Harvard Univ. Press, 1987); see also Karen Lystra, *Searching the Heart: Women, Men, and Romantic Love in Nineteenth-Century America* (New York: Oxford Univ. Press, 1989).

8. Bernstein's sociolinguistic theories are described in John Mack Faragher, *Women and Men on the Overland Trail* (New Haven: Yale Univ. Press, 1979), p. 132.

9. Marilyn Ferris Motz, *True Sisterhood: Michigan Women and Their Kin, 1820–1920* (Albany: State Univ. of New York Press, 1983), p. 78.

10. Barbara Welter lists four attributes of what she calls "The Cult of True Womanhood": piety, purity, submissiveness, and domesticity. Mass-market reading materials such as dime novels and "ladies'" magazines were instrumental in defining and illustrating these attributes. In discussing the effects of such cultural prescription on women's lives, Welter concludes: "The American woman had her choice—she could define her rights in the way of the women's magazines and insure them by the practice of the requisite virtues, or she could go outside the home, seeking other rewards than love. It was a decision on which, she was told, everything in her world depended" ("The Cult of True Womanhood, 1820–1860," *American Quarterly* 18 [1966]: 173).

11. Joan N. Radner and Susan S. Lanser, "Strategies of Coding in Women's Cultures," in *Feminist Messages: Coding in Women's Folk Culture*, ed. Joan Newlon Radner (Chicago: Univ. of Chicago Press, 1993), pp. 1–29; quotations on pp. 23, 7.

12. *Meeting at the Crossroads,* Carol Gilligan and Lyn Mikel Brown's most recent work on adolescent girls' psychological development, bears out the importance of listening to girls' stories in order to understand adolescence as a "crossroads," a time of "disconnection, sometimes of dissociation or repression in women's lives, so that women often do not remember—tend to forget or to cover over—what as girls they have experienced and known" (Brown and Gilligan, *Meeting at the Crossroads: Women's Psychology and Girls' Development* [Cambridge, Mass.: Harvard Univ.

Press, 1992], p. 4). In a different essay, "Telling a Girl's Life," Brown suggests that researchers consider the concept of *relationship* as a central determinant of factors such as the intended audience for a girl's story, the context in which she tells her story, and the potential risks she faced in telling her story. To assess such factors, Brown explains, researchers need to "ask who was this adolescent girl as a child and what has she to lose or gain from speaking about what she knows about herself and her relationships, what she feels and thinks, what she knows from experience. Listening to young girls . . . is the only way to fully understand the nature of the choice a girl at the edge of adolescence makes about what story to tell about her life" ("Telling a Girl's Life: Self-Authorization as a Form of Resistance," in *Women, Girls, and Psychotherapy: Reframing Resistance,* ed. Carol Gilligan, Annie G. Roberts, and Deborah L. Tolman [New York: Haworth Press, 1991] pp. 72–73). While we do not assert that twentieth-century psychological theory can completely explain the circumstances of a nineteenth-century girl's life, we appreciate the correlations between Brown and Gilligan's findings and our own observations about the cultural context surrounding Sarah's diary keeping.

13. Thomas Mallon, *A Book of One's Own: People and Their Diaries* (New York: Ticknor and Fields, 1984), p. 210.

14. In an unpublished 1990 essay, "Dependence and Autonomy in Mother-Daughter Relationships: Emily Hawley Gillespie and Sarah Gillespie, 1865–1888," Emily K. Abel maintains that Emily Gillespie attempted to "conform to the ideal of maternal self sacrifice" and "guardian of morality" (p. 4). Abel suggests that Emily tried to represent herself as the calm, gentle peacemaker and her husband as the irritable, violent instigator of family violence. Further, Abel argues that Emily used her diary, which her children frequently read, as a place where she could shape them into "children who bore none of the imprint of their father's character" (p. 11).

15. In the late 1800s Iowa law held that grounds for divorce included adultery, inhuman treatment endangering life, and desertion without reasonable cause for two years. Among the grounds for annulment of marriage were "impotency, bigamy, insanity, and idiocy" (Jessie Cassidy, *The Legal Status of Women* [n.p.: National American Woman Suffrage Association, 1897], p. 65). On the "wronged woman" tradition, see Daniel Shea, *Spiritual Autobiography in Early America* (Princeton: Princeton Univ. Press, 1968); see also Ann Taves, *Religion and Domestic Violence in Early New England: The Memoirs of Abigail Abbot Bailey* (Bloomington: Indiana Univ. Press, 1989).

16. Our working definition of *dysfunctional family* is a family that suffers from the effects of emotional, verbal, physical, and/or sexual abuse, or from the effects of chemical dependency. The dysfunction seen and felt by family members is often carefully hidden from outsiders. Invisibility is one of the hallmarks of a dysfunctional family.

17. In *Who Cares for the Elderly?* Emily K. Abel describes the dynamic that characterizes many families in which an adult daughter assumes the major role of caregiver to a mother: "Although residues from the past shape the experience of caring for elderly mothers, daughters discover that they cannot go home again. Even caregivers who feel most like children must have the personal strength to make decisions about what they perceive their mothers' needs to be. Moreover, caregiving punctures the illusion of maternal omnipotence. Although many daughters continue to look to their mothers for protection and security, they must acknowledge their mothers' growing infirmities and dependence. Even before a mother's death, the need to render care may signal the end of childhood" (*Who Cares for the Elderly? Public Pol-*

icy and the Experiences of Adult Daughters [Philadelphia: Temple Univ. Press, 1991], pp. 112–13).

18. Robert Fothergill, *Private Chronicles: A Study of English Diaries* (London: Oxford Univ. Press, 1974), p. 82.

19. Sara Ruddick's analysis of power and powerlessness in mother-daughter relationships is helpful in understanding Sarah's relationship with her mother, Emily, particularly as reflected in the language of their diaries. Ruddick notes, "From a mother's point of view, maternal powerlessness is very real indeed. Yet adults are not hallucinating when they remember their mothers as having immense power over their physical activities and emotional lives. Especially if she is isolated with one or two children, a mother's desires, moods, and style determine a child's options. Children learn from their mother a 'mother-tongue,' a sense of what can be named and what can be changed; who is to be feared and whose authority is only a sham" (*Maternal Thinking: Towards a Politics of Peace* [New York: Ballantine Books, 1989], p. 35).

20. Ann Romines, *The Home Plot: Women, Writing, and Domestic Ritual* (Amherst: Univ. of Massachusetts Press, 1992), p. 293.

21. For a detailed discussion of Sarah's career as a teacher, see Mary Hurlbut Cordier, "'To Be a Teacher': Sarah Gillespie Huftalen, 1865–1955," in *Schoolwomen of the Prairies and Plains: Personal Narratives from Iowa, Kansas, and Nebraska, 1860s to 1920s* (Albuquerque: Univ. of New Mexico Press, 1992), pp. 209–44. In her chapter on Sarah's role as an educator, Cordier analyses the importance of literacy in Sarah's own life as well as her emphasis on developing a systematized, rigorous curriculum for use in the country schools of Iowa.

9

MARYAN WHERRY

Women and the Western Military Frontier

ELIZABETH BACON CUSTER

THE FOCUS OF recent studies of western women has been on the woman pioneer or homesteader, and most of the attention given to frontierswomen's writings has focused on diaries, journals, and reminiscences. Only in rare cases did women write about the frontier for publication. A frequently overlooked group of frontierswomen are the military wives who accompanied their husbands on their campaigns. And military wives were surprisingly prolific in their writing about the frontier. More than any other group of frontierswomen, military wives wrote about their experiences and adventures specifically for publication. The published works of these women reveal a portrayal and perception of the West that is strikingly different from the conventional male myth and from various emerging theories of a "woman's frontier." These texts also serve to establish a sense of identity and significance by making a neglected group of women visible—first to themselves and subsequently to the historical process.[1]

The earliest published writing by cavalry wives took the form of the travel narrative. The travel log or journal was a sign of gentility; many of the emigrant women's diaries read like travel journals. Gayle Davis argues that diaries acted as mediators between the "writer's self-perception as a Victorian lady and her feared loss of that identity in the wild."[2] The travel journal, both private and public, filled much the same purpose. It was not until the mid-1880s, when Elizabeth Custer began to publish her experiences, that the cavalry wife's narrative seemed to really become popular.

The writings of Elizabeth Custer, which began to be published in 1885, act as a catalyst for change in the cavalry wife's narrative. Up to this point, the genre had primarily been a travel narrative about everything but the individual writer and her life. But beginning with Custer, the individual woman/writer becomes more of a visible central character in the narrative. As the biographical self becomes more visible in the texts, the textual self undergoes a social change, shifting from traits ascribed to what we have termed the midcentury True Woman to those of the turn-of-the-century New Woman. As Myres writes: "The more independent and less restrained lives they lived in the West made the women more aware of their own assets and abilities and made them more willing to step outside the 'woman's place.'"[3] Excluded as these women were from the male world and from history, the cavalry wife's narrative serves as a vehicle by which they were able to establish a sense of self and identity. These narratives and the wife's use of her literacy serve to combat that invisibility and allow her to emerge into selfhood.

Women on the frontier are generally viewed as fitting one of a few stereotypes. The most prominent is that of the "weary and forlorn frontier wife," a melancholy, overworked, prematurely aged figure, resigned to her fate and teetering on the brink of insanity. She is the hardy heroine with weathered face and vacant eyes as she looks out over the barren horizon. She is the "sturdy helpmate and civilizer" who "trod westward with grim-faced determination, clad in gingham or linsey-woolsey, her face wreathed in a sunbonnet, baby at breast, rifle at the ready, bravely awaited unknown dangers, and dedicated herself to removing wilderness from both man and land and restoring civilization as rapidly as possible."[4] This superwoman, adapted to her environment, was physically and emotionally strong, competently handled crises and emergencies—and did it all without complaint. Whatever the label—Reluctant Pioneer, Gentle Tamer, Madonna of the Prairie, Brave Pioneer Mother—she is the woman credited (or blamed) for bringing civilization, law and order, and religion to the frontier and putting an end to the Wild West.

An image related to the helpmate is that of the refined lady—in Barbara Welter's terms, the True Woman. The lady could be a wife, a schoolteacher, or a missionary; "too genteel for the rough and ready West," she is unable to adapt or adjust to her new environment and is "uncomfortable, unhappy, or is driven literally crazy by the frontier." Ultimately, her gentility leads to her victimization.[5]

The other major category of the western woman is that of the Bad Woman, generally associated with raw nature and open sexuality. Frequently, this image was projected onto the Indian "squaw"; for a white woman, it is associated with saloons, dance halls, and rowdy living. The antithesis of the hardy heroine or refined lady, the bad woman was "the soiled dove or female bandit, the Calamity Jane who drank, smoked, and cursed and was handy with a poker deck, a six-gun, and a horse."[6] Crude, unmannered, illiterate, more masculine than feminine: still, she had a heart of gold and was kind and considerate. Nonetheless, it is a negative figure and image.

Recent scholarship focusing on women's attitudes toward nature, landscape, and Indians, tracing the influence of race and class, and compiling social histories of prostitutes and mining camps has significantly expanded our understanding of the experiences of women on the western frontier, blurring distinctions constructed by the stereotypes. Frontier women's writings have been analyzed by John Faragher, Julie Roy Jeffrey, Lillian Schlissel, Annette Kolodny, Glenda Riley, Sandra Myres, Susan Armitage, Elizabeth Jameson, Ruth Barnes Moynihan, and others. However as the study of western women's history splinters and becomes more specialized, the cavalry wife is lumped together with the pioneer or the civilizer or simply remains invisible. Perhaps this inattention to the woman's experience on the military frontier is explained by these women's intimate connection to one of the most masculine areas of American frontier history: the U.S. Army. However, history is full of wives overshadowed by their husbands' reputations. Women like Elizabeth Bacon Custer are mentioned in biographies of their husbands, and their writings are frequently cited and quoted in those biographies; but the women themselves remain virtually invisible.

The military wife was not a "reluctant pioneer," in that she willingly accompanied her husband to the West; nor was she a "gentle tamer" or a "Madonna of the Prairie," as she rarely was allowed beyond the confines of the fort and left no visible influence on the frontier itself. The cavalry wife's experience differed from the emigrant experience of "passing through" to California or Oregon and from the experiences of the pioneer woman making a permanent home. The cavalry wife was a sojourner in that she lived on the frontier for a period of time, yet that home neither was nor was intended to be permanent. As a sojourner, she was not required to assimilate into or be assimilated into the dominant culture, because the sojourner adjusts the self to the new environment—social and physical—as best she can to fulfill her mission. The sojourner may learn about the new culture, but she remains relatively assured that the new environment or culture poses no threat to her own cultural identity because her stay there is short.

The cultural identity of a cavalry wife like Elizabeth Custer was not challenged: she remained an upper-middle-class white woman, often with servants; she adjusted to the physical and social environment of the fort and frontier; and while displaying a keen interest in the beauty of the land, she exhibited no desire to control or possess it. She was acutely interested in the behavior and culture of the Indians, but she nonetheless disdained them.

The attitude toward the frontier shown by the military wife often was quite different from that of the more permanent settlers. And the attitudes contained in published accounts often reflect the private feelings and reactions recorded in diaries and daily journals. Many of the books that the military wives wrote about their frontier experiences were composed several years after they had returned East, after their husbands—their link to the military—had either died or retired from active service. These books are not only accounts of everyday lives, but also tributes to their husbands. As public, visible narratives by women who left no mark on the West, these books are examples of resistance to women's invisibility. Further, what identity the wife had during that part of her life she chronicles was defined through her husband. Even as she extols the virtues of the source of her identity, the wife / woman / author ultimately subverts the focus on her husband and establishes an identity of her own. As a number of scholars have suggested, by the mid-nineteenth century middle-class women often used their energy to advance the status of the men in their family. As the social status of the men advanced, so, too, did that of the women.[7]

By writing publicly, conscious of the fact they were writing histories, these women were creating their own narrative about the Western Frontier and combatting their invisibility and lack of identity. This invisibility (which continues today) is compounded by the difficulty of classifying the writings of army wives. Most of the scholarship on frontier women's experiences has focused on diaries, fiction, or particular geographical regions. The texts by military wives do not fall neatly into any of these defined genres. They are not private diaries, for they were written for publication. Nor can they be considered as fiction, even if one takes into account their various historical inaccuracies. Further, their frontier experiences range from Texas through the Southwest, to Nevada, Wyoming, and the central Great Plains.

Of the dozen or so cavalry wives who eventually wrote about their experiences, Elizabeth Bacon Custer is perhaps the most influential, although neglected until recently. Even in the surge of scholarship in the area of women and the western frontier, Elizabeth Custer has been virtually ignored. Although she is mentioned by several scholars in their research, she is seldom more than a footnote or a passing reference; only once has Custer received any direct attention or extended individual treatment. In a recent book, Shirley Leckie argues that Elizabeth Custer is able to create the Custer myth by building on middle-class gender roles and that by being the "model" wife, she—not George Custer—made his career and reputation.[8]

Elizabeth Bacon was born in 1842 in Monroe, Michigan, the only child of Judge Daniel Bacon and Sophia Page Bacon. When her mother died in 1854, Elizabeth was sent to the local girls' seminary, where she boarded until her graduation as valedictorian of her class in 1862. Custer was a product of what Welter identifies as the Cult of True Womanhood—pious, chaste, submissive.[9] Elizabeth Custer, as a properly raised, upper-middle-class "true woman," would have acknowledged her own submission to and dependence on her husband and his activities, and she would have defined herself in terms of her relationship to George Custer. Thus, her seeming preoccupation with "the General" may be only a "natural" consequence of nineteenth-century culture and education.

After George Custer was killed at Little Bighorn, Custer needed to support herself. There was no annuity or army benefits per se, George Custer's salary had not been particularly high, nor had he been particularly frugal. Soon Custer found herself in financial straits, and acting on the advice of some friends, she wrote a book about her life with Custer and her adventures on the frontier. Eventually she produced three books and several articles. Written in reverse order of the events they retell, *Boots and Saddles* (1885) covers 1873–76, *Tenting on the Plains* (1887) 1863–67, and *Following the Guidon* (1890) 1867–69. Her articles appeared in *Lippincott's*, *Harper's Bazar,* and *Saturday Review.*[10]

That Custer would turn to writing is not surprising. She received from her father a diary for her ninth birthday in which she made intermittent entries for nearly ten years. Her early entries, typical of a young schoolgirl, were sometimes just a few lines. However, later entries became more detailed, particularly those following the death of her mother. Earning a higher education than most women in the century, she graduated from Boyd Seminar (Young Ladies Seminary and Collegiate Institute) of Monroe, Michigan, modeled on Willard's Troy Female Seminary. She took elocution lessons and, as valedictorian in 1862, read her speech: an essay on "Crumbs," or the importance of everyday events. As Leckie tells us, the *Detroit Free Press* reported Libbie's speech "one of the best."[11] She met her husband at the Boyds' home at a social gathering. As an officer's wife, Custer gained a reputation of being a sparkling conversationalist, a quality that carried over into her writing. She wrote as if carrying on a conversation with friends rather than in a high-toned literary style. It is entirely possible that she helped George Custer write and compile several of his published articles.

Custer's trilogy of frontier experiences has been critically treated as a defense of George Armstrong Custer's reputation. Jane R. Stewart, editor of the reprints of Custer's works, claims that "all of these volumes were defensive in that they projected the Custer image that she wanted the American people to accept." Stewart implicitly condemns Custer for being "the undaunted champion of her husband's reputation." Stewart overtly criticizes Custer for her inaccuracy about and omission of various incidents and details regarding George Custer's military experience.[12] Stewart assumes that any value of Custer's works is necessarily connected to George Custer. To be sure, Custer wrote to keep the memory of George Armstrong Custer "before his country," but her books are much more than just the story of George Custer's frontier career. Stewart dismisses the possibility that these works may not be George Custer's story but rather that of Elizabeth Custer. She thereby completely misses one of the most important and interesting aspects of Custer's writings: they are, by Custer's own acknowledgement, *her* story. In the preface to *Boots and Saddles,* Custer wrote: "Very little has been written regarding the domestic life of any army family, and yet I cannot believe it is without interest."[13] Today, over a century later, this same void exists: very little has been written about women and the military frontier.

Regardless of whether Elizabeth Custer wrote to defend and promote the reputation of George Armstrong Custer, her writings are ultimately not about him. He may be the occasion of her experiences, but he is not finally the subject of them. By concentrating on domestic issues and by placing the importance of her husband in the forefront, Custer was reinforcing socially accepted gender roles and instructing other women by example in how to be model wives. In these texts, Custer never considers herself to be anything but a proper Victorian woman and widow. She justifies her career and texts as "serving didactic and inspirational purposes," using the constraints of gender roles, both male and female, to forward her cause. While extolling George Custer's virtues, she silences his critics: as Leckie asks, "What officer or enemy of Custer would have had the temerity or callousness to disagree openly with a bereaved and loving spouse?"[14]

Elizabeth Custer claims that she "was the only officer's wife who always followed the regiment." Not only did she partake in those adventures because her husband wanted her there, she enjoyed the camping and the adventure. Custer later became a professional writer and journalist, building her career on her frontier experiences. Although she could not have seen it or described it this way, she outgrew her Victorian culture, becoming a True Woman who metamorphoses into a New Woman. Thus she does more than mark a transition in the genre of the personal travel narrative. She herself is a symbol of a cultural transformation in the ideals of American womanhood. While her reputation and legacy derive from her actions as the devoted Victorian wife and loving widow, her conflicted narrative of frontier life underscores the change.

Women's perceptions of the frontier are in sharp contrast to the Great American Myth. Custer's experience on the frontier lies directly opposed to the frontier adventure stories of James Fenimore Cooper, Francis Parkman Jr. and others. The most telling difference between Custer's frontier and that of the male adventurers is in her perception and portrayal of the frontier itself. To Parkman, the frontier was a "land of promise" offering opportunity and rejuvenation. To Custer, it was "the Great American Desert." [15]

Although she chose adventure over staying safely in Michigan, Custer's attitude toward the "challenges" of the frontier is one of fear, dread, and trepidation, if not outright dislike. While her husband was "delighted" at the transfer to the Dakota Territory, to Custer it seemed as if they "were going to Lapland." Rather than admiring the beauty of nature, it seemed to her that "no spot could be more utterly desolate." Later she claims that "it seems strange that anyone stationed at such a post had not gone stark mad." [16]

Custer did not appear to much like any of the Plains. In addition to making disparaging remarks about Kansas and Dakota, she expressed disgust about Texas and its inhabitants: "Small, low log huts, consisting of one room each . . . were the customary architecture. The windows and doors were filled with the vacant faces of the filthy children of poor white trash. . . . The men and women slouched and skulked around the cabins . . . and every sign of abject, loathsome poverty was visible." [17]

What Custer seems to reject most is that which the frontier myth vaunts most: individualism, nature, the "noble savage." She instead presents a story of tolerance, forced submission, and quiet suffering. Custer must teach herself to endure the hardships and discomforts of frontier life as she accompanies her husband. Women often did not have any choice in their westward movement. As wives, daughters, or sisters they went West because there "was no way for them not to go once the decision was made" by the patriarch.[18] The American frontier myth offers men heroism and space, the opportunity for rebellion and nonconformity; but this freedom is not offered to women. In fact, the very values that the male is escaping are assigned to the white females: constrictions, obligations, and capitulation. Women are unable to respond to the West's egalitarian grandeur; they may not participate in the adventure, independence, and freedom—that is reserved only for the men.[19]

Hence, the most detailed parts of *Boots and Saddles* are those incidents that focus on domestic and social concerns, activities in which Custer is a participant, not an outside observer. Custer expresses an almost continual need to create or establish a "home" or at least a sense of hominess. She complains about the condition and treatment of carpets, discusses the difficulties of keeping "the 'invisible of a woman's toilet' from utter destruction" on a windy clothesline, and relates such social pastimes as sewing bees, sleighing parties, and other activities.[20] Even when she is with the troops in a one-night encampment, her descriptions focus on the placement and distribution of her domestic furnishings. However, when relating incidents and adventures such as the capture of Rain-in-the-Face and the recapture of the garrison's stock herd, Custer is clearly a watcher of the action: she is observing, not participating in, the male adventure. Woman, in the frontier myth, is a distant and distinct "Other."

Throughout her writings, Custer's fear of the frontier is pervasive, and she fears many different aspects of it: the land and environment itself, the Indians, and the constant threat to herself or loved ones of death. She also reveals an almost constant struggle to retain and maintain her femininity, a quality that is constantly under attack by the harshness of the frontier. Rather than treating her feminine traits in positive terms, Custer tends to see them in terms of weaknesses: lack of courage, inability to shoot, fear of snakes, lack of physical endurance. She is not allowed an inherent pride in either her femininity or in her strength and perseverance.

However, Custer's rhetoric subverts itself. While chastising herself for being cowardly, weak, or irrational, she reflects on the natural courage, tolerance, and resilience of women: "When a woman has come out of danger, she is too utterly a coward by nature not to dread enduring the same thing again; but it is something to know that she is equal to it. Even though she may tremble and grow faint in anticipation, having once been through it, she can count on rising to the situation when the hour actually comes."[21] Another part of retaining her femininity appears in Custer's emphasis on maintaining connections with other women, the East, and "civilization." Throughout *Boots and Saddles,* she places more value and emphasis on the concept of community than on the individualism advocated by the frontier myth. This community occurs in a variety of contexts. Custer recounts family birthday parties and dinners, evening gatherings, and countless social functions like masquerades, dances, and private theatricals.

Perhaps the most visible type of community is that created by female bonding. While women, especially army wives, do not have to be brave and strong, they do have to wait—and this they often did together: "The women, with one instinct, gathered together" (*Boots*, p. 132). Custer takes comfort in numbers and stresses the importance of the women's interdependence: "The women met together every day and read aloud in turn. . . . We feared to disagree even over trifles, for if we did it might end in our losing our only companionship" (p. 156). There is a sense of empathy and compassion in her treatment of other women and their frontier experiences, and she often refers to them in terms of "patience" and "endurance."

To Custer and her female companions, motherhood on the frontier presented special problems. When witnessing a mother's grief at the death of a child, Custer recalls that "it seemed to me her lot was too hard for human endurance. Every sorrow seemed much worse out there" (p. 100). Not only did the sorrows intensify, but occasions that might have been considered as joyous in the East became reasons for concern. Pregnancy was viewed as a time of "coming peril": "Instead of rejoicing, as we would have done in the States over the sweet privilege of maternity, we cried and were almost disconsolate" (p. 164). Death, birth, and waiting served to strengthen and tighten the small female population into a community.

The sense of community is heightened by Custer's rhetorical use of the plural, "we" and "our." She seldom does anything or goes anywhere alone; she is always accompanied by husband, escort, female friend(s), or servant. Her life was a communal one. This sense of companionship and community is at odds with the individualism of a frontiersman like Boone or Bumppo. Furthermore, it extends beyond the limits of the fort. At several points Custer draws specific comparisons between life in the "States" and her life in that "God-forgotten land" (p. 157). There seems to be an unspoken need to remain connected to the East and the more "civilized" society there. Unlike the frontier myth, mail and letters are very important to Custer.

Custer is clearly conscious of her status as an officer's wife and enjoys being a commanding officer's lady. Yet when she discusses military wives, their value, and their place on the frontier, another contradiction appears.

On the one hand, "A woman on the frontier is so cherished and appreciated. . . . In twenty little ways the officers spoiled us" (p. 101). However, "the book of army regulations makes no provision for them, but in fact ignores them entirely" (p. 105). Officially, wives were simply "camp followers." Custer indignantly responded that if regulations could be so detailed as to list the "number of hours that bean soup should boil, that it would be natural to suppose that a paragraph or two might be wasted on an officer's wife!" (p. 105). Passages like this make clear that there is more to Custer's narrative than a recounting of George Custer's military exploits.

Like many frontierswomen, Custer's treatment of Native Americans seems ambivalent, wavering between fear and contempt, curiosity and sympathy. For obvious reasons, though, one might expect Custer's portrayal and treatment of Indians—especially the Sioux and Cheyenne—to be less positive than that of others. For her, there are no noble savages. There are Indian scouts, peaceful or reservation Indians, and warlike or unfriendly Indians; but to Custer "Indians were Indians" (p. 57). Earlier, in a private letter, Custer expressed sympathy for the Indians massacred in the Battle of the Washita: "It confused my sense of justice. Doubtless the white men were right, but were the Indians entirely wrong? After all these broad prairies had belonged to them."[22] Nonetheless, for the most part the picture Custer paints of the Indians is not complimentary. When recounting the "Strong Heart" Dance of the Arikaree, she virtually compares the atmosphere to hell: "When we left the unearthly music, the gloom, and the barbaric sights . . . it seemed as if we had escaped from pandemonium" (*Boots,* p. 111). Whether Army scouts or unfriendly tribes, Custer regards the Indians as ugly, lazy, slovenly, and filthy. In describing visits to or from Indians, her tone is most frequently one of condescension.

Indians were the source of Custer's greatest fear, and it was a fear particular to women: "My danger in connection with the Indians was two-fold. I was in peril from death or capture by the savages, and liable to be killed by my own friends to prevent my capture" (p. 56). Later, she admits that she did "not think the actual fear of death was thought of so much as the all-absorbing terror of capture" (p. 133). This acute fear of capture indicates the intensity of contemporary racial taboos that had been acculturated into white women.

Despite her derogatory, even hostile, depiction of Indians, Custer spends a surprising amount of space and shows unexpected concern illustrating their mistreatment at the hands of whites. Because most Native

Americans neither read nor wrote English, the whites made the Indians the butt of jokes: "Each [officer] saluted him, and each vied with the other in pouring forth a tirade of forcible expletives . . . in just as suave a voice as if their words had been genuine flattery" (p. 65). The Indian became an object of amusement and humor to the privileged, English-speaking class. Custer also displays sympathy and compassion when the Indians suffer from starvation during the winter of 1874–75, is dismayed at the U.S. government's refusal of food and aid, and expresses disgust at the reservation agent's cheating of the Indians. Custer herself seems to be torn between a humane compassion for the Indians and an acculturated abhorrence of them. For all of her fear of the Indians, she exhibits an almost obsessive fascination with them, especially their habits, behavior, and dress. At one point, she comments that "they were gorgeous in full dress" (p. 175).

Boots and Saddles ends with the official word of the results of the Little Bighorn encounter, which, quite logically, ends her life in Dakota. However, her last words have nothing to do with George Custer or the frontier; nor does she comment on the battle / massacre itself or its deadly consequences for those involved. Custer's final words are about the effect of those male actions on women: "This battle wrecked the lives of twenty-six women . . ." (p. 222). Custer's comments about the "women who weep" and "walk on alone and in the shadow" reveals what is still "a largely unexplored consequence of the western male's obsession with violence: that women are often the victims of the frontier's celebrated freedom."[23]

More than anything else, Custer demonstrates the sort of dual (non)-existence of many nineteenth-century women. She went West willingly, not reluctantly, because it was "infinitely worse to be left behind" (*Boots,* p. 60). But she was no kind of pioneer, for she had very little engagement with the land around her. The possibility of considering the Plains as "Edenic" appears to be anathema to Custer. Paradoxically, despite the fact that her writings contain a positive tone and relay a positive experience, Custer quite clearly disliked the West, preferring instead the "civilized" society of the East, and, when the time came for her to return, she was quite glad to leave the frontier.

Regardless of whether Elizabeth Custer wrote to defend and promote the reputation of George Armstrong Custer, her writings are ultimately not about him, but about women's domestic life on the frontier. Custer's books and articles reveal significant information and insights, implicit and explicit, about a virtually untapped part of our history. The paradox created by the duality of Custer's rhetoric reflects the conflicting demands that Victorian society made on women. And while Custer is ultimately a victim of the male frontier myth, she does seem to have reaped some benefit from it. Implicit throughout her writings is the awareness that women are not a weaker sex; they are only a different sex.

The cavalry wife's public narrative challenges the dominant American myths in multiple ways, varying from text to text. Despite these differences, their variety of approaches to their various subjects, and their different purposes, they represent a genre of writing by a type of writer—but not one that plays on generic stereotypes like "reluctant pioneer" or "gentle tamer." The writers are all sojourners, but of a distinct kind: their different texts offer us a re-vision, a new interpretation, of a frontier that was unique to the female sojourner.[24]

Notes

1. See, for example, Martha Mitten Allen, *Traveling West: Nineteenth Century Women and the Overland Routes* (El Paso: Texas Western Press, 1987); Susan H. Armitage, "Reluctant Pioneers," in *Women and Western American Literature,* ed. Helen Winter Stauffer and Susan J. Rosowski (Troy, N.Y.: Whitson, 1982), pp. 40–51; Annette Kolodny, *The Land before Her: Fantasy and Experience of the American Frontiers, 1630–1860* (Chapel Hill: Univ. of North Carolina Press, 1984); Dawn Lander, "Eve Among the Indians," in *The Authority of Experience: Essays in Feminist Criticism,* ed. Arlyn Diamond and Lee R. Edwards (Amherst: Univ. of Massachusetts Press, 1977), pp. 194–211; Sandra L. Myres, "Romance and Reality on the American Frontier: Views of Army Wives." *Western Historical Quarterly* 13 (1982): 409–24, and her *Westering Women and the Frontier Experience, 1800–1915* (Albuquerque: Univ. of New Mexico Press. 1982).

2. Gayle R. Davis, "Women's Frontier Diaries: Writing for Good Reason," *Women's Studies* 14 (1987): 7.

3. Myres, "Romance and Reality," p. 426.

4. Myres, *Westering Women, p.* 2.

5. Barbara Welter, "The Cult of True Womanhood, 1820–1860," *American Quarterly* 18 (1966): 151–74. The quotation is from Armitage, "Reluctant Pioneers," p. 12. See also Beverly J. Stoeltje, "'A Helpmate for Man Indeed': The Image of the Frontier Woman," *Journal of American Folklore* 88 (1975): 25–41.

6. Myres, *Westering,* p. 4.

7. See Jane E. Rose in this volume.

8. Shirley A. Leckie, *Elizabeth Bacon Custer and the Making of a Myth* (Norman: Univ. of Oklahoma Press, 1993).

9. See Welter, "Cult."

10. Elizabeth B. Custer, *"Boots and Saddles"; or, Life in Dakota with General Custer,* ed. Jane R. Stewart (1885; rpt., Norman: Univ. of Oklahoma Press, 1961); *Tenting on the Plains; or, General Custer in Kansas and Texas,* ed., Jane R. Stewart,

3 vols. (1887; rpt. Norman: Univ. of Oklahoma Press, 1971); and *Following the Guidon,* ed. Jane R. Stewart (1890; rpt. Norman: Univ. of Oklahoma Press, 1966). See also her " 'Where the Heart Is': A Sketch of Woman's Life on the Frontier." *Lippincott's* 65 (1890): 305–13; "Home-Making in the American Army" *Harper's Bazar* (1900): 309–13; and "An Out-of-the-Way Outing." *Harper's Weekly* 35 (18 July 1891): 534–35.

11. Leckie, *Elizabeth Bacon Custer,* p. 22.

12. Custer, *Boots,* pp. xxii-xxiii.

13. Ibid., p. xxix.

14. Leckie, *Elizabeth Bacon Custer,* pp. 14, 237.

15. Francis Parkman Jr., *The Oregon Trail,* ed. David Levin (1849; rpt. New York: Penguin, 1985) p. 43; Custer, "Where the Heart Is," p. 305.

16. Custer, *Boots,* pp. 4–5, 39, 41.

17. Custer, *Tenting,* pp. 120–21.

18. Lillian Schlissel, *Women's Diaries of the Westward Journey* (New York: Schocken, 1982), p. 10.

19. Melody Graulich, " 'O Beautiful for Spacious Guys': An Essay on the 'Legitimate Inclinations' of the Sexes," in *The Frontier Experience and the American Dream,* ed. David Mogen et al. (College Station: Texas A & M Press, 1989), pp. 186–87.

20. Custer, "Where the Heart Is," p. 310.

21. Custer, *Boots,* p. 60; this work will hereafter be cited parenthetically in the text.

22. Quoted in Glenda Riley, *Women and Indians on the Frontier, 1825–1915* (Albuquerque: Univ. of New Mexico Press, 1984), p. 151; see also Riley, *The Female Frontier: A Comparative View of Women on the Prairie and the Plains* (Lawrence: Univ. Press of Kansas, 1988).

23. Graulich, "O Beautiful," p. 198.

24. For more on sojourner theory, see Paul C. P. Siu, "The Sojourner," *American Journal of Sociology* 58 (1952): 34–44.

10

P. JOY ROUSE

Cultural Models of Womanhood and Female Education

PRACTICES OF COLONIZATION AND RESISTANCE

"GIVE ME A GIRL at an impressionable age, and she is mine for life." As pedagogical a statement as ever was made, this assertion by the heroine of Muriel Spark's *The Prime of Miss Jean Brodie* demonstrates the knotty relationship between educational philosophy/practice and youthful womanhood. Set at the Marcia Blaine School for Girls in Edinburgh, Scotland, in the 1930s, the novel chronicles the unconventional teaching habits of Jean Brodie and the response of her pupils—the "Brodie Set," as the other teachers referred to them with frustration. Brodie taught outside the accepted Marcia Blaine School curriculum and, above all, tutored her students to recognize and then live fully in their "prime." Believing that her own prime had just begun, Brodie coached them, "One's prime is elusive. You little girls, when you grow up, must be on the alert to recognize your prime at whatever time of your life it may occur. You must live it to the full. . . . One's prime is the moment one was born for."[1] She is on the verge of being fired; Brodie's crime was fomenting among her students a vision of the possibilities for their lives that usurped the "virtuous" vision of the Marcia Blaine School. Their "prime," while something they were born for, suggests an openness for surprise and purpose, and she encouraged them to be accepting of and curious about that largeness of purpose.

Although this essay is not about literary representations of female education or the betrayal of Miss Jean Brodie, using *The Prime of Miss Jean*

Brodie as a starting place allows me to show how central and interconnected personal well-being and identity are to educational practices. While Spark writes about a fictional school in 1930s Scotland, my interest is in nineteenth-century American girls' schools. The common ground is the relationship between educational philosophy/practice and the socialization of females into presumably biologically determined roles, behaviors, and choices. This relationship is much more complex than the one I imagined as I began my research into the archival documents of female education. I began with preset categories of "narratives of containment" or "narratives of possibilities," but such a categorization, I soon realized, is far too reductive to explain or analyze the phenomena of nineteenth-century female education. Rather than merely reflecting expectations and models for white middle-class womanhood, the archival materials I worked with and analyze below document a tension that lies at the heart of female education in the nineteenth century, a tension between beliefs of biological determinism and the social construction of identity. Furthermore, they document the agency and determination of many young women to construct a life and behaviors that fell outside of the domestic vision handed them by educational institutions.

One of the primary arguments for female education in the nineteenth century was that it would make girls better wives and mothers—it would facilitate the smooth running of the "American family" and therefore contribute to the smooth running of the nation. In this patriarchal vision of harmony between Family and State, middle-class white women were contained within the family and their primary responsibility to the polis was to raise virtuous sons. This vision of American society had its roots in classical republican thought and the early history of the American Republic. As Jill K. Conway observes, Enlightenment ideas had an uneasy translation into American political thought. The problem was how to foster and define the "pursuit of happiness" in a way that simultaneously challenged British governmental tyranny and kept intact the patriarchal power base in the family.[2] In his *Reflections of Courtship and Marriage*, Benjamin Franklin, according to Conway, asserted that the solution was to make women rationally convinced that their happiness lay in marriage and the home. Centering women's possibilities on the "pursuit of happiness" and teaching them that their only happiness could come out of being wives and mothers would guarantee their participation in their own containment.[3] Likewise, Benjamin Rush focused on the patriotic duties of women in the Republic. A successful republic depended upon a virtuous and disciplined citizenry, he argued, and these characteristics are taught within the family. The sole purpose of women's education was to educate women so they would produce useful male citizens.[4] Reformers who wanted education to broaden women's experience were a threat to this delicate balance and were often construed as betrayers of ideal womanhood and of the Republic.

The ideals of womanhood most often cited within historical and theoretical scholarship, "Republican Motherhood" (Kerber) and "True Womanhood" (Welter), have become familiar and are discussed by Rose and many others in this volume.[5] The common ground between the two ideals is the belief that domestic duty is woman's primary function and that her education is to prepare her for this duty. I understand these ideals explicitly as social and political forces strengthened through educational institutions. As such, they represented a colonizing effort to control women that I will address at the end of the first section. The following discussion is, at best, exploratory; my research into female educational institutions isn't exhaustive and my primary goal has been to identify some of the patterns and beliefs surrounding women's historic struggle for literacy. In the second section of my essay I will examine female literacy practices more closely through the work of nineteenth-century pupils and pay particular attention to the ways in which they construct an identity and future vision for themselves separate from the cult of domesticity.

The Culture of Women's Education

It is clear from school pamphlets and advertisements that many educators were invested in maintaining the separate spheres ideology embedded in nineteenth-century ideals of womanhood by promoting education as a domestic duty. For example, in 1845 the principals of the Limestone Springs Female High School, located in Spartanburg, South Carolina, compared their school to those in the North as a way to challenge southerners to support female education; this comparison also implies a criticism of northern female education. The principals assert that they offer "no commonplaces on the general importance of Female Education. . . . But they may consistently inquire whether any full or fair share of support has been afforded to this branch of Education, as compared with that of our young men? Whether some 'ungentle' slumbers have not come over our Southern patriotism here?"[6]

While pointing out that women and men don't have equal access to education, thus indicting the current state of "Southern patriotism," the principals also indicate female characteristics they believe make women's education appropriate. Women, they suggest, are sometimes superior in epistolary writing and in "compositions that require ease of thought and expression." Women's abilities to "contract and lose habits, and accommodate themselves to new situations" represent characteristics that no "thoughtful parent or instructor can safely disregard." Based on these characteristics, the principals claim to "attempt to unite all that is useful in female acquirements with reasonable accomplishments; to give a domestic, kind and firm tone to the entire discipline of the mind, in the home establishment of the School." Distancing themselves from some of the progressive tendencies of northern education, the principals write, "It will be seen from the above [outline of study], that in this establishment are combined the advantages of a Northern and Southern Education. It will be, in all respects, a SOUTHERN SCHOOL. On the part of the pupils, estrangement from home, its duties and associations, will thus be guarded against."[7]

Southern Female Education, in this pamphlet, means a reinforcement of traditional "womanly duties" as well as a manipulation or development of "accommodation." Young women were indoctrinated into the self-effacing practice of accommodation, a practice of always putting others' needs before oneself that lay firmly at the center of domestic duty. Constructing the school as a "home away from home" is a pattern that is repeated in the materials I examine here, and it demonstrates the function of the schools to provide practice as well as training in the domestic vision insisted upon for girls. Like the principals of the Limestone Springs Female High School, other educators, teachers, or administrators aligned themselves with arguments for women's equal education and then used their position to drastically qualify what "women's education" should mean.

The following documents provide two explicit examples of the extent to which the ideal of True Womanhood was reinforced through educational institutions. The first example, Wadawanuck Female College, located in Stonington, Connecticut, clearly demonstrates that domestic education was on the agenda of northern educators in 1860.[8] After claiming that "a complete, thorough and appropriate education" for both men and women "must be regarded as a fundamental truth by all who recognize the common humanity of man and woman," the writers of this circular continue by outlining what kind of education women "really" need. In a statement that invokes the values of True Womanhood, the writers assert:

> As teacher, wife, mother, and guide of the house, woman exercises a power over the very elements of society while in the forming and growing state, which determines in a great degree the moral and intellectual

> character, and the physical well-being of the entire community. While therefore her active powers have less range that those of man, her influence is ever wider and more pervading. Of this influence, character is the most essential element; what woman can *do,* is included in and depends upon what she *is.*[9]

The language of this passage attempts to persuade readers that women's sphere, although more restricted than men's, is actually more pervasive. A woman's education benefits more than her family; the "moral and intellectual character" and "physical well-being" of the community at large are also dependent on women assuming the appropriate role. If women ceased to be positioned, or to position themselves, in this particular relation, the "entire community" would suffer. This lesson was so important that the organizers of the school claimed, "No young lady will be considered a worthy candidate for the *First degree* who does not appreciate and understand the various duties and social amenities that devolve upon the mistress of a well ordered household." In "Words to parents" the circular writers embrace a theory of accommodation as they warn parents to tell their children that "they come here for 'discipline' and 'culture'" and will have to be punctual and "yield at all times a conscientious obedience to the requirements of the institution." Furthermore, they are to bring no books because the instructors will determine what they will read. In a final admonition to the parents the writers suggest that they inquire before indulging their daughters' complaints and that they warn their daughters to be wary of the "one indiscreet, impulsive girl" typically found in boarding school families. The containment strategy used here is to squelch resistance before it surfaces and to dismiss as reckless or misdirected the voice of any young woman who isn't cooperative in the enterprise of the school.[10]

The second example of the constructed dependence between True Womanhood and female education comes from the work of the Bucknall sisters. Joanna Rooker Bucknall (1816?–95) and Martha Elizabeth Bucknall (d. 1880) founded and ran schools for girls in Newark (1840–55), New York (1855–66), and New Brunswick, New Jersey (1866–80). The Bucknall papers included some of the sisters' work as students as well as their addresses to graduating classes, letters to and from students and parents, and student papers. Much can be learned form this collection, not the least of which is the importance of religion in some women's lives and in some aspects of student education in mid-nineteenth century. For my purposes here I've focused on the sisters' graduation addresses,[11] which consistently over their teaching careers position female education as a domestic duty and characterize the students as "clinging vines." In all cases the sisters insisted that their students' education didn't stop at graduation; it was, in fact, just beginning. In an 1868 address one of them asserted:

> In conducting your education we have aimed to qualify you for the responsibilities of womanly duty, which you will ere long assume; for the world of man's ambition is not your befitting sphere. The clinging tendral is not intended to do the office of the sturdy oak. . . . Why should you seek to figure in Conventions or in the Halls of Legislature when so much nobler destiny lies before you in your god-appointed mission your delightful employment to restore in part the forfeited charms of Eden. Does not the human intellect take whatever form is given it by the moulding hand of woman?

In the 1869 address the sisters charged their students to meet "the uncertain future" and to "prove your armor in the battle of life." Reminding them of their "responsibilities of woman's mission," they ordered the graduates "to benefit others rather than please yourself." To the class of 1874 the sisters asserted that they had struggled to prepare their students "for a life of duty, rather than careless ease." It wasn't until the address for the class of 1875 that the sisters began to acknowledge how hard, or unpleasant, "woman's duty" may have been. As their students prepare to leave school, the sisters warn them:

> Although fancy unrestrained may have sketched for you an enchanting picture of the happiness and enjoyment which await you when you shall be released from the restraints of school-life, experience will so dissipate the illusions of fancy, and convince you that you live in a world of sober and stern realities. And this is not to be regretted, for when you cease to build airy castles, and fully realize that life consists of duties and responsibilities, then and not till then, will you enter upon the way that leads to happiness, usefulness and distinction.

The language of accommodation is once again used to define happiness for the graduates. The world of "sober and stern realities" isn't to be resisted, but to be embraced as the way to happiness. The duties and responsibilities, are, of course, those of a wife or mother as the "restraints of school-life" are exchanged for the restraints of home-life.

The Limestone Springs Female High School, Wadawanuck Female College, and the educational practices of the Bucknall sisters are all examples of the cultivation of domestic duty through the ideological work of educational institutions. They each construct women as service vehicles and perform the cultural work of female role socialization that supports the essentialism of the cult of domesticity. By circumscribing possible alternate visions for the female students' future lives, they enable the belief, "This is what we are born for."

The texts discussed so far demonstrate a belief in the limitations of females. Domestic ideals were a force in female education late into the nineteenth century (and, we might argue, remain intact in twentieth-century education systems). This fact bespeaks a recurrent nervousness that young women were seeing a life for themselves outside of the script afforded them by True Womanhood or domestic destiny. Girls were taught that they were *inherently* better suited for the home while their education *constructed* them that way. This dynamic shows that, rather than being self-sustaining, female containment and oppression were supported by the systems of education.

Bonnie Cook Freeman makes a compelling argument that the relationship between men and women is a colonial one. While others (Altbach, Kelly) argue that internal colonization may only be used metaphorically to describe the social and political inequality of oppressed people within a nation, Freeman asserts that "inequality" and "oppression" are inadequate concepts to represent the relationships between men and women, as well as those between upper and lower classes and between Anglo-Americans and other American races or ethnicities. As concepts, they are too static and represent the "evidence" of a relationship rather than the "essence" of it.[12]

A colonial relationship exists, she asserts, when the colonized are assumed to be inferior; the education system is controlled by the dominant group; the history of the colonized is denied; the content of the colonized education is different from that of the colonizer; and the colonized identify, as a result of the education system, with the oppressor and see themselves as the colonizer does. The crucial point here is that female-specific education colonizes female identity. Freeman asserts, "The assault on the identity and culture of the female, the mechanisms by which subordination[s] are created and facilitated, and the ideologies by which they are justified, all lead us to the conclusion that a more fundamental and systematic phenomenon—the internal colonization of women by men—is taking place."[13]

That nineteenth-century female education was founded upon the supposed dictates of female physiology and feminine nature and that the education systems available to girls taught them that their natural or God-given role was to fulfill their domestic duty suggest that colonization is an apt framework for viewing the education of girls in the nineteenth century. The documents I have examined so far represent educational institutions.

In colonial relationships, much can be learned from examining the work and strategies of the colonized to escape their containment. Rather than pursue the popular and antifeminist position that women willingly participate in their own victimization, a position that brackets the social and instead overprivileges the individual, I want to show how the culture of education, despite its function of colonizing women, could at the same time foster female agency. The agency it fostered, primarily through women's active resistance, was neither utopian nor presocial (and therefore part of some essential or inherent identity), but held important feminist potential.

Literacy, Colonization, and Resistance

Writing about nineteenth-century coeducational institutions, Conway asserts that scholars need to focus on the self-perceptions of women students when examining educational institutions rather than assuming that access to education carried liberatory results.[14] The documents I've examined show that liberation was often struggled for, especially in gaining and using literacy skills. Domestic ideals of womanhood determined that the primary function of women's literacy was salvation.[15] Taught to read religious tracts, which enforced women's domestic socialization, young wives and mothers would be able to raise morally sound children and maintain a morally redemptive household for their men. In order to understand and use their literacy skills more broadly, young women such as Anna Gale had to confront their contained identities and redefine themselves as active literate beings whose education was to benefit others *as well as* themselves.

Anna Gale was a student of Margaret Fuller's and attended the Greene Street School in Providence, Rhode Island, in 1837 and 1838. She provides one of the boldest examples of a school girl enacting self-definition. She recorded the following incident in her student journal on 22 January 1838:

> At noon I took my Drawing book, and went home, merely because I was cross. This I cannot say I think exactly right, but I felt as though I could not stay here. I wished to go home, and shut myself up where I could neither see or hear anyone. I should no doubt have been wiser to have stayed and not indulge myself in such feelings. I know it is foolish to despair, because I cannot be or do what I wish.[16]

Anna Gale's reflection is complicated; it resembles Fuller's later exhortation to women, "Let her put from her the press of other minds, and meditate in virgin loneliness."[17] Anna's reflection demonstrates her struggle to enact Fuller's declaration. What I see here is more than a case of a young girl escaping the school and retreating into the home. Anna Gale wrote, "I cannot be and do what I wish," while she did what she wanted to do—go somewhere to think, to be alone. She challenges the model of the obedient daughter, not merely in order to pull a prank, but to claim her right to contemplation. She isn't altogether comfortable with her deed, though; she feels that she has "indulged" in a feeling that is not wise and calls it "folly." After Mr. Fuller, the principal, admonishes her, telling her that "he should go home the next time he was cross," Anna scolds herself, writing, "If all should go for so trifling a course, there would be no school."

It is interesting that a few days later Anna Gale responds to transcendentalism in her journal after a class discussion on music in nature. It is ironic that female students, defined in relation to others in their immediate spheres, were studying this literary and social movement that celebrated the autonomous powers of the individual. She observed, "I am very ignorant respecting the new subject of transcendentalism—though I should be glad to catch its spirit." Her actions and subsequent feelings of guilt demonstrate the complex intersections between gendered expectations and the promises of transcendentalism that so often uncritically assume male privilege. As Anna Gale's experience demonstrates, the different cultural values and expectations of men and women clashed as she dared to catch the spirit of transcendentalism. Actions that would be defended for her male counterparts were considered a trifling course by Anna Gale when she enacted them herself.

Within domestic models, the appropriate actions for women were most often taken within the home in familial relationships, or in nurturing relationships outside the home. The prime action was to give—to give time, energy, life, support. However, school documents and student compositions even from early in the nineteenth century indicate that there was some slippage of the notion of women's exclusive responsibility to the family, as young women saw a life possible outside of the domestic sphere.

As early as 1817 Caroline Prescott wrote from the Female Academy: "The education of women is to qualify them for the purposes of life. A lady studies not that she may qualify herself to become an orator or a leader, not that she may learn to debate, but to act. . . . The great use of study is to enable her to regulate her own mind and to be useful to others." [18] This assertion places very real limitations on women. While oratory or leadership is not claimed for women, the arena of action is yet broader than the home. There is no mention of domestic duty nor suggestion that women's education is only for the benefit of those in their family. Prescott does suggest that a woman gains something, too—control to regulate her own mind—while also being useful to others. This tie between actions and thought resurfaces in a number of documents.

Naming "entire self-government" as their goal, the trustees of the Uxbridge Female Seminary in 1833 determined that moral instruction was the best method to obtain it. By bringing together the "intellectual powers" and "the heart" they hoped to cultivate "an enlightened conscience—a quick sense of moral obligation."[19] As a school that appears from its catalogue to have been entirely run by women, it is significant that there was no mention of domestic education, duty, or household education. Instead, intellectual power, social obligations, and self-government were the stated goals of female education. A sense of social connectedness was being taught, but students' relationships with other people were not predetermined as exclusively domestic.

Several examples of student writing in which young women define themselves outside of the cult of domesticity come from the Brooklyn Female Academy in New York. A commencement program, school catalogue, student compositions, and an alumnae publication provide the texts for the following readings of self-definition. In the 1851 circular and catalogue for the school the trustees claimed to "afford to young ladies the same facilities for acquiring a good English and Classical education that are provided for young men at the best collegiate institutions in the country."[20]

Distinctions are not drawn between the type of education appropriate for men and women. Many comments in the circular, which include observations of journalists and reports of examination committees, provide different perspectives. One of the most interesting comes from the report on penmanship submitted by Edward Copland. Although he praises Mrs. Plummer, the instructor, for her success, Copland remarks that "writing, though an accomplishment, is in fact only a mechanical labor, made necessary by the condition of society, and the progress of knowledge; very little mind being required for its fullest evolution. . . . [I]t is one of those accomplishments which, to keep perfect, should never be neglected." Copland questions whether women need extensive education in this "mechanical labor" and argues, "The absence of a necessity for the use of the pen, with females, is one of the evidences daily before us, and the result presents a fact much to be lamented."[21] He laments that women do not write more, but ironically observes that when a young girl leaves school her domestic duties "are allowed to intervene." As an outsider to the Brooklyn Female

Academy, Copland imposes his view of women's education and of women's writing practices (or lack of them). At the same time, several student compositions explicitly contradict his notion of writing as mechanical labor, as students use their compositions to explore their positions as women or, in some cases, to define writing as a social act.

Student writings are scattered throughout the commencement program of the Brooklyn Female Academy; it was typical to include poems or hymns written by students that reflect school life or to print students' predictions of the future. Although these texts are a strange mixture of resistance to and reinforcement of the cult of domesticity, the selections share one thing in common. They all create an image of the graduates exiting in both fear and hope. I see self-culture or self-definition enacted through the students' alignment with women as a historical and social group and also through a rewriting of their social role. The selection "Hymn—By a Pupil" demonstrates this aspect of self-culture:

> Life's May morn is breaking o'er us,
> Only love tones greet our ear,
> But a future lies before us,
> Fraught alike with hope and fear—
> There the fields where we must labor,
> Labor for the good and true,—
> There amid the golden harvest,
> Sisters! we have work to do.

This student positions herself and her classmates as actors in the future. She writes about their influence as labor, real work, which sets her apart from another student who writes of their "holy influence" as they went out into the world as women. In "Ode, By a Pupil" this same student wrote:

> For woman's mingled lot is ours,
> 'Tis ours her power to wield.
> Each path to light and strew with flowers,—
> A holy influence yield.

As a part of the future, the work for the "good and true" in the first example takes place in a larger context than women's proper sphere of the home. And, unlike Anna Gale's individual claim to the right to self-culture, the action here takes place in "fields." Education is as much for the sake of the community as it is for the individual, but without self-sacrifice or self-effacement. The impression is given of women as a group, a community, working towards some identifiable "good."[22]

In another composition from the Brooklyn Female Academy, Bessie Hunting takes up the phrase "I can't" to address the importance of writing. In her essay, "I Can't," Bessie observes, "How often has my title been used by school girls in writing compositions, when with a sorrowful face perhaps tearful eyes they say, Oh dear 'I can't' write anything, What am I to do?" She continues her pep talk of sorts by replacing this phrase, which she says "leads to evils of a disastrous nature and . . . weakens the intellectual powers of the employers, destroying her efforts to perseverance and causing her to sink into a lethargy." By substituting the phrase, "I'll try," Bessie asserts that school girls will be able to use "the power of language" for their improvement and advancement and that they will also increase their perseverance, have higher expectations of themselves, and improve their intellect.[23] In this essay and another one about the process of writing a composition, Bessie describes composing as collaborative. Students should talk with one another, she observes, share ideas, and question their teacher about topics. By using this process of collaboration Bessie contains the fear of writing she has observed and also disrupts the notion of the isolated writer as she embraces a sense of collectivity.

The alumnae publication of the Brooklyn Female Academy, *The Messinger-Bird,* offers another direct contradiction to Copland's view that writing is merely a mechanical labor, a kind of labor women don't participate in when their domestic duties are "allowed to intervene." In the introduction of *The Messinger-Bird* the editors give their reasons for beginning the publication: in addition to the desire to reconnect with past graduates, the editors have some sense of the "cultural work" of their publication. Having planned in private and now ready to send out their publication, the editors assert, "Plume thyself to-day for thy first flight, bird of the untried pinion! . . . We have called thee our Messinger-bird. To whom do we send—and what Message: To those who have left us, and dwell far away—A Love Token. To those who have watched our progress with approving glance and word—A Thank offering. To those of kindred pursuits and tastes—A Cordial Greeting; and to all who desire to see the intellect of Woman cultivated, and her standard of thought exalted—A Manifestation of our Sympathy."[24]

In a segment titled "The Editor's Table" that appeared in each issue, the editors create a dialogue between themselves and representatives of the school. Conflicting notions of women's education and abilities are at the center of the dialogue. On hearing that the girls are editing a magazine, one teacher, "Mrs. Timorous," exclaims, "Why, my girls could not be induced to touch a pen; unless it was to write invitations to their own weddings." The editors respond that they want to avoid "intellectual lethargy" after leaving school, to continue to be intellectually active, and that *The Messinger-Bird* will help them to maintain an "association together in the attainment of learning." After "Mrs. Timorous" predicts the magazine will fail, the editors respond by observing, "She will never rise out of that heavy atmosphere of fear that she carries with her. She is a moral Slough of Despond, into which she seeks to drag all she meets." Although it is difficult to know exactly what sparked this critique, as figures such as "Miss Fashion" and "Mr. Covetous" enter the dialogue it becomes clear that the editors are critiquing inadequate models of womanhood as well as patriarchal appropriation of women's work. "Miss Fashion" tries to lure the editors away from their work to go shopping and meet men, while "Mr. Covetous" agrees to help them only after they achieve some amount of success, at which point he wants them to use his name. It isn't until "Father Goodwill" enters the dialogue that the editors are praised for their self-reliance and motivation. Within this dialogue the resistance to women's self-reliance is played out through several characters: "Mrs. Timorous" is scared of it; "Miss Fashion" scorns it; and "Mr. Covetous" wants to use it, control it. The students, however, parody these responses.[25]

Female students certainly weren't always eager to share their ideas, to be vocal, or to participate in public readings or declamations. Harriet Tappan and Olympia Brown offer contrasting examples of mid-nineteenth-century students' responses to the rising expectations for women to speak in public. Harriet Tappan attended the Fort Edward Institute, located in New York, in 1855. Her diary and letters provide some details about the requirements of the school, which was described in a circular as "attempting to provide the poor with the same opportunities for an education as the rich." Shortly after arriving at the school Harriet discovered that she would have to participate in a "Public," an occasion where male students recited and female students read compositions. She began in her diary, "Had a fit of the blues because I must write a Rhetoric article and read it Wednesday evening." Over the next several days Harriet grapples with this requirement, trying to avoid it. After appealing to several teachers to save her from this ordeal, she reflects, "Have tried my best to have Miss Pixley and Mrs. Ames excuse me from reading on the stage, what shall I do?" When she finally goes to the principal, Professor King, he also refuses to dismiss her from the requirement. Harriet's final comments in her journal about this incident indicate some of her reservations. "Must write a composition today, can't get excused," she laments. "I never was in such a stew in my life. To read in public on the stage, What an unjust thought of Prof. King." She appeals to her cousin who also attended the school, "Lib, don't for pity's sake laugh."[26]

Although Harriet never appears to have totally embraced the requirement that she participate in public readings, other compositions indicate that she did realize why oratorical and composition practice were important. In an essay titled "Benefits of Composition Writing" she observes: "The rising generation will soon be obliged to fill the place of statesman and orator and then some will have to bring their minds to act upon subjects of importance and is it not necessary that all begin to practice in youth?"[27] Education, Harriet imagines, is preparing her and her classmates for some future role, perhaps that of statesman or orator. Not making a distinction between male and female students she asks, shouldn't "all" practice? Implicitly she also makes an important observation about the connection between education and the life that education prepares a student to lead after graduation. However, Harriet's initial resistance to speaking publicly isn't representative of all young women. While Harriet struggles just to meet the requirement, Olympia vies for more opportunities to speak and works to bring about the same expectations for female students as male students.

Olympia Brown's self-confidence was much more developed than Harriet Tappan's, and she entered college having already defined herself as a literate, speaking woman. When she had to choose between Oberlin and Antioch Colleges in 1856 because they were the only true colleges that admitted women, Olympia chose Antioch. Although Lucy Stone and Antoinette Brown, whom Olympia admired, had attended Oberlin, they were not allowed to read their graduating essays in public; this restriction infuriated Olympia and, like Stone, she refused to capitulate to it. Olympia faced a number of restrictions at Antioch, however, and became involved in several confrontations over limitations placed on women. Olympia's roommate, Lucretia Effinger, described her passion for fighting barriers imposed on women. "Even then [as a student] her heart began to burn with indignation over the subjection of women, over the assumed inferiority of the feminine intellect and to chafe at the restraints which hedged in her sex," Effinger asserted. This made her difficult for the faculty to "manage"; Brown resented the rule that allowed male students to give orations while female students were limited to reading their compositions. Brown cooperated only marginally, Effinger remembers, by carrying her essay book to the stage with her "with due propriety but delivered her oration without a glance at it."[28]

The rules regulating women's delivering orations were played out in other aspects of Antioch. For example, lecturers were invited to campus throughout the school year; after hearing Emerson, Horace Greeley, and Wendell Phillips deliver speeches, a group of girls, led by Brown, approached the administration to ask why no women had been invited. They predictably were informed that there were no women orators as skilled or good as the men. Brown was determined to bring women orators on campus and called a meeting at which several female students suggested inviting Susan B. Anthony, Elizabeth Cady Stanton, Antoinette Brown, or Lucy Stone. After raising the money themselves, they invited Antoinette Brown to Antioch to give a public lecture.[29] Despite the institution's refusal to acknowledge women orators and the implicit suggestion female students were not capable of oratory, Antioch students, including Brown, were already well aware of women's oratorical practice and resisted institutional efforts to devalue it and to keep them from developing as public speakers.

Other Issues in the History of Women's Literacy

Women's education, especially traditional domestic education, trained women to be teachers of civic virtue and to fulfill their responsibility to the Republic through their work in the home. Within notions of women's moral superiority and responsibility to uphold the morals and well-being of the community at large, however, civic virtue became domestic virtue because women were limited to domestic spaces. Nonetheless, through their resistance women and young girls were realizing the complexity of their identities and moving beyond the idea that they could only be mothers, wives, and daughters, that their only role in life was to fulfill their domestic duty.

If I have identified some of the patterns in nineteenth-century female education and women's struggle for literacy through examining the small sample of documents examined here, I have met my initial goal. In the process, however, I have found that a much more complex nexus of issues needs to be addressed in order to fully appreciate the educational philosophy and practices that fostered the cult of domesticity in female education. In light of the interdisciplinary character of the history of rhetoric, we need to attend to such areas as educational and medical history, analyzing, for example, the "ovarian model of female behavior" that collapsed female physiology with the cult of domesticity (Smith-Rosenberg).[30] Republican and Democratic philosophies are also entwined in the educational practices that sought to confine women's futures in the home. I concur with Bonnie Freeman's belief in the usefulness of colonization as a framework for examining women's education and think this approach promises a rich synthesis of the many educational, philosophical, psychological, and political factors surrounding female education in the nineteenth century. Furthermore, by understanding colonization as one function of rhetoric, we see how education can both enforce social prescriptions for femininity and allow for female agency through resistance.

Doctrines of nineteenth-century female education and physiology, along with the cult of domesticity, functioned together as a colonizing rhetoric that attempted to ensure a narrative of female containment. If women were ever to envision their "primes" outside of their prescribed domestic duty, a struggle for identity formation was needed that could open the possibilities for female subjectivity. I have tried to represent part of that struggle through my examination of texts by nineteenth-century women students. But if we are to offer a sophisticated and thorough account of the history of nineteenth-century women's literacy, I concur with the Brooklyn Female Academy pupil and writer of "Hymn—By a Pupil": "Sisters! We have work to do."

Notes

I would like to thank Rosaria Champagne for reading multiple drafts of this essay and providing useful critique as well as much welcomed intellectual camaraderie. I also want to acknowledge Susan Jarratt, who provided support and guidance when I was working on earlier drafts of this piece as a part of my dissertation at Miami University, Oxford, Ohio. Finally, I want to thank Mary Kelly, Dartmouth College, who was a researcher at the American Antiquarian Society while I was there in 1990 doing research. We found ourselves sitting at the same table working on similar topics; she graciously shared sources with me, several of which appear in this essay.

1. Murial Spark, *The Prime of Miss Jean Brodie* (New York: Plume, 1961), pp. 16–19.

2. Jill K. Conway, "Perspectives on the History of Women's Education in the United States," *History of Education Quarterly* 14 (1974): 2–3.

3. Benjamin Franklin, *Reflections on Courtship and Marriage: In Two Letters to a Friend. Wherein A Practical Plan Is Laid Down For Obtaining And Securing Conjugal Felicity* (Philadelphia, 1746), quoted in Conway, "Perspectives," pp. 2–3.

4. Benjamin Rush, "Thoughts on Female Education Accommodated to the Present State of Society. Manners and Government in the United States of America" (1787), in *Essays on Education in the Republic,* ed. Frederick L. Rudolph (Cambridge, Mass.: Harvard Univ. Press, 1965); quoted in Conway, "Perspectives," pp. 3–4.

5. Linda Kerber, *Women of the Republic: Intellect and Ideology in Revolutionary America* (Chapel Hill: Univ. of North Carolina Press, 1980); Barbara Welter, "The Cult of True Womanhood, 1820–1860," *American Quarterly* 18 (1966): 151–74. Although the ideals of Republican Motherhood and True Womanhood have been used to describe the general position of women from the Revolution through 1860, it is clear that these ideals are representative of white, upper- and middle-class women in New England. For insightful and important critiques of these exclusive ideals and challenges to historiography that naturalizes the exclusion of African American women, see Paula Giddlings, *When and Where I Enter: The Impact of Black Women on Race and Sex in America* (New York: Bantam Books, 1985); Dorothy Sterling, ed. *We Are Your Sisters: Black Women in the Nineteenth Century* (New York: Norton, 1984); and Gerda Lerner, *Black Women in White America: A Documentary History* (New York: Vintage Books, 1972). For a discussion of the lives of rural women see Joan M. Jensen, *Loosening the Bonds: Mid-Atlantic Farm Women, 1750–1850* (New Haven: Yale Univ. Press, 1986), and Elizabeth Fox-Genovese, *Within the Plantation Household: Black and White Women of the Old South* (Chapel Hill: Univ. of North Carolina Press, 1988).

6. *Limestone Springs Female High School* (Spartanburg District, S.C., 1845), p. 2.

7. Ibid., pp. 3–5.

8. Although Welter places the Cult of True Womanhood in the period from 1810 to 1860, I have found traces of this ideal working as an active cultural force even further into the nineteenth century.

9. *Catalogue and Circular of the Wadawanuck Female College* (Stonington, Conn., 1860), pp. 8–9.

10. Ibid., pp. 13–14.

11. Joanna Rooker Bucknall and Martha Elizabeth Bucknall Papers, MC 239, folder 42, Schlesinger Library, Radcliffe College, Cambridge, Mass. Since the Bucknall sisters didn't sign the graduation addresses, it is difficult to attribute authorship specifically to one or the other.

12. Bonnie Cook Freeman, "Female Education in Patriarchal Power Systems," in *Education and Colonialism,* ed. Philip G. Altbach and Gail P. Kelly (New York: Longman, 1978), pp. 207–42: see p. 210. In their coauthored introduction to this collection, Altbach and Kelly make their case that internal colonization should only be used metaphorically to describe male-female power relations. See pp. 24–29 for their review of women, African Americans, and the working class in connection to internal colonization.

13. Ibid., pp. 208–10.

14. Conway, "Perspectives," p. 9.

15. Ibid., p. 2.

16. Gale Family Papers, Manuscript Collection, American Antiquarian Society, Worcester, Mass.

17. Margaret Fuller, *Woman in the Nineteenth Century* (1855; rpt. New York: Norton, 1971), p. 121.

18. Francis Merritt Quick Papers, Schlesinger Library, Radcliffe College. This student composition and the scrapbook in which it is contained provide no specific information about the location of the Female Academy.

19. *Catalogue of the Members of the Uxbridge Female Seminary,* p. 9.

20. *Circular and Catalogue of the Brooklyn Female Academy* (Brooklyn, 1851), p. 8.

21. Ibid., p. 31.

22. Hunting-Rudd Family Papers, Schlesinger Library, Radcliffe College.

23. Ibid.

24. *The Messinger Bird: A Periodical Conducted by the Alumnae of the Brooklyn Female Academy* (Brooklyn: T. D. Smith, 1856), pp. 1–2.

25. Ibid., pp. 21–22.

26. Harriet Tappan Papers, Schlesinger Library, Radcliffe College.

27. Ibid.

28. Olympia Brown Papers, Schlesinger Library, Radcliffe College.

29. Ibid.

30. Carroll Smith-Rosenberg, *Disorderly Conduct: Visions of Gender in Victorian America* (New York: Oxford Univ. Press, 1985). See especially "Puberty to Menopause: The Cycle of Femininity in Nineteenth-Century America," pp. 182–96.

II

HEIDEMARIE Z. WEIDNER

Silks, Congress Gaiters, and Rhetoric

A BUTLER UNIVERSITY GRADUATE OF 1860 TELLS HER STORY

All people ought to be educated. . . . I think we can get along through this world much better than if we are not, and will know how to attend to all kinds of business. . . . We ought to advance in wisdom, virtue, and knowledge, and try to learn something new everyday.

—Lydia Short, 1917

AT THE TIME she wrote these words in her diary about the benefits of education, Lydia Short was still a school girl in small-town southern Indiana. Yet even then she felt passionately about learning and, before she was ten, had decided on attending college. Neither her mother's lack of support nor her father's difficult "pecuniary affairs" could dissuade Short from her goal. If necessary, she would wait until she was of age, "and then could do as [she] pleased." Fortunately, "some favoring influence" intervened on her behalf. In 1857 she was able to enter North Western Christian University, one of the few coeducational colleges in America at the time.[1]

Although few in number, coeducational colleges deserve special attention in our efforts to trace the growth of women's literacy in the nineteenth century. Such institutions may shed light on the importance of context and how it did or did not support women's higher education. Furthermore, a look at coeducational schools may also reveal to what extent the interaction between men and women in the classroom did or did not raise the consciousness of female students and clarify their feelings about reading and writing. Finally, some historians suggest that women's colleges, instead of supporting equality for women, may have actually supported segregated education and helped solidify the idea of separate spheres for men and women. Meanwhile, others claim that coeducation either suppressed women's talents or forced them to take inhospitable forms and directions. We cannot begin to resolve such issues until we know more about coeducation. It is important that we understand how coeducational colleges were alike or different. In what ways did they or did they not encourage equal access to various forms of literacy?

Concentrating on one woman's experience at coeducational Butler University, this essay attempts to fill in some of the blank spots left on our map of nineteenth-century women's education. Board minutes, university catalogues, and faculty reminiscences from Butler University archives, as well as Lydia Short's college-days diary, support my discussion of the university's context and Short's struggles and gains on the road to literacy. Although these sources do not lead to a full picture of women's reading and writing experiences in coeducational schools, they may encourage researchers to examine additional evidence to arrive at a more conclusive interpretation.

The Context

The college Short entered in 1857 was a mere fledgling in terms of enrollment, but a giant in terms of goals. Butler University had been founded only two years before and was situated on what was then considered the frontier. Opened to pioneers in 1803, the Northwest Territory did not become a state until 1816, and Indianapolis was chosen as its capital nine years later. Although in the future—due to commerce and its central location—the town was to grow rapidly into an urban settlement, in 1855 Indianapolis consisted of about 15,000 inhabitants who had not forgotten the tree-stump-covered sites of its earliest years, reminders of the dense woods that still covered most of Indiana.[2]

This environment, the challenging and quickly changing world of the frontier, required men and women attuned to the practical present and its problems rather than gentlemen and gentlewomen of leisure contemplating the past. The settlers needed to deal resolutely with a variety of unforeseen situations and be able, in their daily tasks, to speak and write effectively in their mother tongue. Thus concepts of "practicality and utility," stressed throughout the nineteenth century, would take on special overtones and become a logical stipulation in colleges preparing young people for the task of transforming a wilderness into civilization.

Yet educational opportunities of any kind were scarce in midcentury

Indianapolis. Few private schools and only the rudiments of a public school system begun in 1847 existed, so that a traveler from Europe, businessman and classical archaeologist Heinrich Schliemann, could still write home: "There is very little to occupy the mind in Indianapolis. . . . Here in Indiana classical education does not exist at all," while "useful knowledge goes beyond every other consideration" and "everyone from childhood on is instructed to think for himself."[3]

Nevertheless, the conditions for higher education were favorable. The city had, in fact, a great number of settlers whose schooling and intellectual curiosity helped nurture a love for books and writing. Oratory, too, was still a practical tool held in high esteem, making Indiana speakers well known throughout the nation. "Her public men enjoyed a national reputation for eloquence, both at the bar and in political life."[4]

Butler University: Goals

Butler University, one of the many small institutions founded by Protestant denominations between 1800 and the beginning of the Civil War, was the brainchild of the Christian or Disciples of Christ Brotherhood. Concerned about an "illiterate ministry," like the founders of Harvard before them, some Disciples saw a need for a college in the newly settled country west of the Alleghenies. Unlike Harvard's founders, however, the Disciples—under the intellectual, moral, and financial leadership of Ovid Butler, an Indianapolis lawyer "passionately devoted to education"—called for "free popular education." Their college would be interdenominational, multiracial, and coeducational.[5]

With these goals, Butler University differed markedly from its fellow denominational colleges, which Albert Kitzhaber has described in unflattering terms: "The denominational colleges . . . found themselves in opposition to nearly all the new trends that were beginning to appear; coeducation, courses in laboratory science, higher standards of scholarship, all ran counter to their traditional ideals and modes of operation." In fact, its frontier atmosphere and the needs of its pioneer population allowed Butler University to break with several traditions and substitute instead "liberal and enlightened policies."[6] One of the most visible manifestations of these policies was the school's coeducational practice; the other, equally significant, was an emphasis on English education at a time when most American institutions still stressed the benefits of a classical education (see also Harmon in this volume).

Although nineteenth-century society no longer questioned women's right to some amount of schooling, much of the public sentiment before the Civil War argued against women's higher education, and particularly against coeducation. Short found this attitude in her own home and wrote about it in her diary: "My mother, good as she was, could never see the propriety of women knowing more than merely to read, write, and cipher a little." To opponents, college education for women was "hardening and deforming," and reduced their chances of marriage. This view survived despite the success of the female academies and many college experiments since 1825. It influenced such pioneer institutions as Oberlin College in Ohio—coeducational since 1837—where women either sat silently in the classes of the Gentleman's Course or attended the Lady's Course, which catered to women's so-called special talents.[7]

In contrast, Butler University offered men and women equal access to education. Two arguments supported the decision of the board to allow women to enter the new institution "on the same terms as men." One was the Christian idea of "helpmate," a concept that the hardships of frontier life with its demands for cooperation undoubtedly strengthened. This idea found expression during an 1870 meeting of the board at which the directors argued for the addition of women directors: "In council and in action man needs a help meet."[8] The second support for coeducation derived from the insight that the minds of both men and women deserve to be educated and that their interaction in the classroom could create additional benefits. This creed became part of many later catalogues advertising Butler's coeducational policy: "The same mental training is good for both [men and women] and . . . both may receive important benefits from associating in classroom work."[9]

Nevertheless, for a number of years Butler University made concessions to the public and offered female students the choice between a full four-year and a modified three-year course. With the abandonment of the so-called Female Collegiate Course in 1869, Butler acknowledged a reorientation toward its original goals. In its catalogue announcement, the institution reminded the public that it was chartered as a university, a type of school that demanded a "higher standard of scholarship, and a more extended course of study, than usually found in the ordinary Academy Course." Therefore, the board decided "to make no distinction between male and female students, with respect to branches of study, but invite them to pursue those branches upon an 'equal' footing, and side by side make proof of the 'right' to the highest Academic honors."[10]

In addition to coeducation, Butler University signaled yet another radical departure from eastern practices in its emphasis on an English education. Such a move was generally followed by other midwestern or western institutions (e.g., Illinois State Normal University; see Harmon in this volume) and an outgrowth of such schools' cultural, political, economic, and social contexts. Although English as a medium of instruction had entered Harvard and Yale between 1756 and 1776, classical languages and their literatures still formed the backbone of a liberal education. Not until the last quarter of the nineteenth century would Butler University's plan—"a critical and thorough study of the English language"—enter the majority of colleges and universities. It needed the prestige of Harvard and the forcefulness of Charles William Eliot, who in 1869 had addressed the neglect of a "systematic study of the English language," to make English studies a national concern.[11]

Butler founder Ovid Butler stressed English when he admonished the board in 1872, "Every graduate . . . should have a practical knowledge of his or her own language and literature. . . . More time [must] be spent in learning and building up our mother tongue. We are living in a practical age. Men and women are not so much regarded for what they can as for what they *do* learn. It is well for them to understand the classics . . . but it is better for them to know more of the living present that when they go forth in the great battle of life they may be better prepared to meet its realities." And as late as 1889 the president of Butler University reasserted his institution's goals as being different from those of eastern schools: "Our circumstances and needs are different, and our courses of study and methods must be adapted to the necessities of our young [students]."[12]

The emphasis on the practical aspects of a higher education singled out English as the necessary foundation for all other studies. However, we cannot judge Butler's insistence on practicality and utility from our vantage points of business English and technical communication but must evaluate the slogan in light of the preference given to classical education. Seen thus, "practicality and utility" addressed the needs of a pioneer society where the majority of the people were engaged in practical, hands-on tasks, such as clearing forests, building roads, erecting houses, and planning towns and cities. Since few were destined to live lives of leisure, most students' educational needs went beyond Latin, Greek, and higher mathematics to include English as a spoken and written language and such eminently practical subjects as surveying and bookkeeping. But most of all, Butler University's practical and useful goals allowed the institution to treat English as a subject on a par with both Latin and Greek—that is, to teach English grammar, composition, oratory, and literature with the same thoroughness allotted to classical languages. The board accordingly ordered the faculty "in arranging the order of studies . . . to place first and as of primary importance, a critical and thorough study of the English language, including composition, elocution, rhetoric, belles lettres."[13]

Lydia Short: Butler University Graduate of 1860

When Lydia Short entered college, Butler University still offered her a choice of two curricula. Perhaps it was in order to attract more women students that the Board of Directors made certain concessions to the popular sentiment of the time and began the new institution with two distinct courses, a four-year "College Course" and a three-year "Female Collegiate Course." Yet women had the choice of attending either and received the degree of Mistress of Arts or Mistress of Science respectively.

The differences between the two curricula were much like those at Oberlin College. Students in the Female Collegiate Course omitted Greek, the U.S. Constitution, higher mathematics, and such vocational subjects as surveying, applied chemistry, calculus, and mechanics. Other subjects taught in the men's fourth year were incorporated into the women's third year. During the freshman year, all students took rhetoric one term and English literature another. So-called rhetorical exercises—the practical side of a rhetorical education, consisting of declamations, orations, and essays—accompanied the more formal course in rhetoric. Since enrollment was low, and women initially accounted for only about 10 percent (for the 1856–57 school year the entire collegiate population amounted to only twenty-one students), men and women were usually instructed together.[14]

Short chose the "Female Collegiate Course" for reasons her diary does not explain. Perhaps she bowed to her mother's misgivings about crossing a barrier few women had crossed in those days. Perhaps her father's resources made three but not four years of college possible. Whatever the explanation, the outcome could have mattered little. Due to its small enrollment, Butler University could offer entirely separate curricula for men and women in its catalogues but not in practice, thus by default avoiding to some extent the segregation a two-course system implied.

According to a classmate, Short was an attractive young woman, "mentally wide-awake," "capable of appreciating good literature," and "plainly availing herself of her opportunities."[15] As the only woman in a class of fourteen students, she would become the second female graduate of Butler University; the founder's daughter, Demia Butler, was the first. Excerpts of Short's diary, published in the *Butler Alumnal Quarterly* of

1917, discuss at great length, and to considerable depth, her reading, writing, speaking, and listening. The emphasis she placed on these activities seems to argue for an interpretation of rhetoric and composition as central in the university's curriculum—for both men and women. As Short's journal entries progressed toward graduation day, her involvement with language through reading, writing, and speaking seemed to promote a growing awareness of self and others. This awareness concerned her role as a woman, her writing abilities, her critical discrimination, and, finally, her growth as a public speaker.

Rhetorical training of men was a crucial part of any college education and, at the same time, embedded in and supported by the community at large. In 1857, however, society did not generally condone women's striving for rhetorical expertise let alone envision the use they would make of their newly acquired skills in writing and speaking. Moreover, such education did not always change how a woman herself perceived women's role, and some of Short's diary entries struggle with this issue.

According to nineteenth-century conduct books, women were to be virtuous, modest, pious, and silent (see also Rose in this volume). Society considered loud laughter, liveliness, and critical outspokenness in women inappropriate and unacceptable. Yet the situations in which Short found herself at a coeducational institution may have encouraged laughter, even horseplay, and critical analysis was definitely one of the goals of rhetorical training. If success in the classroom built self-confidence and bred independence, a young woman might exercise these character traits off campus as well. Although Short seems to feel a measure of chagrin over her offenses, she also accepts them as part of her individuality: "I spoiled all the fun by laughing myself when I read anything funny. This was always a failing with me. I don't have at times any seeming dignity."[16]

More than about laughing, however, Short worried about drifting off during bad sermons. Her struggle and display of critical sensibilities, were they known to her detractors, would confirm their arguments that women's higher education spelled the decline of religious life and the downfall of civilization:

> Mr. ——— delivered a rather prosy sermon, on account of which quality I was utterly unable to follow the chain of his reasoning. I find myself so often guilty of inattention during divine services unless the expositions are made very forcible by a peculiar attractiveness of style. I am quite apt to give my head the inclination of looking at the parson while I slacken the rein of my thoughts, allowing them to dwell on all

> topics. I do conscientiously condemn such a course, attributing it to a want of pure veneration; yet how I am to remedy the evil I do not know. ("Diary," p. 152)

While Short knew that her inattentiveness at church was caused by the preacher's poor rhetoric, she did not show the same critical perception when it came to judging the worth of her own writing. Among the additional courses listed for students of the "Female Collegiate" curriculum was composition, a subject nineteenth-century culture considered particularly appropriate for women. It was the kind of study that was to cultivate women's imagination, appeal to their emotions, and heighten their natural elegance of style. Furthermore, because writing is a more private art than oratory, exercises in composition were thought to suit women's cultivated aversion to intruding into the public sphere.

Short's discussion of her own writing suggests yet another reason for women's perceived "delicacy." It was the belief that women's subjects, and writings about these subjects, did not count when compared to the more important matters about which men write and talk. This is a point frequently encountered—in papers of women at Oberlin College; in Butler's student paper, the *Collegian;* and in assigned journals of the time, written by women students, which too often begin with the complaint, "Dear Diary, I don't have anything to say." [17] Because Short shared this belief, she discontinued her diary at the end of her second college year after only three months of writing. A year later, when starting up again, she explained that she had been "making a greater 'to do' over small matters than was necessary," her category of "small matters" including the founding of Butler University's first women's literary society. Although Short found herself under "somewhat similar circumstances" now, she had gained during her third year at Butler a new sense of self and the confidence to appreciate her journal "pen scratchings," written, she said, "in the loosest and most careless style possible" ("Diary," p. 158).

In the diary, Short had been happy to abandon the "good rule" of her composition exercises. She knew her weaknesses as a writer by now—her need for revision if she did not apply the favored think-write method of her rhetoric course—and could say: "I never write correctly offhand—my composition always needs correcting and pruning, unless I meditate deliberately on the expression and thought itself before I commit it to paper" (p. 158). What she did not truly appreciate yet was the liveliness of her "loose and careless" journal style. Whether she described a visit to the State Legislature, an evening at a lecture hall, or a fire in a nearby housing district, her vivid imagery, telling comparisons, or the rushing movement of the present tense manage to put her readers there:

> March 4, 1859
>
> Feel well prepared for to-day's ordeal [classes]. While waiting for the hour of recitation to roll around, Hark! Fire! O, the college is on fire! What noise and confusion the students are in, tearing out the recitation rooms by the score! No, it is not the college—good, good! 'Tis a residence a square distant. The wind blowing fiercely, the students and faculty fly to the rescue like startled rabbits, making an impromptu fire company. . . . What towering flames, how they glare! Ho! the engines are here. (pp. 147–48)

Her comments on a eulogy, reflections on the baptism of some classmates, or thoughts on the evening of her graduation are dull in comparison, the rules of formal discourse having drained all lifeblood from them:

> May 31, 1860
>
> How very sage it makes one feel on attaining the climax in one's history. . . . It forms an era in the great drama of human existence, when one feels like the mariner that had been drifted by gentle gales and lured by innumerous infatuations until he finds himself decoyed into the midst of the great deep. (p. 157)

When Short followed the "good rule," writing was much slower and more tormented. Her commencement salutatory was an assignment over which she agonized for almost two months. Being so used to literary models in her rhetoric class made writing without such a model the biggest problem she faced. Her struggles reflect Hugh Blair's notion that invention "comes from a thorough knowledge of the subject, and profound meditation on it."[18] After studying her topic, procrastinating, and talking about it with friends, Short's various invention strategies finally resulted in a "paroxysm of inspiration" and a draft of the speech that would celebrate her graduation ("Diary," p. 158).

The distance Short lacked to appreciate her own writing she seemed to possess when listening to the presentations of others. Her critical analyses of the speeches she heard betray her sharp mind and the excellent training in rhetorical principles she received from the early teachers of rhetoric at Butler University. At the time Short attended the university, her professor of rhetoric used Blair's *Lectures*. According to James L. Golden and his coauthors, this choice provided students who had little rhetorical background with "a comprehensive, coherent, and rational overview of rhetoric, literature, and criticism." Blair also emphasized rhetoric as literary criticism intended to form the student's correct aesthetic "taste."[19] No wonder Short subjected every speech or sermon she heard and every lecture she attended to some kind of critical analysis.

For instance, if Short depicted a speaker, she applied rhetorical principles of description. Beginning with the long shot, Short first described how the speaker "move[d] up the aisle and mount[ed] the rostrum." Her next look focused on his person: "He is a large man, very tall, with a well-built constitution, tho' not disposed to corpulency." Finally, she showed his head and face, tracing first larger, then smaller details: "Well-developed, tho' receding, forehead; rather pointed features, with a piercing countenance and very black hair, with short whiskers and trim mustache of the same hue." Only then did she comment on the speech itself ("Diary," p. 146).

Rhetoric understood as criticism was at the heart of Short's assessment of speeches and sermons. It had become for her second nature to write about a speaker's approach to audience, arrangement, style, and delivery. Among the rhetorical principles she considered most important was that subjects be "purely practical" and adapted to the occasion, a demand that echoes the principles of Butler University and the demands of her times (pp. 152, 156).

Furthermore, speeches or sermons had to follow a plan. Short also liked ideas "correctly expressed" and clever figures of speech employed. Only this way could a speech touch the faculties of its listeners. Of course, delivery was very important, too, for good "articulation and intonation" and effective "gesticulation" would make a speech "masterly." But knowing how to criticize effective application of rhetorical principles in others was only a stepping-stone to Short's own rhetorical practice in the literary society she helped start and in the commencement exercises in which her speech formed the highlight of her college education (pp. 146, 152).

There is no evidence that Butler's women suffered the fate of Oberlin College women students, who were not allowed to speak in class, read their own essays, or speak on a public platform during commencement exercises. But until women had their own literary society, there was no opportunity to practice for those public occasions. While Short was at Butler, the men already had founded two literary societies, the Pythonian and the Mathesian. Admitted as honorary members, women most likely sat decoratively, admiring the literary exercises, and engaging in domestic duties, such as helping the men "make a carpet for their hall" (p. 150). The Pythonian *Observer,* however, informs us that some of the men envisioned more substantial contributions from their women visitors. Criticizing the lack of serious subjects at society meetings, a contributor to the society paper complains that too many members want their "lady visitors" entertained, believing that women "are made up of, and consequently are delighted with the light, frivolous and funny." Women, this early Butler student writes, need to object and reject the "trash everywhere prepared for them." He hopes to "see the day and shall rejoice in the sight, when the ladies shall assert their right to, and feed their mind upon as sound mental pabulum as that which satiates the loftiest intellects in the galaxy of science and literature."[20]

The new literary society for Butler University's women students emerged from the travesty of male rhetoric. Short, while waiting to give a declamation as part of the regular rhetorical exercises, felt bored and with some of the young women went into the Mathesian Hall and "in mimicry went through performances similar to those of the societies, after which I mounted the rostrum, and, after making a short speech made a motion that the ladies . . . endeavor to form a society" ("Diary," pp. 148–49).

Thus the new women's literary society was born amid the speech making of "different persons," with women students loudly claiming their right to face the "public eye." In naming the society after Lydia Sigourney, the students chose a woman who represented sexual equality as well as segregation. A prolific writer, who had advised her female readers to get educated in order to find an occupation "should they be reduced to poverty," Sigourney also upheld in her publications the ideology of separate spheres.[21]

Short's journal entry following the founding of the new society juxtaposes enthusiasm with the reality of college life and hints at the obstacles still ahead for women rhetoricians: "All the girls seem highly elated at the prospects. Geometry is awfully hard" ("Diary," p. 149). One of the young women's father answered his daughter's joy over having founded a literary society with grave disapproval: "Mary, no daughter of mine can be so bold as to belong to a literary society. I cannot have it."[22] Another insult, surely not perceived as such, lay in the fact that fatherly Professor Benton, professor of rhetoric, wrote the constitution and bylaws for the new society. Although, unlike the women students at Oberlin College, Butler women did not have to force the issue of speaking like their men classmates, in the matter of public versus private topics Butler women were almost as careful as their Oberlin counterparts. Thus public exhibitions moved cautiously on the new path to rhetorical freedom. While the men's public performance had five orations, three of which spoke of such male subjects as "Show Thyself a Man," "Highways to Greatness," and "Patriotism," the Sigourneans list only two orations, both bearing the vague title "Variety." The rest of their program consisted of essays and recitations on such "womanly" topics as "Prayer," "The Life Boat," and "The Aspiring" ("Diary," pp. 155–56).

When the Sigourneans met in private, bolder issues were up for debate, a feature their society gatherings had in common with those of Oberlin College women. Topics ranged from, for example, "The Pen is Mightier Than the Sword" and "Do Savage Nations Have a Right to the Soil?" to "Resolved That Marriage is a Failure" and "Improvement of Woman's Condition" (pp. 149, 152). As president of the society and editor of its literary paper, the *Casket,* Short enjoyed the power and frustrations her new duties brought. As a friend recalls, "The membership [in the new society] being necessarily small, it was no light task to make the meetings interesting and helpful. In this she did her full part, and more, often substituting for others less willing."[23]

Considering Short's affinity for critical analysis and quick repartees, it is not surprising that among the society exercises debate ranked highest with her. Reflecting on it, she writes: "Debate is my favorite species of performance and I think it corresponds more with my tenor of mind than any other. There seems to be so much to admire, when one will boldly make an affirmation and then direct every energy to its support, or unravel the arguments of another and set forth her fallacies" ("Diary," pp. 158–59). Short's words carry no overtones of false modesty or extreme delicacy. Her language, direct and forceful, is the language of a speaker who makes her opinions known and eagerly engages in competition.

Short's topic for her commencement salutatory, "The Power of Verse," shows the confidence of the earlier journal entry. In selecting the subject, she acknowledges her femininity but claims the genre that society considered her speciality as an instrument of power. She makes the same point with the clothes she chose for the festive occasion. Should she wear a plain outfit in case she failed? she asks. Convinced of her success, Short flaunts her silks, flounces, lace, and ribbons, matching them with "congress gaiters tight enough to make Tarquinius Superbus feel uncomfortable" (p. 161). If Oberlin College women, by their dress and choice of topics, indicated that "their arena would not be a battlefield,"[24] one Butler woman at least felt confident enough to turn "handicap" into strength, verse into power, and to compare herself to, nay even surpass, the tyrant of Rome.

Short did not go on to become a professional woman, although she continued her studies and is listed in her institution's alumni records as having earned an M.S. degree. Several times she returned to the college, however, to give the alumni address, "elegant and scholarly," or the speech for her literary society.[25] After her marriage, "College, Church, Home, [remained] the great underlying forces of her life" ("Diary," p. 145); one wonders whether the sequence was intentional.

In 1866, six years after Short's graduation, two Butler University women students were the first to choose the professional life of teachers. With the employment of Catharine Merrill, the first Demia Butler Professor of English Literature in 1869, more women entered the university and subsequently engaged in professional activities. Merrill herself formed an important link in this development. When she accepted the college teaching position, one of the duties she dreaded most was the "Sunday lecture" in chapel. In a letter to a friend she wrote, "I hate Women's Rights women who run over the country lecturing, so don't tell anybody about me." Merrill made sure that her first lecture was not announced and that she was well prepared, but her hopes for a small audience were crushed when a large group of people assembled in the chapel to hear the new "Lady professor" speak. She was slightly consoled by the fact that most of them were "personal and intimate friends." Trembling and almost out of breath, Merrill began to speak, getting gradually stronger. Her letter tells the rest: "I . . . got through without any painful exhibition of weakness. Mr. Butler, however, who sat by me felt it and shook hands with me, with tears in his eyes."[26]

This little sketch in a nutshell sets the scene, introduces the major actors, and forecasts the growth of Butler University's women students, developing from timid rhetorical novitiates into speakers and writers who knew their strength. In this story Merrill represents many of the women of her time, but especially those whose teacher she would become. Her hesitation to speak in public, particularly in mixed company, stemmed from the nineteenth-century belief that women's sphere was in the privacy of the home, and that their public demeanor should be one of silence, restraint, and decorum. Her fears in Butler's chapel would allow Merrill to understand the fears of all those entrusted to her care.

Nevertheless, speak Merrill did, and in speaking gained the courage to "get through" that particular Sunday and many occasions thereafter. Ovid Butler, the man whose vision and influence opened the doors of the new university to women, students as well as professors, did not lend Merrill his arm in support but shook her hand as an equal. His tears told her he knew the psychological barriers she had had to overcome. But having found the strength in herself, she would find ways to empower the women who sat in her classes. This Merrill would accomplish not so much by her words, for despite her high position and literary accomplishments, the first Demia Butler professor was one of those pioneer teachers who seemed to firmly believe in women's assigned place. In all her teaching, one of her friends wrote, Merrill upheld "wifehood and motherhood" as the "normal conditions of a woman's life." Notwithstanding her many talks, lectures, and publications, Merrill, her admirer said, "was far from being an organizer of 'movements' or a trampler of platforms."[27]

Yet Merrill's own words seem to contradict her male friend's evaluation. The years of teaching the young women at Butler and her own increasingly active role as lecturer could not but change Merrill's conviction of woman's role. While for the most part her words and writings may have upheld nineteenth-century conventions, her very presence in "the room in the old University, . . . upon the platform in the bay window," in her "black silk gown," demonstrated to her women students that the "higher life," once only available to men, was calling them now as well. Merrill herself noted the new possibilities for women when she wrote in her diary after a speech given to "the Presbyterian ladies": "The assemblage of women was one of the noblest spectacles I ever saw. Realized as I never had before that a higher life is opening up for women. Why should people say, 'What shall we do with our daughters?' when, educated, they have the field of usefulness before them this assemblage shows."[28]

Notes

1. Lydia Short, "Pages from a Diary," *Butler Alumnal Quarterly* 6 (Oct. 1917): 145–61; see p. 161; George M. Waller, "Historical Sketch," MS, Rare Books and Special Collections (RBSC), Irwin Library, Butler University, Indianapolis, 1990, p. 2, writes that aside from Oberlin College in Ohio, North Western was the only coeducational college in America. However, the claim is disputed in Harmon's essay in this volume and there may have been other institutions.

I will refer to North Western Christian University as Butler University throughout the essay. The name North Western Christian University was retained until 1877, when the name was changed to honor Ovid Butler.

2. Jacob Piatt Dunn, *History of Greater Indianapolis* (Chicago: Lewis Publishing, 1910), p. 196.

3. *Schliemann in Indianapolis,* ed. Eli Lilly (Indianapolis: Indiana Historical So-

ciety, 1961), pp. 20, 26, 52. Indiana University, located in the relative isolation of Bloomington, had been founded in 1820.

4. Julia Henderson Levering, *Historic Indiana* (New York: G. P. Putnam's Sons, 1909), pp. 376, 354–55.

5. For background, see Heidemarie Z. Weidner, "Coeducation and *Ratio Studiorum* in Indiana: Rhetoric and Composition Instruction at Nineteenth-Century Butler University and Notre Dame" (Ph.D. diss., Univ. of Louisville, 1991); Albert R. Kitzhaber, *Rhetoric in American Colleges, 1850–1900* (Dallas: Southern Methodist Univ. Press, 1990), pp. 6–9. Quotes on Butler are from Lee Burns, "The Beginnings of Butler College," *Butler Alumnal Quarterly* 15 (Apr. 1926): 3–12; see also Waller, "Sketch," p. 1.

6. Kitzhaber, *Rhetoric in American Colleges,* p. 18: Minutes, Board of Directors of the North Western Christian University, 1852 (Ledgers, MS, RBSC, Irwin Library, Butler University), p. 326.

7. Short, "Diary," p. 161; Thomas Woody, *A History of Women's Education in the United States* (1922; rpt. New York: Octagon Books, 1966), pp. 152, 154–55; LeeAnna Lawrence, "The Teaching of Rhetoric and Composition in Nineteenth-Century Women's Colleges" (Ph.D. diss., Duke University, 1990), p. 61.

8. Catalogues of the Officers and Students of the North Western Christian University, Indianapolis, 1856–1900 (RBSC, Irwin Library, Butler University): *1891–92,* p. 11; Minutes, Board of Directors, 1870, p. 317.

9. *Catalogue, 1891–92,* p. 11.

10. *Catalogue, 1869,* p. 25.

11. Frederick Rudolph, *Curriculum: A History of the American Undergraduate Course of Study since 1636* (San Francisco: Jossey-Bass, 1977), pp. 38–39. For nineteenth-century colleges, the terms "science" and "humanities" differed from our usage today. Since 1800 science had been taught under the headings of "natural philosophy" and "natural history," and in general it referred to "pure science," "an instrument of human understanding and contemplation of the divine" (Rudolph, *Curriculum,* p. 104). Science also meant "any well-organized body of principles concerning any area of knowledge or speculation" (Laurence R. Vesey, *The Emergence of the American University* [Chicago: Univ. of Chicago Press, 1965], p. 133), as in "the science of rhetoric." This latter definition continued, but after 1850 science became "more closely associated with specific evidence, and with evidence observed in nature" (Vesey, *Emergence,* p. 134). While lectures still formed part of science classes, they were complemented by work in laboratories or—in the case of a poor college—by the scientific cabinet (Edward J. Power, *Catholic Higher Education in America* [New York: Appleton-Century-Crofts, 1972], p. 146).

The term "humanities" as a label for certain courses did not exist in nineteenth-century colleges. James McLachlan, "The Choice of Hercules: American Student Societies in the Early Nineteenth Century," in *University in Society,* vol. 2, ed. Laurence Stone (Princeton, N.J.: Princeton Univ. Press, 1974), uses the term "humanities" to encompass rhetoric, elocution, composition, belles lettres, and English literature. Nineteenth-century students received a "literary" or "liberal" education, an education containing all knowledge—in the sense of the German *Wissenschaften* (p. 487). Its product was the man of letters who had gone through the classical curriculum, acquiring a knowledge of Latin and Greek, of higher mathematics, of rhetoric, and of the sciences and other subjects included under moral, mental, and natural philosophy. Since "liberal education was a matter of style more than it was a matter of subjects," the humanist tradition could also exist within the new courses entering colleges in the late nineteenth century: modern languages, English literature, and the fine arts (Rudolph, *Curriculum,* p. 188). On Charles William Eliot's influence, see Rudolph, *Curriculum,* p. 140.

12. Minutes, Board of Directors, 1872, pp. 449–52; Minutes, 1889, p. 197.

13. Minutes, Board of Directors, 1857, p. 230.

14. References to Oberlin College are based on Lawrence, "Rhetoric and Composition." Student enrollment figures are from W. A. Holliday, "Letter," *Butler Alumnal Quarterly* 6 (Jan. 1918): 274–76.

15. Holliday, "Letter," p. 275.

16. Short, "Diary," p. 154. Further references to this work will be parenthetical in the text.

17. Heidemarie Z. Weidner, "Double-Voiced Discourse: A Young Woman's Journal from a Nineteenth-Century Composition Class," March 1991, ERIC ED 340 027.

18. Hugh Blair, *Lectures on Rhetoric and Belles Lettres,* ed. Abraham Mills (Philadelphia: Porter and Coates, n.d.), p. 182.

19. James L. Golden et al., *The Rhetoric of Western Thought* (Dubuque, Iowa: Kendall/Hunt, 1989), p. 143.

20. Pythonian Society, *Observer, 1858–62* (Ledger, MS, RBSC, Irwin Library, Butler University), 19 Nov. 1858.

21. Lydia Sigourney, *Letters to Ladies* (Hartford: W. Watson, 1835), p. 32.

22. Katharine Merrill Graydon, ed., *Catharine Merrill: Life and Letters* (Greenfield, Ind.: Mitchell, 1934), p. 343.

23. N. E. A., "Letter," *Butler Alumnal Quarterly* 2 (Jan. 1914): 198.

24. Lawrence, "Rhetoric and Composition," p. 81.

25. *Catalogue, 1867,* p. 6; N. E. A., "Letter," p. 198.

26. *Catalogue, 1870; Catalogue, 1876–77,* p. 28; Graydon, *Catharine Merrill,* pp. 350–51.

27. Catharine Merrill, *The Man Shakespeare and Other Essays,* ed. Melville B. Anderson (Indianapolis: Bowen-Merrill, 1900), pp. 24, 8.

28. Graydon, *Catharine Merrill,* pp. 342, 346, 388.

12

SUE CARTER SIMMONS

Radcliffe Responses to Harvard Rhetoric

"AN ABSURDLY STIFF WAY OF THINKING"

Some men are born with an insight into the soul feminine, some men marry and achieve this insight, some men correct girls' themes and have this insight thrust upon them.

—H. A. W., Daily Theme, *Radcliffe Magazine,* 1900

COMPOSITION TEACHERS AND feminists alike have frequently complained about and critiqued academic writing. Ken Macrorie galvanized popular sentiment among many writing teachers in the 1960s and 1970s when he described his students' failed attempts at academic writing as "Engfish." Jane Tompkins, in her often-cited essay "Me and My Shadow," spoke for many feminists and other academics dissatisfied with the agonistic stance academic writing obligated them to take. Olivia Frey offered academic women a variety of noncombative discursive strategies in her 1990 *College English* essay. A 1992 feature article in the *Chronicle of Higher Education* and a 1994 companion piece reported a growing trend among women scholars in fields as diverse as literature and law to include autobiographical perspectives and personal voice in their traditional scholarly writings.[1]

Over the past few years, many people in the field of composition have begun to explore the ways that composition teaching could better serve women students alienated by traditional pedagogies. New ways of reading women's autobiographical writings are suggested in essays by Elizabeth Flynn and Shirley K. Rose. The essays in *Teaching Writing: Pedagogy, Gender, and Equity* collectively call for teachers to offer students alternatives to traditional academic writing. Some of those alternatives have been published in mainstream composition journals by Pamela Annas in "Style as Politics: A Feminist Approach to the Teaching of Writing," by Clara Juncker in "Writing (with) Cixous," and by Catherine E. Lamb in "Beyond Argument in Feminist Composition." Taken together, these works give evidence of the ways that feminist scholarship is changing views about academic writing.[2]

Ostensibly, one purpose of learning academic writing—and of teaching it—is for students to be able to enter new discourse communities where they will gain access to greater cultural capital. However, theory about discourse communities in composition teaching has most often served, as Susan Miller argues in her critique of the field, to "bring the student and the student's desires within academic conventions." Likewise, many feminist critiques of academic writing conclude with the conservative injunction that teachers must continue to teach academic writing in order to give oppressed students access to this means of cultural capital.[3]

The impetus to teach conventions of academic discourse, Miller argues, has led many teachers and theorists to overlook the conflictual nature of communities, to gloss over how communities restrict membership and reinscribe patterns of oppression and exclusion, and to undervalue the resistance of students to the discursive strategies of academic writing.[4] This omission is important because resistance to oppressive structures can provide powerful sites of critique. I'd like to build on Miller's observation about student resistance by examining how women students at Radcliffe in the late nineteenth and early twentieth centuries responded to the ways of writing they learned in their composition courses. In these women's writings, I see a range of critiques of academic writing, a variety of strategies for resisting it, and a record of women's voices bearing witness to their experiences in a male-centered curriculum.

During the late nineteenth century, Radcliffe's "brother" institution, Harvard, was known nationally as a leader in curriculum reform. In writing instruction it was a national leader as well, with textbooks by two of its English professors, Adams Sherman Hill and Barrett Wendell, adopted at colleges and universities nationwide. Harvard's influence on writing instruction spread further as men trained there in English moved on to teach writing and set up writing programs at other colleges and universities, and as secondary and preparatory schools struggled to match their curricula to Harvard's entrance examination requirements.[5]

To date, however, little is known about Harvard's influence on writing instruction at its neighbor on nearby Brattle Street, Radcliffe. JoAnn

Campbell's examination of three Radcliffe women's writings for their composition courses indicates that Harvard pedagogy failed to meet these women's needs as learners. Likewise, Joyce Antler argues, in her case history of Radcliffe graduate Lucy Sprague Mitchell, that Mitchell's own struggle against the so-called universal epistemology of her Harvard philosophy professors "suggests that we ought to search harder . . . to locate similar examples of women's far from passive responses to their education."[6] Since writing instruction at Harvard developed in a particular—and masculine—context, examining the early history of writing instruction at Radcliffe will indicate some of the challenges surrounding pedagogical practice in that different—and feminine—context. Indeed, the surviving writings show the Radcliffe students' resistance to and critique of Harvard writing pedagogy, as well as one student's initiation into, and mastery of, academic discourse. These women's writings about their experiences learning academic discourse can illuminate the ambivalent feelings many students, teachers, and scholars in higher education have today and can thus inform our collective critique of academic discourse.

Archival holdings about writing instruction before 1900 at Radcliffe are limited, including catalogs of course offerings; annual reports of Radcliffe's governing bodies; the papers of one student from the 1880s, Annie Ware Winsor Allen; records of some student clubs; and the *Radcliffe Magazine,* a student-run literary magazine begun in 1899.[7] Consequently, in this paper, I will briefly sketch the early history of writing instruction at Radcliffe and then turn to two bodies of writings, the writings of Annie Ware Winsor Allen while she was taking English courses at Radcliffe from 1883 to 1888 and the daily themes published anonymously in the *Radcliffe Magazine.* Annie, like the anonymous *Radcliffe Magazine* writers, experienced many of the conflicts addressed in recent feminist critiques of academic discourse and developed discursive survival strategies that enabled her to transform the hostile educational environment into one more supportive of her needs as a learner. Looking at the writings and listening to the voices of Annie and her fellow students at Radcliffe can provide us with considerable insight into the process of "mastering" academic writing.

Moving Harvard Rhetoric to Radcliffe

In 1879 schoolmaster Arthur Gilman and his wife Stella began corresponding with Harvard president Charles Eliot to determine whether Harvard professors might be allowed to offer private instruction to women students. The Gilmans, perhaps concerned about the higher education of their daughter, soon organized a group of prominent women in Cambridge determined to provide women with the opportunity to receive the same education offered to Harvard men. Arrangements were made for willing Harvard professors to repeat their course lectures, beginning in 1880, at a separate location to an audience of women students only. Entrance requirements were identical to those of Harvard, and those women students who finished a four-year course of study identical to that at Harvard were to receive a certificate of completion.[8]

Classes were small initially, with a total enrollment in 1880 of twenty-five students and only four students studying composition with Adams S. Hill. By 1884–85 there were four English courses offered to a total of fifty-nine students. That year, Annie and eleven others studied Shakespeare with Barrett Wendell, eighteen studied eighteenth-century British literature with Bliss Perry, six studied Chaucer with LeBaron Russell Briggs, and "large classes" took the required course Themes and Forensics from Barrett Wendell. The course offerings and enrollment continued to increase: by 1894–95 English offered sixteen courses to 387 students; by 1900–1901, twenty-one courses to 457 students.[9]

Since the primary mission of Radcliffe was to provide the same education for women as Harvard did for men, the same degree requirements had to be met as well. During the last quarter of the nineteenth century, Harvard had instituted an entrance examination that included writing an essay about literature and correcting sentence errors; Radcliffe women took the same entrance examinations as the male students. In addition Harvard, under the leadership of President Charles Eliot, moved to a largely elective curriculum but maintained some requirements in writing.[10]

During most of the last quarter of the nineteenth century, Harvard and Radcliffe required students to take English A, a first-year writing course, and to write a series of longer papers, called themes and forensics, during the last two or three years of study. In addition, English 12, an advanced elective writing course, was regularly taught at Radcliffe in the 1880s and 1890s. In English A students at Harvard listened to lectures twice a week on the principles of style and met once weekly in smaller sections to hear their teacher's oral criticisms of student themes. Students wrote long themes, called "fortnightlies," every other week. In English 12 students followed the same general outline of activities but also wrote short "daily themes" six days a week for the entire academic year, excluding a brief break at Christmas. Writing teachers at Harvard tended to grade primarily on surface features of language—grammatical correctness and a narrow range of stylistic features.[11]

From the start, the goal of providing the "same" education for Radcliffe women as for Harvard men was compromised in several ways, especially in writing instruction. Professors ordinarily met their classes for three hours weekly at Harvard; at Radcliffe, as an inducement for their participation, they met classes for only two hours. In writing courses, and especially English 12, the two hours of lectures were complemented with a third hour for writing practice or workshop. While the archival sources are not clear, most probably the third-hour workshop activities were dropped at Radcliffe and lectures filled the two hours of class time.

At Harvard, writing teachers routinely met all writing students in conferences about once monthly for the entire year. In the conferences, teachers delivered oral criticisms of the papers and generally came to know their students more personally, or at least they attempted to do so. Conferences were usually held either in a teacher's home or in a room he rented for use as an office on the Harvard Yard; Barrett Wendell, who taught the writing courses most often in Radcliffe's early years, held conferences in his office in Grays Hall. In the 1880s and 1890s, however, Radcliffe students were forbidden to enter the Yard. In fact, Wendell, an outspoken opponent of formalized coeducation at Harvard, defended the practice of forbidding women to walk in Harvard Yard as Harvard's foremost "virile" tradition.[12] Conferences might have been held in the Radcliffe classroom building; however, until 1884, when a larger building was purchased, there was no available space for conferences. It is probable, then, that the women were unable to meet their writing instructors in conference before 1884, and unclear whether or not conferences might have been held after 1884 in the larger building, Fay House.

Additionally, class size changed the effects of writing instruction at Radcliffe. Harvard classes were large, with as many as 500 in English A and 150 in English 12. A central part of the pedagogy in those classes was reading aloud student papers and criticizing them before the class. The class sizes at Harvard offered anonymity to student writers whose writing faults were exposed to their classmates. At Radcliffe, with perhaps two or three dozen students in English A and less than a dozen in English 12, anonymity was not possible, since the few women students were more likely to know each other and even room with each other.

Radcliffe Student Responses to Harvard Rhetoric

Histories of women's education in the United States such as Barbara Solomon's *In the Company of Educated Women* and Helen Horowitz's *Alma*

Mater have noted that women came to college for different reasons than men. While men in the late nineteenth century were more likely to attend college to further their professional futures, women were constrained in the occupations that they could enter. Some women's colleges and seminaries, such as Mount Holyoke, designed curricula to meet women's needs and existing career opportunities. Toward the end of the nineteenth century, normal schools began to provide professional training for women (and men) who planned careers as teachers. Some other colleges, like Radcliffe, simply provided a traditional curriculum designed for male students, with little forethought about how women might use their education after college. The writing curriculum, then, was a Harvard approach that had been transplanted into a very different ground at Radcliffe.[13]

In many ways the system of writing instruction that evolved at Harvard during the 1870s and 1880s was uniquely suited to Harvard, then the most difficult college in the United States to enter and the easiest to graduate from. After meeting the stringent entrance requirements, Harvard students could easily take the "gentleman's C" in their courses and in the writing required of them, graduate with a Harvard degree, and progress into their chosen professions or family businesses. Indeed, the Harvard writing curriculum presumed casual attitudes about study on the part of most students. Gradebooks in the Harvard Archives reveal that great numbers of Harvard men regularly received C's in writing courses at all levels, and that very few men in the large classes seemed interested in distinguishing themselves in their professors' eyes.[14]

Some Radcliffe students found the Harvard writing pedagogy to be, at best, alienating and ineffective. In her essay "Controlling Voices: The Legacy of English A at Radcliffe," JoAnn Campbell argues that Annie Ware Winsor Allen, along with two early-twentieth-century Radcliffe students, Mary Lee and Helen Dorothea Crawford Seidler, desired more personal relationships with their professors.[15] Examining papers these women wrote for their writing classes, Campbell notes that responses from the instructors usually consisted of comments on mechanics and grammar, with no or little mention of the content of the writing. As Campbell's discussion shows, Mary Lee and Dorothea Seidler were frustrated and angry at the writing courses and teachers, feelings most powerfully expressed in Dorothea's ironic theme of advice to other Radcliffe women on how to survive college: "It is absolutely necessary that you become fully convinced of the fact that you are nobody and that you know nothing. Select the most insignificant animal you know, and consider it many degrees above you. Practice mental salaaming until you reach the humanity of a worm." [16]

Ridicule, direct critique, and anger are not to be found in Annie Ware Winsor Allen's school papers, however. Instead, in them a variety of writing voices emerge, voices that indicate the difficulties Annie encountered as a woman learning to perform in the ways her Harvard professors expected. Moreover, Annie's papers reveal her own struggle to work in an alienating educational setting on a daily basis, and to face continuing lack of success at her writing efforts. Annie's papers also indicate how, by learning academic literacy, she transformed the hostile curriculum she met into a more personally fulfilling one that enabled her to meet her own goal of becoming a schoolteacher. In this respect, looking at the process by which Annie came to write academic discourse shows both the challenges one student faced and the power she eventually acquired by learning academic discourse.

Developing a Public Voice, Negotiating Authority

Annie wanted to be a schoolteacher and believed a Harvard education from Radcliffe would best prepare her for such work. In her writings Annie directly comments on the difficulty of speaking about her experiences in the academic context, she consciously adopts several writing voices, and she eventually negotiates ways of voicing her experiences and opinions in academic language and in academic settings. Like the *Radcliffe Magazine* writers, she found ways of using writing to transform an alienating, masculinized, teacher-centered academic environment into a more student-centered, connected one. And Annie found ways of writing with authority and privilege in an academic circle.[17]

When Annie began her second year at Radcliffe in the fall of 1884, she began keeping a journal that she dedicated to "my Mother dear." She wrote in the journal almost daily and shared it with her family regularly, like many women of her time. Historically, journals have often been kept as a record of family life and have thus been shared with family members, especially women's journals.[18] That Annie would, in her second year of study, begin a family journal about her academic experiences is significant. In the journal she used written literacy both to record her experiences with higher education and to share those experiences with her family. Thus the journal provided a means of integrating the separate spheres of Annie's life, an integration that her academic experiences challenged daily.

In her first impressions of her teacher Barrett Wendell in Shakespeare class, Annie records the challenge to her own personal moral values she faced in the academic context. In her journal entry for the first day of class, Annie records that Wendell "showed himself a man and a gentleman in what he said about the reasons for not using expurgated editions" of Shakespeare. Matters of taste arose as the course progressed, and Annie again turned to her journal:

> [Wendell] has a bothersome way of addressing all his questions on any one subject to one person, and he fixed upon me to explain—apropos of Falstaff's remarks about Prince John—how men who were not teetotalers felt about men that were. And told me at full length how they felt a man of that sort had not sympathy and fellow-feeling etc. etc. He is a greater smoker himself and does not disapprove of wine on occasion. I was aghast. I hadn't a notion of what to do. Anywhere else I would have told him what I thot, and explained just my own position. But of course I couldn't do that, and I couldn't look as tho' I entirely liked it, or entirely didn't like it. So I just said—"I know they do" in as non-committal a tone as I could find.[19]

Annie, fully aware that she and her teacher disagreed on their views of the acceptability of drinking and smoking, found herself unable or unwilling to express her own views directly to Wendell in the public space of the classroom. However, she did turn to the more private space of her journal and to the more familiar audience of her family to record this experience—an audience so familiar to her that she could not only write freely about her shock at Wendell's opinions, she could refer to her "own position" without even needing to explain to her readers what it was.

Annie showed a keen understanding of the public space of the classroom, knew it to be anything but a free marketplace of ideas, and took care with the comments she made there. Further, she saw in her encounters with Wendell that the moral values that she brought with her to Radcliffe might not be shared by others there. However, at this point, Annie's insights into the classroom went no further than herself and her family.

Annie's first long theme assignment from Wendell was to write on whether it is good for men to "sow wild oats" when young. In keeping with the primary goal of Radcliffe to provide Harvard education for women, this topic is similar to those assigned at Harvard then. Nonetheless, one must wonder at the possible subject positions this topic might elicit from late-nineteenth-century men and women—as prospective sowers of oats, and as prospective fields upon which those oats might be sown.

Not unaware of the difficulty of finessing this rhetorical situation as a woman, Annie wrote her theme as two letters from herself (return address

"Speculationsville") to a fictional friend, "Bob," in response to his claim that a young man should sow wild oats in his youth. In the first letter, Annie can't agree: she argues that to do so would be to contradict the laws of nature and development, to follow one's worst impulses rather than one's best. The second letter addresses Bob's claim that a man who has sown his oats and reformed in his youth is stronger and deserves more credit than a man who has never done wrong. Again Annie cannot agree, and argues from personal example: her own father is the best man she can think of, he did no wrong when young, and he is a wholly good man.

To complete this assignment, Annie adopts a discursive form familiar to her, the letter, and constructs Bob as a person who also knows her father and who would therefore understand and perhaps accept her argument. The elaborate rhetorical context also allows Annie a means of stating her own opinion on the matter—she signs her initials to both letters—without directly addressing her views to her teacher, who, by now, she knows decries conventionality in areas of morals and taste. Bob, however, would have been a more supportive reader than her teacher Wendell was.

In his comment on the paper, Wendell characterizes Annie's reasoning as feminine, her knowledge as naive, and her argument from example as weak:

> Your reasoning, if you will permit me to say so, is charmingly feminine. That is, you base it upon the notion of the world which insists in a well-brought up feminine mind, & not upon the world as it is. In the real world, things are askew; they always have been & always will be. Again, as I hope Shakespere [sic] will begin to show you, nobody was every wholly good or wholly bad. To go no further, study Falstaff & Prince Hal. Finally,—I hate to dispel illusions, but your argument from family examples is a terribly weak kind of thing. If there is ever one class of people that we don't know in all their complexity, it is the people that we live with & care for.[20]

While the elaborately constructed rhetorical context of the letters seems to have enabled Annie to complete the assignment, it is a strategy that did not succeed in her teacher's eyes. Wendell's comment cuts through the fictional context directly to the substance of not just Annie's paper, but her family as well—the argument from the example of her father, the family views on good moral conduct. Wendell's comment, indeed, takes aim at the very source of Annie's knowledge, her family, her father: "If there is ever one class of people that we don't know in all their complexity, it is the people that we live with & care for." As JoAnn Campbell notes in her reading of this same essay, in this last line Wendell shows "disbelief in even the possibility of intimate relationships, a stance with serious consequences for a connected knower."[21] Ironically, as Annie constructed a rhetorical context for the assignment that allowed her to connect her family and academic lives, her teacher carefully delineated the only spheres that she would be permitted to connect in her academic writing—writing class and Shakespeare class.

After these exchanges, not surprisingly, Annie's daily themes changed. She began to write daily themes of two types: themes discussing Radcliffe life, and themes on more innocuous topics such as moods, the value of being broadly educated, family scenes, a sketch of a room, character sketches, a sunset in the city. In these themes Annie developed a distinctive voice, or, more precisely, she developed a distinctively *indistinctive* voice. That is, as she followed Wendell's instructions to "observe" the world around her and record those observations in the daily themes, Annie's writing became increasingly more anonymous—no more direct references to any details of her life or to her own opinions or beliefs.

In one of these themes, Annie uses a variety of rhetorical strategies that distance her from what she is saying: the argument from analogy, the third-person pronouns:

> When a man's business is the putting-in of electric lights, he puts them in, wherever they are ordered. He does not question the right of these places to exist. Owners of rum-shops, gambling dens, and low places of amusement are his most usual customers. He does business as business, and does not ask the moral worth of each man whom he serves.
>
> When a pupil enters a class he is expected to learn. He is to take every means within his reach to improve his knowledge of the branch which he has chosen. His mind is to be stocked: it is a matter of business between him and the teachers. His mind is a thing apart from himself, a thing to be criticized and improved in every way. There should be no consideration of the credit or discredit which its state reflects upon him. When he feels it incumbent upon him to be always in the right and always sensible, he will not learn much. Until he can put his sensitiveness behind him he will not develop much.[22]

Wendell, perhaps willfully missing the point of the argument from analogy, commented simply "Analogy obscure." While Annie drew no direct connections between her own experience and the subject of the theme, she must certainly have been commenting on her own experience in her Radcliffe classes. Given that her early writings show her facing conflicts between her moral views and those of her teachers, the moral message of this theme is especially important: students must passively accept what their teachers present. Annie's description of the process of education—"His mind is to be stocked: it is a matter of business between him and the teachers"—echoes Paulo Freire's critique of the banking concept of education, a view of students as consumers, paying their money and waiting passively for authoritarian teachers to symbolically deposit knowledge in them.[23]

A more striking feature of this theme is the voice used. Annie directly states that a student's mind is a thing separate from "his" body; in other words, the kinds of knowledge that students learn in school are separated from the kinds of knowledge they learn elsewhere, with their whole beings. Annie speaks here with the "voice from nowhere," to paraphrase Donna Haraway's term, a generic voice grounded nowhere, that presents "the view from above, from nowhere, from simplicity." Richard Ohmann, in a classic Marxist critique of composition teaching in the 1970s, argued that static teaching curricula typically characterize a student writer as "newborn, unformed, without social origins and without needs that would spring from his origins. He has no history. Hence the writing he does and the skills he acquires are detached from those parts of himself not encompassed by his new identity as a student." Students, Ohmann observes, are portrayed as "having been extracted from any community they might have inhabited prior to entering the classroom."[24]

Extending Ohmann's critique of the position of student writers, Sharon Crowley protests: "That this a-rhetorical nonperson could author a text in the sense of taking responsibility for its shape or of marking it with her voice is difficult to imagine." Rather than marking a written text with a personalized voice, Crowley argues, many student writers produce "anti-writing" marked with no voice, or with a generic "student voice." Mary Lee, writing at Radcliffe in the early part of the twentieth century, realized that the required writing course English A promoted what Crowley calls antiwriting: "English A does not teach us to write, it teaches us not to write. It is not a path to future composition courses, it is a stumbling block, over which most of us get so bumped and battered & discouraged, that we let English class alone through college."[25]

The "voice from nowhere" is decidedly masculine, and its knowledge and view of schooling are decidedly masculine as well. Annie uses the word "man" twice in the first paragraph and uses masculine pronouns exclusively in the paragraph on schooling—a practice that is quite uncharacteristic of her other college writings.[26] Her choice to speak in this masculine voice contrasts starkly with her earlier letters from Speculationsville, signed with her own initials and written about her own father. Further, as Annie develops the analogy, she chooses masculine occupations—putting in electric lights, business—and masculinized public locations—rum shops, gambling dens, low places of amusement. Her analogy compares the relationship of student and teacher to that of tradesman and customer, pointedly placing schooling in the public, and masculine, sphere.

Annie does write in a more grounded and distinctly female voice, "the voice from Radcliffe," in some daily themes. She writes about Radcliffe experiences, Radcliffe women, stereotypes about Harvard men, and, at times, the ways Latin is taught at Radcliffe. In these themes, however, Annie writes generalizations about these subjects, using third-person pronouns, or occasionally the plural "we," rather than specifically identifying the opinions expressed or the experiences referred to as her own.

In many of these themes, I sense great tension between the voice used and the subjects being addressed, as in her theme on "Open Criticism," which openly criticizes a common practice in the writing courses. Wendell and other Harvard writing instructors, during the 1880s and 1890s, read aloud passages of several student papers and criticized them before the class. The instructors seem not to have identified the authors of the papers as they were read aloud, a practice that probably ensured anonymity at Harvard with its classes of 150 or more and its discussion groups numbering 50 and higher. However, as pointed out earlier, anonymity would be difficult at best at Radcliffe where the classes were considerably smaller—a total of forty-two students in all English courses for the year 1886–87, with eighteen in Briggs's Rhetoric and English Composition and only four in Wendell's English Composition class. Here is Annie's response to this practice, written during her fourth year at Radcliffe:

> At first a system of public criticism is certainly trying. It is always hard for people to get out of themselves and look at themselves with impartial eyes. This is what we are expected to do when our themes are criticized aloud in open class. It makes the shivers creep over one's cheeks, and the shakes go all over one's body at first. We are not used to sharing our peculiar difficulties with the general public. The process of getting used to it is not a pleasant one.
>
> But it is only right that we should learn to look at our work in this impersonal way. It is a good thing to learn that our faults are not precious possessions like our life-blood. We can part with our faults without injury; it is not a vital pain when they are touched. And our good

> qualities—we do well to understand that they are not sacred invaluable possessions which are profaned by being looked upon. If somehow we can get to see that a mental fault is not a virtue we have gone far toward a healthy state of mind. We are learning to live to see ourselves and other people in the natural light of day. The nearer we get to this state of mind the easier it will be for us to learn and for our instructors to teach.[27]

The turn that this theme takes in the last paragraph is typical of Annie's writings in the "voice from Radcliffe." The theme initially brings up an experience or opinion centered in Radcliffe, implies a negative evaluation of it, then turns at the end to reinscribe the existing power relations. In reading through Annie's daily themes of this type, I find myself waiting for the moment when her writing will erupt with the anger of Mary Lee. What I hear at the end of these themes instead is the voice of compliance and accommodation, the voice of a student who may question her teachers but does not presume to challenge them. Annie's voice of accommodation may well reflect the fact that the themes in her collection were actually submitted for credit to her teachers. The *Radcliffe Magazine* writings are called "dailies," implying that they too were written for credit in the writing courses. However, the public forum of the magazine may have provided a place where students could critique their teachers and classes more stridently than they dared in writings actually submitted for course credit.

Beginning in late 1886 and early 1887, Annie comes to use a different voice in her daily themes, the voice of the cultural translator. While her daily themes were ostensibly addressed to Wendell, and perhaps read only by him, Annie's sense of audience is broader than Wendell alone, as her sense of purpose for writing is broader than merely fulfilling an academic requirement. Annie positions herself as an insider on the culture of Radcliffe women and uses her writing to educate her Harvard teachers about the pedagogical situations that they encounter. It is in these themes that Annie begins to write with increasing authority, to take ownership of her writing, and to integrate her personal knowledge with her academic writing:

> That man will be successful in the education of women, who learns to know and use their peculiar characteristics. I think there are few men, even among those who have taught women a long time, who understand how much might be brought to light if the right means were used; women are so easily frightened back into their ignorance, and on the other hand so easily led to believe themselves quite wonderfully

> clever, that they need very judicious and even crafty management. I do feel certain that the man who practices the right method would be surprised himself at the result which he produced.
>
> These women, timid, narrow, inconsequent as they are, have great power of persistent endurance and a most delicate perception. Women as students do not show for half what they are worth; the man who teaches them has but little notion of some of their most valuable possibilities. Of this I am sure,—if women are not interesting inspiring pupils, it is not that they cannot be, but that they do not know how to be. I see enough of Annex girls to know that most of them never show in the class their individual ability and their most attractive mental characteristics.[28]

In this theme, Annie uses first-person pronouns, clearly stating, and claiming, her own opinions, grounding them in her own experiences ("I see enough of Annex girls to know . . ."). Further, she speaks boldly as educational critic, using her personal observations and experience as grounds to critique the education she is receiving.

In another daily theme, Annie discusses with great insight the classroom demeanor of her classmates at Radcliffe, noting that women students do not passively receive whatever knowledge comes their way in classes. Rather, women students actively challenge and resist, though they may do so without speaking up in class:

> I think women, besides really lacking independence, add to their apparent servility by their timid silence. Women students often disagree radically and emphatically with their instructors' statements and opinions, often have independent and sensible notions of their own; but they do not dare to express their dissent, or, feeling themselves ignorant, they do not feel justified in propounding original theories to men who have spent years in study. They are not the mere receptacles which they seem to be.[29]

Up until this point, Wendell's comments on Annie's daily themes had been noncommittal at best; Wendell usually responded to writing that he considered poor by ignoring it. As I have read Annie's themes along with student themes in the Harvard Archives, I see Wendell's positive comments when student writers write with assured confidence about insights of their own, based on their own observations of life and human behavior. His monthly report for Annie's daily themes in January 1887 included comments that Annie's subjects are "varied; & almost always suggestive. Close to life. . . . The variety of your work is excellent. You seem to me entirely on the right road." Annie's response to these positive comments can be inferred from her writings: she continued to write with the voice that Wendell had praised.

Annie used the writing courses she took with Wendell to pursue her interest in literature, in part by necessity. Since the literature course offerings at Radcliffe then were limited, Annie took Wendell's course on daily and fortnightly themes several times, with a different plan of literary reading each time. Many of Annie's longer themes, the fortnightlies, were written about the literature she had been reading and thus reflect Annie's attempts to enter the discourse community of literary scholarship. To some extent, the voice of scholar that Annie uses allows her new ways of writing about her own moral values—a way of voicing her personal values within an academic context.

Annie had been unsuccessful earlier at such writing in the two letters to "Bob" from "Speculationsville." Later that same year, however, Annie addressed a similar topic in her theme "Evelina's Picture of Her Times," an essay favorably received by Wendell. Writing on Fanny Burney's novel *Evelina,* which conveys a young woman's views of eighteenth-century English life, Annie comments on the overconcern of that time with matters of etiquette and delicacy. Specifically, she cites a passage from the novel in which Evelina is accosted by one man while another man of a lower social class looks on—he simply watches because intervening would be a breach of etiquette. Annie sharply criticizes the man who refused to help the woman because, she argues, in matters of etiquette, commonsense should help one distinguish between essentials and nonessentials. On this point—Annie's view supported by an example from a literary text—Wendell agrees, writing "Good" in large letters across the entire page. Annie was thus able to criticize the "sowing of wild oats" in a way that would not offend her instructor's penchant for mocking conventional morality but would actually support his penchant for mocking etiquette.[30]

An additional strategy that Annie adopted as she wrote about literary texts—one she kept using throughout her college writing—was to end her papers with one or more questions for her teacher about some point in the text of her paper or about some technical matter of style. She might ask, for example, whether a particular passage in the paper needs more descriptive detail. In one paper on late medieval literature, Annie ends by stating that, as a result of her reading, "a new want has been created. I want now to study philology and etymology in connection with the English language." This last sentence of the paper is followed with a few blank lines and then, in parentheses and smaller handwriting, a question addressed directly to her teacher: "(Is there no word for philology and etymology?)" Her instructor replied by giving her the accepted usages of words such as linguistics, philology, and etymology, and by asking her a question: "Do you ever work with Skeat's large etymological dictionary—a fascinating & suggestive book?"[31]

This exchange is notable: at Annie's invitation, Wendell responded not as teacher/corrector of her style; he responded as supporter of her developing disciplinary interests. This exchange typifies many other in which Annie found ways of representing herself as a student serious about her studies and about her writing. More importantly, I believe, such exchanges—initiated by Annie—provided new positions from which her teachers could write and speak to her. In short, this strategy provided Annie a means of getting more personal attention from her teachers and of presenting herself as a serious student of literature who deserved that attention. This strategy helped enable her to transform a masculine curriculum and environment into one that better met her needs as a learner and as a serious student.

Both Annie and Wendell came to see her role in the community of literary scholars in a fashion consonant with conventional gender roles. Wendell mentored outstanding Harvard men believing that he was helping to create the next great generation of American writers and men of letters. In fact, his English 12 course at Harvard nurtured dozens of writers, scholars, and men of letters. Both Wendell and Annie came to believe that her destiny would be as a schoolteacher, not a writer or a scholar.[32]

In maintaining her commitment to school teaching, Annie may be simply following conventional gender roles, that is, forsaking a career as a scholar for that of a school teacher. However, as Joyce Antler's study of Lucy Sprague Mitchell shows, some women have seen school teaching as a means of maintaining autonomy over their own lives while contributing to the lives of children. Lucy Sprague Mitchell, who graduated from Radcliffe in 1900, was active in Progressive Era educational reforms and left a career of higher education to teach younger children and train elementary teachers. Antler argues that Mitchell's career change reflected her understanding of school teaching as "a creative, experimental, and scientific endeavor, to be pursued ardently over the course of a continuing career." Mitchell came to believe that "teachers were active learners who expanded their personal horizons continuously, at the same time that they aided the larger cause of social reconstruction."[33] In effect, teachers could be agents for social reform through their work in the classroom. While Annie's educational philosophy is never fully articulated in her writings, a view of teaching as significant work emerges toward the end of her studies at Radcliffe.

From her family and personal journals to the daily and fortnightly themes she wrote for her classes, Annie's writings reflect her commitment to teaching. When her insights about teaching move from her family journals to her academic writing, and when she moves from merely informing her audience about Radcliffe women to convincing her audience to accept her opinions, Annie begins to write boldly, with assurance: "In the course of eight years' study and observation I have become fully convinced that in nine cases out of ten Latin is taught very badly."[34]

She wrote her first senior forensic on teaching—and in it directly adopts the persona of the teacher she wants to become. Annie wrote the paper as a series of arguments for the value of general reading in the form of a teacher's lecture to young girls beginning a course in English literature. In many ways the essay is a remarkable performance. In it, Annie creates a fictional rhetorical setting that occasions the writing, much as she had earlier created the letters to "Bob" from "Speculationsville." Further, Annie specifically creates a setting in which the speaker of the essay is a woman addressing a class of girls—a setting with which her teacher Wendell is totally unfamiliar.

The essay was well received by Wendell, who wrote comments in the margins such as *Excellent exposition* and *Superior* (high praise from Wendell). In his end comment, however, he addressed Annie as a professional, giving her an A on the paper in spite of his criticism of it: "Admirable: interesting & discriminating. Yet you run the risk of 'patronizing' your pupils; need you regard them as quite so infantile & giddy? I should not dare treat boys as you propose to treat girls. Be as strong & as interesting, & less professorial, & you will prove a stimulating teacher."[35] There is a certain caution in Wendell's judgment: Annie does not patronize her pupils, she "runs the risk" of doing so. Similarly, Wendell does not tell her she should treat her pupils differently; he says that he would not treat boys the way she is treating girls. Wendell critiques Annie's paper from his own experience in teaching college men, opening up the possibility in his comment that perhaps classes of girls and of boys might require different treatment from their teachers, and that Annie might well have chosen the appropriate tone for her fictional audience of girls. This caution—along with the grade of A—reasserts Annie's authority as writer/teacher able to make decisions about her own textual/classroom space.

In this paper, as Wendell notes, Annie speaks with authority, the authority of the teacher she wants to become. Ironically, in writing this paper—as a school*girl*, not yet a school*teacher*—Annie pulls off the quintessential academic performance of writing as though she had the authority she does not yet have—the authority that she will be granted only if she can write as though she already possesses it.

Writing from a position of authority, of privilege, is a central part of learning to write academic discourse, according to composition theorist David Bartholomae. A successful student writer, Bartholomae argues, "must see herself within a privileged discourse, one that already includes and excludes groups of readers. She must be either equal to or more powerful than those she would address. The writing . . . must somehow transform the political and social relationships between students and teachers."[36] In the papers she wrote on the literature she read and in her papers on teaching, Annie found ways of writing with authority that positioned Wendell as her equal. Annie found ways to integrate successfully her commitment to teaching and her observations and experiences as a student with the academic writing requirements she had to meet. The high praise from Wendell on these papers reveals that in them Annie found a way to write in the public space of the academy about subjects she found truly meaningful, and on which she had important things to say.

"Mastering" the Daily Theme

Direct criticism of Harvard writing instruction (and instructors) is rarely voiced in the writings that Annie Ware Winsor Allen turned in for grades, and is evident only rarely in the journals she shared with her family. Perhaps because of the real audiences with whom these writings were shared, these writings present a necessarily limited view of the curriculum and instructors. More direct critiques of the curriculum and instructors can be found in the *Radcliffe Magazine.* Early volumes of the *Radcliffe Magazine,* which began publication in 1899, feature a regular column of "Dailies," daily themes written, ostensibly, for the writing courses. These daily themes, published with the authors identified only by their initials, offer a variety of critiques of Harvard writing instruction.

One line of critique concerns the contrast between what the women writers know and what they must voice in school. In the daily below, B. M. D. shows herself distracted from the history she studies, from watching the fly to looking at the marshes and the sea outside speculating on what it must have been like to sail to distant places:

> I sit in the bit rocking-chair, tilted well back, with my feet on another chair, and the atlas and a book of badly written notes sprawled open on my knees. I keep one hand pressed over the passage which I am try-

> ing to learn, and, with my eyes turned up to the ceiling, ask myself: What did Estevan Gomez do, and when did he do it? A fly rambles across the ceiling; I watch him to the window, and my eyes stray farther to the brown marshes in the distance and the blue sea. You were a sailor, Don Estevan, I know; you set out in your rickety little pinnace among those tumbling bright waters. Did you steer among the smooth channels of the Bahamas, or did you launch boldly into northern waters and fight your way through tempests and great waves? You must have loved the tumult of the life, Don Estevan; I only wish I might have sailed with you. It is a hard fate to be born in the nineteenth century, and born a woman.
>
> The clock begins to strike. Twenty minutes wasted, and, Estevan Gomez, I cannot for the life of me remember what it was you discovered.[37]

The history B. M. D. studies is in every way unconnected to her. While she can detail the setting in which she studies, she cannot recall the information she is expected to memorize about Estevan Gomez. She is very aware of her present-tense existence ("The clock begins to strike"), while she studies about the past. And she is clearly aware that cultural expectations about her gender separate her from the history she studies—unlike Don Estevan, instead of exploring, she must study about his explorations, or daydream about them. Ironically, the daydream allows her to construct a personal relationship with the subject of her study, a relationship embodied in the daily theme she writes.

Like this daily, the other published dailies reveal a great gulf between the women students' ways of knowing and the substance of their school writings. These women comment directly on their sense that their personal knowledge, opinions, and experiences are not acceptable subjects for papers in writing class, echoing Helen Dorothea Crawford Seidler's advice in 1910 to "become fully convinced of the fact that you are nobody and that you know nothing." In a similar vein, Joyce Antler finds a central epistemological conflict in the papers Lucy Sprague Mitchell wrote for her Harvard philosophy professors. Lucy Mitchell critiqued their epistemology "on the ground that they excluded her own experience—women's experience—from the sphere of their moral universe."[38] Thus the women students faced a gulf that they had to bridge in the act of writing themes. Significantly, writing pedagogy during the 1880s and 1890s at Harvard and thus at Radcliffe included writing short themes daily, six days a week, from October to June. Women students, then, had to find ways almost every day of bridging the gap between what they knew or were interested in and what knowledge their instructor expected them to display in their writings. What is most fascinating about the daily themes published in the *Radcliffe Magazine,* however, is that they reveal not so much the women's "mastery" of this one genre of school writing, but their domestication of it to suit their own purposes: to vent their frustration with their writing classes, to voice their critique, and to build community among other Radcliffe students.

The daily below playfully mocks this dilemma of the student writer:

> In response to a request for a composition about elephants the following was handed in by a small boy:
>
> "Elephants are small, playful animals; they are very affectionate and have long, white wool. They live on nuts."
>
> The astonished teacher naturally questioned the youthful genius.
>
> "Did you ever see an elephant?"
>
> "Oh, yes."
>
> "Do you think they are small and playful?"
>
> "Oh, no."
>
> "Do you think they are affectionate and have long, white wool, and feed on nuts?"
>
> "Oh, no."
>
> "Then why did you write this?"
>
> "You told me to write a composition."[39]

The young writer is gullible enough to simply do as he is expected; the woman who wrote the story, M. V. A., uses this writing to indirectly critique the discursive conventions of writing classes. Perhaps she also willfully genders the student writer as a boy as a joke for her Radcliffe classmates, whose understanding of school writing exceeds that of the boy.

Another writer, H. A. W., directly addresses the ethical dilemma of the student writer whose course of daily writing trains her to lie:

> The most appropriate course to follow and counteract English 22 [an advanced writing course] would seem to be one in Ethics. When you have lied about brothers, sisters, and roommates that you never had, about sunsets that you never saw, and adventures that never came within your experiences; when you have contracted the habit of staring covertly over your book at the girl in the next alcove, and of eavesdropping in street cars; when you have come to hail the misfortunes and misadventures of your best friends as heaven-sent grist for the daily grind, is there not need for some corrective? A course in Ethics would at least help toward restoring the equilibrium of a moral sense

> warped by a hundred—or have we not written two or three hundred—daily themes.[40]

H. A. W. finds that the daily writing intrudes on all aspects of her life, disturbing her relationships with her friends by reducing them to subjects for her school writing and twisting her moral sense by teaching her to spy and to lie.

In this daily H. A. W. also comments on the artificial nature of the writing produced in the daily themes, another line of critique that emerges from the women's writings. In the daily below, M. V. A. critiques the artificial genre of school writing by appropriating the nonacademic, and feminine, genre of recipes:

> HINTS TO WRITERS
>
> *How to make a Daily Theme.*
>
> Take one empty head, and fill with a stuffing composed of indescribably tempting sunsets, five different aspects of Harvard Bridge, and a firm conviction that the writing of daily themes is destined to be the cause of your premature death. Stir this mixture rapidly for about ten minutes with a fountain pen. One of these ingredients, in most cases your opinion on the subject of themes, will rise to the surface. Take this out, flavor to taste with commas, and serve on a sheet of white paper. This receipt may be varied occasionally by substituting for the sunsets, electric cars, and for the views from the bridge, small girls with conventional golden curls.[41]

M. V. A. displays her mastery of the daily theme, reducing it to a formula and domesticating it in the feminine form of the recipe, which she can pass on to her *Radcliffe Magazine* readers. In her corresponding recipe for longer, "fortnightly" themes, M. V. A. comments directly on male privilege in describing how women students are perceived by their male instructors: "Take the brain of one Sophomore, which, if the theme is to be perfectly successful, should be of the Harvard brand, but in case that cannot be procured, Radcliffe will do."

In a similar vein, H. A. W. tells this anecdote:

> A girl wrote a theme and introduced a more or less facetious remark with the words, "as my brother said." The theme came back with her brother's remark bracketed, and the magic red word "good" in the margin opposite. Now can anything sadder be imagined than the fact that, since she never had a brother, he never can know that his humor was appreciated in English twenty-two [advanced writing]?[42]

In this anecdote, the male instructor's response to the theme treats the woman's writing as a vehicle to deliver humor to a male audience. Yet H. A. W. has the last laugh, using her writing as a vehicle to make the instructor the butt of her joke for the audience of Radcliffe students.

Most telling are the critiques that personify the daily and fortnightly themes as males. In a daily from 1900, C. F. McI. refers to the two kinds of writings as "brothers" in an imagined conversation between them. In another daily from 1900, E. B. C. imagines an encounter on a country walk with a daily theme, who, she says, was "nodding and leering at me wickedly." The daily theme is personified as a male who stalks her while she is alone and finally accosts her:

> "Come now, you may as well be civil," and he began pulling at my elbow.
>
> "Please go away," I begged.
>
> "Hm, want to get rid of me, do you?"
>
> I looked down imploringly. "It's all your own fault, you know," he continued, smiling ominously.
>
> "But I do so want to enjoy the fields and the trees, alone," I said, with tearful emphasis on the last word. There was an uncomfortable silence.
>
> "Well," drawled out my tormentor reluctantly, "I'll leave you now, not from any feeling of pity, but because I see a lady at the other end of the meadow whom I should rather enjoy bothering. I shall return soon, so don't be lonesome." And smiling maliciously he hopped away.[43]

In both dailies, the women writers use ridicule in their constructions of the themes, perhaps to claim their mastery over school writing. Both writers characterize the themes as males who think themselves able to exert power over Radcliffe women. Yet the writers also characterize the males as comic characters woefully inadequate to the task. In the writing above, while the daily theme is called a "tormentor," he nonetheless "hops" away. Likewise, in the daily by C. F. McI., the daily and fortnightly themes boast about who is more powerful and who causes more misery to the "girls" who must write them, in a stereotypically masculine display of oneupsmanship.

The writings from the *Radcliffe Magazine,* along with those by Mary Lee and Dorothea Seidler, display feelings of frustration with the academic writing required of Radcliffe students and illustrate the gulf between the women's ways of learning and writing and the school-sanctioned ways of demonstrating knowledge in writing. The more satiric writings also function as a means of claiming mastery over academic writing through ridicule or critique of it, such as concocting a recipe for themes, describing a small boy writing about elephants, and personifying themes as males. In this way, then, the daily theme functioned for these writers as a forum in which the women could remake a school writing form to serve needs of their own that were not being met in the established writing curriculum.

Farewell to the Daily Theme

Annie Ware Winsor Allen initially kept several kinds of journals—the school journal she shared with her family, a personal journal she apparently did not share, and, during summers, travel journals. While she was taking courses at Radcliffe, her personal writing waned, most certainly from the burden of study and frequent writing during the school year. Annie's experience thus presents a fine irony of Harvard rhetoric at Radcliffe.

Wendell required the dailies at Harvard in order to make writers more fluent and to make them more keenly observe the world around them, in short to use them as a substitute for the journals that many working writers keep. Yet as Gannett finds in *Gender and the Journal,* journals are a more feminine tradition, and as teachers in composition have often found, far more girls are likely to have had experience keeping diaries or journals than boys.[44]

From Annie's experience, we can see what happens when a fluent, perceptive, and observant writer meets a pedagogy designed to develop abilities that she already has: the great volume of written schoolwork leaves her with less and less time, and finally no time at all, for the self-sponsored writing she had found personally meaningful and that had been a primary means by which she maintained connection with her family. Moreover, because of the limited course offerings in literature at Radcliffe in the 1880s, Annie took writing courses several times, doing unrequired reading in different literary areas along with writing the required daily and fortnightly themes. Eventually, the sheer volume of her academic written work silenced her journal writing. In another way, Annie's repeated engagement with the writing courses worked against her. Her papers contain correspondence with Radcliffe decades later in which she tries, in vain, to receive a certificate of completion for her five years' of work at Radcliffe. According to the official records that survived, Annie did not receive credit for writing courses taken more than once, and consequently did not have enough credits for a certificate.

The voices with which Annie speaks in the daily themes are not the same as the voices of her family or personal journals. The muted voices of her daily and fortnightly themes are the written embodiment of Annie's survival strategies as an academic writer—the "daily theme eye" that she was coached to construct. Frequently written as first-person narratives, the daily themes present a strongly personal ethos. On the surface, they read like journal entries, like the "natural" self-expression of an "authentic" voice. Personal writings in composition classes may seem to present a unique, individual voice. Yet in "Judging Writing, Judging Selves," Lester Faigley discusses how such an ideology belies the constructed nature of self and voice. The personal voices that speak in the daily themes and other school writings were constructed in a particular discursive setting; they are performances for a teacher/evaluator.[45]

Drawing on Gannett's discussion of women's journal-keeping practices, I see Annie's personal and family journal voices as silenced in and by the academic context—squeezed out by the voices Annie needed to speak with for academic survival. Her last daily theme is resonant with the artificiality of her academic voices: "this is my last daily theme. . . . Good bye daily themes. I can't say I've been very fond of you but I don't doubt you were an excellent medicine. Good bye. Some one else will support you though I give you up."[46]

In this farewell to daily themes, Annie writes with the compliant voice of the dutiful student, a voice emphasized by her halting syntax. She hints at a critique of the educational process she has undergone yet finally demurs from such a project by reinscribing her trust in her teachers and their pedagogy—"I don't doubt you were an excellent medicine." That critique reemerges months later, when she begins writing in her family journal again: "If I can manage to make this journal writing a matter of duty as daily themes were last year it will be a good thing. I've got into an absurdly stiff way of thinking when I have a pen in my hand, and I must get out of it, or I shall utterly despair."[47]

Despite the "absurd stiffness" of her Harvard writing voices, Annie was able to use her writing to transform a masculinized, teacher-centered curriculum to be more hospitable and meaningful to her. Her school writings reveal the struggles Annie faced and the strategies she devised to connect her own ways of knowing with the conventions of academic discourse. Her ways of positioning—as well as her ways of repositioning—herself and her knowledge enabled her to favorably impress her writing teachers, earn good grades, receive favored treatment from some of them, and solicit the personal attention she needed. They also enabled her to survive the masculine context of higher education at Radcliffe long enough to gain the credentials she came there to attain, so that she could go on with her life.

After leaving Radcliffe Annie taught school most of her life, combining her career with marriage and motherhood in an era when women were hard pressed to do so. Biographical records in the Radcliffe Archives indicate that Annie published four books during her lifetime, including one growing out of her professional experience in teaching: *Home, School, and Vacation: A Book of Suggestions.*[48] Annie's mastery of academic discourse at Radcliffe is not necessarily related to her professional success as an educator. However, in acquiring mastery of academic discourse at Radcliffe, Annie gained experience in integrating her personal experience and opinion with the conversation of an intellectual community. She learned how to express herself in ways that would be heard by readers of greater rank and power. In the unsettled pedagogical arena of Radcliffe, she learned to question and to critique the professors with whom she worked and, finally, to trust her own experiences and observations as valid sources of knowledge and critique.

By contrast, the voices in the *Radcliffe Magazine* dailies present a collective critique of the entire enterprise of Harvard writing instruction, whose objective epistemology denies the women writers' experiences and reinscribes a male-based curriculum where men are writers and women are written about. The practice of daily writing forces the women writers to face the dilemma of what to write, which voice to use, which to silence. Yet the published dailies also reveal the women's mastery and domestication of academic discourse through their use of satire and ridicule and their decision to publish the dailies for an audience of female readers.

The published dailies also show that for at least some Radcliffe writers, the daily theme was a flexible writing form that they adapted to their own needs and purposes. Whatever the educational objectives of the writing teachers in assigning daily themes, these writers were able to "master" the form and mold it to fit their own needs. These writers used the daily theme as an academic writing form where they could openly critique, vent their frustration at, and satirize their writing courses and teachers. The daily theme thus provided one forum in which academic writing could have a real purpose and personal meaning for the student writers.

The voices of the *Radcliffe Magazine* writers and of Annie Ware Winsor Allen, Helen Dorothea Crawford Seidler, and Mary Lee call on those of us engaged in teaching, reading, and writing academic discourse to listen carefully to our own voices and to those of our students and colleagues. Some of us have found value in asking students to say what they think about what we teach them and ask them to write. Many teachers have discovered the value of providing students, at least occasionally, with alternatives to traditional academic writing—journals, informal reading responses, parodies, nonacademic styles. And we have discovered the value of trying such ways of writing ourselves. Yet providing opportunities for students to voice their own resistance to academic writing does not mean abandoning the project of teaching it. As in the case of the *Radcliffe Magazine* writers, such opportunities may be the best way to lead students to the critique of academic discourse that is central to mastery of it.

Notes

I'd like to thank Jane Knowles, Radcliffe College archivist, for her assistance. I'd also like to thank the Schlesinger Library and Pat King, director, and the Bowling Green State University Faculty Research Committee for grants to complete the archival research for this essay. All manuscript materials quoted from the Schlesinger Library are used by permission.

1. Ken Macrorie, *Telling Writing* (New York: Hayden, 1970), pp. 1–4; Jane Tompkins, "Me and My Shadow," *New Literary History* 19 (1987): 169–78; Olivia Frey, "Beyond Literary Darwinism: Women's Voices and Critical Discourse," *College English* 52 (1990): 507–26; Scott Heller, "Experience and Expertise Meet in a New Brand of Scholarship," *Chronicle of Higher Education,* 6 May 1992, A7–A9; and Liz McMillen, "A Passion for French," *Chronicle of Higher Education,* 9 February 1994, A8–A9, A19.

2. Elizabeth Flynn, "Composing as a Woman," *College Composition and Communication* 39 (1988): 423–35; Shirley K. Rose, "Reading Representative Anecdotes of Literacy Practice; or 'See Dick and Jane Read and Write!'" *Rhetoric Review* 8 (1990): 244–59; Cynthia L. Caywood and Gillian R. Overing, eds., *Teaching Writing: Pedagogy, Gender, and Equity* (Albany: State Univ. of New York Press, 1987); Pamela J. Annas, "Style as Politics: A Feminist Approach to the Teaching of Writing," *College English* 47 (1985): 360–71; Clara Juncker, "Writing (with) Cixous," *College English* 50 (1988): 424–36; and Catherine E. Lamb, "Beyond Argument in Feminist Composition," *College Composition and Communication* 42 (1991): 11–24.

3. Susan Miller, *Textual Carnivals: The Politics of Composition* (Carbondale: Southern Illinois Univ. Press, 1991), pp. 111–12.

4. Ibid, p. 112.

5. Albert R. Kitzhaber, *Rhetoric in American Colleges, 1850–1900* (Dallas: Southern Methodist Univ. Press, 1990), pp. 32–36, 59–73; Lovie Sue Simmons, "A Critique of the Stereotype of Current-Traditional Rhetoric: Invention in Writing Instruction at Harvard, 1875–1900" (Ph.D. diss., Univ. of Texas at Austin, 1991), pp.

256–63; and Mary Trachsel, *Institutionalizing Literacy* (Carbondale: Southern Illinois Univ. Press, 1992), pp. 58–63.

6. JoAnn Campbell, "Controlling Voices: The Legacy of English A at Radcliffe College, 1883–1917," *College Composition and Communication* 43 (1992): 472–85; Joyce Antler, "The Educational Biography of Lucy Sprague Mitchell: A Case Study in the History of Women's Higher Education," in *Women and Higher Education in American History,* ed. John Mack Faragher and Florence Howe (New York: Norton, 1988), p. 53.

7. These sources are located in the Radcliffe Archives and the Schlesinger Library at Radcliffe College, Cambridge, Mass. The Harvard Archives, in the Pusey Library at Harvard University, also contain a few gradebooks for writing courses at the Annex during the 1880s.

8. Helen Lefkowitz Horowitz, *Alma Mater: Design and Experience in the Women's College from Their Nineteenth-Century Beginnings to the 1930s* (New York: Knopf, 1984): 95–98; Radcliffe College, *Annual Report of 1880–1881* (Cambridge, Mass., [1851]).

9. Radcliffe College, *Annual Report of 1880–1881,* p. 12; *Annual Report of 1884–1885* (Cambridge, Mass., [1885]), p. 10; *Annual Report of 1894–1895* (Cambridge, Mass., [1895]), pp. 13–14; *Annual Report of 1900–1901* (Cambridge, Mass., [1901]), pp. 15–18.

10. Kitzhaber, *Rhetoric,* pp. 31–36.

11. C. T. Copeland and H. M. Rideout, *Freshman English and Theme-Correcting in Harvard College* (New York: Silver, Burdett, 1901); James A. Berlin, *Writing Instruction in Nineteenth-Century American Colleges* (Carbondale: Southern Illinois Univ. Press, 1984).

12. Barrett Wendell, "The Relations of Radcliffe College with Harvard," *Harvard Monthly* 29 (1899): 4.

13. Barbara Solomon, *In the Company of Educated Women: A History of Women and Higher Education in America* (New Haven: Yale Univ. Press, 1985); Horowitz, *Alma Mater.*

14. Barrett Wendell's gradebook for English A at Harvard in 1889–90 shows that 402 students originally enrolled in the course and 340 finished it. Of the 340, 46 percent earned C's, 30 percent D's, and 14 percent B's. Five percent each earned A's and F's. The Harvard Archives also contain professional course lecture notes for almost all of the courses popular among Harvard students in the 1880s and 1890s, evidence that those who could buy the notes were able to cut lectures and still obtain the material to be memorized for examinations.

15. Campbell, "Controlling Voices," p. 7.

16. Helen Dorothea Crawford Seidler Collection, SC 42, Radcliffe College Archives.

17. Annie Ware Winsor Allen took English A in 1883 to 1884 with Adams Sherman Hill. The following two years she took Sophomore Themes, English 12, Shakespeare, and Senior Themes and Forensics with Wendell. Her papers contain little record of her English A experience.

18. Personal journal, 26 Sept. 1884, Annie Ware Winsor Allen Collection, MC 322, Schlesinger Library, Radcliffe College; Cinthia Gannett, *Gender and the Journal: Diaries and Academic Discourse* (Albany: State Univ. of New York Press, 1992), pp. 132–33.

19. Personal journal, 26 Sept. 1884 and 27 Oct. 1884, Annie Ware Winsor Allen Collection, MC 322, Schlesinger Library, Radcliffe College.

20. First Sophomore Theme, Annie Ware Winsor Allen Collection, SC 35, Radcliffe College Archives.

21. Campbell, "Controlling Voices," p. 479.

22. No date, Annie Ware Winsor Allen Collection, SC 35, Radcliffe College Archives.

23. Paulo Friere, *Pedagogy of the Oppressed,* trans. Myra Bergman Ramos (New York: Continuum, 1983), pp. 57–74.

24. Donna Haraway, "Situated Knowledges: The Science Question in Feminism and the Privilege of Partial Perspective," *Feminist Studies* 14 (1988): 589, and Richard Ohmann, *English in America: A Radical View of the Profession* (New York: Oxford Univ. Press, 1976), p. 148.

25. Sharon Crowley, *The Methodical Memory: Invention in Current-Traditional Rhetoric* (Carbondale: Southern Illinois Univ. Press, 1990), p. 151; Mary Lee, "English A," Mary Lee Collection, Radcliffe College Archives.

26. Annie uses the pronoun "one" or "we" when making generalizations about Radcliffe students. In a daily theme for 10 Nov. 1886, Annie notes the illogicality of gender in pronoun references: "If a college which is composed of men is called *she,* I should think a college composed of women would be called *he.* However, perhaps all large bodies of people should be called *she.* Yet that will scarcely hold, for I should scarcely expect to hear a caucus called *she.*"

27. Daily Themes, 11 Nov. 1886, Annie Ware Winsor Allen Collection, SC 35, Radcliffe College Archives.

28. Daily Themes, Jan. 1887, Annie Ware Winsor Allen Collection, SC 35, Radcliffe College Archives.

29. Daily Themes, 5 Jan. 1887, Annie Ware Winsor Allen Collection, SC 35, Radcliffe College Archives.

30. "Evelina's Picture of Her Times," Annie Ware Winsor Allen Collection, SC 35, Radcliffe College Archives.

31. "Theme on Percy's Reliques," 30 Nov. 1886, Annie Ware Winsor Allen Collection, SC 35, Radcliffe College Archives.

32. Robert Self, *Barrett Wendell* (Boston: G. K. Hall, 1975), pp. 138–39.

33. Antler, "Educational Biography," p. 61.

34. Daily Themes, 18 Nov. 1886, Annie Ware Winsor Allen Collection, SC 35, Radcliffe College Archives.

35. First Senior Forensic, Annie Ware Winsor Allen Collection, SC 35, Radcliffe College Archives.

36. David Bartholomae, "Inventing the University," in *When a Writer Can't Write,* ed. Mike Rose (New York: Guilford, 1984), pp. 139–40.

37. B. M. D., *Radcliffe Magazine* 1 (1899): 21–22.

38. Antler, "Educational Biography," p. 52.

39. M. E. C., *Radcliffe Magazine* 1 (1899): 23.

40. H. A. W., *Radcliffe Magazine* 1 (1899): 24.

41. M. V. A., *Radcliffe Magazine* 2 (1900): 31–32.

42. H. A. W., *Radcliffe Magazine* 1 (1899): 22.

43. E. B. C., *Radcliffe Magazine* 2 (1900): 87–88; C. F. McI., *Radcliffe Magazine* 2 (1900): 87–88.

44. See especially Gannett's discussion, "Gender and Journal-Keeping Traditions," *Gender and the Journal,* pp. 99–151.

45. The phrase "the daily theme eye" comes from an anonymous essay by the same title in *Essays and Essay-Writing,* ed. William M. Tanner (Boston: Atlantic

Monthly Press, 1917), pp. 21–25; Lester Faigley, "Judging Writing, Judging Selves," *College Composition and Communication* 39 (1989): 395–412.

46. Daily Themes, 22 March 1887, Annie Ware Winsor Allen Collection, SC 35, Radcliffe College Archives.

47. Personal journal, 24 Jan. 1888, Annie Ware Winsor Allen Collection, MC 322, Schlesinger Library, Radcliffe College.

48. Biographical folder, Annie Ware Winsor Allen Collection, MC 322, Schlesinger Library, Radcliffe College; Annie Winsor Allen, *Home, School, and Vacation: A Book of Suggestions* (Boston: Houghton Mifflin, 1907).

Postscripts

A Toast to Jerusha Jane Jones

THIS TOAST TO the mythical Jerusha Jane Jones was found in the Rockford Female Seminary archives in a letter written by Rockford teacher Mary Ashmun in 1874 from her home in rural Wisconsin. The letter was addressed to English teacher and magazine editor Caroline A. Potter, who later taught Jane Addams, a student literary editor of the magazine. The toast may have been spoken at Rockford Seminary as part of an 1874 literary society program or commencement and provides a fine example of women's extracurricular rhetoric of the period.[1]

The name Jerusha is one of the rare references in a biblical genealogy to a mother, in this case, the queen to King Uzziah, mother of Jotham (2 Kings 15:33). Yet as the toast shows, Jerusha and her colleagues thought a woman should be able to serve not just as a mother but to occupy any sphere that she "has the capacity to fill." The toast stresses that women will not be happy even with an expanded sphere until they have suffrage. Here the toast refers to another important text for women, the Old Testament Book of Esther (see "the Haman at the court of Ahasuerus" and "the Mordecai of the right of suffrage"). Such references were appropriate for the audience. The permeating religious atmosphere at Rockford College, successfully resisted by the singular Jane Addams, was created by Anna Peck Sill when she founded Rockford Seminary in 1851. But it is doubtful that suffrage was the kind of goal or aspiration hoped for or approved of by the strict, but admirable, Sill when she founded the frontier seminary on the Holyoke model to train missionaries and teachers.

In the essay following the toast, reprinted from the *Rockford Female Seminary Magazine* of 1875, Jerusha Jane Jones shows how women's education could be different even when men and women were educated together because of differences in cultural expectations. Jones, a composite figure representing the ideal RFS student, details the differences between her life and that of her college brother John Jones, differences that add up to her having less time to spend on studies and self-development. The article may have been written by Julia Lathrop, who spent 1874 at Rockford, earned her degree from Vassar College in 1880, and returned to the

Midwest to live with Jane Addams and Ellen Gates Starr at Hull House, becoming a nationally recognized child welfare expert. In 1912 she was appointed first head of the federal Children's Bureau within the Department of Commerce and Labor. Reappointed by President Wilson, she left in 1921 and went on to continue her long career criticizing and administering social services worldwide until her death in Rockford, Illinois, in 1932.[2]

Toast!

Jerusha Jane Jones! May she not only find her place; but may some 19th century Solomon be found to place her in it.

Reply.

Jerusha Jane Jones! Heaven help her! For nearly six thousand years she has been wandering disconsolately up and down with this pathetic appeal upon her lips—"If there is a realm where woman can walk uncriticised, may some Solomon arise to show her what and where it is; for I, Jerusha Jane Jones, would go to the ends of the earth to be able to rise up and sit down, to put on my hat and take it off, to ride and walk, to read and talk, without having it continually sounded in my ears, 'You are out of your sphere,' or 'You are not fulfilling the high destiny for which you were created.'" But all the Solomons in all their wisdom and in all their glory have been unable to solve the problem satisfactorily; and so in the middle of this 19th century Jerusha Jane Jones has changed her tactics, and in a fit of desperation has ceased to call upon the Solomons at all, but with the cry, "Make way for liberty," has rushed into the field of action. When lo! the crowds of Solomons on the right hand and on the left have parted before her oncoming footsteps, and gallantly lifting their hats, have made a place for her in their very midst. To be sure, it was not without some struggle that they have seen her working quietly by the side of her brother physicians in the hospital and in the dissecting room, with scalpel and knife in hand. And some have groaned in very anguish of soul as they have seen her ascending the rostrum and have heard her speak of "Righteousness, temperance and judgment to come," while others more emotional have, like Isaac when he saw his coming wife approaching, "lifted up their voices and wept" as she has thrown aside the domestic needle and has wielded the sword of the spirit from the sacred desk.

But the struggles are dying away, the groans are vanishing into thin air, and the voice of weeping is changed into shouts of joy as it is acknowledged that she does these things *as well as some men!* And now what is there left to be desired? Surely any reasonable being ought to be satisfied. Jerusha Jane is permitted to teach, to preach, to practice law and medicine, and to be at the head of business firms. What can she ask for more? But Jerusha Jane Jones is irrepressible, and the Haman at the court of Ahasuerus, none of these things will pacify her as long as the Mordecai of the right of suffrage refuses to do homage. But inasmuch as the radius of her "sphere" has been constantly increasing in proportion as she has shown a capacity to fill a gradually enlarging space, let her not doubt but that the privilege of voting will soon be thrust into her outstretched hand. And this the question of the ages—"What is woman's sphere?" shall be satisfactorily answered by the reply. Her sphere is any sphere that she can show that she has a capacity to fill.

Is John Smarter than I?

"John Jones, I assert a woman is not created physically or mentally inferior to man, but there is another reason why she falls below him in intellectual attainments."

"But assertion is not proof; while this is evidence *per se* that she is not capable of strong, vigorous thought, and the old Roman says: '*Ex uno disce omnes*'"; and John waved before me my graduating essay that he had been criticising with that exasperating air of superiority that an A. B. a few months old knows so well how to display.

"I deny that even that is proof," said I, and I arose, took the manuscript from his hand, not with the gentle air an angel would have been likely to exhibit, I admit, and left the room. John shouted after me, "Denial is not proof, Jerusha, I still claim; *adhuc sub judice lis est*."

Now, I acknowledge John's criticisms on my essay were just; that, in fact, women do not attain the same standard of scholarship as men; that their writings, as a class, fall below those of the masculine pen; but the reason, I contend, is not in the original constitution of the brain. Look at a boy baby; does it learn to handle its rattle, to walk, or to talk any sooner than a girl baby? Has this very wise brother of mine demonstrated that he is, by nature, greatly my intellectual superior because he can write a better essay than I? No; I maintain that there are just as good and sufficient reasons for this as that he can read Greek, while Patrick, the gardener, cannot read his own name.

When I commenced my mortal career, John had been two years battling with life's experience; yet, even with this advantage, tradition says I mastered the intricacies of the a, b, cs as soon as he. How well I recall those first years in the district school; John and I leaving home of a morning; he carelessly swinging his arms, free to skip a stone at a squirrel that may chance to dart along the roadside, or with hat in hand to "scoop" a butterfly or a bumblebee; I with steady, careful step, arms firmly held, because at my elbow hangs the dinner-basket, a charge given me by mother with these words: "Jerusha, you will have to take care of the dinner-basket, John is so thoughtless, he will either leave it beside the road, or forget to bring it home at night." Yes, woman must always care for the dinner-basket! Speaking of that dinner-basket reminds me of an act of moral heroism performed even by a girl.

Plain Susan Brown is eating a piece of bread and butter in school hours. "Susan, are you eating in school when you know it is strictly forbidden?" inquires the teacher.

"Yes ma'am," says Susan, knowing that by these words she has pronounced her own sentence; that she is doomed to the mortifying disgrace of standing in the middle of the floor and eating her lunch amid the laughter of the school. I have never seen this occurrence in print. It has never been related as anything remarkable that, even under circumstances so trying, a girl should speak the truth, but, for nearly a century, George Washington with his little hatchet has been held up for the admiration of all mankind, as an instance of a boy who could tell the truth. Why should this fact of a boy's wanton destruction of a valuable cherry-tree and not denying it, be pictured, printed, published in every conceivable way, unless it be an exceptional case? Why do we not see pictures of hungry Susan Brown with her piece of bread in her hand, looking up in her teacher's face, and saying, "I cannot tell a lie, I am eating a piece of bread and butter?" Is it not because no one is surprised that a girl should tell the truth? John, however, admits in a patronizing kind of way that I am morally his superior; but I claim intellectual equality.

Up to the ages of fourteen and twelve respectively, notwithstanding the disadvantages of my juniority, and the extra thought necessary for the security of the dinner-basket, I still held my place in class beside him. From this stage in life I admit there was a separation, he passing from class to class more rapidly than I. Physiologists have explained this fact from their stand-point of observation, to their entire satisfaction; philosophers and sentimentalists from their stand-points to their entire satisfaction; I shall not explain it from any stand-point, but will lay before you events as they occurred in John's educational career, and that of mine.

It was the summer I attained my twelfth year that the piano made its advent into the Jones household; with it the decree that I was to sit two hours daily before it, training my intellectual powers, as well as my eyes, to read at the same instant two lines, several inches apart, of the most puzzling hieroglyphics, disciplining the muscles of my hands and fingers to so obey the commands of my will that they should strike, without failure, a thousand in a minute of the ivory keys, corresponding to the readings. About this same time I was instructed that it was quite the thing for a Miss of my years to do "fancy work." Accordingly, the Jones parlors were not a whit behind their neighbors in sofa pillows too nice to lay your head on, tidies that were marvels of workmanship, rugs, footstools, and ottomans displaying wonderful specimens of natural history. These were the representatives of weeks and months of my time and labor. While I was at the piano, John was playing base ball; while I was learning the various stitches of crochet and the nice harmonies in the shades of worsted, he was educating his perceptive and reflective faculties by chess-playing, or widening his knowledge of the world by some book of travels. Shall we impiously say it was God's work that I could not bring as much mental vigor to my studies, or failed to master as readily as he the difficult problems in mathematics, when all his training was promotive of physical and mental strength, and mine exhaustive of the same?

So two or three years went by, and the time came that we were to leave home for wider opportunities, John to go to college, I to a seminary. Vividly that summer rises up before me with all its work and weariness. I almost fancy I can feel, even now, the sharp pain between my shoulders, from thence shooting up to the temples in tiny streams, like lightning darts, and, finally, settling down in that dull, heavy ache across the forehead and through the eyes. When mother laid the matter before Dr. Physiologist, he shook his head with great gravity and said, "I told you so, Madam; girls have not the physical organization to endure study. I advise you to take all books away from your daughter." So the reviewing was dropped out, and a little more sewing machine put in. Through those long summer days, while John was lounging upon the grass or swinging in his hammock under the maples, reviewing his geometry and Virgil, I was giving all my time, thoughts, and strength to ruffles, tucks, and puffs.

When the September morning came that was to send us forth to our new fields of operation, I had, standing in the hall, two trunks filled with what was considered a proper wardrobe for a boarding-school Miss. This entire outfit was largely the product of my summer's work, for my father was strictly orthodox on the question of a girl's making and mending her own clothing. John's one trunk stood beside mine in the hall. Not an article in it had cost him a moment's labor, and scarcely a single thought. Even the folding and packing had been done by my mother, and each garment so placed as to give him the least inconvenience possible in taking out for use.

Arrived at our respective institutions, we were marshalled for examinations. John passed his every way creditably. I, together with nine-tenths of my companions, fell a degree lower than we had expected. Facts that were once perfectly familiar, denied even my slightest acquaintance. There seemed really nothing in my cranium but a couple of muffled drums that kept beating away in either ear as if playing a dead march for my departed wits.

"Ah," says Professor Spectacles, "girls learn largely by the faculty of memory; they never grasp a subject in its various relations, and so make it thoroughly their own; they make a brilliant recitation, but a few months after, and the greater part has evaporated."

I entirely disagree with the learned Professor. Suppose John had been hard at work from daylight till bed-time for three months before his examinations, making coats, pantaloons, and waistcoats—given to realize that his gentility, respectability, and every masculine desirability depended on his filling at least two Saratoga trunks with these garments in every conceivable style of cut and material, and then at the end of that time call him up to demonstrate a proposition in Euclid, and see if there has not been some evaporation even from a masculine brain.

John's school had a four years course of study, so had mine. With the exception of a year and a half of the ancient languages, and a half year of mathematics, the two were parallel. This difference, however, was met by the more advanced requirements for entrance at John's school; so the amount of daily study required of me for the four years was equivalent to his.

The institution selected for me by my parents was what might have been designated a compromise school; it being adjusted to run to the temple of knowledge either broad or narrow gauge. While it held a college charter, had a fair course of study, and recognized the idea that woman was capable of acquiring a liberal education, yet, it had so great a fear that its pupils might be called "strong minded," or forget their province of general superintendents of the dinner-basket, that the wise board of trustees established that *every* pupil should devote one hour per day to domestic work. It fell to my lot to mix bread; accordingly, every morning at a certain bell, I donned a large apron and went to the domestic hall. Here I found several pans containing a flour and water mixture upon which I was to spend an hour kneading into a state of greater consistency. What became of it after this I know not. How it came to be in the state I found it I knew not, but for twenty weeks one hour daily, Sundays excepted, I spent in this work, which I was told was a part of the process of bread-making. The next twenty weeks I cut bread, then I sifted flour, washed glass, swept, turned the crank of the chopping machine, etc., until my fourth year, when I was allowed to scour knives without change for the forty weeks. This work was regarded as one of the senior privileges, not because of the greater mental discipline necessary to its accomplishment, but forty-five minutes of this labor was considered equivalent to sixty of the ordinary kinds, so it left fifteen minutes daily for recreation and reading, which was thought proper for seniors to have.

When the Rev. Mr. Smilax spoke so glowingly in his anniversary address of the value of learning that useful accomplishment, housekeeping, at the same time that we were acquiring an education in mathematics and languages, I could but think it very strange that our trustees, who were also trustees of John's school, had never thought to set him planing boards and boring holes, an hour daily, so that when he graduated he could be a house-builder, as well as I a housekeeper. I ventured at one time to suggest this to one of our venerable fathers, but he so frightened me with the immense interrogation points that stared at me from his eyes as he answered, in very decided tones, "Miss Jones, such a thing would be perfectly impracticable," that I never ventured farther with my philanthropic suggestions. So John did not shove a plane, or turn a bit or auger during his college days; but he pitched a base ball, kicked a foot ball, or rowed a boat, to prepare himself for the business of future years.

Again, there was the time actually demanded of me by the dictates of fashion, for the dressing and adorning of my person. Every day, and occasionally oftener, I was to hook, pin, button, or otherwise fasten upon my person, from sixteen to twenty different articles of apparel, exclusive of pins, hair-pins, rings, chains, braids, curls, and frizzes, the number of these being, mathematically considered, an indeterminate quantity. Then there was the care of these articles, seeing that they were in proper condition for use and ornamentation. Perhaps you will say I had no need to comply with fashion's dictates. So the Rev. Mr. Smilax said, but as I early observed, he shed the most of his benignant wisdom on the girls with the greatest numbers of flounces and frizzes, and as the conversation of the Reverend gentleman was considered highly instructive, I subjected myself to all this labor in order to attain my highest cultivation.

If John and I were to give statements of our daily account, with time, the following would be the result:

Dr. JOHN JONES *Cr.*

		hrs.	min.			hrs.	min.
18—				18—			
Sept.	To Time,	24		Sept.	By Dressing,		15
					" Morning Prayers,		30
					" recitations at 3 hours,	9	
					" 3 meals at 30 minutes,	1	30
					" Sleep,	7	45
					Balance,	5	
		24				24	

Dr. JERUSHA JANE JONES *Cr.*

					hrs.	min.
18—			18—			
Sept.	To Time,	24	Sept.	By Dressing,		30
				" morn'g and ev'ng prayers at 30 minutes,	1	
				" 3 recitations at 3 hours	9	
				" Music,	2	
				" Domestic work,	1	
				" 3 meals at 30 minutes,	1	30
				" Private meditations and devotions		30
				" Room work,		30
				" Care of wardrobe,		15
				" Sleep,	7	45
				Balance,		
		24			24	

Now, Mr. Physiologist, does it prove that a girl is physically incapable of going to school, because she "breaks down" under a burden about one-half greater than a boy's? Is my brain made of poorer clay because I have not attained, at the end of a four years course, as broad and thorough scholarship as John, when he has had five hours daily, and I—how much!—to give to recreation and general culture? Does not the proverb "all work and no play" apply to me as well as to Jack?

Elihu Burritt is regarded as one of the most remarkable men of the century. School boys have been pointed to him as a model of perseverance. He acquired a knowledge of Latin and French during his apprenticeship, and at the age of thirty was master of several languages, although a good mechanic, working at his forge from eight to ten hours per day. A woman is expected to learn and practice housekeeping, a trade, with its thousand details, far more difficult than blacksmithing, and then, because she does not master as many languages as a Burritt, must there ever be before her the fingers of a man's hand, writing upon the wall that bars her progress, "*Mene, mene, tekel upharsin?*" JERUSHA JANE JONES.

Notes

1. The article and toast are in the Rockford College Archives. I extend my gratitude to Joan B. Clark, Rockford College public services librarian and archivist, who not only helped locate materials and pinpoint dates but who first linked the article with Julia Lathrop as a "best guess." Thanks are also due to my father Dan S. Hobbs, who read Jerusha as the ideal RFS student and helped locate Biblical references. Jerusha Jane Jones, "Is John Smarter than I?" was published in the *Rockford Seminary Magazine* 8 (1875), pp. 300–306. Caroline A. Potter was editor at the time. A graduate of the RFS class of 1855, Potter taught English language and literature as well as modern history and served as magazine editor from volume 2 until Jane Addams took over as student editor in 1879. Mary Ashmun, from rural Wisconsin, graduated in the class of 1864, and taught in the normal and preparatory department and also in the Department of Mathematics from 1864 to 1868.

2. Biographical information on Julia Lathrop is from Edward T. James, Janet James, and Paul S. Boyer, eds., *Notable American Women, 1607–1950,* vol. 2, G–O (Cambridge, Mass.: Harvard Univ. Press, 1971), pp. 370–72. Information on Addams is from Allen F. Davis, *American Heroine: The Life and Legend of Jane Addams* (New York: Oxford Univ. Press, 1973).

JOANN CAMPBELL

Afterword: Revealing the Ties That Bind

I BRING A history to this collection, for in 1989 I was one of a group of graduate student and junior faculty women who coalesced at a conference on history and historiography of rhetoric at the Flagship Inn in Arlington, Texas. This particular group gathered in a hotel restroom fuming, sputtering, and bonding in our exclusion from the center of action after two days of discussion by invited speakers. This "alternative" conference was billed as offering a format more conducive to conversation than traditional gatherings. Yet none of us had been invited to speak, and none of us had so far spoken in discussion sessions. Our vital interest in the history of women speaking and writing was marginal to the conference as a whole, and we were perhaps unwilling or unready to risk the critical gaze of others in the room or field. Commiserating in the "ladies' room," we decided one way to enter the conversation was to start our own and place at its center the issues, people, and histories important to us. In recovering and discovering the women who moved from silence to speech and text, we hoped to learn strategies, gain courage, and situate ourselves within a particular academic community. This volume represents one tangible outcome of that discussion, one that may as much reflect issues of academic literacy (particularly the writing of history) for some of its contributors as explore dimensions of literacy for nineteenth-century women.

I tell this tale of origin to locate the subjects of writing, both authors and historical characters, because the women in *Nineteenth-Century Women Learn to Write* in many ways mirror those who reconstruct them. Most of the nineteenth-century women presented here were highly skilled readers and writers for whom learning to write meant entering new discourses, meeting new forms and conventions, and constructing an acceptable written voice. This focus on already-literate women working in society or within institutions of higher education offers a complementary and correcting story to previous histories of writing instruction in U.S. colleges, histories that depend primarily on material from men's colleges or elite coeducational institutions. The questions raised in this volume challenge assumptions about the neutrality of literacy practice and instruction and offer a new lens through which to view women's history.

If conventions of historiography were more conducive to explicating biographical connections between a writer and her topic, we would find that the desire to trace one's own lineage or genealogy fuels many historical projects. A hunger for the details of women's lives and literacy development can provide sustenance for long hours in archives and attics and proffer a welcome that literate women of the nineteenth century did not always receive. Seeking roots, looking for continuities, assuring ourselves of our place at the table by surveying who was there a century ago—all these are worthy endeavors. In "Resisting Amnesia," Adrienne Rich honors those needs, while suggesting that historians go further: "Breaking silences, telling our tales is not enough. We can value that process—and the courage it may require—without believing that it is an end in itself. Historical responsibility has, after all, to do with action—where we place the weight of our existences on the line, cast our lot with others, move from an individual consciousness to a collective one. But we all need to begin with the individual consciousness. How did we come to be where we are and not elsewhere?" [1] To begin answering "how did we come to be where we are and not elsewhere?" the historian can, and should, make her own location part of the story. Historiographers have urged us to do that for several political and academic reasons. The late James Berlin, whose history of nineteenth-century composition practices opened the door and provided a framework within and against which many of us in English studies work, argues that a historian must "make every effort to be aware of the nature of her point of view and its interpretive strategies, and to be candid about them with her reader." Only with such practices, Berlin claims, can historians "honestly present their own political agendas." [2] Those political agendas may be quite personal, such as a desire to describe past difficult environments in which women learned to write academic prose in order to understand one's own struggles with writing. Susan C. Jarratt acknowledges the temptation of such desire and warns the writer of history to be "aware of what the work cannot say and keep before her the ways her own consciousness urges her to create an object which recreates her own struggle." [3]

These tales of nineteenth-century women, whose efforts at literacy inside and outside institutions of higher learning were sometimes thwarted, sometimes rewarded, and sometimes ignored, shape a story of women collectively "coming to voice," to use bell hooks's term. As hooks remarks, however, the movement from silence to speech is not everywoman's journey: "Certainly for black women our struggle has not been to emerge from silence into speech but to change the nature and direction of our speech, to make a speech that compels listeners, one that is heard."[4] Indeed, Logan's profile of Sojourner Truth asks us to question the practices by which literacy is defined. Logan argues that Truth's "persona demands a definition of literacy—and of intellect—that transcends knowledge of the written word and takes into account the ability to exploit the word's rhetorical potential." Historians located in traditional arenas of literate activity such as educational institutions must be conscious of that bias in their definitions and searches for exemplars of literacy.

Because the writer is never a disinterested, objective observer of fact but always a selector of objects and interpreter of tales, the writing of history requires recognizing the location of the teller, the impetus of her investigation, and her vested interest in the tale. While any historical project brings to contemporary readers important moments from a collective past, historians must work to complicate their readings with an interrogation of the contradictory forces operating both in the nineteenth century and in writing today. Yet such a weaving of past and present is difficult precisely because of the histories of text production described in these essays. Self-erasing, self-effacing narration is a product not of individual lack (of self-esteem, confidence, or experience) but of discursive practices produced in nineteenth-century women's education and alive today: meeting a teacher's expectation of the good student (Simmons), masking one's ambition for the sake of social harmony (Tonkovich), working in an environment where one's political interests are not encouraged (Ricks), having different uses for literacy than the dominant race, class, or gender (Logan). Interwoven in these narratives of clever women resiliently writing in times and places more repressive than today are underlying facts: that women had to resist institutional and cultural norms in order to speak, that at times they have to subvert intellectual powers in order to be recognized, and that always they faced consequences for a violation of standard feminine uses of literacy. A legacy of historical, institutional, and social obstacles to women's writing affects each woman who writes in academia today. Happily, that effect is not, and has not always been, silence. Yet constraints against women's academic literacy continue to operate today, as Theresa Enos documents in a 1988 report on the percentages of articles written by men and by women in composition journals over the past eight years.[5] In the two most prestigious journals, 69 percent and 63 percent of the scholarly articles were written by men, while 31 percent and 37 percent were written by women. These figures matched percentages in six other journals Enos reviewed, with the largest gap being 81 percent male-authored articles to 19 percent female-authored articles in one journal. Percentages were closer and the gap less dramatic in journals devoted to pedagogy. Enos notes that the review process may contribute to this discrepancy, yet the journal she edits, *Rhetoric Review,* receives far more submissions by males, which is why male-authored articles dominate. Because composition studies has always been a field where women predominate, we might infer that historical constraints on women's advanced literacy still exist.

These historical struggles and the importance of literacy to nineteenth-century women are revealed in the variety of previously unexamined texts that form the core of these investigations of individuals, institutions, and writing groups. Ricks, for example, draws on archival research to show the challenges women faced in the last century in their literacy education. Simmons's use of gradebooks and class rosters and Mihesuah's examination of census figures, college catalogues, and student publications are wonderfully thick descriptions woven from a variety of sources. Published materials examined from a feminist perspective provide the source of Hobbs's examination of hymns and Rose's account of conduct books, while Logan's profile of five African American women, Mihesuah's account of the Cherokee Female Seminary, and Harmon's detailed discussion of the Illinois State Normal University complement and correct histories of literacy and writing instruction that rely almost exclusively on elite white women's experiences. Future scholarship should continue along these paths, with historians exploring institutional archives in their own locales, or, as Patricia Bizzell has suggested, looking at work previously not considered and "redefining the whole notion of rhetoric in order to include this new work by women."[6]

Further, these essays alert us to the difficulties of interpreting history, raising issues of representation and resistance. Annie Ware Winsor, one of Radcliffe College's first students, observed that "in everything which we undertake, we seem deliberately to misrepresent our powers."[7] How, then, does an historian contextualize those powers so as to reveal their misrepresentation? Because not all students saved and donated their essays, we need to ask what manuscripts housed in archives reveal about the writer's relationship to her college, her writing, and her readers. How does an historian "make sense" of manuscripts with no dates or names where the gender of the author is purposefully disguised? How, since minutes of meetings are inevitably filtered through the recorder, can oral/written interactions be recovered? In addition to revealing the complexities of one's sources, Berlin suggests that the historian should examine any rhetoric "for the explicit as well as implicit devices it employs to establish subjectivity." Because all subjectivities are conflictual, "it is the business of the historian to locate these contradictions."[8] The historian pries at the cracks in a culture, loosing the possibilities inherent in every contradiction.

According to Rich, "feminist history charges us, as women committed to the liberation of women, to know the past in order to consider what we want to conserve and what we want not to repeat or continue. It is not simply contributory; it demands that we turn the questions upside down, that we ask women's questions where they have not been asked before."[9] These essays share much that is worth conserving: literate links between women, arenas in which female writers play with gender roles, skillful moves from student to teacher in a single essay, the power of rhetorical triumph in public discourse. They also suggest practices we might not want to continue, such as publishing studies, especially histories, from the perspective of an omniscient author in academic prose that obliterates the peculiar conditions of a woman writing. Perhaps we might establish a historical genre parallel to narrative or autobiographical literary criticism in order to interrupt the omniscient historical voice with another that asks questions, suggests connections, and indicates the emotional qualities of the work.[10] I know personally that finding nineteenth-century women's themes describing the difficulties of public writing offers comfort and a historical-institutional perspective through which to view my own students' and colleagues' texts and processes.

Raising the question of women's literacy history can mean asking what forms were not used as well as noticing and critiquing the ones employed. It can mean directing our attention to the literacy events of working-class women, inquiring into the ways Asian American women negotiated cultural and academic conflicts, and questioning which institutional structures supported teachers of writing and which kept them isolated and unable to connect with students. Future studies of school literacies should include historically black colleges, southern female seminaries, high schools, and teacher training colleges. Working outside formal educational arenas of writing/reading instruction and practice might bring the scholar to church archives, an important site of power for both African American and white women. Diaries and letters continue to be important documents to understand the private practices of literacy, and articles in women's magazines and journalism by nineteenth-century writers show how women initiated, added their voices to, or helped shape public discussions. We must also begin to add an international perspective to what has largely been an effort to find intellectual forebears in the United States.

The women who populate this volume offer one version of the past, with which each reader has a different relation. Hélène Cixous comments that "we don't know, either universally or individually, exactly what our relationship to the dead is. Individually, it constitutes part of our work, our work of love, not of hate or destruction; we must think through each relationship. We can think this with the help of writing, if we know how to write, if we dare write."[11]

There is love here between writer, reader, and historical subject, and that love fuels the search for historical predecessors. As we articulate our individual relationships with the dead, we challenge writing conventions that would compartmentalize the history and the historian, the text, and the love that produced and discovered the text. These essays ask us to blur these lines, along with the lines between public writing in school and private writing for friends, family, and self, as they examine the multiple ways a subject is constructed in writing. In many respects, this is a history of possibility, a celebration of the ways women have used literacy to challenge oppositional structures, subvert dominant discourses, and create spaces in which to work and play. As Hobbs charges in the introduction, we need histories like this one to better understand complex contemporary issues of women's literacies worldwide. By reckoning with these varied historical accounts of women's literacy, we can learn something about conditions for women writing today.

Notes

1. Adrienne Rich, "Resisting Amnesia: History and Personal Life," in *Blood, Bread, and Poetry: Selected Prose, 1959–1985* (New York: Norton, 1986), p. 145.

2. James Berlin, *Writing Instruction in Nineteenth-Century American Colleges* (Carbondale: Southern Illinois Univ. Press, 1984), p. 17, and "Postmodernism, Politics, and Histories of Rhetoric," *Pre/Text* 11 (1990): 185.

3. Susan C. Jarratt, "Speaking to the Past: Feminist Historiography in Rhetoric," *Pre/Text* 11 (1990): 202.

4. bell hooks, *Talking Back: Thinking Feminist, Thinking Black* (Boston: South End Press, 1989), p. 6.

5. Theresa Enos, "Gender and Journals, Conservers or Innovators," *Pre/Text* 9 (1989): 212–13.

6. Patricia Bizzell, "Opportunities for Feminist Research in the History of Rhetoric," *Rhetoric Review* 11 (1992): 51.

7. Untitled theme, Annie Ware Winsor Allen Collection, Schlesinger Library, Radcliffe College, Cambridge, Mass.

8. Berlin, "Postmodernism," p. 11.

9. Rich, "Resisting Amnesia," p. 145.

10. On autobiographical criticism, see Diane Freedman, Olivia Frey, and Frances Murphy Zuahar, eds., *The Intimate Critique: Autobiographical Literary Criticism* (Durham, N.C.: Duke Univ. Press, 1993).

11. Hélène Cixous, *Three Steps on the Ladder of Writing,* trans. Sarah Cornell and Susan Sellers (New York: Columbia Univ. Press, 1993), p. 12.

Bibliography
Contributors
Index

Selected Bibliography

Abbott, Devon, "'Commendable Progress': Acculturation at the Cherokee Female Seminary." *American Indian Quarterly* 11 (1987): 187–201.

——. *See also* Mihesuah, Devon A.

Abbott, John S. C. *The School-Girl; or, the Principles of Christian Duty Familiarly Enforced.* Boston: Crocker and Brewster, 1840.

Abel, Emily K. *Who Cares for the Elderly? Public Policy and the Experiences of Adult Daughters.* Philadelphia: Temple Univ. Press, 1991.

Abell, Mrs. L. G. *Woman in Her Various Relations: Containing Practical Rules for American Females.* New York: J. M. Fairchild, 1851.

Adams, Henry. *The Education of Henry Adams.* 1918. Reprint, Boston: Houghton Mifflin, 1961.

Adams, John R., ed. Introduction. *Regional Sketches: New England and Florida by Harriet Beecher Stowe.* New Haven: College and University Press, 1972.

Alcott, Louisa May. *Work: A Story of Experience.* 1872–73. Reprint, New York: Schocken Books, 1977.

Alcott, William. *Letters to a Sister; or Woman's Mission.* Buffalo: George H. Derby, 1850.

——. *The Young Wife, or Duties of Woman in the Marriage Relations.* 1837. Reprint, New York: Arno Press, 1972.

Allen, Annie Ware Winsor. Annie Ware Winsor Allen Collection. Schlesinger Library. Radcliffe College, Cambridge, Mass.

Allen, Martha Mitten. *Traveling West: Nineteenth Century Women and the Overland Routes.* El Paso: Texas Western Press, 1987.

Anderson, Judith, ed. *Outspoken Women: Speeches by American Women Reformers, 1635–1935.* Dubuque, Iowa: Kendall/Hunt, 1984.

Anderson, James D. *The Education of Blacks in the South, 1860–1935.* Chapel Hill: Univ. of North Carolina Press, 1988.

Anderson, William L., ed. *Cherokee Removal: Before and After.* Athens: Univ. of Georgia Press, 1991.

Andreadi, Harriet. "True Womanhood Revisited: Women's Private Writing in Nineteenth-Century Texas." *Journal of the Southwest* 31 (1989): 179–204.

Angerman, Arina, et al., eds. *Current Issues in Women's History.* London: Routledge, 1989.

Annas, Pamela J. "Style as Politics: A Feminist Approach to the Teaching of Writing." *College English* 47 (1985): 360–71.

Antler, Joyce. "The Educational Biography of Lucy Sprague Mitchell: A Case Study in the History of Women's Higher Education." In Faragher and Howe, *Women and Higher Education in American History,* pp. 43–63.

Aptheker, Herbert, ed., *The Correspondence of W. E. B. Du Bois*. Amherst; 1973–78.

Aresty, Esther. *The Best Behavior: The Course of Good Manners—from Antiquity to the Present—as Seen through Courtesy and Etiquette Books*. New York: Simon and Shuster, 1970.

Armitage, Susan H. "Reluctant Pioneers." In *Women and Western American Literature*, ed. Helen Winter Stauffer and Susan J. Rosowski, pp. 40–51. Troy, N.Y.: Whitson, 1982.

Arthur, Timothy Shay. *Advice to Young Ladies on Their Duties and Conduct in Life*. Boston: Phillips and Sampson, 1848.

Auwers, Linda. "Reading the Marks of the Past: Exploring Female Literacy in Colonial Windsor, CT." *Historical Methods* 13 (1980): 204–14.

Ballara, Marcela. *Women and Literacy*. Women and World Development Series. London: Led Books, 1992.

Banner, Lois. *American Beauty*. New York: Knopf, 1983.

Bartholomae, David. "Inventing the University." In *When a Writer Can't Write*, ed. Mike Rose, pp. 143–65. New York: Guilford, 1985.

Bassard, Katherine Clay. "Gender and Genre: Black Woman's Autobiography and the Ideology of Literacy." *African American Review* 26 (1992): 119–29.

Baym, Nina. "Between Enlightenment and Victorian: Toward a Narrative of American Women Writers Writing History." *Critical Inquiry* 18 (1991): 22–41.

——. *Feminism and American Literary History*. New Brunswick, N.J.: Rutgers Univ. Press, 1992.

——. *Novels, Readers, and Reviewers: Responses to Fiction in Antebellum America*. Ithaca: Cornell Univ. Press, 1984.

——. *Woman's Fiction: A Guide to Novels by and about Women in America, 1820–1870*. 2d ed. Urbana: Univ. of Illinois Press, 1993.

Beauchamp, Virginia Walcott. *A Private War: Letters and Diaries of Madge Preston, 1862–1867*. New Brunswick, N.J.: Rutgers Univ. Press, 1987.

Beecher, Catharine. *An Essay on the Education of Female Teachers*. New York: Van Nostrand and Dwight, 1833.

——. *A Treatise on Domestic Economy*. 1841. Reprint, New York: Schocken Books, 1977.

Beecher, Harriet. "Modern Uses of Language." *Western Monthly Magazine* 1 (March 1833): 121–25.

——. "A New England Sketch." *Western Monthly Magazine* 2 (April 1834): 169–92.

——. *See also* Stowe, Harriet Beecher.

Belenky, Mary Field, Blythe McVicker Clinchy, Nancy Rule Goldberger, and Jill Marruck Tarule. *Women's Ways of Knowing*. New York: Basic Books, 1986.

Bennett, Paula. "Critical Clitoridectomy: Female Sexual Imagery and Feminist Psychoanalytic Theory." *Signs* 18 (1993): 235–59.

Bergamasco, Lucia. "Female Education and Spiritual Life: The Case of Minister's Daughters." In Angerman et al., *Current Issues in Women's History*, pp. 39–60.

Berlin, James A. "Postmodernism, Politics, and Histories of Rhetoric." *Pre/Text* 11 (1990): 169–88.

——. *Rhetoric and Reality: Writing Instruction in American Colleges.* Carbondale: Southern Illinois Univ. Press, 1987.

——. *Writing Instruction in Nineteenth-Century American Colleges.* Carbondale: Southern Illinois Univ. Press, 1984.

Bizzell, Patricia. "Opportunities for Feminist Research in the History of Rhetoric." *Rhetoric Review* 11 (1992): 50–58.

Blackwell, Elizabeth. *Pioneer Work in Opening the Medical Profession to Women.* London: Longmans Green, 1895.

Bledstein, Burton. *The Culture of Professionalism: The Middle Class and the Development of Higher Education in America.* New York: Norton, 1976.

Bleich, David. *The Double Perspective: Language, Literacy, and Social Relations.* New York: Oxford Univ. Press, 1988.

Bloch, Ruth. "The Gendered Meanings of Virtue in Revolutionary America." *Signs* 13 (1987): 37–58.

Bloom, Leonard. "The Acculturation of the Eastern Cherokee: Historical Aspects." *North Carolina Historical Review* 19 (1942): 323–58.

——. "The Cherokee Clan: A Study in Acculturation." *American Anthropology* 41 (1939): 266–68.

Bobbitt, Mary Reed. "A Bibliography of Etiquette Books Published in America before 1900." *Bulletin of the New York Public Library* 51 (1947): 687–720.

Bock, E. Wilbur. "Farmer's Daughter Effect: The Case of the Negro Female Professional." *Phylon* 30 (1969): 17–26.

Bode, Carl. *The Anatomy of Popular Culture, 1840–1861.* Berkeley: Univ. of California Press, 1959.

Boydston, Jeanne, et al. *The Limits of Sisterhood: The Beecher Sisters on Women's Rights and Woman's Sphere.* Chapel Hill: Univ. of North Carolina Press, 1988.

Bradstreet, Anne. *The Complete Works of Anne Bradstreet.* Ed. Joseph R. McElrath, Jr. and Allan P. Robb. Boston: Twayne, 1981.

Brandt, Deborah. "Literacy and Knowledge." In Lunsford et al., *The Right to Literacy,* pp. 189–96.

——. *Literacy as Involvement: The Acts of Writers, Readers, and Texts.* Carbondale: Southern Illinois Univ. Press, 1990.

Brereton, John C., ed. *The Origins of Composition Studies in the American College, 1875–1925: A Documentary History.* Pittsburgh: Univ. of Pittsburgh Press, forthcoming.

Brickley, Lynn Templeton. "Sarah Pierce's Litchfield Female Academy, 1792–1833." Ph.D. diss., Graduate School of Education, Harvard University, 1985.

Brody, Miriam. *Manly Writing: Gender, Rhetoric, and the Rise of Composition.* Carbondale: Southern Illinois Univ. Press, 1993.

Brown, Lyn Mikel. "Telling a Girl's Life: Self-Authorization as a Form of Resistance." In *Women, Girls, and Psychotherapy: Reframing Resistance,* ed. Carol Gilligan, Annie G. Rogers, and Deborah L. Tolman, pp. 71–86. New York: Haworth Press, 1991.

Brown, Lyn Mikel, and Carol Gilligan. *Meeting at the Crossroads: Women's Psychology and Girls' Development.* Cambridge: Harvard Univ. Press, 1992.

Buck, Gertrude. *A Course in Argumentative Writing.* New York: Henry Holt, 1899.

——. "The Study of English." *Vassar Miscellany Weekly* 2 (19 Jan. 1917): 6.

Buck, Gertrude, and Elisabeth Woodbridge [Morris]. *A Course in Expository Writing.* New York: Henry Holt, 1899.

——. *A Course in Narrative Writing.* New York: Henry Holt, 1906.

Buell, Lawrence. *New England Literary Culture: From Revolution through Renaissance.* New York: Cambridge Univ. Press, 1986.

Bunkers, Suzanne L. *"All Will Yet Be Well": The Diary of Sarah Gillespie Huftalen, 1873–1952.* Iowa City: Univ. of Iowa Press, 1993.

——. "Diaries: Public *and* Private Records of Women's Lives." *Legacy: A Journal of Nineteenth-Century American Women Writers* 7 (Fall 1990): 17–25.

——. "'Faithful Friend': Nineteenth-Century Midwestern American Women's Unpublished Diaries." *Women's Studies International Forum* 10 (1987): 7–17.

——. "Midwestern Diaries and Journals: What Women Were (Not) Saying in the Late 1800s." In *Studies in Autobiography,* ed. James Olney, pp. 190–210. New York: Oxford Univ. Press, 1988.

——. "Reading and Interpreting Unpublished Diaries by Nineteenth-Century Women." *A/B: Auto/Biography Studies* 2 (1986): 15–17.

——. "Subjectivity and Self-Reflexivity in the Study of Women's Diaries as Autobiography." *A/B: Auto/Biography Studies* 5 (1990): 114–23.

Burns, Lee. "The Beginnings of Butler College." *Butler Alumnal Quarterly* 15 (Apr. 1926): 3–12.

Butcher, Patricia Smith. *Education for Equality: Women's Rights Periodicals and Women's Higher Education, 1849–1920.* Westport, Conn.: Greenwood Press, 1989.

Butler, Charles. *The American Lady.* Philadelphia: Hogan, 1836.

Butler, Judith. *Gender Trouble: Feminism and the Subversion of Identity.* New York: Routledge, 1990.

Button, H. Warren, and Eugene F. Provenzo Jr. *History of Education and Culture in America.* Englewood Cliffs, N.J.: Prentice-Hall, 1983.

Campbell, JoAnn. "Controlling Voices: The Legacy of English A at Radcliffe College, 1883–1917." *College Composition and Communication* 43 (1992): 472–85.

——. "Women's Work, Worthy Work: Composition Instruction at Vassar College, 1897–1922." In *Constructing Rhetorical Education,* ed. Marie Secor and Davida Charney, pp. 26–42. Carbondale: Southern Illinois Univ. Press, 1992.

Campbell, Karlyn Kohrs. *Man Cannot Speak for Her.* Vol. 1, *A Critical Study of Early Feminist Rhetoric.* Contributions in Women's Studies, no. 101. Westport, Conn.: Greenwood Press, 1989.

——, comp. *Man Cannot Speak for Her.* Vol. 2, *Key Texts of Early Feminists.* Contributions to Women's Studies, no. 102. Westport, Conn.: Greenwood Press, 1989.

——, ed. *Women Public Speakers in the United States, 1800–1925: A Biblio-Critical Sourcebook.* Westport, Conn.: Greenwood Press, 1993.

Carby, Hazel V. *Reconstructing Womanhood: The Emergence of the Afro-American Woman Novelist.* New York: Oxford Univ. Press, 1987.

Carson, Gerald. *The Polite Americans: A Wide-Angle View of Our More or Less Good Manners over 300 Years.* New York: Morrow, 1966.

Cassidy, Jessie. *The Legal Status of Women.* n.p.: National American Woman Suffrage Association, 1897.

Caywood, Cynthia L., and Gillian R. Overing, eds. *Teaching Writing: Pedagogy, Gender, and Equity.* Albany: State Univ. of New York Press, 1987.

Chodorow, Nancy. "Family Structure and Feminine Personality." In Rosaldo and Lamphere, *Woman, Culture, and Society,* pp. 43–66.

——. *The Reproduction of Mothering: Psychoanalysis and the Sociology of Gender.* Berkeley: Univ. of California Press, 1978.

Cixous, Hélène. "Sorties: Out and Out: Attacks/Ways Out/Forays." In *The Newly Born Woman,* trans. Betsy Wing, pp. 63–78. Minneapolis: Univ. of Minnesota Press, 1986.

——. *Three Steps on the Ladder of Writing.* Trans. Sarah Cornell and Susan Sellers. New York: Columbia Univ. Press, 1993.

Clark, Gregory, and S. Michael Halloran, eds. *Oratorical Culture in America: Essays on the Transformation of Nineteenth-Century Rhetoric.* Carbondale: Southern Illinois Univ. Press, 1993.

Clarke, Edward. *Sex in Education; or, A Fair Chance for the Girls.* Boston: Osgood, 1873.

Clinton, Catherine. *The Other Civil War: American Women in the Nineteenth Century.* New York: Hill and Wang, 1984.

Clower, John W. "Women's Contributions to the Theory of Language Pedagogy in the U.S.: The First Women Theorists." Ph.D. diss., Indiana Univ., 1989.

Cogan, Frances. *All-American Girl: The Ideal of Real Womanhood in Mid-Nineteenth-Century America.* Athens: Univ. of Georgia Press, 1989.

Cohen, Paul. "Barrett Wendell: A Study of Harvard Culture." Ph.D. diss. Northwestern Univ., 1974.

Cole, Arthur C. *A Hundred Years of Mount Holyoke.* New Haven: Yale Univ. Press, 1940.

Collins, Patricia Hill. *Black Feminist Thought: Knowledge, Consciousness, and the Politics of Empowerment.* New York: Routledge, 1991.

Connors, Robert J. "Rhetoric in the Modern University: The Creation of an Underclass." In *The Politics of Writing Instruction: Postsecondary,* ed. Richard Bullock and John Trimbur, pp. 55–84. Portsmouth, N.H.: Heinemann, 1991.

Conway, Jill K. "Coeducation and Women's Studies: Two Approaches to the Question of Woman's Place in the Contemporary University." *Daedalus* 103 (1974): 239–49.

——. *The First Generation of American Woman Graduates.* Higher Education, Culture, and Professionalism, 1850–1950. New York: Garland, 1987. Originally published as Ph.D. diss., Harvard Univ., 1968.

——. "Women Reformers and American Culture, 1870–1930." *Journal of Social History* 5 (1972): 164–77.

Cooper, Anna J. *A Voice from the South.* 1892. Reprint, New York: Oxford Univ. Press, 1988.

Copeland, C. T., and H. M. Rideout. *Freshman English and Theme-Correcting in Harvard College.* New York: Silver, Burdett, 1901.

Corbett, Edward P. J. *Classical Rhetoric for the Modern Student.* 3d ed. New York: Oxford Univ. Press, 1990.

——. "Literature and Composition: Allies or Rivals in the Classroom?" In *Composition and Literature: Bridging the Gap,* ed. Winifred Bryan Horner, pp. 168–84. Chicago: Univ. of Chicago Press, 1983.

Cordier, Mary Hurlbut. "'To Be a Teacher': Sarah Gillespie Huftalen, 1865–1955." *Schoolwomen of the Prairies and Plains: Personal Narratives from Iowa, Kansas, and Nebraska, 1860s to 1920s,* pp. 209–44. Albuquerque: Univ. of New Mexico Press, 1992.

Cornelius, Janet Duitsman. *"When I Can Read My Title Clear": Literacy, Slavery, and Religion in the Antebellum South.* Columbia: Univ. of South Carolina Press, 1991.

Cornell, Drucilla. *Beyond Accommodation: Ethical Feminism, Deconstruction, and the Law.* New York: Routledge, 1991.

Cott, Nancy F. *The Bonds of Womanhood: "Women's Sphere" in New England, 1780–1835.* New Haven: Yale Univ. Press, 1977.

——, ed. and intro. *History of Women in the U.S.: Historical Articles on Women's Lives and Activities.* Vol. 12, *Education.* Munich: K. G. Sauer, 1993.

Coultrap-McQuin, Susan. *Doing Literary Business: American Women Writers in the Nineteenth Century.* Chapel Hill: Univ. of North Carolina Press, 1990.

Croly, Mrs. J. C. *A History of the Woman's Club Movement in America.* New York: H. G. Allen, 1898.

Crosby, Fanny J. *Memories of Eighty Years.* Boston: James H. Earle, 1906.

Crowley, Sharon. *The Methodical Memory: Invention in Current-Traditional Rhetoric,* Carbondale: Southern Illinois Univ. Press, 1990.

Culley, Margo. Introduction to *A Day at a Time: The Diary Literature of American Woman from 1764 to the Present,* ed. Culley, pp. 3–26. New York: Feminist Press, 1985.

Cummings, A. I. *The Young Lady's Present: or Beauties of Female Character.* Boston: J. Buffam, 1854.

Custer, Elizabeth Bacon. *"Boots and Saddles"; or, Life in Dakota with General Custer.* 1885. Ed. Jane R. Stewart. Reprint, Norman: Univ. of Oklahoma Press, 1961.

——. *Following the Guidon.* 1890. Ed. Jane R. Stewart. Reprint, Norman: Univ. of Oklahoma Press, 1966.

——. *Tenting on the Plains; or, General Custer in Kansas and Texas.* 1887. 3 vols. Ed. Jane R. Stewart. Reprint, Norman: Univ. of Oklahoma Press, 1971.

——. "'Where the Heart Is': A Sketch of Woman's Life on the Frontier." *Lippincott's* 65 (1890): 305–13.

Darwin, Charles. *The Descent of Man and Selection in Relation to Sex.* 2 vols. London: John Murray, 1871.

Davidson, Cathy N., ed. *Reading in America: Literature and Social History.* Baltimore: Johns Hopkins Univ. Press, 1989.

——. *Revolution and the Word: The Rise of the Novel in America.* New York: Oxford Univ. Press, 1986.

Davis, Allen F. *American Heroine: The Life and Legend of Jane Addams.* New York: Oxford Univ. Press, 1973.

Dean, Sharon G. Introduction to *A Hairdresser's Experience in High Life,* by Eliza Potter. 1859. Reprint, New York: Oxford Univ. Press, 1991. xxxiii–lix.

De Jong, Mary G. " 'I Want to Be Like Jesus': The Self-Defining Power of Evangelical Hymnody." *Journal of the American Academy of Religion* 54 (1986): 461–93.

Donovan, Josephine. "Toward a Women's Poetics." *Tulsa Studies in Women's Literature* 3 (1984): 99–110.

——. *"Uncle Tom's Cabin": Evil, Affliction, and Redemptive Love.* Boston: Twayne, 1991.

Douglas, Ann. *The Feminization of American Culture.* 1977. Reprint, New York: Anchor Press, 1988.

Du Bois, W. E. B. *Black Reconstruction in America: An Essay toward a History of the Part Which Black Folk Played in the Attempt to Reconstruct Democracy in America, 1860–1880.* 1935. Reprint, Cleveland: Meridian Books, 1962.

Dunn, Jacob Piatt. *History of Greater Indianapolis.* Chicago: Lewis Publishing, 1910.

Eddy, Daniel Clark. *The Young Woman's Friend; or the Duties, Trials, Loves, Hopes of Woman.* Boston: Wentworth and Company, 1857.

Eldred, Janet Carey, and Peter Mortensen. "Gender and Writing Instruction in Early America: Lessons from Didactic Fiction." *Rhetoric Review* 12 (1993): 25–53.

——. "Monitoring Columbia's Daughters: Writing as Gendered Conduct." *Rhetoric Society of America.* Forthcoming.

Eliot, William. *Lectures to Young Women.* Boston: Crosby, Nichols, 1856.

Ellison, Rhoda Coleman. Introduction to *The Planter's Northern Bride,* by Caroline Lee Hentz. Chapel Hill: Univ. of North Carolina Press, 1970.

——. "Mrs. Hentz and the Green-Eyed Monster." *American Literature* 22 (1950): 345–50.

——. *The Planter's Northern Bride: or, Scenes from Mrs. Hentz's Childhood.* Philadelphia: Peterson, 1854.

English, Karen Ann. "To Live by Talking: The Arts of Transcendental Conversation." Ph.D. diss., Univ. of North Carolina, 1992.

Enos, Theresa. "Gender and Journals, Conservers or Innovators." *Pre/Text* 9 (1989): 209–14.

Epstein, Barbara. *The Politics of Domesticity: Women, Evangelism, and Temperance in Nineteenth-Century America.* Middletown, Conn.: Wesleyan Univ. Press, 1981.

Faderman, Lillian. *Surpassing the Love of Men: Romantic Friendship and Love between Women from the Renaissance to the Present.* New York: William Morrow, 1981.

Faigley, Lester. "Judging Writing, Judging Selves." *College Composition and Communication* 40 (1989): 395–412.

Faragher, John Mack. *Women and Men on the Overland Trail.* New Haven: Yale Univ. Press, 1979.

Faragher, John Mack, and Florence Howe, eds. *Women and Higher Education in American History: Essays from the Mount Holyoke College Sesquicentennial Symposia.* New York: Norton, 1988.

Flynn, Elizabeth. "Composing as a Woman." *College Composition and Communication* 39 (1988): 423–35.

Foote, John P. *Memoirs of Samuel E. Foote.* Cincinnati: Robert Clarke, 1860.

Foreman, Grant. *Indian Removal: The Emigration of the Five Civilized Tribes of Indians.* Norman: Univ. of Oklahoma Press, 1932.

Foster, Charles H. *The Rungless Ladder: Harriet Beecher Stowe and New England Puritanism.* New York: Cooper Square, 1970.

Foster, Frances Smith. *Written by Herself: Literary Production by African American Women, 1746–1892.* Bloomington: Indiana Univ. Press, 1993.

——. ed. *A Brighter Coming Day: A Frances Ellen Watkins Harper Reader.* New York: Feminist Press, 1990.

Fothergill, Robert. *Private Chronicles: A Study of English Diaries.* London: Oxford Univ. Press, 1974.

Freedman, Diane, Olivia Frey, and Frances Murphy Zuahar, eds. *The Intimate Critique: Autobiographical Literary Criticism.* Durham, N.C.: Duke Univ. Press, 1993.

Freire, Paulo. *Pedagogy of the Oppressed.* Trans. Myra Bergman Ramos. New York: Continuum, 1983.

Frey, Olivia. "Beyond Literary Darwinism: Women's Voices and Critical Discourse." *College English* 52 (1990): 507–26.

Fuller, Margaret. *Woman in the Nineteenth Century.* 1855. Reprint, New York: Norton, 1971.

Gannett, Cinthia. *Gender and the Journal: Diaries and Academic Discourse.* Albany: State Univ. of New York Press, 1992.

Gates, Henry Louis. "In Her Own Write." Foreword to *The Journal of Charlotte Forten Grimké.* Ed. Brenda Stevenson. Schomburg Library of Black Women Writers. New York: Oxford Univ. Press, 1988. vii–xxx.

Gere, Anne Ruggles. *Writing Groups: History, Theory, and Implications.* Carbondale: Southern Illinois Univ. Press, 1987.

Giddings, Paula. *When and Where I Enter: The Impact of Black Women on Race and Sex in America.* New York: Bantam, 1985.

Gilbertson, Catherine. *Harriet Beecher Stowe.* Port Washington, N.Y.: Kennikat Press, 1968.

Gilligan, Carol. *In a Different Voice: Psychological Theory and Women's Development.* Cambridge: Harvard Univ. Press, 1982.

Gilman, Charlotte Perkins. *His Religion and Hers: A Study of the Faith of Our Fathers and the Work of Our Mothers.* 1923. Pioneers of the Woman's Movement Series. Reprint, Westport, Conn.: Hyperion Press, 1976.

——. "The Yellow Wallpaper" (1892). In *The Charlotte Perkins Gilman Reader,* ed. Ann J. Lane, pp. 3–31. New York: Pantheon, 1980.

Gilmore, William J. "Elementary Literacy on the Eve of the Industrial Revolu-

tion: Trends in Rural New England, 1760–1830." *Proceedings of the American Antiquarian Society* 92 (1982): 114–26.
——. *Reading Becomes a Necessity of Life: Material and Culture in Rural New England, 1780–1835.* Knoxville: Univ. of Tennessee Press, 1989.
Ginzburg, Carlo. *The Cheese and the Worms: The Cosmos of a Sixteenth-Century Miller.* Trans. John and Anne Tedeschi. Baltimore: Johns Hopkins Univ. Press, 1980.
Golden, James L., Goodwin F. Bergquist, and William E. Coleman. *The Rhetoric of Western Thought.* Dubuque, Iowa: Kendall/Hunt, 1989.
Goody, Jack, and Ian Watt. "The Consequences of Literacy." *Composition Studies in Society and History* 3 (1963): 304–45. Reprinted in *Literacy in Traditional Societies,* ed. Jack Goody. Cambridge: Cambridge Univ. Press, 1968.
Graff, Gerald. *Professing Literature: An Institutional History.* Chicago: Univ. of Chicago Press, 1987.
Graff, Harvey J. *The Legacies of Literacy: Continuities and Contradictions in Western Culture and Society.* Bloomington: Indiana Univ. Press, 1987.
——. *The Literacy Myth: Literacy and Social Structure in the Nineteenth-Century City.* New York: Academic Press, 1979.
Graulich, Melody. "'O Beautiful for Spacious Guys': An Essay on the 'Legitimate Inclinations' of the Sexes." *The Frontier Experience and the American Dream,* ed. David Mogen et al., pp. 186–201. College Station: Texas A & M Press, 1989.
Graves, Mrs. A. J. *Woman in America; Being an Examination into the Moral and Intellectual Condition of American Female Society.* New York: Harper, 1843.
Green, Harvey. *The Light of the Home: An Intimate View of the Lives of Women in Victorian America.* New York: Pantheon Books, 1983.
Grimké, Sarah. *Letters on the Equality of the Sexes and Other Essays.* 1838. Ed. Elizabeth Ann Bartlett. Reprint, New Haven: Yale Univ. Press, 1988.
H. E. B. "Aunt Mary." *Western Monthly Magazine* 2 (July 1834): 362–67.
Hall, James. *The Catholic Question, to Which Are Annexed Critical Notices, of a Plea for the West.* Cincinnati: n.p., 1838.
Halttunen, Karen. *Confidence Men and Painted Women: A Study of Middle-Class Culture in America, 1830–1870.* New Haven: Yale Univ. Press, 1982.
Haraway, Donna. "Ecce Homo, Ain't (Ar'n't) I a Woman, and Inappropriate/d Others: The Human in a Post-Humanist Landscape." In *Feminists Theorize the Political,* ed Judith Butler and Joan W. Scott, pp. 86–100. New York: Routledge, 1992.
——. "Situated Knowledges: The Science Question in Feminism and the Privilege of Partial Perspective." *Feminist Studies* 14 (1988): 575–99.
Harper, Charles A. *Development of the Teachers College in the United States with Special Reference to the Illinois State Normal University.* Bloomington, Ill.: McKnight and McKnight, 1935.
Harper, Frances E. W. *Iola Leroy, or Shadows Uplifted.* 2d ed. 1892. Reprint, College Park, Md.: McGrath, 1969.
Harris, Maria. *Dance of the Spirit: The Seven Steps of Women's Spirituality.* New York: Bantam Books, 1989.
Heath, Shirley Brice. "Toward an Ethnohistory of Writing in American Educa-

tion." In *Variation in Writing,* ed. Marcia Farr Whiteman, pp. 25–45. Vol. 1 of *Writing: The Nature, Development, and Teaching of Written Communication.* Hillsdale, N.J.: Erlbaum, 1981.

Hedrick, Joan D. "Parlor Literature: Harriet Beecher Stowe and the Question of 'Great Women Artists.'" *Signs* 17 (1992): 275–303.

Heller, Scott. "Experience and Expertise Meet in a New Brand of Scholarship." *Chronicle of Higher Education,* 6 May 1992, A7-A9.

Hentz, Caroline Lee. *Ernest Linwood: The Inner Life of the Author.* Philadelphia: Peterson, 1869.

Herbst, Jurgen. *And Sadly Teach: Teacher Education and Professionalization in American Culture.* Madison: Univ. of Wisconsin Press, 1989.

Hertz, Deborah. *Jewish High Society in Old Regime Berlin.* New Haven: Yale Univ. Press, 1988.

Higginbotham, Evelyn B. "African-American Women's History and the Metalanguage of Race." *Signs* 17 (1992): 251–74.

Hobbs, Catherine. *See* Peaden, Catherine Hobbs.

Hoffman, Nancy. *Women's "True" Profession: Voices from the History of Teaching.* Old Westbury, N.Y.: Feminist Press, 1981.

Hogan, Rebecca S. "Engendered Autobiography: The Diary as a Feminine Form." *Prose Studies* 14 (1991): 95–107.

Hogeland, Ronald W. "Coeducation of the Sexes at Oberlin College: A Study of Social Ideas in Mid-Nineteenth-Century America." *Journal of Social History* 6 (1972): 160–76.

Hooker, Bessie R. "The Use of Literary Material in Teaching Composition." *School Review* 10 (1902): 474–85.

hooks, bell. *Ain't I a Woman? Black Women and Feminism.* Boston: South End Press, 1981.

——. *Talking Back: Thinking Feminist, Thinking Black.* Boston: South End Press, 1989.

hooks, bell, and Cornel West. *Breaking Bread: Insurgent Black Intellectual Life.* Boston: South End Press, 1991.

Horowitz, Helen Lefkowitz. *Alma Mater: Design and Experience in the Women's Colleges from Their Nineteenth-Century Beginnings to the 1930s.* New York: Knopf, 1984.

——. *Campus Life: Undergraduate Cultures from the End of the Eighteenth Century to the Present.* New York: Knopf, 1987.

Howe, Florence. *The Myths of Coeducation—Selected Essays, 1964–1983.* Bloomington: Indiana Univ. Press, 1984.

Hume, Ruth Fox. *Great Women of Medicine.* New York: Random House, 1964.

Hutchinson, Louise Daniel. *Anna J. Cooper: A Voice from the South.* Washington, D.C.: Smithsonian Institution Press, 1981.

Ihle, Elizabeth. "Black Women's Education in the South: The Dual Burden of Sex and Race." In *Changing Education: Women as Radicals and Conservators,* ed. Joyce Antler and Sari Biklen, pp. 69–80. Albany: State Univ. of New York Press, 1990.

Jacobs, Harriet. *Incidents in the Life of a Slave Girl.* 1861. Schomburg Library of Nineteenth-Century Black Women Writers. Reprint, New York: Oxford Univ. Press, 1990.

Jarratt, Susan C. "Speaking to the Past: Feminist Historiography in Rhetoric." *Pre/Text* 11 (1990): 189–210.

Johnson, Nan. "Nineteenth-Century Elocution and the Private Learner." In Clark and Halloran, *Oratorical Culture in America,* pp. 139–57.

——. *Nineteenth-Century Rhetoric in North America.* Carbondale: Southern Illinois Univ. Press, 1991.

Jones, Jacqueline. *Labor of Love, Labor of Sorrow: Black Women, Work, and the Family, from Slavery to the Present.* New York: Vintage, 1985.

——. *Soldiers of Light and Love: Northern Teachers and Georgia Blacks, 1865–1873.* Chapel Hill: Univ. of North Carolina Press, 1980.

——. "Women Who Were More Than Men: Sex and Status in Freedman's Teaching." *History of Education Quarterly* 19 (1979): 47–59.

Jordan, David Starr. *The Days of a Man: Being Memoirs of a Naturalist, Teacher, and Minor Prophet of Democracy.* Yonkers-on-Hudson, N.Y.: World Book Company, 1922.

Juhasz, Suzanne. "'Some Deep Old Desk or Capacious Hold-All': Form and Women's Autobiography." *College English* 6 (1978): 663–68.

——. "Toward a Theory of Form in Feminist Autobiography." In *Women's Autobiography,* ed. Estelle Jelinek, pp. 221–37. Bloomington: Indiana Univ. Press, 1980.

Kaestle, Carl F., et al. *Literacy in the U. S.: Readers and Reading since 1880.* New Haven: Yale Univ. Press, 1991.

Kann, Mark E. *On the Man Question: Gender and Civic Virtue in America.* Philadelphia: Temple Univ. Press, 1991.

Kelley, Mary. *Private Woman, Public Stage: Literary Domesticity in Nineteenth-Century America.* New York: Oxford Univ. Press, 1984.

Kerber, Linda. "The Paradox of Women's Citizenship in the Early Republic: The Case of Martin vs. Massachusetts, 1805." *American Historical Review* 97 (1992): 349–78.

——. "The Republican Mother: Women and the Enlightenment—An American Perspective." *American Quarterly* 28 (1976): 187–202.

——. "Separate Spheres, Female Worlds, Woman's Place: The Rhetoric of Women's History." *Journal of American History* 75 (1988): 9–39.

——. "'Why Should Girls Be Learn'd and Wise?': Two Centuries of Higher Education for Women as Seen through the Unfinished Work of Alice Mary Baldwin." in Faragher and Howe, *Women and Higher Education in American History,* pp. 18–42.

——. *Women of the Republic: Intellect and Ideology in Revolutionary America.* Chapel Hill: Univ. of North Carolina Press, 1980.

Kersey, Shirley Nelson. *Classics in the Education of Girls and Women.* Metuchen, N.J.: Scarecrow Press, 1981.

Kintgen, Eugene R., Barry M. Kroll, and Mike Rose, eds. *Perspectives on Literacy.* Carbondale: Southern Illinois Univ. Press, 1988.

Kitzhaber, Albert R. *Rhetoric in American Colleges, 1850–1900.* Dallas: Southern Methodist Univ. Press, 1990.

Kolodny, Annette. *The Land before Her: Fantasy and Experience of the American Frontiers, 1630–1860.* Chapel Hill: Univ. of North Carolina Press, 1984.

Kraditor, Aileen. *The Ideas of the Woman Suffrage Movement, 1899–1929.* Garden City, N.Y.: Doubleday, 1971.

Kristeva, Julia. "Women's Time." Trans. Alice Jardine and Harry Blake. In *The Kristeva Reader,* ed. Toril Moi, pp. 188–213. New York: Columbia Univ. Press, 1986.

Laird, Susan. "The Ideal of the Educated Teacher—'Reclaiming a Conversation' with Louisa May Alcott." *Curriculum Inquiry* 21 (1991): 271–97.

Lamb, Catherine E. "Beyond Argument in Feminist Composition." *College Composition and Communication* 42 (1991): 11–24.

Lander, Dawn. "Eve among the Indians." In *The Authority of Experience: Essays in Feminist Criticism,* ed. Arlyn Diamond and Lee R. Edwards, pp. 194–211. Amherst: Univ. of Massachusetts Press, 1977.

Lane, Ann J. *To "Herland" and Beyond: The Life and Work of Charlotte Perkins Gilman.* New York: Meridian, 1990.

Lauer, Janice M., and Andrea A. Lunsford. "The Place of Rhetoric and Composition in Doctoral Studies." In *The Future of Doctoral Studies in English,* ed. Andrea Lunsford, Helene Moglen, and James F. Slevin, pp. 106–10. New York: MLA, 1989.

Lawrence, LeeAnna. "The Teaching of Rhetoric and Composition in Nineteenth-Century Women's Colleges." Ph.D. diss., Duke University, 1990.

Lebsock, Suzanne. *The Free Women of Petersburg: Status and Culture in a Southern Town, 1784–1860.* New York: Norton, 1984.

Leckie, Shirley A. *Elizabeth Bacon Custer and the Making of a Myth.* Norman: Univ. of Oklahoma Press, 1993.

Lee, Mary. Mary Lee Collection. Schlesinger Library. Radcliffe College, Cambridge, Mass.

Leiber, Justin, James Pickering, and Flora Bronson White, eds. " 'Mother by the Tens': Flora Adelaide Holcomb Bronson's Account of Her Life as an Illinois Schoolteacher, Poet, and Farm Wife, 1851–1927." *Journal of the Illinois State Historical Society* 76 (1983): 293–94.

Lensink, Judy Nolte. "Expanding the Boundaries of Criticism: The Diary as Female Autobiography." *Women's Studies* 14 (1987): 39–53.

——. *"A Secret to be Burried'": The Diary and Life of Emily Hawley Gillespie, 1858–1888.* Iowa City: Univ. of Iowa Press, 1989.

Lerner, Gerda. *The Majority Finds Its Past.* New York: Oxford Univ. Press, 1981.

Leslie, Eliza. *Miss Leslie's Behavior Book: A Guide and Manual for Ladies.* Philadelphia: T. B. Peterson, 1859.

Levering, Julia Henderson. *Historic Indiana.* New York: G. P. Putnam's Sons, 1909.

Lockridge, Kenneth A. *Literacy in Colonial New England: An Enquiry into the Social Context of Literacy in the Early Modern West.* New York: Norton, 1974.

Logsdon, Guy William. *The University of Tulsa: A History, 1882–1972.* Norman: Univ. of Oklahoma Press, 1977.

Lunsford, Andrea A., Helene Moglen, and James Slevin, eds. *The Right to Literacy.* New York: MLA, 1990.

Lystra, Karen. *Searching the Heart: Women, Men, and Romantic Love in Nineteenth-Century America.* New York: Oxford Univ. Press, 1989.

Mabee, Carleton. "Sojourner Truth, Bold Prophet: Why Did She Never Learn to Read?" *New York History* 69 (1988): 55–77.

Majors, Monroe A. *Noted Negro Women: Their Triumphs and Activities.* 1893. Reprint, Freeport, N.Y.: Books for Libraries Press, 1971.

Mallon, Thomas. *A Book of One's Own: People and Their Diaries.* New York: Ticknor and Fields, 1984.

Malone, Henry T. *Cherokees of the Old South.* Athens: Univ. of Georgia Press, 1956.

Mansfield, Edward Deering. *The Legal Rights and Duties of Women, with an Introductory History of Their Legal Condition in the Hebrew, Roman, and Feudal Civil Systems.* Cincinnati: Moore, 1845.

——. *Personal Memories, Social, Political, and Literary, with Sketches of Many Noted People, 1803–1843.* 1879. Reprint, Arno Press, 1970.

Marshall, Helen E. *Grandest of Enterprises: Illinois State Normal University, 1857–1957.* Normal: Illinois State Normal Univ., 1956.

Marshall, Madeleine Forell, and Janet Todd. *English Congregational Hymns in the Eighteenth Century.* Lexington: Univ. Press of Kentucky, 1982.

Martin, Jane Roland. "Methodological Essentialism, False Difference, and Other Dangerous Traps." *Signs* 19 (1994): 630–57.

——. *Reclaiming a Conversation: The Ideal of the Educated Woman.* New Haven: Yale Univ. Press, 1985.

Martin, Theodora Penny. *The South of Our Own Voices: Women's Study Clubs, 1860–1910.* Boston: Beacon Press, 1987.

Mathes, Valerie Sherer. "Susan LaFlesche Picote: Nebraska's Indian Physician, 1865–1915." *Nebraska History* 63 (1982): 502–30.

Matthews, Glenna. *"Just a Housewife": The Rise and Fall of Domesticity in America.* New York: Oxford Univ. Press, 1987.

McDowell, George S. "Harriet Beecher Stowe at Cincinnati." *New England,* n.s., 2 (March 1895): 65–70.

McLachlan, James. "The Choice of Hercules: American Student Societies in the Early Nineteenth Century." *University in Society.* Vol. 2. Ed. Lawrence Stone. Princeton, N.J.: Princeton Univ. Press, 1974.

McLoughlin, William G. *The Cherokee Ghost Dance: Essays on the Southeastern Indians, 1789–1861.* Macon, Ga.: Mercer Univ. Press, 1984.

——. *Cherokee Renascence in the New Republic.* Princeton, N.J.: Princeton Univ. Press, 1986.

——. *Cherokees and Missionaries: 1789–1839* New Haven: Yale Univ. Press, 1984.

McMillen, Liz. "A Passion for French." *Chronicle of Higher Education,* 9 February 1994, A8–A9, A19.

Merrill, Catharine. *The Man Shakespeare and Other Essays.* Ed. Melville B. Anderson. Indianapolis: Bowen-Merrill Company, 1900.

Mihesuah, Devon A. *Cultivating the Rosebuds: The Education of Women at the*

Cherokee Female Seminary, 1851–1909. Urbana: Univ. of Illinois Press, 1993.

——. "'Out of the Graves of the Polluted Debauches': The Boys of the Cherokee Male Seminary." *American Indian Quarterly* 15 (1991): 503–21.

——. *See also* Abbott, Devon.

Miller, Susan. "The Feminization of Composition." In *The Politics of Writing Instruction: Postsecondary,* ed. Richard Bullock and John Trimbur, pp. 39–53. Portsmouth, N.H.: Heinemann, 1991.

——. *Textual Carnivals: The Politics of Composition.* Carbondale: Southern Illinois Univ. Press, 1991.

Minnich, Elizabeth, Jean O'Barr, and Rachel Rosenfeld, eds. *Reconstructing the Academy.* Chicago: Univ. of Chicago Press, 1988.

Mitchell, Silas Weir. "Address to the Students of Radcliffe College." Cambridge, Mass. 1886 (delivered 17 Jan. 1885). History of Women Collection. Schlesinger Library. Radcliffe College, Cambridge, Mass.

Monaghan, E. Jennifer. "Literacy Instruction and Gender in Colonial New England." *American Quarterly* 40 (1988): 18–41.

Morris, Robert C. *Reading, 'Riting, and Reconstruction: The Education of Freedmen in the South.* Chicago: Univ. of Chicago Press, 1981.

Moses, Wilson J. *Alexander Crummell: A Study of Civilization and Discontent.* New York: Oxford Univ. Press, 1989.

Motz, Marilyn Ferris. *True Sisterhood: Michigan Women and Their Kin, 1820–1920.* Albany: State Univ. of New York Press, 1983.

Moynihan, Ruth Barnes. *So Much to Be Done: Women Settlers on the Mining and Ranching Frontier.* Lincoln: Univ. of Nebraska Press, 1990.

Myres, Sandra L. "Romance and Reality on the American Frontier: Views of Army Wives." *Western Historical Quarterly* 13 (1982): 409–24.

——. *Westering Women and the Frontier Experience, 1800–1915.* Albuquerque: Univ. of New Mexico Press, 1982.

Newcomer, Mabel. *A Century of Higher Education for American Women.* New York: Harper and Bros., 1959.

Newton, Sarah Emily. "Wise and Foolish Virgins: 'Usable Fiction' and the Early American Conduct Tradition." *Early American Literature* 25 (1990): 139–67.

Nin, Anais. *The Novel of the Future.* New York: Collier Books, 1968.

Ninde, Edward S. *The Story of the American Hymn.* New York: Abingdon, 1921.

Norton, Mary Beth. *Liberty's Daughters: The Revolutionary Experience of American Women, 1750–1800.* Boston: Little, Brown, 1980.

——. "The Paradox of 'Women's Sphere.'" In *Women of America: A History,* ed. Carol Ruth Berkin and Mary Beth Norton, pp. 139–49. Boston: Houghton, 1979.

Ochs, Carol. *Women and Spirituality.* New Feminist Perspectives. Totowa, N.J.: Rowman and Allanheld, 1983.

Ohmann, Richard. *English in America: A Radical View of the Profession.* New York: Oxford Univ. Press, 1976.

Ortner, Sherry B. "Is Female to Male as Nature Is to Culture?" In Rosaldo and Lamphere, *Woman, Culture, and Society,* pp. 67–87.

Painter, Nell Irvin. "Sojourner Truth in Life and Memory: Writing the Biography of an American Exotic." *Gender and History* 2 (1990): 3–16.

Papashvily, Helen Waite. *All the Happy Endings: A Study of the Domestic Novel in America, the Women Who Wrote It, the Women Who Read It, in the Nineteenth Century.* New York: Harper, 1956.

Parker, E. P. "Harriet Beecher Stowe." In *Eminent Women of the Age; Being Narratives of the Lives and Deeds of the Most Prominent Women of the Present Generation,* ed. James Parton et al., pp. 296–331. Hartford: S. M. Betts, 1868.

Parkman, Francis Jr. *The Oregon Trail.* 1849. Ed. David Levin. Reprint, New York: Penguin, 1985.

Pattison, Robert. *On Literacy: The Politics of the Word from Homer to the Age of Rock.* New York: Oxford Univ. Press, 1982.

Peaden, Catherine Hobbs. "Feminist Theories, Historiographies, and Histories of Rhetoric." In *Rhetoric and Ideology: Compositions and Criticisms of Power,* ed. Charles W. Kneupper, pp. 116–26. Arlington, Tex.: Rhetoric Society of America, 1989.

Perdue, Theda. "Cherokee Women and the Trail of Tears." *Journal of Women's History* 1 (1989): 14–30.

——. *Slavery and the Evolution of Cherokee Society: 1540–1866.* Knoxville: Univ. of Tennessee Press, 1983.

——. "The Traditional Status of Cherokee Women." *Furman Studies* (1980): 19–25.

Perkins, Linda M. "The Education of Black Women in the Nineteenth Century." In Faragher and Howe, *Women and Higher Education in American History,* pp. 64–86.

Phelps, Elizabeth Stuart. *Beyond the Gates.* Boston: Houghton, Mifflin, 1883.

[Potter, Eliza]. *A Hairdresser's Experience in High Life.* 1859. Reprint, New York: Oxford Univ. Press, 1991.

Power, Edward J. *Catholic Higher Education in America.* New York: Appleton-Century-Crofts, 1972.

Pratt, Anne. *The Excellent Woman; as Described in the Book of Proverbs.* Boston: Gould and Lincoln, 1851.

Radner, Joan N., and Susan S. Lanser. "Strategies of Coding in Women's Cultures." In *Feminist Messages: Coding in Women's Folk Culture,* ed. Joan Newlon Radner, pp. 1–29. Chicago: Univ. of Chicago Press, 1993.

Randall, Randolph C. *James Hall: Spokesman of the New West.* Columbus: Ohio State Univ. Press, 1964.

Rich, Adrienne. "Resisting Amnesia: History and Personal Life." In *Blood, Bread, and Poetry: Selected Prose, 1979–1985,* pp. 136–55. New York: Norton, 1986.

Richardson, Marilyn, ed. *Maria W. Stewart, America's First Black Woman Political Writer: Essays and Speeches.* Bloomington: Indiana Univ. Press, 1987.

Riegel, Robert E. *American Feminists.* Lawrence: Univ. of Kansas Press, 1963.

Riley, Glenda. *The Female Frontier: A Comparative View of Women on the Prairie and the Plains.* Lawrence: Univ. Press of Kansas, 1988.

——. *Women and Indians on the Frontier, 1825–1915.* Albuquerque: Univ. of New Mexico Press, 1984.

Robbins, Sarah. "Domestic Didactics: Nineteenth-Century American Literary Pedagogy by Barbauld, Stowe, and Addams." Ph.D. diss., Univ. of Michigan, 1993.

Romines, Ann. *The Home Plot: Women, Writing, and Domestic Ritual.* Amherst: Univ. of Massachusetts Press, 1992.

Rosaldo, Michelle Zimbalist, and Louise Lamphere, eds. *Woman, Culture, and Society.* Stanford: Stanford Univ. Press, 1974.

Rose, Jane E. "Gender Politics in American Literature of Domesticity, 1830–1860." Ph.D. diss., Purdue Univ., 1992.

Rose, Shirley K. "Reading Representative Anecdotes of Literacy Practice; or 'See Dick and Jane Read and Write!'" *Rhetoric Review* 8 (1990): 244–59.

Rosenberg, Rosalind. *Beyond Separate Spheres: Intellectual Roots of Modern Feminism.* New Haven: Yale Univ. Press, 1982.

Ross, Ishbel. *Child of Destiny: The Life Story of the First Woman Doctor.* London: Victor Gollancz, 1950.

Ross, William Potter. "Public Education Among the Cherokee Indians." *American Journal of Education* 1 (Aug. 1855): 121.

Rothenbusch, Esther. "The Joyful Sound: Women in the Nineteenth-Century United States Hymnody Tradition." In *Women and Music in Cross-Cultural Perspective,* ed. Ellen Koskoff, pp. 177–94. Contributions in Women's Studies, no. 79. New York: Greenwood Press, 1987.

Rothman, Ellen. *Hands and Hearts: A History of Courtship in America.* Cambridge, Mass.: Harvard Univ. Press, 1987.

Royster, Jacqueline Jones. "Dark Spinners of Word Magic: Literacy as an Authorizing Event." Paper presented at the Composition, Rhetoric, and Literacy Seminar, Univ. of Oklahoma, Sept. 1992.

Ruddick, Sara. *Maternal Thinking: Towards a Politics of Peace.* New York: Ballantine Books, 1989.

Rudolph, Frederick. *Curriculum: A History of the American Undergraduate Course of Study since 1636.* San Francisco: Jossey-Bass, 1977.

Ruether, Rosemary Radford, and Rosemary Skinner Keller, eds. *The Nineteenth Century.* Vol. 1 of *Women and Religion in America.* San Francisco: Harper and Row, 1981.

——. *1960–68.* Vol. 3 of *Women and Religion in America.* San Francisco: Harper and Row, 1986.

Ruffin, Bernard. *Fanny Crosby.* Philadelphia: United Church Press, 1976.

Ryan, Mary P. *The Empire of the Mother: American Writing about Domesticity, 1830–1860.* New York: Haworth Press, 1982.

Sahli, Nancy Ann. *Elizabeth Blackwell, M.D. (1821–1910): A Biography.* New York: Arno Press, 1982.

Salvino, Dana Nelson. "The Word in Black and White: Ideologies of Race and Literacy in Antebellum America." In *Reading in America,* ed. Cathy N. Davidson, pp. 140–56. Baltimore: Johns Hopkins Univ. Press, 1989.

Saxton, Alexander. *The Rise and Fall of the White Republic: Class Politics and Mass Culture in Nineteenth-Century America.* London: Verso, 1990.

Schlesinger, Arthur M., Jr. *Learning to Behave: A Historical Study of American Etiquette.* New York: Macmillan, 1946.

Schwager, Sally. "Educating Women in America." *Signs* 12 (1987): 333–72.
Scott, Anne Firor. "The Ever-Widening Circle: The Diffusion of Feminist Values from the Troy Female Seminary, 1822–1872." *History of Education Quarterly* 19 (1979): 3–25.
——. *Making the Invisible Woman Visible*. Urbana: Univ. of Illinois Press, 1984.
——. *Natural Allies: Women's Associations in American History*. Urbana: Univ. of Illinois Press, 1991.
——. "On Seeing and Not Seeing." *Journal of American History* 11 (1984): 7–21.
——. *The Southern Lady: From Pedestal to Politics, 1830–1930*. Chicago, Univ. of Chicago Press, 1970.
——. "Women and Libraries." *Journal of Library History* 21 (1986): 400–405.
Scott, Joan Wallach. *Gender and the Politics of History*. Gender and Culture. New York: Columbia Univ. Press, 1988.
Scott, Leonora Cranch. *The Life and Letters of Christopher Pearse Cranch*. Boston: Houghton, Mifflin, 1917.
Scribner, Sylvia, and Michael Coles. *The Psychology of Literacy*. Cambridge, Mass.: Harvard Univ. Press, 1981.
Sedgwick, Catharine. *Means and Ends, or Self-Training*. New York: Harper, 1854.
Seidler, Helen Dorothea Crawford. Helen Dorothea Crawford Seidler Collection. Radcliffe College Archives, Cambridge, Mass.
Self, Robert T. *Barrett Wendell*. Twayne U.S. Authors Series, no. 261. Boston: G. K. Hall, 1975.
Shea, Daniel. *Spiritual Autobiography in Early America*. Princeton, N.J.: Princeton Univ. Press, 1968.
Short, Lydia. "Pages from a Diary." *Butler Alumnal Quarterly* 6 (Oct. 1917): 145–61.
Showalter, Elaine. "Feminist Criticism in the Wilderness." *Critical Inquiry* 8 (1981): 179–205.
Sigourney, Lydia. *Letters to Ladies*. Hartford: W. Watson, 1835.
Simmons, Lovie Sue. "A Critique of the Stereotype of Current-Traditional Rhetoric: Invention in Writing Instruction at Harvard, 1875–1900." Ph.D. diss., Univ. of Texas at Austin, 1991.
Sizer, Sandra S. *Gospel Hymns and Social Religion*. American Civilization Series. Philadelphia: Temple Univ. Press, 1978.
Sklar, Kathryn Kish. *Catharine Beecher: A Study in American Domesticity*. New Haven: Yale Univ. Press, 1973.
——. "The Founding of Mount Holyoke College." In *Women of America: A History*, ed. Carol Ruth Berkin and Mary Beth Norton, pp. 177–201. Boston: Houghton, 1979.
Smith, Elizabeth Oakes. *Woman and Her Needs*. 1851. In *Liberating the Home*. New York: Arno Press, 1974.
Smith-Rosenberg, Carroll. *Disorderly Conduct: Visions of Gender in Victorian America*. New York: Knopf, 1985.
Solomon, Barbara Miller. *In the Company of Educated Women: A History of*

Women and Higher Education in America. New Haven: Yale Univ. Press, 1985.

Soltow, Lee, and Edward Stevens. *The Rise of Literacy and the Common Schools in the United States: A Socioeconomic Analysis to 1870.* Chicago: Univ. of Chicago Press, 1981.

Starr, Emmet. *History of the Cherokee Indians: Their Legends and Folklore.* Oklahoma City: Warden, 1979.

Stearns, Jonathan. *Female Influence and the True Christian Mode of Its Exercise.* Newburyport, Mass.: J. G. Tilton, 1837.

Sterling, Dorothy, ed. *We Are Your Sisters: Black Women in the Nineteenth Century.* New York: Norton, 1984.

Stewart, Maria W. *Productions of Mrs. Maria Stewart, Presented to the First African Baptist Church and Society of the City of Boston.* 1835. Reprint, in *Spiritual Narratives,* pp. 1–84. New York: Oxford Univ. Press, 1988.

Still, William. *The Underground Rail Road.* Philadelphia: Porter and Coates. 1872.

Stock, Brian. *Listening for the Text: On the Uses of the Past.* Baltimore: Johns Hopkins Univ. Press, 1990.

Stowe, Charles Edward. *Life of Harriet Beecher Stowe, Compiled from Her Letters and Journals.* Boston: Houghton, Mifflin, 1890.

Stowe, Charles Edward, and Lyman Beecher Stowe. *Harriet Beecher Stowe: The Story of Her Life.* Boston: Houghton, Mifflin, 1911.

Stowe, Harriet Beecher. Introduction to *The May Flower and Miscellaneous Writings.* Boston: Phillips, Sampson, 1855.

——. *The Mayflower; or, Sketches of Scenes and Characters among the Descendants of the Pilgrims.* New York: Harper, 1844.

——. *Uncle Tom's Cabin; or, Life among the Lowly.* 1852. Reprint, in *Uncle Tom's Cabin, or Life among the Lowly; The Minister's Wooing; Oldtown Folks,* ed. Kathryn Kish Sklar, pp. 11–519. New York: Literary Classics of the United States, 1982.

——. *See also* Beecher, Harriet.

Street, Brian. *Literacy in Theory and Practice.* Cambridge: Cambridge Univ. Press, 1984.

Tamke, Susan S. *Make a Joyful Noise unto the Lord: Hymns as a Reflection of Victorian Social Attitudes.* Athens: Ohio Univ. Press, 1978.

Taves, Ann. *Religion and Domestic Violence in Early New England: The Memoirs of Abigail Abbot Bailey.* Bloomington: Indiana Univ. Press, 1989.

Taylor, J. M. "The Conservatism of Vassar." Women's Suffrage Collection. Box 5. Vassar College Library, Poughkeepsie, N.Y.

Taylor, Susie King. *Reminiscences of My Life: A Black Woman's Civil War Memoirs.* 1902. Ed. Patricia W. Romer and Willie Lee Rose. Reprint, Princeton: Marcus Weiner, 1992.

Temple, Judy Nolte. *See* Lensink, Judy Nolte.

Terry, Esther. "Sojourner Truth: The Person Behind the Libyan Sibyl." *Massachusetts Review* 26 (1985): 425–44.

Theriot, Nancy M. *The Biosocial Construction of Femininity: Mothers and Daughters in Nineteenth-Century America.* Contributions in Women's Studies, no. 93. New York: Greenwood Press, 1988.

Tinnin, Ida Wetzel "Educational and Cultural Influences of the Cherokee Seminaries." *Chronicles of Oklahoma* 37 (1959): 59–67.
Tompkins, Jane. "Me and My Shadow." *New Literary History* 19 (1987): 169–178.
——. *Sensational Designs: The Cultural Work of American Fiction, 1790–1860.* New York: Oxford Univ. Press, 1985.
Trachsel, Mary. *Institutionalizing Literacy.* Carbondale: Southern Illinois Univ. Press, 1992.
Truth, Sojourner. *Narrative of Sojourner Truth.* Ed. Frances W. Titus. 1878. Reprint, Salem, N.H.: Ayer, 1988.
——. Speeches delivered on May 9 and 10 at the First Annual Meeting of the American Equal Rights Association. *National Anti-Slavery Standard,* 1 June 1867, p. 3.
Tucker, Louis L. "The Semicolon Club of Cincinnati." *Ohio History* 73.1 (1964): 13–26, 57–58.
Tuman, Myron. *A Preface to Literacy: An Inquiry into Pedagogy, Practice and Progress.* Tuscaloosa: Univ. of Alabama Press, 1987.
U.S. Department of Commerce, Bureau of the Census. *Negro Population in the United States, 1790–1915.* 1918. Reprint, New York: Arno Press, 1968.
Venable, W. H. *Beginnings of Literary Culture in the Ohio Valley.* Cincinnati: R. Clarke, 1891.
Vesey, Laurence. *The Emergence of the American University.* Chicago: Univ. of Chicago Press, 1965.
Vinovsky, Maris, and Richard Bernard. "Beyond Catharine Beecher: Female Education in the Antebellum Period." *Signs* 3 (1978): 856–69.
Walker, Robbie Jean, ed. *The Rhetoric of Struggle: Public Address by African American Women.* New York: Garland, 1992.
Washington, Mary Helen. Introduction to *A Voice from the South,* by Anna Julia Cooper. New York: Oxford Univ. Press, 1988. pp. xxvii-liv.
Wecter, Dixon. *The Saga of American Society: A Record of Social Aspirations, 1607–1837.* New York: Scribners, 1937.
Weidner, Heidemarie Z. "Double-Voiced Discourse: A Young Woman's Journal from a Nineteenth-Century Composition Class." March 1991. ERIC, ED 340 027.
Wein, Robert A. "Women's Colleges and Domesticity, 1875–1918." *History of Education Quarterly* 14 (1974): 44.
Wells, Ida B. *Crusade for Justice: The Autobiography of Ida B. Wells.* Ed. Alfreda Duster. Chicago: Univ. of Chicago Press, 1970.
Welter, Barbara. "The Cult of True Womanhood, 1820–1860." *American Quarterly* 18 (1966): 151–74.
——. *Dimity Convictions: The American Woman in the Nineteenth Century.* Athens: Ohio Univ. Press, 1976.
——. "The Feminization of American Religion, 1800–1860." In *Clio's Consciousness Raised,* ed. Mary Hartman and Lois Banner, pp. 137–57. New York: Harper Colophon, 1974.
Wendell, Barrett. Gradebook for English A, 1889–90. Barrett Wendell Collection. Harvard Archives. Pusey Library, Cambridge, Mass.

——. "The Relations of Radcliffe College with Harvard." *Harvard Monthly* 29 (1899): 1–10.

Williams, Fannie Barrier. "The Club Movement among Colored Women of America." 1900. In Woloch, *Early American Women,* pp. 490–92.

Wilson, Dorothy Clarke. *Lone Woman: The Story of Elizabeth Blackwell, the First Woman Doctor.* Boston: Little, Brown, 1970.

Wilson, Forrest. *Crusader in Crinoline: The Life of Harriet Beecher Stowe.* New York: Lippincott, 1941.

Wise, Daniel. *The Young Lady's Counsellor: or, Outlines and Illustrations of the Sphere, the Duties, and the Dangers of Young Women.* 1851. In *The American Ideal of the "True Woman" as Reflected in Advice Books to Young Women,* ed. Carolyn De Swarte Gifford. New York: Garland, 1987.

Woloch, Nancy. *Early American Women: A Documentary History, 1600–1900.* Belmont, Calif.: Wadsworth, 1992.

——. *Women and the American Experience.* New York: Knopf, 1984.

Woodson, Carter G. *The Education of the Negro Prior to 1861.* 1919. Reprint, New York: Arno Press, 1968.

Woody, Thomas K. *A History of Women's Education in the U.S.* 2 vols. New York: Science Press, 1929. Reprinted in one vol. New York: Octagon Books, 1966.

Wright, Muriel H. "Rachel Caroline Eaton." *Chronicles of Oklahoma* 10 (Mar. 1932): 8.

Wright, William Winfield, "Extra-Institutional Sites of Composition Instruction in the Nineteenth Century." Ph.D. diss., Univ. of Arizona, 1994.

Yellin, Jean Fagan. *Women and Sisters: The Antislavery Feminists in American Culture.* New Haven: Yale Univ. Press, 1989.

Young, Iris Marion. "Gender as Seriality: Thinking about Women as a Social Collective." *Signs* 19 (1994): 713–38.

Young, Mary E. "Women, Civilization, and the Indian Question." In *Clio Was a Woman: Studies in the History of American Women,* ed. Mabel E. Deutrich and Virginia C. Purdy, pp. 98–110. Washington, D.C.: Howard Univ. Press, 1989.

Contributors

SUZANNE L. BUNKERS is professor of English at Mankato State University in Minnesota, where she also serves as a member of the Center for Faculty Development. She has worked on women's diaries for a decade, including editions of *The Diary of Caroline Seabury, 1854–1863* (Madison: Univ. of Wisconsin Press, 1991), and *"All Will Yet Be Well": The Diary of Sarah Gillespie Huftalen, 1873–1952* (Iowa City: Univ. of Iowa Press, 1993).

JOANN CAMPBELL, assistant professor of English at Indiana University, Bloomington, has published articles on writing instruction at Vassar and Radcliffe colleges. She is completing a book on cultural expectations for the first generations of college women in the United States, examining student essays to better understand both the demands and the opportunities provided by college writing instruction.

SANDRA D. HARMON is lecturer in the History Department at Illinois State University, where she teaches courses on U.S. history and history of women in the United States and Europe, as well as supervising student teachers. A specialist in Illinois women's history, she has written on Illinois women and politics, on club women, on issues of history and biography, on American women in music history, and on Florence Kelley.

CATHERINE HOBBS is assistant professor in the rhetoric, composition, and literacy program in the English Department and a member of the Women's Studies faculty at the University of Oklahoma. She focuses on eighteenth- and nineteenth-century history and theory of rhetoric, composition, and literacy. She has published on feminist theory and women's history and also writes on eighteenth-century theories of language and rhetoric.

JUNE HADDEN HOBBS is assistant professor of English at Gardner-Webb University in Boiling Springs, North Carolina, where she teaches composition, American literature, and women's studies. She received her Ph.D. in 1994 from the University of Oklahoma. Her dissertation, " 'I Sing for I Cannot Stay Silent': The Feminization of American Hymnody, 1870–1920," is an interdisciplinary study of the rhetoric of gospel hymns.

SHIRLEY WILSON LOGAN is assistant professor in the Department of English at the University of Maryland where she directs the Professional Writing Program.

She teaches courses in the history of rhetoric, advanced composition, and African American literature. She has currently edited a critical anthology of speeches by nineteenth-century black women, *With Voice and Pen,* forthcoming from Southern Illinois University Press.

Devon A. Mihesuah is assistant professor of American Indian history at Northern Arizona University, Flagstaff. She has published four books about the education of American Indians and the desecration of American Indian burial sites. A member of the Choctaw Nation of Oklahoma, she has received grants and fellowships from the Ford Foundation, the National Endowment for the Humanities, the Smithsonian Institution, the American Historical Association, and the American Council of Learned Societies.

Vickie Ricks, formerly of Grand Valley (Michigan) State University, is an independent scholar who writes on rhetoric and composition and women's history. She has published on Gertrude Buck's social theory of discourse and on William Faulkner, and she has presented papers on the history of women's rhetoric and writing instruction and on literature and feminist theory at meetings including the Conference on College Composition and Communication, the Kentucky Philological Association, and the Twentieth-Century Literacy Conference.

Jane E. Rose is an assistant professor of English at Panhandle Oklahoma State University. In addition to American literature, she also teaches business and technical writing and composition. Her research focuses on nineteenth-century American cultural studies with an emphasis on women's studies.

P. Joy Rouse is an assistant professor of writing/English and textual studies at Syracuse University where she teaches undergraduate rhetoric courses and graduate seminars in the history of rhetoric. Her work has appeared in *Rhetoric Society Quarterly, Writing Lab Newsletter,* and *English Language Arts Bulletin.* She is currently working on a book about literacy and rhetorical education framed by theories of colonization.

Sue Carter Simmons is assistant professor of English at Bowling Green State University in Ohio, where she teaches writing, courses on the history of rhetoric and composition, and a course in gender and writing, with women's studies. She has published on composition pedagogy and on the history of Harvard rhetoric. She is currently working on a writing textbook, *Writing Together,* forthcoming from Macmillan Publishing.

Judy Nolte Temple (formerly Lensink) is associate professor of English and Women's Studies at the University of Arizona. She has edited two volumes on contemporary southwestern culture and is author of *"A Secret to be Burried": The Diary and Life of Emily Hawley Gillespie, 1858–1888,* an interdisciplinary study of a pioneer woman's diary. She is currently researching the private autobiographical writings of the legendary Colorado Silver Queen, "Baby Doe" Tabor.

Nicole Tonkovich is assistant professor in the Department of Literature at the University of California, San Diego, and directs the Fifth College Writing Program there. She has published on Sarah Josepha Hale and on Margaret Fuller in *Legacy: A Journal of Nineteenth-Century American Women Writers,* on the rhetoric of *Godey's Lady's Book,* and on other topics in nineteenth-century women's history and literature.

Heidemarie Z. Weidner is assistant professor of rhetoric and composition in the English Department of Tennessee Tech University in Cookesville, where she directs the first-year composition program. She has published on Lydia Short and the history of rhetoric and composition at Butler University and has presented on journal writing and coeducation as well as the history of Native American literacy instruction.

Maryan Wherry is assistant professor of American Studies at the University of Maryland. She did her doctoral dissertation on Elizabeth Bacon Custer. She works in the Overseas Program teaching on military bases across Europe, and also has extensive experience working with writing instruction.

Index

Index

Index

Index

Index

Index

Index

Feminist Issues: Practice, Politics, Theory

ALISON BOOTH AND ANN LANE, EDITORS

CAROL SIEGEL
Lawrence among the Women: Wavering Boundaries in Women's Literary Traditions

HARRIET BLODGETT, ED.
Capacious Hold-All: An Anthology of Englishwomen's Diary Writings

JOY WILTENBURG
Disorderly Women and Female Power in the Street Literature of Early Modern England and Germany

DIANE P. FREEDMAN
An Alchemy of Genres: Cross-Genre Writing by American Feminist Poet-Critics

JEAN O'BARR AND MARY WYER, EDS.
Engaging Feminism: Students Speak Up and Speak Out

KARI WEIL
Androgyny and the Denial of Difference

ANNE FIROR SCOTT, ED.
Unheard Voices: The First Historians of Southern Women

ALISON BOOTH, ED.
Famous Last Words: Changes in Gender and Narrative Closure

MARILYN MAY LOMBARDI, ED.
Elizabeth Bishop: The Geography of Gender

HEIDI HUTNER, ED.
Rereading Aphra Behn: History, Theory, and Criticism

PETER J. BURGARD, ED.
Nietzsche and Feminism

FRANCES GRAY
Women and Laughter

NITA KUMAR, ED.
Women as Subjects: South Asian Histories

ELIZABETH A. SCARLETT
Under Construction: The Body in Spanish Novels

PAMELA R. MATTHEWS
Ellen Glasgow and a Woman's Traditions

MAHNAZ AFKHAMI
Women in Exile

DEIRDRE LASHGARI, ED.
Violence, Silence, and Anger: Women's Writing as Transgression

CATHERINE HOBBS, ED.
Nineteenth-Century Women Learn to Write